Multiple Dilemmas

ANSWERING THE DILEMMAS OF CHRISTIANS & MUSLIMS

JEFF & ANNETTE
HAMMOND

Ark House Press
arkhousepress.com

Some names and identifying details have been changed to protect the privacy of individuals.

Cataloguing in Publication Data:
Title: Multiple Dilemmas
ISBN: 9781764562058 (pbk)
Subjects: REL077000 RELIGION / Faith; REL023000 RELIGION / Christian Ministry / Discipleship.

Design by initiateagency.com

CONTENTS

Introduction to Multiple Dilemmas v

The Reason for Writing Multiple Dilemmas ix

Dilemma 1. The Ishmael and Esau Dilemma 1

Dilemma 2. The Bible Dilemma? 31

Dilemma 3. The Qur'an Dilemma 54

Dilemma 4. The Trinity or Tauhid Dilemma 94

Dilemma 5. The Jesus Dilemma 128

Dilemma 6. The Crucifixion Dilemma 156

Dilemma 7. Who killed Jesus Dilemma 180

Dilemma 8. The Straight Path Dilemma 209

Dilemma 9. The Women's Dilemma 233

Dilemma 10. The Heaven & Hell Dilemma 285

Dilemma 11. Muhammad in the Bible Dilemma 323

Dilemma 12. The Jesus' Deity Dilemma 340

Dilemma 13. The Islamic Expansion Dilemma 385

Dilemma 14. Errors and Contradictions Dilemma 433
Dilemma 15. The Lamb of God Dilemma 453
Dilemma 16. Escaping Hell Dilemma....................................483
Dilemma 17. Conquering Spiritual Powers Dilemma 508
Dilemma 18. Islamic Eschatology Dilemma 534
Dilemma 19. Bible Prophecy Dilemma 570
Dilemma 20. Effective Witnessing Dilemma 596

INTRODUCTION TO MULTIPLE DILEMMAS

By Bishop Harry Westcott

When understanding Truth and Obedience in a modern world of confusion, deceit, lies and misinformation, I find it is most helpful to listen to those labourers who have lived their lives at the coalface in 'Pioneer Situations'. Obedience to the Lord's Command and following the 'Call of God' into dangerous fields put them in danger and could have cost them their lives. The Authors of this Book are just such people. Dr Jeff and Annette Hammond have been in many strange Lands that few of us have ever visited, let alone having spent 50 years of their ministry in many of them.

This book will be a revelation to many Christians in Australia. It is only in the last few years we have begun to experience the impact of Islam and its antisemitic views. We thought they were trying to escape the tyranny and violence of the Middle East, but instead some of them have imported it here. This religion has caused us a lot of confusion and heartache because of our ignorance of Islam's beliefs and cultural practices. It has caused a lot of fear.

As Christians, we have welcomed them to Australia. We have loved to help them be at home in our country, but maybe God has another purpose both for us and for the new arrivals. Maybe the Lord is giving us the opportunity to love them and help both them and us, to solve the many dilemmas that this situation has presented us. It has saddened us to see young children coming out of their schools and into the streets chanting "From the River to the Sea, Palestine will be Free!" We have seen tragic attacks against Jewish restaurants and synagogues in Melbourne, planned attacks to take bombs into the MCG, and lately the tragedy of the Bondi massacre in Sydney. Perhaps it is time for us to stir up our Christian faith and demonstrate the truth of Christ's love for all people and to share the saving and transforming power of the Gospel of Jesus Christ.

I believe that *Esther 4:14* applies to Dr Jeff and Annette Hammond,

"Who knows whether you have come to the kingdom for such a time as this?"

They have spent their 50 years, mainly in Indonesia, Malaysia, Lebanon, Jordan, Yemen, Egypt and Israel. They have survived heart aches and sorrows, but because of their love and faith for Muslim communities God has thrilled them with so many experiences, witnessing many amazing miracles! Today they have been given an important 'Kairos Time' – a special opportunity!

I am sure that this book, **Multiple Dilemmas,** will become important material for all who will be training for ministry in all Denominations, and even for all Christians wanting to effectively serve the Great Commission of *Matthew 28:19-20* as we move into this new era of Australian history.

I strongly urge you to study this book and share it with many others.

In His Grip,
Bishop Harry Westcott

About Bishop Harry Westcott

Bishop Harry Westcott was born on the 19th April 1935. He have enjoyed a wonderful non-threatened, fruitful and long life in this greatest of all lands we all love. With his wife, Doreen born in England on the 14th March, 1935, they have served the Lord for over six decades of ministry, beginning with the Methodist Church, the Uniting Church and Vision Ministries in God's great mission field. They have ministered in every State and Territory of Australia as well as 27 other nations around the world. Whenever returning to Australia they were always thrilled to call Australia, "home".

THE REASON FOR WRITING MULTIPLE DILEMMAS

....

We are excited to have the opportunity of sharing from our over 50 years of studying Islam and Arabic as well as ministering in Islamic nations like Indonesia, Malaysia, Jordan, Egypt, Lebanon, Yemen and the Palestinian territories in the West Bank.

In those years we have experienced extreme persecution. We have been attacked, bombed and targeted. Some of our staff, students, colleagues and friends have been assassinated, beheaded and maimed for life. Do we hate these attackers? No, not at all. We realize they are victims of the Satanic attack aimed at the whole of humanity. For all the anguish we have witnessed, we wish them no harm. We love them and forgive just as Jesus taught us by His example on the Cross and as is declared in John's Gospel.

John 3:16,

"For God so loved the world (that includes Muslims), that He gave (sacrificed) His only begotten Son, that whosoever believes in Him will have eternal life."

On the Cross Jesus spoke of those who hated Him, persecuted Him, tortured Him, whipped Him, spat on Him, nailed Him to the Cross and humiliated Him. He responded by saying in *Luke 22:34,* "Father, forgive them, for they do not know what they do."

We disagree with the teachings and practices of Islam just as they disagree with ours. Every person has the right and the freedom to choose their own pathway to God, but everyone will bear the consequences of their decision. It is our desire to solve the dilemmas facing Muslims and Christians as we seek to find the one true pathway to salvation. Muslims pray the first Chapter or Surah of the Qur'an, *Al Fatiha* 17 times every day. The key, central prayer is: "Show us the Straight Way!" It is our prayer and love for them that they will find that Straight Way in Jesus Christ who said in *John 14:6,* "I am the Way, the Truth and the Life. No one comes to the Father except through Me."

Why is it difficult for Muslims to accept Jesus as their Saviour?

To many Christians it is difficult to understand why our Muslim friends do not accept that Jesus Christ is God the Son, the Creator of Heaven and Earth and the only Saviour of Mankind.

An internet site called *Relentless Reasoning (medium.com/@relentlessreasoning18)*, explains some of the dilemmas that confront our Muslim friends. This site focuses on exposing religious ideologies that resist examination and invites readers to investigate evidence, and intellectual honesty in the pursuit of truth. One important element they discuss is the emotional impact that overwhelms logical discussion.

One of their enlightening blog articles is titled *Why Apologists Fight Even After the Evidence Dies.* It describes the difficulties Muslims face when confronted with the evidence that Islam is false and the Qur'an has a multitude of errors. The following are quotations from this article.

"Modern psychology is clear: Most people do not believe because of evidence — they use evidence to protect what they already believe. Once a belief becomes tied to: family, community, ethnicity, culture, belonging, moral framework, emotional security, purpose, stability, then questioning it becomes impossible because to question the belief is to question: one's past, one's parents, one's community, one's self. This is why the less evidence a belief has, the more aggressively its defenders protect it. They are not defending the belief. They are defending themselves."

"When evidence undermines Islam's foundations, the apologist experiences not just intellectual discomfort but *existential threat.*"

"The fear that: "If Islam collapses, I collapse." "If Islam is false, my entire life loses meaning." "If the Qur'ān is not preserved, my identity is a lie." "If Muhammad didn't do these things, who am I?"

"Thus any attack on the religion triggers: panic, hostility, denial, moral outrage, emotional defensiveness, tribal loyalty."

This leads to the following response: "I've invested too much to walk away now."

They have dedicated decades praying, fasting, defending the Qur'an, teaching their children Islam, decades believing Muhammad as perfect, decades avoiding forbidden pleasures, then discovering the Qur'an cannot be reconstructed, the Hadith cannot be authenticated, the Surah was created late, early Islamic history contradicts the narrative, the legal system is fabricated and the canon is unstable."

They simply say: "I have invested too much to accept the collapse now."

It is important that we understand how important this is to everyday Muslims.

In many Muslim societies: religion = community; community = protection; protection = survival. Leaving Islam is not just theological suicide — it is social death. Ex-Muslims lose family, marriage prospects, friends, community status, inheritance, physical safety, economic networks, belonging."

"Many Muslims genuinely believe: "Without Islam, society collapses."

So when evidence undermines Islam, they fear moral relativism, sexual chaos, loss of meaning, atheistic nihilism, family collapse, community disintegration, purposelessness."

These fears drive everyday Muslims to fight for their identity in every area of their lives.

"They are not defending the Qur'an. They are defending family stability, moral order, social structure, personal values, community cohesion. Losing Islam means losing certainty about right and wrong — and for many, that fear is worse than losing doctrine."

This is why it is very difficult for Muslims to accept the Gospel of Jesus Christ. Mentally, they may see that it is true but the cost is great. They seem to have everything to lose. With the guidance of the Holy Spirit we need to help them be aware of the even greater cost, the eternal cost, of not accepting the truth of who Jesus is and what He has done for them. We need to bring them to the fulness of the amazing love and acceptance of Jesus.

We must remember that our Muslim friends are not our enemies. They are the victims of a Satanic conspiracy. Satan wants to damn them to an eternity in hell, but we are God's chosen vessels to introduce them to a glorious, joyful and fulfilling life in Christ. This life and faith will bring them to an eternity in the glories of heaven in the presence of God. **Muslims are more than a quarter of humanity** and God has chosen us to bring them the love of Jesus Christ.

Our dilemma is how to fulfil this calling.

Jeff & Annette Hammond

Some other Books written by the Authors:

The Andrew Chan Story – The testimony of transformation through Christ
New Wine – What sort of Church does Jesus want today?
Experiencing the Amazing Power of Forgiveness
Explosions of God's Almighty Power
Coming soon: Building the Third Temple and Preparing for the Second Coming

For further information contact: *Abbahouse2000@outlook.com*

DILEMMA 1

THE ISHMAEL AND ESAU DILEMMA

The first dilemma we will discuss originates in the stories of two rejected men – the son and grandson of Abraham. The two that we refer to are Ishmael and Esau. Both of them had bitter experiences after facing rejection. They give us an interesting snapshot into two elements or characteristics that we find within Islam.

Understanding the background and bitter experiences of these two men can help us understand many of the conflicts in history, ancient and modern, as well as God's attitude to both elements today. The dilemma facing Christians is that both Ishmael and Esau are seen as symbols of Islam, and in the eyes of many Christians, they are seen as symbols of radical Islam. This perception needs to change.

In Muslim majority communities or countries, Christians tend to keep their distance from Muslims unless contact is unavoidable. In countries like Indonesia which has some 230 million Muslims and 35 million Christians and another 20 million from other religious groups like Buddhism, Hinduism, Confucianism and animism, there is a tendency for each community, where possible, to keep to themselves. They often have different residential communities, separate marketplaces, and for Christians, designated areas where a church may be built. This separation is often designed to reduce risks of conflict and isolation for the prevention of evangelism among Muslim communities. We see this in Jakarta, Sydney, London, Sweden, New York and many other places across Europe and Asia.

The Decline of Christianity in the West

This decline in Western countries has been happening for more than a century. Europe, Australia, New Zealand, South Africa, the USA, the UK, Germany, France, Italy and others were considered Christian regions. 100 years ago Christianity was more vibrant, more missionary oriented and growing throughout Asia and Africa. After World War One a dramatic change began and this accelerated after World War Two. The Middle East went from 14% Christian down to 3%. This was due to the gradual rise in Islamic nationalism and Islamic extremism. We could say that it was the rise of the "Esau spirit" and its dominance over the "Ishmael spirit".

A country like Lebanon went from 70% Christian to 30%. Towns like Bethlehem have gone from 80% down to 12%. Trends in the Middle East terrorized the Christians. Their homes were marked by painting the Arabic letter nun (noon) ن a symbol for Nasrani (Christian). These homes were offered the choice of:

a) converting to Islam
b) submitting to Islam and paying the **jizya**, a protection tax, or
c) being killed with the sword.

Hundreds of thousands of Christians, in fear, abandoned the Middle East and migrated to Europe, Australia, New Zealand, Canada and the USA.

The Islamic slogan has long been, "First the Saturday people. Then the Sunday people." That's why both Jewish and Christian communities around the world have been targeted for extinction. Islam enters societies by immigration as a peace-loving community. They lay their foundations quietly but as they get established, they spread their wings and begin to exercise their plans to influence and eventually take over the society. Integration and multiculturalism is not their goal. It's a tool. Once they are established, the expansion begins and political control follows. In a city like New York in the USA there are now over 750,000 Muslims and their mayor is a radical, Hamas supporting Muslim.

For growth of Islam in Australia see the Youtube videos:
www.youtube.com/watch?v=yB3ZGCC8VNg&t=172s

To see what happens, globally, as the Islamic faith, education, halal culture, political activity, sharia law and economic integration spreads, view the following video:
www.youtube.com/watch?v=No3LIM3lmOs

In recent times, the Islamic Jihad began creating circumstances for mass migration of Islamic youths, mainly males, who were fleeing to the West as well and setting up communities for expansion. Gaining permanent residence and citizenship they then began importing, through sponsorship, large numbers of their families, nuclear and extended, and their populations exploded. This created no-go zones in many countries in the Scandinavian countries, the UK, Australia, the USA and others. They began taking control of local politics as evidenced in about 12 major UK cities now having Muslim Mayors. This trend is spreading. New York now has a Hamas supporting Islamic Mayor. This is part of a deliberate strategy in their global vision of taking the world for Islam. Christianity is being hammered.

At the same time, Western societies impacted by Darwinism, materialism, secularism, civil society concepts, and left-wing ideologies have become anti-Christian and Christianity has become a dirty word and many

Christians have been cowered into silence. The forces of "Esau" and its alignment with the anti-Christian philosophy rising in the West has put the Christian faith on an extinction trajectory. Churches have become mosques and Islamic Centres and Christians have been silenced and in many cases the Great Commission has been abandoned.

This was indeed prophesied in the New Testament:

Matthew 24:9-12,

"They will deliver you up to tribulation and kill you, and you will be hated by all nations for My name's sake. And then many will be offended, will betray one another, and will hate one another. Then many false prophets will rise up and deceive many. And because lawlessness will abound, **the love of many will grow cold**."

1Timothy 4:1-2,

"Now the Spirit expressly says that **in latter times some will depart from the faith,** giving heed to deceiving spirits and doctrines of demons, speaking lies in hypocrisy, having their own conscience seared with a hot iron."

The Christian Dilemma

The dilemma now facing Christian communities is the recognition that we are commanded by Jesus to preach the Gospel to all of mankind including Muslims. However, there is a crippling fear that left wing Governments and "Esau" Muslims will attack them if they try to share the Gospel. Christians are branded as radicals causing disharmony in the community. This prevents many of them from obeying the Great Commission.

Matthew 28:19,

"Go therefore and make disciples of all the nations, baptizing them in the name of the Father and of the Son and of the Holy Spirit."

Mark 16:15,

"Go into all the world and preach the gospel to every creature."

In this Chapter we will see that the Christian view of Islam is too limited and based on a lack of understanding of two major spiritual streams that we can identify within Islam. One stream is really hungry and thirsty for the truth. They are crying out for salvation. They are desperately seeking the true path to God. We will see that this stream is illustrated by the spirit of Ishmael.

The other stream in the Bible is described as immoral, despisers of the Divine Covenant, murderous, and very dangerous. This is manifest in the spirit of Esau and this spirit seeks to terrorize Christians and to prevent them from helping those of the spirit of Ishmael to find their way back to the Father and find salvation in Jesus. This is at the core of this dilemma facing Christians.

Hebrews 12:14-17,

"Pursue peace with all people, and holiness, without which no one will see the Lord: looking carefully lest anyone fall short of the grace of God; lest any root of bitterness springing up cause trouble, and by this many become defiled; lest there be any fornicator or profane person like **Esau**, who for one morsel of food sold his birthright. For you know that afterward, when he wanted to inherit the blessing, he was rejected, for he found no place for repentance, though he sought it diligently with tears."

Understanding the Cry of Ishmael

Ishmael is understood by most historians to be the father of the Arabic people. However, as we have inferred above, Ishmael, the son of Abraham and Hagar, and Esau, the twin of Jacob and grandson of Abraham, represent two different aspects and attitudes among the Arabs throughout history. These different aspects are in full display today. This is important and will become obvious as we dig deeper into this topic.

Some people in the Bible were referred to by name by God before their birth, but there are only five people in the Bible who were specifically given their name by God before their birth:

1. Ishmael – *Genesis 16:11*
2. Isaac – *Genesis 17:19*
3. Solomon – *1Chronicles 17:19*
4. John the Baptist – *Luke 1:13*
5. Jesus – *Luke 1:31*

In Biblical hermeneutics, there is a principle of interpretation called "The first-mention principle". It indicates a special importance and priority to the first-mentioned person, event, teaching etc. in the Bible. That Ishmael is the first person named by God in the Bible, before he was born, shows that God rated Ishmael as a very significant person in His eternal plan. Ishmael's name means "God hears" and we will see that occurs in his life.

Interestingly, in Christian circles, we have tended to ignore Ishmael and concentrate solely on Isaac. Nevertheless, we need to see that in God's plan, Ishmael has an important role to play.

We see that God named Ishmael and described his nature as being like a wild donkey and would always be quarrelling with his brothers, ***Genesis 16:11-12.*** Ishmael was despised by Sarah because he mocked her and the baby Isaac. She wanted Ishmael and Hagar to be cast out, ***Genesis 21:9-10.*** This conflict distressed Abraham, for he loved Ishmael, but the Lord commanded him to do as Sarah had said. God would still hear the cry of Ishmael and would still greatly bless him, but the covenant was to be with Isaac, ***Genesis 21:11-13; 17:18-21.***

Ishmael was about 15 years-old, when he was cast out and abandoned by Abraham and Sarah. He never met his father again! ***Genesis 21:14.*** Can you imagine the pain and sense of rejection that this teenager felt as he and his mother were sent into the wilderness – to die! Ishmael loved his father, and Abraham loved him, but by casting him out, he was cast into humiliation, no longer treated as his son but as the son of the slave-woman. Can you feel what he felt? Sadly, this pain has continued on for 4000 years.

However, Ishmael's cry was to be reconciled to his father. He loved his father. When Ishmael heard that his father had died, he returned home and together with Isaac buried their father, Abraham. In this event, Ishmael was not only burying his father; he was burying his last chance to be accepted by his father and to be acknowledged as a son! (*Genesis 25:5-11.)*

Is it any wonder that Muslims throughout history, beginning with Muhammad, have rejected God as a father, and reject the notion that God has a son. The God of Islam declares that He only has slaves.

Surah Al Anaam 6:101, "How can he have a son, when he has no wife?"

To the Muslim, being a slave to God is the highest position of honour a human can achieve. Muslim must totally submit to God in all aspects, and to accept everything, whether good or evil, that comes from Him.

This God declares that he has no sons. It is blasphemy to say that God has a son. God's rejection of having a son is repeatedly stated in many Surahs (Chapters) of the Qur'an:

Surah 2:116; 17:111; 19:35; 19:88-92; 23:91; 25:2; 39:4; 43:81; 72:31; etc

The Qur'an also declares that instead of sons, God has slaves. Indeed Muhammad is declared to be the slave of God - *Surah Al Baqarah 2:23.* In other places humanity is referred to by God as "My slaves" *Surah 15:42.* Noah is spoken of as "a grateful slave" *Surah 17:3.*

Other references include *Surah 17:65; Surah 19:93; Surah 25:63-67; Surah 39:53* etc.

What did God say about Ishmael?

Before Ishmael was born, God had named him. Ishmael means **"God hears".**

The call of God to Israel is "Shema Israel" that is "Hear O Israel!" The words come from the same root.

Deuteronomy 6:4,

"Hear, O Israel: The LORD our God, the LORD is one!"

God declared the revelation of Ishmael's name over him, and His concern for him, when he is dying under a bush in the wilderness. Yes, God hears the cry of Ishmael.

Genesis 21:16-20,

"Then she went and sat down across from *Ishmael* at a distance of about a bowshot; for she said to herself, "Let me not see the death of the boy." So she sat opposite *him,* and lifted her voice and wept. And **God heard the voice of the lad.** Then the angel of God called to Hagar out of heaven, and said to her, "What ails you, Hagar? Fear not, for **God has heard the voice of the lad** where he is. Arise, lift up the lad and hold him with your hand, for I will make him a great nation." Then God opened her eyes, and she saw a well of water. And she went and filled the skin with water, and gave the lad a drink. **So God was with the lad**."

Bad circumstances are not a sign of God's rejection. God has His own purposes in the shaping of our lives. Moses was death-doomed by Pharoah's decree to slay all the new-born males, but the Lord watched over him *(Exodus 2).* Jesus was born in a stable and satanic forces were seeking to kill Him through Herod from the beginning *(Matthew 2).* So the Lord was with Ishmael, heard him, protected him and placed in his heart the desire to be reconciled to his father, Abraham. His father loved him and raised him up and for 13 years they had hunted together. Abraham loved Ishmael and wanted him to be his heir, Ishmael too loved his father *(Genesis 21:11-13; 25:9).*

Jeff's Personal Testimony

"In my limited, personal experience, I somewhat understand the account of Ishmael's sense of rejection. He was denied access to his father. He was denied any inheritance.

I was born in Rabaul, Papua New Guinea. When my birth was registered, my mother's name was not recorded on my birth certificate. It was like I was the child of the slave woman. My father's first wife's name was placed there. Why? In post World War Two Australia defacto relationships were not recognized and when my father was posted to Papua New Guinea by the Australian Government, he took my mother and my elder brother with him. My mother had to travel under the name of my father's first wife as the Government would not pay for the fares or allowances for a defacto wife. When I was born in Rabaul, the name of my mother on my birth certificate was not my birth mother but my father's first wife.

In 1952 my father abandoned my mother, my brother and myself. My mother was pregnant with a daughter at the time. We became street kids and were forced to live in a cleaned-out dog's kennel in North Melbourne. In 1955 my mother became the "defacto wife" of another man who had three sons. This uniting of two families became a "Brady-bunch" family with six children. I was forced to take his surname "Harvey". This happened after I was badly beaten until I submitted to his demand. They had another three children together and then there were nine children living in Ferntree Gully.

In 1963 my mother was ill with gall stones and had to have surgery and called on her younger sister to care for us while she was in hospital. She brought her children with her. It was very crowded. Well, she cared more for my mother's defacto husband and when my mother returned from hospital, she abandoned my mother, all the children and fled with my mother's defacto husband. We were in a desperate situation with no finances. No support. My mother was in total despair. The household was full of hate, anger and bitterness.

I wanted to play local Under 16 Football but there was a problem. To be registered, the Football Association had to see a copy of my Birth Certificate. I had never seen my Birth Certificate and when the Mayor of the Ferntree Gully Shire, Mr. Wally Tew, who was also the President of the Football Club came to see my mother, I was ordered out of the room. My mother didn't want me to know that her name was not on the Birth Certificate. Another woman's name was on it as my mother. It was only two years later that I actually got to see my Birth Certificate with the name of my father's first wife, and not my mother's name.

In 1965 I became a Christian and knew Jesus as my Lord and Saviour. I began searching for my father. I wanted my father. In 1987 I discovered my family in Perth. I had five more brothers, another sister, three step-sisters, a nephew, two cousins, two uncles and aunts. It was a happy moment, yet sad as well. I learned that my father had been dead and buried for eight years. And of course, like Ishmael, I received no inheritance.

As the gravity of all this sunk in I identified with Ishmael – cast out, rejected, destitute, fatherless, with a loss of identity and disinherited. I wept as I felt the pain of being similar to Ishmael. The one redeeming fact was that my family in Perth were so embracing and said they would never use the name "Harvey" because I was a Hammond. They said they had waited for this day for years and I was welcomed back into the Hammond clan. I shared this with my wife, Annette, and our children, and unanimously, we all decided to return to our birth heritage and be known again as Hammonds.

It was very fulfilling being restored into my family and discovering more brothers and a sister in New Zealand.

It is my prayer that many Ishmaels might find their way back to their true heritage in Abraham through the restoration that is only possible in believing in Jesus as Lord and Saviour."

Ishmael went from being a son *(ibn)* to being a slave *(abd)*

In Arabic culture, in a home, to be an ***ibn*** (Arabic for son) is a far higher status than to be an ***abd*** (Arabic for servant/slave). Ask your Muslim friends, if they would rather be a son or a slave in their home? Of course they want to be sons. Sons have dignity, status, preferential rights, the family name and inheritance. A slave has none of that.

We ask our Muslim friends a second question, "What would you prefer to be before God? A son or a slave?" They find that impossible to answer for God says He has no sons, only slaves. It is here that we can challenge our Muslim friends about the love of God. He wants them to be sons, not slaves with no dignity.

Look what happened to Ishmael after being cast out by Abraham and Sarah:

- His "father" image was SHATTERED
- His identity was in CONFLICT
- His status was DOWNGRADED TO HUMILIATION
- His inheritance was CUT OFF
- His brother, Isaac, gets everything and Ishmael gets NOTHING
- Had God now abandoned him too?

If you were in Ishmael's shoes how would you feel? Would you be abandoned? Feel rejection, resentment and anger?

Learn to understand the heart of Ishmael and you will learn a powerful message about the heart of Muslims around the world. It will help you understand why they can seem so hard to reach, but remember, this same point is where we can reach in and touch their hearts.

It was on this point that **Bilquis Sheik** who wrote the book, *"I Dared To Call Him, Father"*, was reached by the Lord as she walked in the garden of her home in Pakistan. She had been married to General Khalid Masud Sheikh, the Interior Minister of Pakistan. After leaving Islam she was sentenced to death and with the assistance of the intervention of the United Nations, Amnesty International, the USA and many others she was released to the USA where she became a witness for Christ.

In Islam one must never call God, Father. That is haram, forbidden, blasphemy. This eventually led her to know Jesus Christ as her Lord and Saviour. This was blasphemy in Islam and she was sentenced to death. Her testimony has blessed many around the world. She passed into glory in 1997.

Another example is **Ayan Hirsi Ali**, a Sumali refugee who fled her homeland because of the practice of female circumcision. She went to the Netherlands and became a member of Parliament. Her relentless exposures and attacks of Islamic practices made it unsafe for her to stay there. She fled to the USA.

Her rejection of Islam led her to become an atheist, but in America she heard the Gospel which then led her to accept Jesus as her Lord and Saviour. She is an internationally, well known, and outspoken witness for Christ. She recently conducted podcasts with John Anderson, the former Deputy Prime Minister of Australia and Leader of the National Party.

See: *www.youtube.com/watch?v=2TL7eSm9koI*

The Next Generation after Ishmael and the Generations that followed

After Ishmael passed away, the story passes on to succeeding generations, and so does the pain, the humiliation and sense of rejection. Until today, this wound has not healed. This pain of humiliation and rejection found a home in Islam.

Originally abandoned by his father and finally by his mother, Ishmael was all alone in the desert. Hagar cannot face the agony of seeing him die in the desert. The pain of abandonment continued throughout his life and this passes on to succeeding generations.

What happened in the next generation? ***Genesis 25:17-18*** – the hostility continues and becomes an unhealed sore festering for 4000 years! Could the Lord be calling us to bring healing to Ishmael? To restore him to sonship and for him to find his inheritance in Christ?

Genesis 21:15-20 – In the wilderness, Ishmael was abandoned to death. Will our fear of Islam cause us to abandon Ishmael as well?

Was Ishmael abandoned by God? ***Genesis 21:17-19***– No! The Bible is emphatic, "God was with the boy". What did God promise Ishmael? He would become a great nation. When he was on the point of death, God intervened with a miraculous provision of water - ***Genesis 21:19.*** After this event, Ishmael and Hagar lived in the Wilderness of Beersheba and Paran - ***Genesis 21:14, 21.***

Does God still hear the cry of Ishmael?

Today there are over 2 billion lost, fatherless, cast out, humiliated, rejected and hurting people who are lashing out. Many want to find their way back to the Father but they don't know the way. Can we hear the cry of Ishmael? As God used a woman, Hagar, to bring water to Ishmael 4000 years ago, will He use another woman today - the Church - to bring water to Ishmael?

The descendants of rejected Ishmael built a monument to his cry - Islam!

Islam fits harmoniously into the cry and pain of Ishmael's sense of rejection and humiliation. Ishmael wanted to be accepted as a son and be acknowledged by his father? Do you think Ishmael's cry can be answered in our generation?

Muhammad is usually claimed to be a direct descendant from Ishmael. It is recorded in the official history of Mohammad, *Sirat Rasul Allah,* written by Ibn Ishaq around 770 AD. It is stated that he descends from Nebaioth, the eldest son of Ishmael. According to the Old Testament, the first inhabitants of the Arabian peninsula descended from Joktan *(Genesis 10:26-29),* a descendent of Shem, from which we get the term Semite.

Later, the area was also settled by Abraham's sons through Keturah *(Genesis 25:1-4),* the 12 sons of Ishmael *(Genesis 25:13-16),* and the sons of Esau *(Genesis 36:1-19).* All of them are descendants of Abraham. Arabs are a mixture of all the above plus many inter-tribal marriages.

Ishmael, today, is a major part of Islam. Ishmael is spirit that seeks to please God and earn respect before God as a servant-slave by giving absolute submission to God hoping to earn acceptance through good works. However, the cry in his spirit can never be satisfied until he becomes a son and has a father. Many Muslims today are thirsty, but they cannot see the well. Will you take the water to them? They have no father to give them bread. Will you give it to them?

This is a dilemma for Christians because we have identified the descendants of Ishmael as Muslims and consider that Muslims are radicals and terrorists. The resulting fear has driven us away from Muslims and we refuse to be witnesses to them of the amazing love of Jesus. This spirit of fear must be broken as there are many "Ishmael Muslims" who are crying out for salvation. They want to be restored to the Father. We need to solve this dilemma. Fear and hatred are not the answer. We need to find the love of God in our hearts and hear the words of the apostle John:

1John 4:18,

"There is no fear in love; but perfect love casts out fear, because fear involves torment. But he who fears has not been made perfect in love."

Some of our modern-day "Ishmaels"

1. Arif

We met Arif in the Korobokan Prison in Bali where we were mentoring Andrew Chan the leader of the Bali Nine. Arif was the Imam in the Prison Mosque when he began experiencing visitations from a man in white robes who was calling him to receive Christ and be saved. This happened eight times and Arif thought he was going crazy. Andrew Chan heard about this and confronted Arif and told him, "This is Jesus who is coming to you. He loves you and wants to save you." Arif struggled with this at first but knew it was true. He surrendered his life to Christ and was baptized in the prison and filled with the Holy Spirit. Today Arif is leading many Muslims to faith in Jesus and training them to be witnesses for Jesus in their communities.

Arif's grandfather was one of the founders of the Muslim Brotherhood in Indonesia. His parents were devout and radical Wahabi Muslims. When Arif came to Christ, he was totally rejected and cut off from his family. Today he has a new family who are fellow believers in the Body of Christ. In the last 10 years many thousands of Muslims have come to know Jesus through his ministry and over 800 have currently been mentored and sent out as evangelists for Christ.

2. Muhammad and Shirin

Muhammad and Shirin had studied in Dubai, but Muhammad had a serious question he wanted answered: where is my name mentioned in the Bible? He had grown up in Iran being told that the name Muhammad was in the Bible and he wanted to see it. There was a Christian professor at the university in Dubai and Muhammad asked him about the Bible and where the name Muhammad was mentioned. He was told that the name Muhammad was not in the Bible. Muhammad said, "It must be. I have been told this all my life." The professor lent Muhammad his Bible, and Muhammad read it but couldn't find any mention of his name. After graduating in Dubai, Muhammad wanted to become a master diving instructor.

Diving was his hobby and he was invited to do a course in Thailand. After he graduated he was invited to become a master-diving instructor for a diving school in Phuket. He accepted on one condition, that he return to Iran, marry his fiancé, Shirin, and return with her. They accepted and the next day, December 23, 2004, he departed and flew to Iran. On his arrival he heard the news of the Asian tsunami and 230,000 people were dead. The company that offered him employment was destroyed and all except one of the staff perished. This shook Muhammad. He wanted to find answers and visited an underground church. The meeting was invaded by the secret police and Muhammad was arrested. He was due to be imprisoned, perhaps for life or worse.

Shirin went to the police and bargained for Muhammad's release. She surrendered their home and then had to flee Iran. Muhammad's faith in Christ grew and after coming to Indonesia they joined our team in reaching out to Iranian refugees. Within 6 months, over 70 Iranians had come to Christ and many more followed over the next several years. Muhammad and Shirin conducted radio broadcasts that were reaching many thousands of refugees in Indonesia and the broadcasts were even reaching Iran.

3. Jusuf Roni

Jusuf Roni was a radical leader of Islamic Youth in Indonesia. He led mobs burning down churches and persecuting Christians. He took a Bible from one of the fires as he wanted to gather more information to use against the Christians. When he read ***John 14:6,*** the Holy Spirit convicted him saying, "This is the Way that you have been searching for."

He gave his life to Christ and was sent to prison for 6 years where he was tortured as they tried to convince him to return to Islam. In his trial he took no lawyer but used the opportunity to testify how Jesus was the true Lord and Saviour, and that Jesus was his Defence Lawyer. He released his book, as in the picture, MY GREAT DEFENDER, which became a best seller throughout Indonesia.

After his release we came to know him and his wife Et. We stayed with them in Jakarta. He stayed with us in his visit to Melbourne, Australia. Jusuf Roni became a powerful evangelist and inspired many Muslims to come to faith in Christ. He passed into glory in 2025.

4. Joshua

As the son of an imam, Joshua was expected to be an example to other young men in his mosque, so he joined the *Laskar Jihad.* During the Islamic attacks against Christians in the Maluku Islands of East Indonesia, Joshua was appointed as the General in charge of bombing Christian Churches. The Lord began talking to him and Joshua responded and accepted Jesus as his Lord and Saviour. He now pastors a growing flock of Muslim background believers.

5. Masoud and Raha

Many would-be refugees to Australia from Iran hoped to cross from Indonesia to Australia by boat. Many thousands had landed in Indonesia but

Australia slammed the door shut warning "Any trying to come to Australia illegally by boat would never be given immigrant status in Australia." These would-be refugees were stuck in Indonesia. They registered with the UNHCR office in Jakarta hoping to find a country that would accept them – Australia, New Zealand, Canada or the USA. Among them were two Iranians, strong in their Islamic faith, Masoud and Raha.

Stranded in a foreign land with a foreign language and culture, they struggled to survive. They were invited to attend our home where we would have discussions about the Christian and Islamic faiths. We regularly had over 50 Iranians coming to our home. Some came to show that their faith was the true faith and Masoud in particular came armed with many questions that he was sure would destroy our arguments and show that Islam was the one true faith.

One by one his questions were answered. Initially he was angry as he saw his faith being undermined by the truth of the Gospel. Eventually, both he and Raha saw that the cry in their hearts to know God was answered in accepting Jesus Christ as their Lord and Saviour. This family grew in faith and have now become active evangelists sharing Christ with many Muslims both Arabic speaking and Farsi speaking.

6. Ahmad and Hanan

Masoud had a brother who had gained migrant status in Australia. His wife Hanan has given birth to two children in Australia in addition to their Iranian born daughter. Ahmad, like Masoud, had been against Christianity believing it to be a false religion, but Masoud coming to know Jesus created an opportunity for Ahmad to search a little deeper.

We shared a meal together and Ahmad and Hanan had many questions. Before we left, we asked if we could pray for them. They accepted and we prayed. Within two weeks they had surrendered their lives to Christ. The transformation was awesome. The joy of the Lord in them was infectious.

A few months later an amazing moment happened. Ahmad rang us and said that he and Hanan wanted to be baptized. He added that their daughter, Ghazal, wanted to talk to us. She was so excited she could hardly speak. She was trying to speak but she sounded like she was almost choking, then she blurted it out, "Jesus came to me, Jesus came and talked to me. He told me that I too could get baptized." It was such an exciting experience and testimony. On the day they were baptized in the Goulburn River in Shepparton, Victoria, she shared this testimony with the church. No wonder the angels in heaven rejoice and this joy infected the whole of the church.

7. Windy

Windy was a Muslim student renting an apartment with a girl from our church in Jakarta. There was a weekly Christian home fellowship there of other university students. Usually, Windy would stay in her room, but she listened to what was going on. When there were times of worship and prayer and she would hear "speaking in tongues". One day she challenged her roommate, "What's all this gibberish that you call "speaking in tongues"? She was told that it was a sign that was given to believers who were filled with the Holy Spirit to enable them to pray more effectively. Windy told her roommate that she was crazy.

A few days later when Windy was praying according to her Islamic prayers, when a man with shoulder length hair and a beard, wearing a white garment appeared in front of her. It was Jesus calling Windy to surrender her life to Him and to follow Him. He laid His hands on her head and Windy accepted Christ and was immediately filled with the Holy Spirit, speaking in tongues.

Windy immediately rang her family and told them what had happened. They were a very strong fundamentalist Muslim family. They exploded in anger accusing Windy of having a mental breakdown.

They sent Windy's uncle to see her and he immediately took her out of the home and to an Islamic psychiatric centre to have her healed and restored to Islam. After several months Windy escaped and was mentored by some strong Christians. Windy grew in Christ and met a fine young Christian man. A few years later they married and became active church-workers serving as worship leaders in the church. That was 30 years ago and they are still serving the Lord faithfully and joyfully.

8. Adam Malik – 1917-1984

Adam Malik was one of the founding fathers of the nation of Indonesia.

In August 1945, after the surrender of the Japanese, Adam Malik was one of the student leaders who arrested national leaders, Soekarno and Hatta, and compelled them to declare the independence of Indonesia from the Dutch. This declaration was made on the 17th August 1945.

Adam Malik became an Ambassador to the UN and was later elected the President of the United Nations General Assembly for 1971-1972. He is the only Indonesian to have ever held that most honoured position. From 1978-1983 he was the Vice-President of Indonesia.

On Friday 31st August 1984, Adam Malik called Jeff to his home in Jakarta. "We spent over an hour talking about his eternal future. He declared that although he had gained fame, fortune and position there was one thing missing in his life. He had no peace with God and so he asked, "How can I have peace with God?"

The English Bible in *Isaiah 9:6* calls Jesus the "Prince of Peace" but the Indonesian Bible in *Isaiah 9:5*, calls Jesus the "King of Peace". "I shared with him that only the King could give him the peace he was seeking and that to receive that peace he would need to believe that Jesus is the Son of God and only Saviour from sin, that He died on the Cross and rose again. He said that he believed and wanted to accept Jesus as his Lord and Saviour. We prayed together and he asked Jesus to forgive him his sins and to come into his life as his Lord and Saviour. He immediately said he felt a wonderful joy and peace."

"We went out to the reception area and he called his staff and declared to them, "I now have peace with God." What a joy to see the Vice-President of Indonesia come to faith in Christ and to declare Him openly to his staff."

Adam Malik is an amazing example of how those of the spirit of Ishmael can be reconciled to God the Father through accepting Jesus.

Islamic preachers are worried by this trend, throughout the world, and in particular in Islamic countries. An excellent book on what is happening in the Islamic world was written by *Robert Coleman* titled, ***Mosques and Miracles***. There are also numerous websites detailing how hundreds of thousands of Muslims all over the world are leaving Islam and turning to Jesus as their Lord and Saviour. You can view one such website on *www.youtube.com/watch?v=8GvrQjnc5Z0*

One of the foremost anti-Christian Islamic scholars, named **Zakir Naik**, who debates Christian leaders all over the world has been forced to confess:

"Previously according to me when a person from Saudi Arabia or from a Gulf country went to America or went to a western country the chances that you know they would deviate from their diin (religion) would be maybe 1 or 2% that's it. But nowadays the chances are more than 25%. And if we don't take constructive steps to deal with this, it is going to become an avalanche."

Global Islamic concern for the massive numbers of Muslims abandoning Islam and turning to Christ in Indonesia caused them to create an exaggerated account of these conversions claiming that 2 million Muslims were converting every year and accepting Jesus. Their campaign can be viewed by watching their short Youtube video called:

"**Save Maryam**" *www.youtube.com/watch?v=BCjEMnBFMck*

There are many more such testimonies, but I mention these few examples of people we know personally and have witnessed how there are so many Muslims who are looking for answers. They have a strong yearning to know God. They come from different backgrounds, and the Lord has worked with each one according to their individual situations. The one thing in common is that they all are from the spirit of Ishmael. There are many more around us waiting for someone, like you, to pray for them and to share the love of Jesus with them.

Understanding the Cry of Esau

The spirits of Ishmael and Esau both exist within Islam today and that's why we need intercession with discernment. They are different. Ishmael has a cry for sonship and fatherhood. He is lonely, rejected and humiliated. He's hurting but God loves him and hears his cry.

Esau is a wounded and angry spirit despising the birthright blessing. This is a spirit of hatred, revenge, violence, murder, terror and absolute control.

We are in a spiritual battle

Ephesians 6:12,

"Our struggle is not against flesh and blood, but against the rulers, against the authorities, against the powers of this dark world and against the spiritual forces of evil in the heavenly realms."

2Corinthians 10:4,

"The weapons we fight with are not the weapons of the world. On the contrary, they have divine power to demolish strongholds."

We are not in a battle with worldly weapons, but it is still a real battle. The stakes are high, for we are talking about the eternal destination of the souls of men and women. Muslims are people whom God created, and for whom Jesus died. That makes them very precious, for the blood of Christ was shed to redeem them. God loves them and wants to save them. They are worth saving and we need to fight this spiritual war and to set them free from the strong man's house, ***Luke 11:20-22.*** Jesus is the stronger man and we belong to Him. We need to bind the strong man (Satan) for he will not let his captives go free, ***Isaiah 14:12-17.***

The battle between Esau and Jacob

Isaac and Rebekah had twin sons and the battle between the twins began before they were born, ***Genesis 25:20-26***. The Lord revealed to Rebekah that the older (firstborn – Esau) would serve the younger (Jacob). The covenant promises would be given to Jacob. When the time came for Isaac to pass on the covenant blessings, he called Esau to prepare his favourite meal but Rebekah manipulated the situation to make sure that Jacob would receive the covenant blessing.

This was the second time that Jacob had used the circumstances to possess the birthright blessings. The first time was when Esau returned famished from a failed hunting expedition. He asked for some of Jacob's red-bean soup, but Jacob demanded that his twin brother surrender his first-born rights. Jacob's action was quite despicable in the way he treated his twin brother, but the attitude of Esau was perhaps even more despicable because he despised the birthright blessing of God, *Genesis 25:29-34; Hebrews 12:14-17.*

After twice losing his birthright and covenant blessings to Jacob, Esau was filled with bitterness, hatred, a spirit of revenge and murder. Note what happened when Esau discovered he had been deceived.

Genesis 27:34,

"When Esau heard his father's words, he burst out with a loud and bitter cry."

Genesis 27:36,

"Esau said, "Isn't he rightly named Jacob? This is the second time he has taken advantage of me: He took my birthright, and now he's taken my blessing!"

Genesis 27:41,

"Esau held a grudge against Jacob because of the blessing his father had given him. He said to himself, "The days of mourning for my father are near; then I will kill my brother Jacob."

The bitter cry of Esau reflected his character, and it indicated an unchanging attitude or spirit that causes fear and terror among his enemies. It was a murderous spirit and when the descendants of Ishmael married the descendants of Esau, *Genesis 36,* this second spirit also found its home among the Arabs, including the Amalekites and the Edomites, and eventually in the house of Islam. In 4000 years, the Middle East has been a battleground of horrific warfare, hatred, violence and terror and this is reflected in many verses in the Qur'an, for example:

Al-Anfaal (8):60,

"Against them make ready your strength to the utmost of your power, including steeds of war, to **strike terror** into (the hearts of) the enemies of Allah and your enemies."

However, God has declared His hatred for this violent and immoral spirit within Esau and that He will wipe it out forever. Take note of these following verses:

Hebrews 12:14-17,

"Make every effort to live in peace with everyone and to be holy; without holiness no one will see the Lord. See to it that no one falls short of the grace of God and that no bitter root grows up to cause trouble and defile many. See that no one is sexually immoral, or is godless like Esau, who for a single meal sold his inheritance rights as the oldest son. Afterward, as you know, when he wanted to inherit this blessing, he was rejected. Even though he sought the blessing with tears, he could not change what he had done."

Malachi 1:2-4,

"I have loved you," says the LORD. "But you ask, 'How have you loved us?' "Was not Esau Jacob's brother?" declares the LORD. "Yet I have loved Jacob (Israel), but Esau I have hated, and I have turned his hill country into a wasteland and left his inheritance to the desert jackals." Edom may say, "Though we have been crushed, we will rebuild the ruins." But this is what the LORD Almighty says: "They may build, but I will demolish. They will be called the Wicked Land, a people always under the wrath of the LORD."

Joel 3:19,

"Edom [will become] a desert waste, because of violence done to the people of Judah, in whose land they shed innocent blood."

Obadiah 1:6-10,

"Esau will be ransacked, his hidden treasures pillaged! All your allies will force you to the border; your friends will deceive and overpower you; those who eat your bread will set a trap for you, but you will not detect it. "In that day," declares the LORD, "will I not destroy the wise men of Edom, those of understanding in the mountains of Esau? Your warriors, Teman, will be terrified, and everyone in Esau's mountains will be cut down in the slaughter. Because of the violence against your brother Jacob, you will be covered with shame; you will be destroyed forever."

Modern Day Esau – C21st

Some of the movements that display the characteristics of Esau:

Al-Qaeda, Islamic Jihad, ISIS, Hezbollah, Hamas, Houthi, Boko Haram, Muslim Brotherhood, Al Shabaab, Jemaah Islamiyah, Ansar al-Sharia, Taliban, etc.

On the flags of Islamic nations and movements, we see the fulfilment of the prophecy over Esau:

Genesis 27:40,

"You will live by the sword and you will serve your brother."

This has been evident in modern times and today nearly every Islamic country in the Middle East has incorporated the sword into their national flags. Terrorist organizations like Al-Qaeda and ISIS proudly display this flag.

The reign of terror from the spirit of Esau has been blatantly obvious since the rise of Islamic attacks by the PLO since the Munich Olympics in 1972, the campaign of suicide bombings of civilian airplanes, the Iranian Revolution with Ayatollah Khomeini in 1979, the 911 attack from Al-Qaeda, the rise of ISIS in the 2000's and many others around the world.

How many Jihad attacks since 911 (September 11, 2001)?

Jihad Report
February, 2026

Attacks	**115**
Killed	**748**
Injured	**510**
Suicide Blasts	**4**
Countries	**19**

List of Attacks

Mosab Hassan Yousef, son of the Founder of Hamas:

"Look at the division and the global confusion because of Hamas. They brought us to our knees somehow by their brutality and their barbarism. Brutality is even understating Hamas' acts. Hamas is a religious movement, and they are a raging religious movement against Israel. The mainstream media cannot say this, because they are afraid to ignite a religious war. And what I say, it already is. They want to annihilate the Jewish people because they are Jewish people, because they are a Jewish state."

Two Nations – the Nation of Islam and the Nation of Israel

Today we have two nations that have been born out of the pain of Ishmael and Esau and the deception of Jacob. No wonder there is confusion among the nations as to who owns what.

The issue of justice and land rights, and refugees mixed in with the covenant purposes of God have made this an extremely complicated and emotional issue. It is the perfect breeding ground for rejected spirits to inter-mingle with the spirit of hatred, revenge, and murder. This is why people are confused. This is why when terrorism occurs, even when committed by Muslims quoting from the Qur'an and the Hadith and crying out "Allahu Akhbar!" and saying they are true Muslims, others reject them saying they have corrupted true Islam. If they are confused is it any wonder the rest of the world also is confused?

The answer is simple. There are two separate spirits trapped inside the strong man's house. The spirit of Ishmael and the spirit of Esau – the son and grandson of Abraham. One is crying out for reconciliation and the restoration of sonship and inheritance. The other is crying out for revenge.

The spirit of Esau, with its spirit of hatred, terrorism, violence, immorality and warfare was described by Jesus and the apostle John, as belonging to the spirit of Antichrist, who sincerely believe they are doing the will of God. This is what makes it so frightening. It is not because they want to do evil but they are being held captive by Satan, the strong man, who so deceives them that they really believe that this is God's will.

John 16:1-4,

"These things I have spoken to you, that you should not be made to stumble. They will put you out of the synagogues; yes, the time is coming that ***whoever kills you will think that he offers God service.*** And these things they will do to you because they have not known the Father nor Me. But these things I have told you, that when the time comes, you may remember that I told you of them."

1John 2:18-22,

"Little children, it is the last hour; and as you have heard that ***the Antichrist is coming, even now many antichrists have come***, by which we know that it is the last hour. They went out from us, but they were not of us; for if they had been of us, they would have continued with us; but they went out that they might be made manifest, that none of them were of us. But you have an anointing from the Holy One, and you know all things. I have not written to you because you do not know the truth, but because you know it, and that no lie is of the truth. Who is a liar but he who denies that Jesus is the Christ? ***He is antichrist who denies the Father and the Son.***"

This is why we need to belong to the "stronger man", Jesus, who is able to set people free from the hand of Satan and we need to introduce our friends to Jesus because He is the answer to the cry of their heart.

Can you hear the Cry of Ishmael?

In the midst of this confusion and chaos, do not let your fear of the spirit of Esau, the murderous, terroristic spirit control your thinking or your responses. Esau is in the hand of God. We need to have an ear to hear the cry of Ishmael. Ismael seeks his father and wants to be a son and not a slave. There are millions of Ishmaels and they are crying. The harvest is ripe. It's rich. It's ready. But the harvesters are few.

John 4:35,

"Do you not say, 'There are still four months and then comes the harvest'? Behold, I say to you, lift up your eyes and look at the fields, for they are already white for harvest!"

Luke 10:2,

Jesus said, "The harvest truly is great, but the laborers are few; therefore, pray the Lord of the harvest to send out laborers into His harvest."

The Abrahamic Covenant will be fulfilled

The borders of the Promised Land God gave to Abraham:

SOUTH TO NORTH: *Genesis 15:*18 - From the River Nile to the River Euphrates.

EAST TO WEST: *Joshua 23:4* - From the River Jordan to the Mediterranean Sea.

Today, radical Islam claims this territory as their own. This is their vision. They teach their followers to come out into the streets and chant, "From the River to the Sea, Palestine will be free!" Sadly, they have no idea what that statement means. It really means that Israel would have full authority and ownership of that land.

Radical Islam states that this is their right as the children of Abraham, but God has another plan, an amazing plan that will bring great revival to the Middle East. Egypt, and Israel, and the area of Assyria encompassing Iraq, Iran, Syria and Lebanon, and the areas of Jordan, Saudi Arabia, Yemen and the other Gulf States will be swamped with the awesome power of God. We will see the sons of Ishmael come home, find their father, have their sonship restored and they will find their place in the global Body of Christ, ***Isaiah 17-19; Isaiah 60; Ezekiel 37; Revelation 5:9-10; 7:1-17.*** This will be discussed, more fully, in a later chapter in this book.

Questions to ponder and discuss?

1. What steps can I take to find people who are of the "spirit of Ishmael"?
2. What question do I feel comfortable asking a Muslim friend to begin a discussion?
3. What do I think needs to happen in the church today to enable us to better respond to the cry of Ishmael? Outline the steps you feel should be taken then pray about how you can implement such a course of action. Crystalize your thoughts and write them down. Put them on a piece of paper and slip it into your Bible and pray over it until the Lord shows you how and when you are to act!

DILEMMA 2

THE BIBLE DILEMMA?

A major dilemma facing Muslims is the Bible. Muslims believe the Qur'an is true. The Qur'an says that the Bible is also true. Can the Bible and the Qur'an both be true? How can that be?

The Qur'an frequently mentions the book of the Jews, the *Tawrat* or the Law, and the book of the Christians, the *Injil* or the Bible. These books were present with the Muslims of Muhammad's day. They are described in the Qur'an as books that were "between their hands" or "with them" or "sent down beforehand." These books are said to have been "given" by God, to have "come down from God", to have been "revealed" by God. They cannot be changed or altered. Jews and Christians must follow them. Jews and Christians are commanded to judge by what is written therein. If Muhammad had any questions, he was told to ask "the People of the Book", the Jews and the Christians. The Qur'an claims to be given as a confirmation of all that is written in these books, that is, the Old Testament and the New Testament, the Bible.

Several hundred years after the time of Muhammad, Muslims began to read the Bible and discovered that the Qur'an contradicted the Bible.

To solve this dilemma, Muslims claimed that the book of the Jews, (the Law or the *Tawrat* (the Old Testament) and the book of the Christians (the

Gospel or the *Injil* (the New Testament) have been changed. They did not contain the original words of God!

Were they changed? The Qur'an clearly states that God's words cannot be changed!

This remains a major dilemma for Muslims today.

If the Qur'an confirms the Bible and the Bible is true, then the Qur'an must be false because the Qur'an says the Bible is true.

If the Qur'an confirms the Bible and the Bible has been altered and corrupted, then the Qur'an must be false for confirming a false book.

What is the Law, the Book of the Jews?

The Law or Torah (Arabic - *Tawrat*) in the Qur'an is the book of the Jews, the 39 Old Testament books that include the writings of Moses, David and all the prophets. This book existed in many manuscripts, in many languages, in the days of Muhammad.

The Old Testament was written by many authors. Among the authors were Job, Moses, Joshua, Samuel, David, Solomon, the Prophets, Ezra, Nehemiah. It was written in the Hebrew language, with small sections in Aramaic. The Old Testament was written over a period of about 1,100 years from the time of Moses in 1500 BC until the last prophet, Malachi in 400BC. It was compiled as one book before the year 250BC. About 200BC, the Old Testament was translated into the Greek language and is known as "the Septuagint". This was the book of the Jews that existed in the days of Muhammad and had existed for hundreds of years before Muhammad came on the scene and was available in many countries, including the Arabian Peninsula, its message being primarily circulated through oral traditions, local Christian and Jewish communities, and in canonical languages like Syriac, Hebrew, or Greek.

The Bible that existed in Muhammad's day, is the same Bible we have today. Manuscripts from nearly all the books in the Old Testament were discovered in Qumran near the Dead Sea in 1947. These handwritten copies contain the same content as the Old Testament we have today. A manuscript of the Greek Old Testament, the Septuagint, was also discovered in Egypt in 200AD. None of the manuscripts discovered differ from the Old Testament that both Jews and Christians have today.

The Torah or Old Testament, the book that exists today, is the same Book that existed in the days of Muhammad.

This is the revelation that all Muslims must believe in.

Surah Al Baqarah 2:136

"Say, O believers, 'We believe in Allah and what has been revealed to us, and what was revealed to Abraham, Ishmael, Isaac, Jacob, and their descendants, and what was given to Moses, Jesus, and all other prophets from their Lord. We make no distinction between any of them, and to Allah we submit.'"

This is the Book that is declared to be the criterion for judgment.

Surah Al-Maidah 5: 43.

"How come they unto thee for judgment when they have the Law, wherein Allah hath delivered judgment (for them)? Yet even after that they turn away. Such (folk) are not believers."

This is the Book that is confirmed to be from God Himself and is binding upon them. Whoever does not use the Torah to judge matter are called wrong-doers.

Surah Al-Maidah 5:45.

"And We prescribed for them therein: The life for the life, and the eye for the eye, and the nose for the nose, and the ear for the ear, and the tooth for the tooth, and for wounds retaliation. But whoso forgoeth it, it shall be expiation for him. Whoso judgeth not by that which Allah hath revealed: such are wrong-doers.

Also, this is the Book that the prophet Muhammad himself had seen.

According to a Hadith, "A group of Jews came and invited the Apostle of Allah to Quff. So he visited them in their school. They said: Abul Qasim, one of our men has committed fornication with a woman; so pronounce judgment upon them. They placed a cushion for the Apostle of Allah who sat on it and said: Bring the Torah. It was then brought. He then withdrew the cushion from beneath him and placed the Torah on it saying: I believed in thee and in Him Who revealed thee. *(Sunan Abu Dawood 4449).*

The Hadiths clearly show that the Torah was read and recited by the Jews in the days of Muhammad.

Another Hadith says, "The people of the Scripture (Jews) used to recite the Torah in Hebrew, and they used to explain it in Arabic to the Muslims. On that Allah's Apostle said, "Do not believe the people of the Scripture or disbelieve them, but say: We believe in Allah and what is revealed to us." *(Sahih al-Bukhari, 4485).*

The Psalms are also declared to be the Word of God. The Psalms (Arabic – *Zabur*) according to the Qur'an, are in the book of David (*Dawuud*), one of the holy books revealed by God before the Qur'an.

God gave David the Psalms.

Surah An-Nisa 4:163.

"...To David We gave the Psalms."

Surah Al Isra 17:55.

"We did bestow on some prophets more (and other) gifts than on others: and We gave to David (the gift of) the Psalms."

The Qur'an states that God Himself wrote in the Psalms.

Surah Al-Anbiya 21:105.

"Before this We wrote in the Psalms, after the Message (given to Moses): My servants the righteous, shall inherit the earth."

Also, the Hadiths confirm that the Psalms are the word of God.

"Narrated Abu Huraira: The Prophet said, "The reciting of the *Zabur* (i.e. Psalms) was made easy for David. He used to order that his riding animals be saddled, and would finish reciting the Psalms before they were saddled. And he would never eat except from the earnings of his manual work." (*Sahih al-Bukhari, 3417*).

Thus, all Muslims must believe in and be guided by the Psalms of David.

Strangely the Qur'an also affirms another book, not found in the Bible which is called "the Scrolls of Abraham", According to the Qur'an, the writings of Abraham are said to be the Word of God. What this means is not clear. Some scholars suggest that the Scrolls of Abraham refer to some Hebrew writings called the Sefer Yetzirah. Jewish tradition ascribes the reception of its revelation to Abraham. Other scholars, however, suggest it refers to another writing called the Testament of Abraham, which was also available at the time of Muhammad.

Surah Al-Ala 87:9-19.

"And this is in the Books of the earliest (Revelation) … The Books of Abraham and Moses."

Surah An Najm 53:36.

"Nay, is he not acquainted with what is in the Books of Moses. And of Abraham who fulfilled his engagements?"

What is the Gospel, the Book of the Christians?

The book of the Christians or the Gospel (Arabic, *Injil*) is the New Testament. Its 27 books were written by Matthew, Mark, Luke, John, Paul, Peter, James and Jude in the Greek language.

The earliest book was probably written by Mark in 45AD and the latest around 95AD by John, the apostle. The New Testament is quoted and affirmed by the writings of the early church fathers. It was compiled as one book before the year 375 A.D. It also was the same New Testament that existed in the days of Muhammad and had been existence hundreds of years before him.

More than 24,000 ancient manuscripts of the New Testament have been found.

A team of scientists and scholars claim to have discovered manuscript verses from the world's earliest-known copy of the Gospel of Mark, possibly dating back as early as 80 A.D. They were found on a sheet of papyrus used to make an ancient mummy's mask in Egypt. A manuscript of a section of the Gospel of John was also discovered recently. It was copied about 125AD, about 35 years after it had been written. Almost all portions of the New Testament in their present form were in general circulation among the churches of the Second Century after Christ. A Council of the bishops of 318 churches, the First Council of Nicaea, agreed that all these were fully recognized and accepted as the Word of God and inspired by the Holy Spirit.

The Law and the Gospel together form the Bible. This is the Bible, the Book of the Christians that existed in the days of Muhammad.

There have also been early manuscripts found that contain both the Old and the New Testaments. Three of the earliest are as follows:

- **The Codex Vaticanus**, one of the oldest manuscripts of the Greek Bible (Old and New Testament), written in about 350 AD.
- **The Codex Sinaiticus**, a handwritten copy of the Greek Bible written about 330-360.
- **The Codex Alexandrinus**, a fifth-century manuscript of the Greek Bible, containing the majority of the Septuagint and the New Testament.

These complete Bible manuscripts contained both the book of the Jews, the Old Testament and the book of the Christians, the New

Testament. They were written hundreds of years before Muhammad received his revelations.

The Jews and the Christians are called in the Qur'an, "the People of the Book." Muslims are never called that. The Book, sometimes translated "the Scriptures" is always referred to in the Qur'an as the true and authentic Book of God, sent down by Him.

What does the Qur'an Say about the Law and the Gospel?

The Law and the Gospel are "sent down" by God as a guide to mankind

The Qur'an says the Bible was sent down by the God, the same God as the God of the Jews and the Christian. According to the Qur'an, the God of the Muslims who sent down the Qur'an, is the same God who sent down the Law and the Gospel.

Surah Ali Imran 3:2-3.

"Allah! There is no God but He, - the Living, the Self-subsisting, Eternal ... He sent down the Law (of Moses) and the Gospel (of Jesus) ... as a guide to mankind.

If the same God sent down the book of the Qur'an, the book of the Law and the book of the Gospels, then all must be equally true, valid and authentic. They are all described as guides to mankind. Can that be?

Muslims must believe in the Law and the Gospels

All Muslims who believe in God and his apostle Muhammad, are commanded in the Qur'an to also believe in "the Book which was sent down before them".

Surah An Nisa 4:136

"0 ye who believe! Believe in Allah, and His Apostle - and the scripture which He sent before them".

All Muslims are also told not to dispute with the "People of the Book", which means, Jews and Christians. They are told to tell them that they believe in the revelation which came from Muhammad and that they also believe in what came down from God to them, that is, the Law and the Gospels.

Surah Al Ankabut 29:46.

"And dispute ye not with the People of the Book… but say, We believe in the revelation which has come down to us and that which came down to you."

We are left with a major dilemma because the revelation that came to Muhammad is contradictory to both the book of the Jews and the book of the Christians.

The Law and the Gospel are true and confirmed by the Qur'an

The Qur'an that Allah revealed to Muhammad is said to confirm what He revealed to the Jews and to the Christians. He is not bringing a different message.

Surah Al-Baqarah 2:41.

"And believe in what I reveal [the Qur'an], confirming *[Arabic: musaddiqan]* the revelation which is with you [the Law]."

The Arabic word *musaddiqan,* means "confirming, verifying or attesting to the truth of something". It means "to validate or support". The noun form is *tasdiq*. It is an unambiguous word that can have no other meaning.

Here are verses in the Qur'an that authenticate the Old and New Testaments.

Surah Al-Baqarah 2:89

And when there came to them (the Jews), a Book (this Qur'an) from Allah confirming [*musadiqqan*] what is with them [the Taurat (Torah) and the Injil (Gospel)…

Surah Al-Baqarah 2:91

"And when it is said to them (the Jews), "Believe in what Allah has sent down," they say, "We believe in what was sent down to us." And they disbelieve in that which came after it, while it is the truth confirming (*musaddiqan*) what is with them."

Surah Al-Baqarah 2:97

"Say "Whoever is an enemy to Jibrael (Gabriel), for indeed he has brought it (this Qur'an) down to your heart by Allah's Permission, confirming [*musaddiqan*] what came before it [i.e. the Tawrat (Torah) and the Injil (Gospel)] and guidance and glad tidings for the believers."

Surah Al-Baqarah 2:101

And when there came to them an Apostle from Allah verifying (*musadiqqan*) that which the- have, a party of those who were given the Book threw the Book of Allah behind their backs as if they knew nothing.

Surah Ali-Imran 3:81.

God received the covenant of the prophets, "Inasmuch as I have given you of scripture and wisdom; should a messenger come to you verifying (*musaddiqan*) what you have, you shall believe in him and support him."

Surah An-Nisa 4:47.

"O you who were given the Book! Believe in what We sent down, confirming [*musaddiqan*] what is with you, before We obliterate faces, and turn them upon their backs, or curse them as We cursed the Sabbath-men, and God's command is done."

Surah Yunus 10:37,

"The Qur'an is ... a confirmation (*tasdiq*) of (revelations) that went before it".

Surah Al-Faathir 35:31,

"Indeed, in their stories, there is a lesson for men of understanding. It (the Qur'an) is not a forged statement but a confirmation (*tasdiq*) of the Allah's existing Books [the *Tawrat* (Torah), the *Injil* (Gospel) and other Scriptures of Allah]".

Surah Yunus 10:37,

"This Koran could not have been forged apart from God; but it is a confirmation(*tasdiq*) of what is before it, and a distinguishing of the Book, wherein is no doubt, from the Lord of all Being."

Surah Yusuf 12:111,

"And what We have inspired in you (O Muhammad), of the Book (the Qur'an), it is the (very) truth [that you (Muhammad) and your followers must act on its instructions], a confirmation (*tasdiq*) of that which was (revealed) before it".

Surah As-Saffat 37:37,

"In fact, he came with the truth, confirming (*sadiqa*) ⌜earlier⌝ messengers."

Surah Al-Aqhaf 46:12,

"And before this, was the Book of Moses as a guide and a mercy: And this Book confirms (*musadiqqan*) (it) in the Arabic tongue."

Surah Al-Aqhaf 46:30,

"They said, "O our people, we have heard a Scripture, sent down after Moses, confirming (*musadiqqan*) what came before it. It guides to the truth, and to a straight path."

By reading the above verses, it becomes obvious that when Muhammad received the Qur'an, he had no doubt at all, that the verses he was reciting were confirming, verifying, authenticating and absolutely supporting the truth of all the previous Scriptures revealed by God. Thus, the Qur'an states unequivocally that the Bible, which includes both the books of the Jews and the Christians, is true.

The Bible is affirmed to be the truth, glad tidings, a guide and a mercy that leads to a straight path.

The Law and the Gospel must be used to judge matters

Not only does the Qur'an verify the Old and New Scriptures, but it is also used to judge matters. The Jews are told to judge matters with the Torah, and the Christians are told to judge matters by the Gospel.

Surah Al-Maidah 5:44,46,47,49,

"It was We who revealed the Law (to Moses); therein was guidance and light ... if any do fail to judge by the light of what Allah hath revealed, they are (no better than) unbelievers ... We sent Jesus, the son of Mary, confirming the Law that had come before him: We sent him the Gospel: Therein was guidance and light ... a guidance and an admonition to those who fear Allah. Let the people of the Gospel judge by what Allah hath revealed therein. If any do fail to judge by the light of what Allah hath revealed, they are (no better than) those who rebel. Judge. . . what Allah hath revealed..."

There is no suggestion in the Qur'an that the Law or the Gospel are false, misleading, altered, corrupted or contaminated in any way.

Christians and Jews must stand by their books

The people of the book, Christians and Jews are instructed to stand by their books, the revelation that has come from their Lord, their God.

Surah Al Maidah 5:68."People of the Book! ... Stand fast by the Law, the Gospel, and all the revelation that hath come to you from YOUR LORD. It is the revelation that has come to thee from THY LORD."

Muhammad was told to ask the Christians and the Jews if he had any doubts

Furthermore, if Muhammad had any doubts, he was told to ask the Christians and the Jews, who are the people who had read the Book before him. The Bible in its current form, existed in the days of Muhammad and was being read by Christians and Jews. Allah told Muhammad that if he had any questions or doubts about the revelations he was receiving, that he was to ask the Jews and the Christians who had read the Bible before him. As Muslims claim that Muhammad was illiterate, he could not have read it for himself. According to the Hadith, occasionally he used to ask for it to be read to him. The Bible is referred to as the Book or the Scripture (*al kitab*) and as the Message or Remembrance (*al thikr*).

Surah Yunus 10:94

"If you are in doubt about what We revealed to you, ask those who read the Scripture (*al kitab*) before you. The truth has come to you from your Lord, so do not be of those who doubt."

Surah An-Nahl 16:43

AND [even] before thy time, [O Muhammad,] We never sent [as Our apostles] any but [mortal] men, whom We inspired: and if you have not [yet] realized this, ask the followers of [earlier] revelation (*al-thikr*)."

Surah Al Anbiya 21:7.

Before thee, also, the apostles We sent were but men, to whom We granted inspiration: If ye realize this not, ask of those who possess the Message (*al thikr*)

Again, we see the enormous dilemma posed by these verses for all Muslims who want to understand the message of the Qur'an. Muslims are directed to look for answers from Christians and Jews. Why does it not just advise them to ask their Muslims teachers or leaders?

Both the Law and the Gospel are Confirmed as the Word of God

Surah Al-Maidah 5:43

But why do they come to thee for decision, when they have (their own) Law before them?- Therein is the (plain) command of God; yet even after that, they would turn away. For they are not (really) people of faith

The Gospel was between the hands of Muhammad ("*baina yadihi*" – Arabic words that mean "between the hands") and thus was clearly available in his time.

Surah Al-Maidah 5:46-48.

"And We sent, following in their footsteps, Jesus, the son of Mary, confirming that which came before him in the Torah; and We gave him the Gospel, in which was guidance and light and confirming that which preceded it of the Torah as guidance and instruction for the righteous.

And let the People of the Gospel judge by what Allah has revealed therein. And whoever does not judge by what Allah has revealed - then it is those who are the defiantly disobedient.

And We have revealed to you, [O Muhammad], the Book in truth, confirming that which preceded it of the Scripture and as a criterion over it.

So judge between them by what Allah has revealed and do not follow their inclinations away from what has come to you of the truth. To each of you We prescribed a law and a method. Had Allah willed, He would have made you one nation [united in religion], but [He intended] to test you in what He has given you; so race to [all that is] good... "

It is obvious that both the Law and the Gospel that was sent down by God, existed in the days of Muhammad and was available to them. God calls upon Jews and Christians, the People of the Book to stand upon them and hold fast to them.

Surah Al-Ma'idah 5:68

Say: "O People of the Book! Ye have no ground to stand upon unless ye stand fast by the Law, the Gospel and all the revelation that has come to you from your Lord...."

The fact that there were Jews and Christians "on the right course" in Muhammad's time confirms the Torah and the Gospel was unchanged in the 6th century A.D.!

The Dilemma of the Differences between the Bible and the Qur'an

It is obvious that the teaching of the Bible and the Qur'an are different and contradictory one to one another.

The main doctrinal differences between the Bible and the Qur'an can be seen in the teachings about the Trinity, the Sonship and Deity of Jesus, the crucifixion death of Jesus and his resurrection and the doctrine of salvation and redemption through the sacrificial blood of Christ. These are the central messages of the Gospel.

There are also many other differences in the records of the Qur'an and the Bible. The stories told are not the same. The Qur'an nowhere quotes verses from the Bible, only retells them with variations.

These are topics which will be discussed in other chapters.

God's Word cannot be changed

Could the message of the Bible, the Law and the Gospels, ever been changed? The following verses state clearly that God's word cannot be changed. Since the Qur'an has claimed that all the books of the Christians and the Jews have come down from God, clearly, they cannot be changed.

Al Anaam 6:34. "There is none that can alter the words of Allah."

Al Anaam 6:115. "None can change His words."

Yunus 10:64."No change can there be in the words of Allah."

Al Khaf 18:27. "None can change His words."

Muslim scholars affirmed in their commentaries that it is impossible to change God's Word in the "books".

Al-Tabari (839–923AD), a Persian Qur'anic scholar and historian who wrote the first history of Muhammad "Tarikh al-Rusul wa'l-Muluk," commenting on these verses, said: ""None can change His words", He is saying that there is no one who could change what He has informed in His books about anything which is bound to happen during it's time or has been postponed. It all happens as Allah says it would." *(Ibn Jarir al-Tabari, Jami' al-bayan fi ta'wil al-Qur'an, Commentary on Surah 6:115).*

However, when it became evident that what was written in the Torah and the Injil was different to what was written in the Qur'an, the Muslim scholars had to give an explanation.

Ibn Khazem (994-1064) a well-known Muslim historian, poet, philosopher and theologian from Spain: said, "The manuscripts today have clearly been changed because they are not the same as the contents of the Qur'an. Therefore, the Gospel was changed after the time of Muhammad."

As we can see from the above verses, this explanation was an attempt to justify the Qur'an. However, since there are thousands of copies of both the Old Testament and the New Testament that exist both before and after the time of Muhammad, that statement is clearly refuted by the facts. The Bible before the time of Muhammad and after the time of Muhammad shows no evidence of change. It is exactly the same book.

Archeological Confirmation that the Bible is Accurate

Archaeologists have discovered literally hundreds of objects, inscriptions, and sites that confirm the accuracy of biblical statements. In the last few years, the number of these archaeological confirmations has dramatically increased. Below, are listed a few.

In **Nazareth,** the remains of a first-century stone house was found, the first concrete archaeological proof that Nazareth was settled in the time of Jesus.

In Jerusalem, ossuaries, or **burial boxes**, were discovered, The ossuary of the high priest Caiaphas and the ossuary of James the Just, the brother of Jesus were discovered. Both were dated to the first century, a period in history when it was the custom to place bones in ossuaries. Inscribed on the side of James' ossuary was written in Aramaic "Ya'akov bar-Yosef akhui diYeshua" (James son of Joseph, brother of Jesus). Some evangelical scholars argue, it represents the first ever archaeological confirmation of Jesus.

In 2009 there was the discovery of a large and remarkably ornate first-century synagogue at **Magdala**, on the Sea of Galilee, where Jesus almost certainly preached. In the centre of the building was a large decorated stone, now known as the 'Magdala Stone'. On it were images including a seven-branch menorah, rosette, and fiery wheels. The menorah image is thought to be the oldest known depiction of the menorah, at least outside of Jerusalem, as it appeared in the Temple. It included a coin minted in Tiberias in 29 AD helping to date the structure to the first century, the time of Jesus' ministry. Archaeologists suggest that the synagogue was likely a place where Jesus taught.

The Gabriel Tablet. In 2008, Israeli archaeologists announced the discovery of a first-century stone tablet, written in ancient Hebrew, that mentioned the angel Gabriel and a messianic figure who would suffer, die and perhaps rise again in three days, dramatic confirmation of other textual discoveries that suggested many Jews in the first century were expecting a suffering and dying messiah.

An impression of **King Hezekiah's royal seal** was discovered in excavations in Jerusalem, the first seal impression of an Israelite or Judean king ever exposed on site in a scientific archaeological excavation. On it are inscribed the words, "Belonging to Hezekiah [son of] Ahaz king of Judah."

Archaeological discoveries have proved repeatedly that the Bible record of people and places is accurate.

The Concept of Change or Corruption - *Muharraf* or *Tahriif*

Could the Law and the Gospel be changed (Arabic word, *tahriif*)?

According to the original teachings of Islam, every Muslim must believe in the Law and the Gospels. Muhammad believed the Bible was true and claimed the Qur'an was given to confirm the Bible. The Qur'an itself states quite clearly that the Law and the Gospel come from God and must be believed by all Muslims.

Yet, Muslims say that the Bible has been corrupted.

In Arabic, the terms for change or corruption are "*muharraf*" or "*tahriif*". The concept of *muharraf* or *tahrif* comes from the Arabic verb "*harrafa*" which means: to change, corrupt, or to alter the true meaning. (A Dictionary of Modern Written Arabic, Hans Wehr, Beirut, 1974, p.168-169).

This accusation of corruption is made four times in the Qur'an, not against the Books, but against the Jewish leaders for their use of them.

Those four verses indicate, not that the Bible itself is corrupted, not that the words of the Bible are changed, nor that the written text is altered. They clearly state that it is the Jews who deliberately distort, take words out of context and change words around.

1. ***Al Baqarah 2:75*** "Some of them used to hear the Word of God, and then deliberately distort it, even after understanding it..."

2. ***An Nisa 4:46*** "Among the Jews are some who take words out of context… twisting with their tongues and slandering the religion."
3. ***Al Maidah 5:13*** They change the words from their (right) places…
4. ***Al Maidah 5:41*** They distort words from their places…

It is clear from the Qur'an that the original words of the Law and the Gospel remain the inspired, authenticate, unchangeable words of God. There is not one verse in the Qur'an that states the Law and the Gospel have been changed!

If the "Law" and the "Gospel" are changed (tahriif), then God has not kept His promise to protect ALL of His Word.

Muslims are required by God in the Qur'an to believe and obey the "Law" and the "Gospel". If they do, they would have to acknowledge Jesus is the Son of God and the one Savior of mankind. This is the reason that Muslims today reject the Bible as the Word of God and say it was changed. However, there are many reasons why it is impossible for the Bible to be changed.

1. If the Jews had changed the Tawrat, the Law, the Old Testament books, then Christian scholars, who also believe in the Old Testament, would attack the Jews for defiling the Scriptures and destroying the Word of God.
2. If the Christians had changed the Injil, the Gospel, the New Testament books, Jewish scholars would attack Christians for creating a new story and they would ridicule Christianity for hypocrisy.
3. If both the Law and the Gospel were changed, both believing Jews and believing Christians would protest because God promised the greatest curses on anyone who changed God's Word. "I warn everyone who hears the words of the prophecy of this book; if any one adds to them, God will add to him the plagues described in this book, and if any one takes away from the words of the book of this

prophecy, God will take away his share in the tree of life and in the holy city, which are described in this book." Revelation 22:18-19.

4. It is not possible to change the Law and the Gospel, because secular and other critics would produce the ancient manuscripts and prove that it had been changed and that we have a corrupted Bible.
5. It is not possible that the Law and the Gospels were changed because in the days of Muhammad, the true Law and the true Gospel were "between his hands"(*baina yadihi*). ***Al-Maida 5:46-48***.
6. It is not possible that the Law and the Gospels were changed because if the scriptures had been changed by Jews and Christians in Arabia (Medina), then there would still be many true copies of the Law and the Gospel in many other countries. It would not be possible to destroy ALL the evidence of the true Law and the true Gospel.
7. In addition to this, all of Islam's early commentators stated that the Law and the Gospels have not been changed

    a. Ali al-Tabari (838-870),
    b. Amr al-Ghakhiz (d.869),
    c. Bukhari (810-870);
    d. Al-Mas'udi (896-956);
    e. Abu Ali Husain Bin Sina (980-1037
    f. Al-Ghazzali (1058-1111);
    g. Fakhruddin Razi (1149-1209);
    h. Ibn-Khaldun (1332-1406).

One of the most authentic interpreters of Islam, Ibn Kathir, clearly expressed that the Bible has not been changed. "Wahb bin Munabbih said, "The Tawrat and Injil remain as Allah revealed them, and no letter in them was removed. However, the people misguide others by addition and false interpretation, relying on books that they wrote themselves." Then, they say: "This is from Allah," but it is not from Allah. As for Allah's books, they are still preserved and cannot be changed." (Tafsir Ibn Kathir – Abridged, Volume 2, Parts 3, 4 & 5).

8. A modern commentator states that the Law and the Gospels have not been changed. In the modern era, the famous Islamic scholar, Sir Sayyid Ahmad Khan (1817-1898), also stated that the Bible was not changed.

Evidence says the Bible of Muhammad's day was exactly the same as we have today. If the Bible is changed (*tahriif*), where are the true and unchanged copies? If the Bible has not been changed (*tahriif*) and corrupted, and the Qur'an asserts it confirms the Law and the Gospel, then Muslims must acknowledge Jesus is the Son of God and the one and only Savior of the world!

When we were studying the Qur'an in Yemen, our teacher told us that the Bible had been changed. Jeff asked him to show us the verse. He told us that he would bring it the next day. Jeff asked him again on the following day, but he said he had forgotten but would bring it the next day. This continued till the last day of the course, when he finally banged the desk and said, "You have asked me ten times! There is no verse! But there are thousands of interpretations." Jeff replied, "I don't want the interpretations. I want to hear what God says." The teacher answered, "You are right. You are my professor."

This exchange revealed to us how great a dilemma exists for Muslims. They believe the Qur'an is true, but if that is so, they must also believe the Bible is true. The contradictions between the two books is so evident, that if they are honest, they must confront an overwhelming challenge to their beliefs.

Is the Pattern of the Revelation of the Bible and the Qur'an the same?

The Qur'an is an oral revelation sent down during the years 610 – 632 to one man, Muhammad. He claimed Gabriel would appear to him and speak the verses from time to time as the exact words of God. There is no sequence or order in the 114 chapters (surah) of the Qur'an. Muhammad would tell others his verses and they would then commit them to memory or write them down on leaves, stones, bones or animal skins.

The Qur'anic revelation was a dictation sent down word for word by an "angel." Gabriel appears before him and commands him to recite the first lines of surah 96.

Surah Al-Alaq 96:1,

Read! In the name of your Lord who has created (all that exist).

Muhammad's experience is also mentioned in the following verse.

An Najm 53:4-10,

"It is only an Inspiration that is inspired: He has been taught (this Qur'an) by one mighty in power [Jibrael (Gabriel)]... So did (Allah) convey the Inspiration to His slave."

The concept is that it is literal words in Arabic that are "sent down." Therefore, the Qur'an can only truly be understood in Arabic because translations inevitably distort the meaning. That means every single Arabic word is divinely inspired and not one word can be changed.

The Bible, however, is a Revelation that came by fellowship and communication between God and man and was revealed by the Holy Spirit in various ways to over 40 people, from Moses to John during a period of about 1600 years. It is not the actual Hebrew, Aramaic or Greek words that are inspired, but the meaning and the message. The prophets then wrote down the meaning and the message. Thus, the Bible can be translated into every language and the message will still be a revelation that everyone can understand.

Hebrews 1:1-2,

"God, who at many times and in many ways spoke in time past to the fathers by the prophets, has in these last days spoken to us by His Son."

The Biblical revelation includes the Law, the Psalms, the Prophets and the Gospel. The Word of God was revealed to many different men who spoke with the inspiration of the Holy Spirit.

2Peter 1:21,

"For the prophecy came not in old time by the will of man: but holy men of God spoke as they were moved by the Holy Spirit."

Conclusion

The Bible is the Word of God – its message is the same as 2000 years ago. Its authenticity, accuracy and authority is confirmed by many thousands of ancient manuscripts and an ever-increasing number of archaeological discoveries. The Qur'an confirms that the Bible is the Word of God.

The Qur'an and the Bible do not agree.

Therefore, the dilemma remains:

If the Bible is true,
then the Qur'an must be a false book
because the Qur'an says the Bible is true.

If Bible has been altered and corrupted,
then the Qur'an must be false
for confirming an altered and corrupted book.

Either way,
The Qur'an must be a false book

Questions for Discussion:

1. In what ways does the Qur'an confirm the accuracy, authority, inspiration and preservation of the Bible?
2. What is the difference between the method of revelation of the Bible and the Qur'an?
3. What historical and archaeological evidence is there to confirm the accuracy of the Bible?
4. Discuss with some friends the importance of the Qur'an stating that God gave the Law, the Psalms, the Prophets, and the Gospel to the Jews and Christians and that His Words can never be changed?

DILEMMA 3

THE QUR'AN DILEMMA

What is the Qur'an?

We have seen how the Qur'an authenticates, affirms and confirms the Bible to be inspired by God and is true. What about the Qur'an itself? How was it received? Is the Qur'an itself authentic and truly the word sent down from God? Islam claims that the Qur'an is eternal. It claims the original is in heaven and was sent down portion by portion through Gabriel to Muhammad, perfect, uncreated, unchangeable and impossible to be altered! This creates many dilemmas for Muslims.

"The Qur'an" means "the recitation." Muhammad recited words that were given to him. The Qur'an consists of 114 chapters, which in Arabic are called "Surahs". The Qur'an was written in Arabic, and it is said, can only really be understood in Arabic. It has no chronological or historical order, very few geographical locations and little clear thematic order. Its content has a few basic components: teaching about Allah, Paradise and Hell, instructions on how to live and stories mainly borrowed from the Bible.

Is the Qur'an really the word of God? Does it contain the actual words of God? What is its true origin? Has it been perfectly preserved? Let's look at the origin and history of the Qur'an according to Muslim sources.

The Beginning of the Qur'an in 610 AD: Initial revelations

Muhammad was forty years old in the year 610 AD when he claimed to receive his first revelation from the angel Gabriel. How did this impact Muhammad? It seems that initially, receiving the revelation was a terrifying experience for him! He called himself "majnun" meaning "possessed by jinn" or "crazy". His experience was so bad that he determined to commit suicide and throw himself off the mountain.

According to the history written by Muhammad's biographer *Al Tabari (839-923),*

Al-Tabari, Volume VI, p. 68,

"He (Muhammad) said: I had been thinking of hurling myself down from a mountain crag, but he appeared to me, as I was thinking about this, and said, "Muhammad, I am Gabriel and you are the Messenger of God." Then he said, "Recite!" I said, "What shall I recite?" He took me and pressed me three times tightly until I was nearly stifled and was utterly exhausted; then he said: "Recite in the name of your Lord who created," and I recited it. Then I went to Khadijah and said, "I have been in fear for my life."

Al-Tabari includes several versions about Muhammad's suicide attempts in his history *Ta'rikh al-Rusul wa'l-Muluk.* Firstly, Muhammad wanted to kill himself before receiving his first Qur'anic revelation. A spirit appeared to him and said, "Muhammad, you are the Messenger of God." Muhammad then fled to his wife Khadijah and begged her to cover him.

According to the hadith, Muhammad continued his attempts to commit suicide. His wife, Khadijah, had a cousin named Waraqa who was a Nestorian Christian who shared Biblical stories with him. After Waraqa's death, Muhammad tried to kill himself multiple times because Gabriel was no longer bringing revelations to him.

Al Bukhari in Sahih al-Bukhari 6982, records:

"After a few days Waraqa died and the Divine Revelation was also paused for a while and the Prophet became so sad as we have heard that he intended several times to throw himself from the tops of high mountains and every-time he went up to the top of a mountain in order to throw himself down, Jibril would appear before him and say, "O Muhammad! You are indeed Allah's Messenger in truth", whereupon his heart would become quiet and he would calm down and would return home. And whenever the period of the coming of the revelation used to become long, he would do as before, but when he used to reach the top of a mountain, Gabriel would appear before him and say to him what he had said before".

This raises a dilemma. Were the revelations from God, or do they confirm Muhammad's first impression that this was a satanic manifestation? Was the Qur'an really from God or was it from Satan? Was the angel who appeared to Muhammad, truly the angel Gabriel or was it a deceiver?

The revelation of the Qur'an in Mecca, 610 AD to 622 AD: Prophetic revelations

For twelve years, according to Islamic tradition, the Qur'an continued to be revealed to Muhammad in Mecca. Gabriel would come to him and give him verses that Muhammad would recite to his companions. The companions would then memorize the verses or write them down on stones, bones, leaves or skins of animals.

During the years from 610 AD to 622 AD Muhammad received these revelations in the town of Mecca. These verses are referred to as the Meccan verses. These are the Surahs that contain many of the Bible based stories, many of the peaceful verses of the Qur'an and those that approve of the People of the Book, the Christians and the Jews.

Muhammad himself never wrote down any verses as Islamic tradition states that he was illiterate. Therefore to say that Muhammad wrote the Qur'an is technically incorrect. He was a reciter. The Qur'an is an oral revelation, that claims to be word for word exactly what was revealed to the prophet Muhammad.

Al Ankabut 29:48,

"And you did not recite before it any scripture, nor did you ascribe one with your right hand. Otherwise the falsifiers would have (cause for) doubt.".

Muhammad was illiterate. He could neither read nor write. The Qur'an also calls Muhammad, "the unlettered prophet".

Surah Al-Araaf 7:157,

"Those who follow the Messenger, the unlettered (illiterate) prophet, whom they find written in what they have of the Torah and the Gospel…"

Muhammad did not receive the Qur'an all at once. It was revealed gradually over the years.

Surah Al-Furqan 25:32

"And those who disbelieve say, "Why was the Qur'an not revealed to him all at once?" Thus [it is] that We may strengthen thereby your heart. And We have spaced it distinctly."

Surah Al Furqan 25.32,

"We have rehearsed it to you in slow, well-arranged stages, gradually".

During his time in Mecca, Muhammad faced rejection and mockery. The Meccans in general considered him to be merely repeating old tales, stories he made up. Many of these accusations against Muhammad are mentioned in the Qur'an.

Some people said he forged the Qur'an.

Surah Yunus 10:38,

"Or do they say [about the Prophet], "He invented it?" Say, "Then bring forth a surah like it and call upon [for assistance] whomever you can besides Allah, if you should be truthful."

He was called a Poet with muddled dreams.

Surah Al-Anbyaa 21:5,

"Nay, they say, "Muddled dreams; nay, he (has) invented it; nay, he (is) a poet. So let him bring us a sign like what was sent (to) the former."

Surah Ath-Thur 52:30,

"Or do they say:- "A Poet! we await for him some calamity (hatched) by Time!"

Surah Al-Haqqah 69.41,

"And is not – however little you may [be prepared to] believe it - the word of a poet."

The Meccans accused him of being mad (*majnuun*), possessed by jinns, demons or evil spirits who were revealing to him the words of the Qur'an.

Surah Asy-Syuaraa 26:210-212,

"And [this divine writ is such a reminder:] no evil spirits have brought it down."

Surah Al Hijr 15:6,

"They say: "O thou to whom the Message is being revealed! truly thou art mad (or possessed)."

Surah Ad Dukaan 44:14,

"Yet they turn away from him and say: "Tutored (by others), a man possessed!"

Surah Al Qalam 68:51,

"And the Unbelievers would almost trip thee up with their eyes when they hear the Message; and they say: "Surely he is possessed!"

He was also accused of sorcery.

Surah Al-Anbyaa 21:3,

"The evildoers whisper one to another, 'Is this aught but a mortal like to yourselves? What, will you take to sorcery with your eyes open?"

Other times he was accused of just bringing the words of a mere human being.

Surah Al-Mudatstsir 74:25,

"This is nothing but the word of mortal man!"

Strangely, the Qur'an issues a challenge to ponder on the thought that Muhammad was demon possessed. The challenge is given to do it both singly and in pairs.

Surah Saba 34:46,

"Say: 'With one thing I admonish you: stand up before God in pairs or singly and ponder whether your compatriot is indeed possessed. He is sent forth only to forewarn you of a grievous scourge'".

Muhammad had to be constantly reassured and give assurance to others that he was not mad, demon possessed or a fortune teller.

Surah Ath-Thur 52:29,

"So (continue to) remind (all, O Prophet). For you, by the grace of your Lord, are not a fortune-teller or a madman."

The Qur'anic verses revealed to Muhammad in Mecca raise the question of whether the words he was saying, were truly words from God or not. Was it merely human rhetoric or poetry, the results of demon possession, human invention or the work of sorcery or madness? Why were these constant attacks made upon the prophet?

The Qur'anic verses revealed in Mecca also include many stories retold from the Bible, the Jewish and Christian apocryphal books and Zoroastrian sources. This also became the basis for the accusations being made against Muhammad.

As a result of the increasing mockery, opposition, and death threats he was facing, Muhammad eventually had to flee from Mecca.

The Qur'an revealed in Medina, 622 AD - 632 AD: Political revelations

Things changed in 622AD. Because of the persecution he was experiencing, Muhammad and about 100 of his followers fled from Mecca. They migrated to the town of Yathrib, later changed to Medina. Migration in Arabic is the word *hijra.* This was the year of the migration. It marks year zero of the Islamic calendar and all Islamic time is dated as After Hijrah (AH). It was in Medina that Muhammad was received and welcomed by the local inhabitants, most of them were Jews, with some Christians.

After a couple of years, Muhammad had been able to gather many followers from the countryside and bring them to Madina. As his numbers grew he became the leader and ruler of Medina. From there he began conducting raids into surrounding areas, gathered booty, began to persecute the Jews and to evict them from the towns.

It was in Medina that Muhammad began to receive verses about moral, ceremonial and legal laws that were to become the foundation of Sharia Law. It was there also that he received revelation about conducting jihad wars and fighting for the cause of Allah.

It is important to be aware of the difference in the Meccan and the Medinian verses in the Qur'an. Verses revealed in Mecca are sometimes abrogated (replaced) and negated by those revealed in Medina. Prophetic and religious revelations tend to give way to policital revelations.

Meccan verses tend to be shorter and included towards the end of the Qur'an. They focus on the stories from the Bible, the Oneness of Allah, descriptions of hell and of paradise. The verses revealed in Medina tend to be longer and more detailed. They focus on the state and law, social order and family life, economy and politics, and community. These issues are the basis for the legal system of of Sharia Law. These verses also include much of the teaching on jihad and violence. The final Surah of the Qur'an is generally accepted to be ***Surah At Tawbah 9.*** At Tawbah, is the Surah that presents most clearly the message of jihad.

The Qur'an was unwritten at the time of Muhammad's Death in 632 AD

When Muhammad died in 632, there was no written Qur'an. At his death, the revelation of the Qur'an was automatically concluded but there was still no book. The hadith records, "Allah's Apostle did not collect the Qur'an into one volume." In other words, the "Book of Allah" did not come into existence until a long time after Muhammad died.

First Written Qur'an Collected by the 1st Caliph, Abu Bakr 632 AD-634 AD

When Muhammad died, his replacement as leader of the Muslims was Abu Bakr, the first Caliph. He began the work of collecting materials for the Qur'an. According to the Hadith: ***Sahih Bukhari, Vol. 6, p.478,***

"I started looking for the Qur'an and collecting it from (what was written on) palm-leaf stalks, thin white stones, and also from the men who knew it by heart, till I found the last verse of Surat at-Tauba (repentance) with Abi Khuzaima al-Ansari, and I did not find it with anybody other than him."

Abu Bakr created the "original" Qur'an of 634 AD. He gathered the verses from the companions of Muhammad. This Qur'an was given into the keeping of Hafsah, one of Muhammad's wives and is known as the Hafsah Codex. No copies of this Qur'an remain today.

The Qur'an Revised by Uthman 644 AD – 656 AD: The Revised Qur'an

Uthman, the 3rd Caliph, collected more versions of the Qur'an. He asked Muhammad's secretary, Zaid ibn Thabit to prepare a new version. Uthman then sent the new version of the Qur'an to 4 Islamic Centres in the Caliphate (Islamic Kingdom): Kufah, Basrah, Damascus and Mecca.

All other Qur'ans were ordered to be burned. The other versions had to be destroyed so that there could be no contradictory or variant readings. Muslim source materials report that at least four different versions of the Qur'an existed before the order was given to have them burned.

7 Reasons why we know that the Qur'an has been changed

1. Many memorizers of the Qur'an died

Many of the men who had memorized the Qur'an, died in wars that took place just after Muhammad died. Some portions of the Qur'an were only known by memorizers who had heard the words directly spoken by Muhammad himself. Ibn Kathir reported that 450 memorizers were killed in what are called the "Wars of Apostasy" at the Battle of Yamama in December 632.

A man named Musaylimah had emerged after Muhammad's death and claimed to be a prophet. Abu Bakr led Muslim jihad troops against him and the tribe, the Bani Hanifah, who supported him. Although Abu Bakr's army won, many soldiers died, among them, 450 memorizers of the Qur'an.

As a result, Zayd ibn Thabit was ordered by Abu Bakr to collate the Qur'an from the remaining material. He was afraid Muhammad's words would be lost. Many of them had not yet been written down.

Islam's hadiths record The story of the collection of the Qur'an is recorded in the Hadith.

Sahih Bukhari Book 6 Volume 6:20,

"Narrated By Zaid bin Thabit Al-Ansari: Who was one of those who used to write the Divine Revelation: Abu Bakr sent for me after the (heavy) casualties among the warriors (of the battle) of Yamama (where a great number of Qurra'(memorizes of the Qur'an) were killed). 'Umar was present with Abu Bakr who said, 'Umar has come to me and said, The people have suffered heavy casualties on the day of (the battle of) Yamama, and I am afraid that there will be more casualties among the Qurra' (those who know the Qur'an by heart) at other battle-fields, whereby a large part of the Qur'an may be lost, unless you collect it. And I am of the opinion that you should collect the Qur'an." Abu Bakr added, "I said to 'Umar, 'How can I do something which Allah's Apostle has not done?' 'Umar said (to me), 'By Allah, it is (really) a good thing.' So 'Umar kept on pressing, trying to persuade me to accept his proposal, till Allah opened my bosom for it and I had the same opinion as 'Umar." (Zaid bin Thabit added:) Umar was sitting with him (Abu Bakr) and was not speaking. me). "You are a wise young man and we do not suspect you (of telling lies or of forgetfulness): and you used to write the Divine Inspiration for Allah's Apostle. Therefore, look for the Qur'an and collect it (in one manuscript)." By Allah, if he (Abu Bakr) had ordered me to shift one of the mountains (from its place) it would not have been harder for me than what he had ordered me concerning the collection of the Qur'an. I said to both of them, "How dare you do a thing which the Prophet has not done?" Abu Bakr said, "By Allah, it is (really) a good thing. So I kept on arguing with him about it till Allah opened my bosom for that which He had opened the bosoms of Abu Bakr and Umar. So I started locating Qur'anic material and collecting it from parchments, scapula, leaf-stalks of date palms and from the memories of men (who knew it by heart). I found with Khuzaima two Verses of Surat-at-Tauba which I had not found with anybody else, (and they were): "Verily there has come to you an Apostle (Muhammad) from amongst yourselves. It grieves him that you should receive any injury or difficulty He

(Muhammad) is ardently anxious over you (to be rightly guided)" At Tawbah 9.128."

Zuhri reported,

Abu Bakr Abdullah b.abi Da'ud, Kitab al-Masahif. (Ibn Abi Dawud, Kitab al-Masahif p.23),

"We have heard that many verses of the Qur'an which were revealed but those who memorized them have been slain in the battle at Yamama. Those verses had not yet been written down, and after the death of those who memorized them, those verses are no longer known; they also had not yet been collected by Abu Bakr and Umar or Uthman into one manuscript of the Qur'an. Those verses have not been found with anyone after the deaths of those who had memorized them were killed.".

Report of Abdullah ibn Umar:

As-Suyuti, Al-Itqan fil Ulum the Qur'an, page.524,

"It has been reported from Ismail ibn Ibrahim from Ayyub from Naafi from Ibn Umar who said: "Let no-one say, "I have received the whole Qur'an". How can he know he has it all since much of the Qur'an has been lost? It would be better if he said, "I have received what could be saved."

Ahmad b.Ali b.Muhammad al-Asqalani, ibn Hajar, Fath al Bari (13 vol., Cairo 1939), vol.9, p.9,

"Zayd ibn Thabit said: "The Prophet died and the Qur'an had not yet been gathered into one place."

Ibn Abi Da'ud, Kitab al-Masahif, p.5,

"When the task was finished, Uthman kept one copy in Medina and sent others to Kūfa, Baṣra, Damascus, and, according to some accounts, Mecca, and ordered that all other variant copies of the Qur'an to be destroyed."

2. We know the Qur'an was changed because a goat ate some of the verses

***Sahih Bukhari* Vol.8, Book 82, Numbers 816-817,**

"Ibn Majah reported: "Aisha said "The verses of Al-Rajm (stoning) and Al-Rada'a (breastfeeding men) which had been revealed… and the sheets on which they were written were under my bed. Then the Apostle of Allah died. While I was busy because of his death, a goat entered and ate those sheets of paper."

The 2nd Caliph, Umar, feared that the verse on stoning adulterers, which was originally in the Qur'an, was now lost from the Qur'an. "I am afraid that after a long time has passed, people may say, "We do not find the Verses of the Rajam (stoning to death) in the Holy Book," and consequently they may go astray by leaving an obligation that Allah has revealed. Lo! I confirm that the penalty of Rajam be inflicted on him who commits illegal sexual intercourse. If he is already married and the crime is proved by witnesses or pregnancy or confession.... Surely Allah's Apostle carried out the penalty of Rajam, and so did we after him."

If the Qur'an were divinely revealed and uncorrupted, why then is the stoning verse among the missing verses?

3. The Qur'an is not the original because Muhammad forgot some of the verses

When he was questioned about forgetting what cannot be forgotten, Gabriel came to Muhammad with a new revelation that overcame the problem. He revealed that if Muhammad forgets some verses, then Allah willed them to be forgotten.

Surah Al-Alaa 87:6-7,

"We shall teach you (the Qur'an) and you will not forget it, unless Allah wills it to be otherwise. He knows all that is made public and all that remains hidden."

Sahih Muslim, Vol. 2:2286, p.50,

In the Hadith, Muhammad said, "We used to recite a Surah which resembled in length and severity to (Surah) Bara'at. I have, however, forgotten it with the exception of this which I remember out of it."

4. The Qur'an was changed because some verses were not included

Ibn Abi Dawud, Kitab al-Masahif p.11). Other verses had different versions reported. (Muwatta Imam Malik, [d.795 AD] p.64),

"Some of the original verses memorized by the Qurra' (memorizers/reciters) and the Hafith (memorizers) were not included in the Qur'an assembled by Zayd bin Thabit."

Some verses were said to be overlooked and not included.

5. We know the Qur'an was changed because alternate versions of the Qur'an were burned

Uthman, the 3rd Caliph, ordered that all editions of the Qur'an not in the Quraish (Muhammad's tribe) dialect had to be burned. In so doing, many verses not in the Quraish version of the Qur'an were lost.

The different versions of the Qur'an had to be destroyed because there were so many different variant readings of the Qur'an. Uthman ordered that all the different versions be gathered. He decided that a compiled Quraish version of the Qur'an would be the official version! All other versions were destroyed by burning them.

Ibn Abi Dawud, Kitab al-Masahif p.117,

"Even the Qurra' (reciters/memorizers of the Qur'an) with variant renditions were ordered to forget those versions which differed, but not all obeyed, for example al-Hajjaj ibn Yusuf "made eleven modifications in the reading of the Uthmanic text".

6. We know the Qur'an was changed because the Qur'an had to be edited

The original Qur'an is said to have been given in easy to understand Arabic. It was written down without any pronunciation markings or diacritical marks (in Arabic it's called "*harakat*") which are accents, dots or squiggles. It had to be edited and have the *harakat* added. This meant that hundreds of thousands of pronunciation edits had to take place. It was supposed to be easy to read in clear Arabic, but clearly it was not!

The Arabic tribes had many different Arabic dialects and could not understand the Quraish dialect selected by Uthman as the official language of the Qur'an. The first written Qur'ans had no *harakat* system, no clear indications of how to read, recite and understand what was written. After many complaints and disputes, Islamic leaders felt compelled to clarify the meanings of the Qur'an and how to recite it, so they introduced a system whereby all Arabs could read and recite the Qur'an in the same way. So Allah's "clear Arabic" had to be improved and made clear!

The first system is said to have been devised in the mid to late 7th century, a system of dots using two colours to signal the three short vowels. This was different from the way Arabic is written today. It was devised to indicate how to correctly pronounce and recite the Qur'an.

Later, when the the task of writing using two different colours was found to be tedious and impractical, it was replaced by small superscript letters, the system that is known today. Essentially the Qur'an has been edited at least three times with different *harakat* systems to make it easier to understand!

7. The oldest manuscripts of the Qur'an are not the same version as the Qur'an today

The Birmingham Manuscripts

The manuscripts kept in the University of Birmingham, UK, consists of two leaves of parchment which were carbon dated between 568 and 645 AD.

They are similar to the text today with minor variations. However some experts say that the grammatical marks, the diacritical markers and the verse separators are inconsistent with the dates and only arose much later. There is also evidence that this manuscript could have already been in existence at the time of Muhammad.

The manuscript consists of verses from *Surah Al Kahf 18:17-31* which tells of the seven sleepers, *Surah Maryam 19:91-98* containing stories of Moses and Aaron and *Surah Ta Ha 20:1-40* which also has the story of Moses. All of these stories were already in existence and were circulating long before Muhammad's time. Is it possible that they were merely copied into the Qur'an?

The Sana'a Qur'an Manuscripts

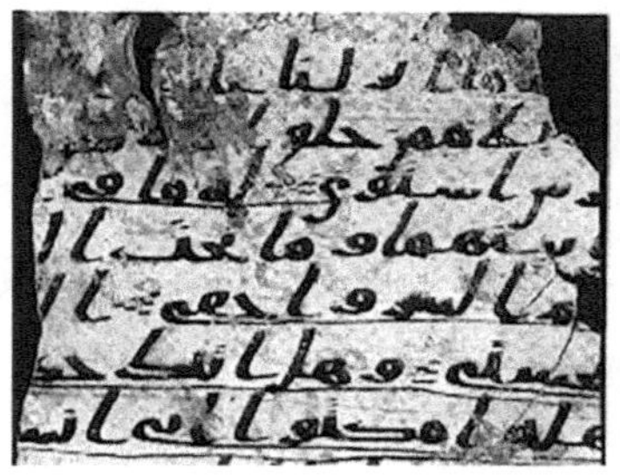

In 1972 Qur'anic parchments and papers were found in an old mosque in Sanaa. They are said to date to the late 7th Century. Again, they had no diacritical marks. ***Dr. Gerd Puin,*** a German expert who examined them claimed that more than half of the text was ambiguous, the letters needed diacritical marks for understanding and the vowels were needed to correct mistakes.

Karl-Heinz Ohlig stated that the Qur'an began to be compiled in the last two decades of the 7th century, after the death of Muhammad, with other versions continuing until the 9th century.Using Ultra-Violet light, another 'Qur'anic' script which had been washed, scrubbed and written over was discovered underneath the existing script. There are differences in the words of the various Qur'ans found in the various layers of the Yemen manuscripts. This again raises the question of the originality and the preservation of the Qur'an.

The Topkapi Manuscript

Another ancient Qur'an was discovered in the Topkapi Palace, Istanbul, Turkey. It is one of the oldest nearly complete Qur'an manuscripts. It is dated to the mid 8th century AD. It also contains variant readings and shows signs of editing. It is written in the Kufic script which is different to modern Arabic script.

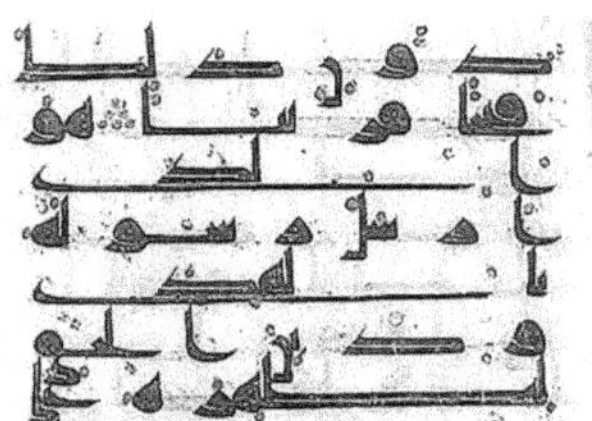

ٮسم الله الرحمں الرحٮم لا اله الا الله وحده لا
سرٮك له له الملك وله الحمد ٮحٮى و ٮمٮٮ وهو
على كلسى ٯدٮر محمد عٮد الله ورسوله

The Transmission of the Qur'an

Allah to Gabriel
Gabriel to Muhammad
Muhammad to Memorizers, His Companions

Memorizers to Abu Bakr, His Successors
Abu Bakr to Uthman
Uthman's Qur'an to Writers of Manuscripts

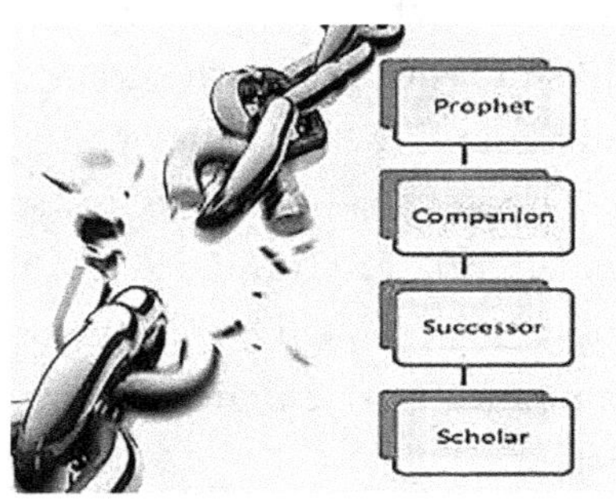

During the time of transmission, portions of the Qur'an were declared to be:

- Lost
- Disappeared
- Forgotten
- Cancelled
- Missing
- Overlooked
- Changed
- Modified

How is it possible that we can be confident that the Qur'an was collated perfectly in the same way, totally unchangeable, as it was given by Gabriel to Muhammad?

The Qur'an Today

Today in Iran, the Middle East and Africa there are up to 30 different Qur'ans with different verses, and hundreds of variations. For Islam, this is a problem because it believes that the revelation of the Qur'an came down direct from Allah, word for word, and is declared to be unchangeable, not even one letter! Has the Qur'an passed the test of authenticity as a direct, perfect revelation from God? Is it, word for word, Divinely protected and passed down perfectly as Muhammad stated?

CAIR (Council of Islam-American Relations) explains the origin of the Qur'an:

www.cair.com/AboutIslam/Islam Basics.asps

The Qur'an "was memorized by Muhammad and then dictated to his companions. The text of the Qur'an was cross-checked during the life of the Prophet. The 114 chapters of the Qur'an have remained unchanged through the centuries."

This statement by CAIR contradicts all the Islamic history we have recorded from the start of this chapter. This is the sort of message that we hear all over the world. Despite the evidence of history, from their own sources, they still claim that the Qur'an is perfectly preserved without alteration.

The standard text of the Qur'an today is the 1924 Cairo edition, known as the Hafs Qur'an. It is said to be based on Uthman's text. However, there are still variations in the way that the text is read. The main differences involve pronunciation, vocalisation, and minor grammatical variations, extra words or differing verse counts.

The Dilemma of the Qur'anic Claims

The dilemma for us today is whether the claims of the Qur'an are true. The Qur'an makes many claims for itself. If any of the claims about itself are untrue, then the book itself must be untrue. The Qur'an not only claims to be the Word of God, it claims it is perfect, unequalled, eternal, easy to understand and unchanged and unchangeable. According to Islamic scholars there is no room for doubt.

The Qur'an claims that it cannot be doubted.

Surah Al Baqarah 2:2,

"This is the Book, there is no doubt in it, a guide to those who fear Allah."

Which Book? The Qur'an, as a Book, as we have seen, never existed in the time of Muhammad, and only years after his death were there efforts to compile a Book called The Qur'an.

The Qur'an claims that it is from God

Surah Al Ahqaf 46:2,

"The revelation of the Book is from Allah the Almighty, the Wise."

One of Islam's most influential experts, *Ibn Kathir (1300-1373)*, declared:

Tafsir Ibn Kathir, vol.5, 134-135,

"The Arabic language is the most eloquent, plain, deep and expressive of the meanings that might arise in one's mind. Therefore the most honourable Book, was revealed in the most honourable language, the most honourable Prophet and Messenger, delivered by the most honourable angel, in the most honourable land on earth, and its revelation started during the most honourable month of the year, Ramadan. Therefore, the Qur'an is perfect in every respect."

Let us examine some of the dilemmas raised by these claims of the Qur'an.

1. The Dilemma of God being the Author of the Qur'an

Is God the author of the Qur'an? If the Qur'an is from God, then it cannot have contradictions.

The Qur'an says in ***Surah An Nisa 4:82,***

"Do they not then consider the Qur'an carefully? "Had it been from other than Allah, they would surely have found therein much contradictions."

Should not the Qur'an be taken seriously and considered carefully? Surely this point must be examined further and its truth verified? Are there any contradictions in the Qur'an? We will examine some of the contradictions in another chapter.

The Qur'an claims that God is the author and the teacher of the Qur'an.

Surah Ar Rahman 55:1-2,

"The Most Compassionate (or The Most Merciful). Has taught the Qur'an."

Surah Al Qiyama 75:16-19,

"Move not your tongue with it, [O Muhammad], to hasten with recitation of the Qur'an". "Indeed, upon Us is its collection [in your heart] and [to make possible] its recitation." "So when We have recited it [through Gabriel], then follow its recitation." "Then upon Us is its clarification [to you]".

Surah Hud 11:1,

"Alif, Lam, Ra. [This is] a Book whose verses are perfected and then presented in detail from [one who is] Wise and Acquainted."

Surah Yunus 10:37,

"This Qur'an is not such as can be produced by other than Allah; on the contrary it is a confirmation of (revelations) that went before it, and a fuller explanation of the Book - wherein there is no doubt - from the Lord of the worlds."

Does the Qur'an confirm the earlier revelations found in the Law and the Gospels? Does the Qur'an give a fuller explanation of "the Book"? Clearly, the earlier revelations and the Book are the Bible. Obviously, this is a major dilemma as the Bible repeatedly contradicts what is in the Qur'an!

2. The Dilemma of the Sources of the Qur'an

Is the Qur'an original? Is there anything original in the Qur'an? Most of the stories recorded in the Qur'an have their origin in the Bible, the Jewish Midrash, the Christian apocryphal gospels, Greek legends and Zoroastrian sources.

The story of the murder of Abel by Cain is a typical mixture of elements from the Bible and Talmudic writings known as the Midrash which predates the Qur'an by many centuries.

In ***Al Maidah 5:30-35*** Adam and Eve did not know what to do with Abel's body. A raven, whose companion had died, came, and took its body, scratched in the earth, and buried it before their eyes. Adam then decided to do likewise and he buried Abel's body in the earth.

The story of Abraham destroying idols told in *Surah 37:91-92* and *21:62-70,* is a remarkable retelling of a story found in the Jewish literature, the ***Midrash Rabbah.***

There are two passages in the Qur'an where certain things are said about Jesus that are ***derived from Buddhist sources.*** The first relates to the actual birth of Jesus which is described in the Qur'an as follows:

Surah Maryam 19:22-26,

"So she conceived him and withdrew with him to a remote place. The pangs of childbirth came over her at the trunk of the palm-tree. She said: "Would that I had died before this and become something forgotten". One cried to her from below it: "Do not grieve, for your Lord has provided a stream below you. Shake also towards you the palm-trunk, it will let fresh ripe dates fall upon you. Eat, drink and be comforted."

Jesus speaks to declare his prophethood, his blessing, and his ordained purpose.

Surah Maryam 19:33,

"Peace on me the day I was born, the day I die, and the day I am raised alive"

This is widely seen as having roots in older Christian liturgical material or infancy narratives.

The Miracle of Clay Birds *(Al Maidah 5:110).*

The story of Jesus breathing life into clay birds, made by his own hands and creating life. by permission of God, is recognized as being adapted from the **Infancy Gospel of Thomas**, a text popular in early Christian communities.

Surah Al Qadr 97 appears to be similar to an ancient Syriac Christian hymn, ***Phos Hilaron,*** also known as ***"O Gladsome Night",*** which dates to the 3rd or 4th century. It speaks of the night when the angels descend and peace and goodness from God appear till dawn.

Descriptions of the Virgin Birth *(Maryam 19, Ali Imran 3*

Many verses regarding the Annunciation, Mary's purity, and the virgin birth are found in both the Bible and earlier Christian texts. The Qur'an gives significant focus to these narratives, often emphasizing them more frequently than the ***New Testament Syriac Hymns of the Annunciation (6th Century).***

Some scholars have pointed to 6th Century Syriac hymns, particularly those by St. Ephrem (or attributed to him), that describe the incarnation of Christ as a celestial gift descending from the heights, which shares parallel themes with the Qur'anic narrative of divine decree descending, particularly in the context of Mary's annunciation, *Surah Ali-Imran 3:42-7, Surah Maryam 19:16-22.*

Surah Al-Muminiin 23:1-5 speaks about ***the duties of the believers.*** These passages were exactly the same written by saint Ephraim in the 4th century. Ephraim spoke Syriac, which is part of the Aramaic group of families. It was a 4th century poem that was originally written in Aramaic and spoke about Jesus.

Research indicates that while the Qur'anic depiction of Paradise (e.g., in other Surahs) shares some imagery with Ephraim's depictions—such as streams of wine, milk, and honey—this indicates common Middle Eastern religious traditions rather than a direct copy of specific verses.

From **749 AD** during the Abbasid period, it appears the ancient Aramaic was absorbed into the Qur'an. Some verses of the Qur'an were originally lectionaries and hymns to Jesus. It was added to and adulterated and became the Qur'an.

According to Google, thirty to ninety percent of the Qur'an comes from the Bible. Over 50 people and events are found in both books, including Adam and Eve, Abraham, Noah, Moses, and Jesus. The Qur'an has 114 Chapters or Surahs and is much smaller, roughly 13% of the size of the Bible, with 1189 chapters.

3. The Dilemma of the Qur'an being easy to understand

The Qur'an plainly and repeatedly says that it is easy to understand.

Surah Al Qamar 54:17,22,32,40,

"And we have indeed made the Qur'an easy to understand and remember."

This same verse is repeated four times.

The Qur'an claims to have clear explanations of everything

Surah An-Nahl 16:89.

"And We have revealed the Book to you which has clear explanation of everything, and a guidance, mercy and good news for those who submit."

If this is the case, why is there so much confusion as to what the Qur'an means? The problem is that there is another verse in the Qur'an that states that some of the verses are not clear but elusive and only God understands them.

Surah Ali-Imran 3:7,

"He is the One Who has revealed to you ˹O Prophet˺ the Book, of which some verses are precise—they are the foundation of the Book—while others are elusive. Those with deviant hearts follow the elusive verses seeking (to spread) doubt through their (false) interpretations—but none grasps their (full) meaning except Allah. As for those well-grounded in knowledge, they say, "We believe in this (Qur'an)—it is all from our Lord." But none will be mindful (of this) except people of reason."

Thus, there are precise verses and elusive verses in the Qur'an. This raises the dilemma of which verses are elusive and how are they to be understood?

4. The Dilemma of the Hadith

The Qur'an claims it is easy to understand. The dilemma is, if it is so easy, why are the Hadith necessary?

The Qur'an says,

Surah Al-Jathiyah 45:6,

"These are the verses of Allah which We recite to you in truth. So in what hadith after Allah and His verses will they believe?"

Surah *Al-Mursalat 77:50,*

"Then in what hadith after this will they believe?"

This creates a dilemma. Islamic scholars can only understand the Qur'an by reading the Hadith. Yet the Qur'an denies that there can be hadith after the Qur'an. No Hadith has the authority of the Qur'an. Only the Qur'an is divinely authored and has binding authority.

Islamic scholar, ***Mohammed Nasir-ul-Deen al-Albani*** said: "There is no way to understand the Qur'an correctly except in association with the interpretation of the Sunnah." (*The Status of Sunnah in Islam – www.orst.edu/groups/msa/books/sunnah1.html*)

The Sunnah are the words and deeds of Muhammad recorded by his disciples and wives in the Hadith. The Hadith are records of all Muhammad did and said that were written and compiled over 200 years after Muhammad lived.

There are six generally accepted Hadith collections

The two biggest and most accepted among Muslims as authentic are the collections of Sahih Bukhari (870AD) and Sahih Muslim (875AD).

The other four are also widely believed to be authentic, that is: Abu Dawood (888AD), Jami'at-Timidhi (892AD), Sunan al-Sughra (915AD) (also known as *Sunan* an-Nasa'i), and Sunan Ibn Majah (795AD).

Many reports were fabricated and contradictions exist within the collections. The Hadith collectors had to choose what to include and what to reject. Over 16 years Bukhari whittled down the collection of Hadith verses from 600,000 verses to 7000 or 8000 verses.

Even the Hadith itself records Muhammad forbidding the Hadith.

Sahih Muslim, the Book of Zuhd, Hadith 3004,

"Do not write anything from me except the Qur'an. Whoever has written anything besides the Qur'an, let him erase it."

How much credence can we give to the Hadith, since it claims to be the words and deeds of Muhammad, his wives and friends that was collected and written down about 200 to 300 years after he lived, while Muhammad himself told them to erase such accounts.

5. The Dilemma of the Arabic Language

One of the major problems in understanding the Qur'an, is that, according to Islam, the Qur'an can only truly be understood in the Arabic language. All other translations are merely interpretations.

Ibn Taymiyah (1263-1338), one of the most influential scholars and thinkers in early Islam, declared: *."Ahmed ibn Abdullah al-Baatilee,* ***Arabic: The Language of the Qur'an****, Al Haramain, www.alharamain.org; http://63.104.232.198/issue35/quraan.htm,*

"The Arabic language is from (Allah's) Religion, and the knowledge of it is an obligation. For surely the understanding of the Qur'an and Hadith is an obligation, and these two are not understood except with the understanding of the Arabic language."

The Qur'an claims that it was specifically written in clear Arabic so that people can understand it. The Qur'an, Muslims claim, came down through Gabriel in clear Arabic. When we were in Jordan, Lebanon, Egypt and Yemen, the local Muslims complained that they could not understand the Arabic in the Qur'an. When we sat down with them in their homes and even the woman wanted to hear our discussions, the men would have to interpret what we were saying to the women who didn't even understand regular Arabic. It had to be put into their tribal language!

Surah Fussilat 41:3,

"A book whereof the verses are explained in detail – a Qur'an in Arabic for a people who know."

Surah *Az-Zukruf 43:3,*

"We have made it a Qur'an in Arabic, that ye may be able to understand."

Surah An-Nahl 16:103,

"This (the Qur'an) is a clear Arabic tongue."

Surah Asy-Syuaraa 26:192-195,

"Verily this is a revelation from the Lord of the Worlds: With it came down the spirit (Gabriel) of Faith and Truth - on thy heart, that thou mayest be a Warner in plain and clear Arabic."

Muhammad declared that the Qur'an was written to confirm the Bible as a warning to Mecca and the Arabs in the cities around about it

God tells Muhammad that He has revealed to him a book confirming the past messages specifically with the purpose to warn Mecca and surrounding cities.

Surah Al-Anaam 6:92.

"This is a book which We have revealed, bringing blessings, and confirming (the revelations) which came before it: that thou mayest warn the Mother of Cities and all around her."

Yet the Qur'an also says in many places that Muhammad came as the apostle of God to bring a message for all mankind.

Surah Al-Araf 7:158,

"Say [O Muhammad]: "O mankind! Verily, I am an apostle of God to all of you, [sent by Him] unto whom the dominion over the heavens and the earth belongs! There is no deity save Him; He [alone] grants life and deals death!" Believe, then, in God and His Apostle-the unlettered (illiterate) Prophet who believes in God and His words-and follow him, so that you might find guidance."

This raises the dilemma of why was it revealed in the Arabic language to be easily understood? If the Qur'an is only written in Arabic, for Arabic speaking people, then does it really have any relevance to those who do not know the Arabic language? If it was specifically given in the Arabic language and for the purpose of warning Mecca and the surrounding cities, what relevance does it have for the rest of the nations and cities of the world? Is the Qur'an universally applicable?

6. The Dilemma of the Qur'an being the Original Eternal Heavenly Book

Mother of all Books (Arabic-*Umm-al-Kitab)?*

One of the major themes of the Qur'an is "the Book", in Arabic, "*Al Kitab*". The Qur'an, the Law and the Gospels are all called, "the Book." Yet the Qur'an also speaks of, "the Mother of the Book" or the "Preserved

Tablet". This is spoken of as the source of all revelation and preserved in heaven.

Surah Ar-Rad (13):39,

"Allah effaces and confirms what He will, And with Him is the Mother of the Book (*Al-Lauh Al-Mahfuz*)."

This verse is interpreted to mean that it is the Qur'an which is "the Mother of the Book". Yusuf Ali and other translators translate it as "the Master Record" (Sahih International), "the Source of Ordinance" (Pickthall) and "the Essence of the Book" (Dr. Ghali).

Other verses also talk about this Book.

Surah Az-Zukhruf 43:4,

"And indeed, it is—in the Mother of the Book (*Umm Al Kitab*) with Us—highly esteemed, rich in wisdom".

Surah Ali-Imran 3.7,

"He is the One Who has revealed to you (O Prophet) the Book, of which some verses are precise—they are the foundation of the Book (*Umm Al Kitab*)—while others are elusive."

Surah Al-Buruj 85.21-22,

"But this is a glorious Qur'an In the Preserved Tablet (*Al Lauh Al Mahfuz*)."

Surah Al Waqiah 56.78,

"This is a noble Qur'an in a guarded book *(Kitāb Maknūn)*."

Surah Al-Fatihah is also known as the Mother of the Book, being the opening foundational chapter of the Qur'an.

However in the Qur'an, "the Book" also refers to the Books of the Law and the Gospel. Therefore "the Mother of the Book" must include, not just the Qur'an, but the Torah, the Psalms, the Prophets and the Gospel as well. In fact the "People of the Book" are not Muslims, they are Jews and Christians. So this becomes a dilemma! What really is the eternal, preserved "Mother of the Book"? If the Law and the Gospel orginate in this eternal book, then shouldn't Muslims be also following them?

Is the Qur'an eternal?

Muslims believe the Qur'an is an eternal book.

Al-Buruuj 85:21-22,

"Nay, this is a Glorious Qur'an (inscribed) in *Al-Lauh Al-Mahfuz* (The Preserved Tablet)!"

Islamic scholars say that this verse means that the Qur'an is "eternal in heaven with Allah". Again, the dilemma remains, how can God have an eternal book in heaven that includes contradictions and errors and does not agree with the Law and the Gospel?

7. The Dilemma of the Perfection of the Qur'an

The Qur'an is considered so perfect that it gives a challenge and dares anyone to write something of equal quality. The Qur'an claims it has no equal, and we are challenged to write a small portion equal to it, even though it has been declared to be the impossible task!

Surah Al-Israa' 17:88,

"If the whole of mankind and Jinns were to gather together to produce the like of this Qur'an, they could not produce the like thereof, even if they backed up each other with help and support."

Surah Al-Baqarah 2:23-24,

"And if ye are in doubt as to what We have revealed from time to time to Our servant, then produce a Surah like thereunto; and call your witnesses or helpers (if there are any) besides Allah, if your (doubts) are true. But if ye cannot, and of a surety ye cannot, then fear the Fire whose fuel is men and stones, which is prepared for those who reject Faith."

The Qur'an claims to be the final authority, fully detailed and clarifying everything.

The Qur'an is explained in detail

Surah Al-Anam 6:114,

"Shall I seek other than Allah as judge, while it is He who sent down to you the Book explained in detail."

The Qur'an clarifies everything

Surah Al-Nahl 16:89,

"We have sent down to you the Book as clarification for all things, and as guidance and mercy and good tidings for the Muslims."

The Qur'an is 100% complete and 100% perfect and unchangeable!

Surah Al-Anam 6:115,

"The Word of your Lord has been completed in truth and justice. None can change His words."

The Qur'an is revealed, guarded, preserved and protected

Surah Al-Hijr 15:9.

"Indeed, we have revealed the Reminder, and indeed We will guard it."

The Qur'an is the final authority. It is complete and perfect. It is unequalled and no one can write anything like it.

The dilemma is that there remains no way to question it! This is the dilemma of Qur'anic logic.

- The Qur'an comes from God so it is true.
- Because it says that it comes from God and that what it says is true.
- The Qur'an, therefore, comes from God.

Is the Qur'an unchanged and unchangeable?

According to Islam, Allah's Word can't possibly be changed or have mistakes.

Why? Because it is protected and preserved by Allah. Although Muslims like to claim immutability exclusively for the Qur'an, that promise in the Qur'an is not exclusively for the Qur'an but for ALL the Scriptures and therefore includes the Law, the Psalms, the Prophets and the Gospel, all of which must be believed to be accurate if Allah is able to keep His promise.

ALL Muslims are commanded to believe ALL the Scriptures. This is a problem since the Qur'an stands in contradiction to the message of the other Scriptures, like what is recorded in the Bible.

The Message, they say, cannot be changed.

Surah Al Hijr 15:9.

"We have, without doubt, sent down the Message; and We will assuredly guard it (from corruption)."

According to Islam that Message, exclusively, is the Qur'an. However, the original Arabic word "the Message" (*dhikr*) covers the Law, the Psalms, the Gospel and the Prophets as well. That is the whole of the Bible is declared to be the *dhikr,* the original message and Word sent down by God.

The Word of God cannot be changed. Therefore the Bible too cannot be changed and the Qur'an therefore declares it to be incorruptible, preserved and protected by Allah.

Surah An-Naam 6:115,

"The word of thy Lord doth find its fulfilment in truth and in justice: None can change His words: for He is the one who heareth and knoweth all."

According to modern Islamic interpreters, that "word" only means the Qur'an. The problem is that "the word" in the Qur'an includes ALL the scriptures.Therefore it must include the Law, the Psalms, the Prophets and the Gospel. According to the Qur'an, a Muslim MUST believe ALL the words of God and none of them can be changed..

Muslims must believe everything sent down from God without distinction. Note carefully again this important verse in the Qur'an.

Surah Al-Baqarah 2:13,

"Say, "We believe in Allah and that which has been sent down to us and that which has been sent down to Abraham, Ishmael, Isaac, Jacob, and to the twelve sons of Jacob, and that which has been given to Moses and Jesus, and that which has been given to the Prophets from their Lord. We make no distinction between any of them, and to Him we submit."

If it is true that God's words cannot be changed, then it is impossible for the Bible to have been changed.

Has the Qur'an itself been changed? MUHARRAF / TAHRIF?

"The words *muharraf* or *tahrif* come from the letters HRF / *harrafa* which in Arabic means to change, falsify, steal the true meaning, especially phonetically (voice/memorization)," *A Dictionary of Modern Written Arabic,* Hans Wehr, Beirut, 1974, pp.168-169.

- It's very important for us to know the authenticity of all books which claim to be the revelation of God. Do we still have access to the original documents or accurate copies or are they *tahrif*?
- Do we still have the original and authentic Qur'an or has it been changed and/or has it been falsified?
- Is the Qur'an today the same as it was in the days of Muhammad?

We have seen that the Qur'an today is NOT the same as it was in 632AD when Muhammad died. It simply did not yet exist.

8. The Dilemma of Abrogation

Abrogation means that Allah replaces words in the Qur'an with new and better ones.

Surah Al-Baqarah (2):106,

"Whatever a Verse (revelation) do We abrogate or cause to be forgotten. We bring a better one or similar to it. Know you not that Allah is able to do all things?"

Sahih al-Bukhari 4090 *records:*

"We used to read a verse of the Qur'an revealed in their connection, but later the verse was cancelled."

Muhammad blamed this on Satan.

Surah Al-Hajj 22:52,

"Never did We send a Messenger or a Prophet before you, but when he did recite the revelation or narrated or spoke, Satan threw some falsehood in it. But Allah abolishes that which Satan throws in. Then Allah establishes His revelations. And Allah is All- Knower, All-Wise."

Abrogation in the Qur'an

Muslim scholars differ on how many verses in the Qur'an are abrogated but there are estimated to be 21 to 100s of examples of abrogation in the Qur'an. Some include the Satanic verses, the acceptance of different religions, forgiveness and overlooking differences to be replaced by vengeance and fighting, the prohibition of alcohol, the shift from voluntary to mandatory charity, and changes in inheritance laws.

One well known example is the waiting period for widows to remarry, which was reduced from one year (*Al Baqarah 2:240*), to four months and ten days (*Al Baqarah 2:234*).

Satanic Verses. Muhammad facing persecution in Mecca, tried to make his message more acceptable to the pagans by praising their gods. Later, Muhammad had to try and squeeze out of this problem.

Surah An Najm 53:19-23,

"Have ye seen Al-Lat and Al-'Uzza, and another, the third (goddess), Manat? What! for you the male sex, and for Him, the female? Behold, such would be indeed a division most unfair! These are nothing but names which ye have devised, ye and your fathers, for which Allah has sent down no authority (whatever)."

The three goddesses mentioned in this verse were considered by the Meccans to be the daughters of Allah. Early Islamic histories, such as those of al-Tabari, mention an incident where Muhammad was tempted to say, "These are the exalted cranes *(gharānīq),* whose intercession is hoped for," which he later removed as being inspired by Satan. Later Muhammad claimed this revelation was corrupted by Satan and so therefore has been abrograted by Allah.

Examples of Abrogation

a. Acceptance of different religions replaced by Islam exclusively

The Qur'an states that people of all religion who believe in Allah and the Last Day and do righteous deeds, including Jews and Christians, will have no sorrow or grief. This implies that they will be accepted by God.

Surah Al-Baqarah 2:62, and Surah Al-Maidah 5:69,

"Indeed, those who believed and those who became Jews and the Christians and the Sabians - who believed in Allah and the Last Day and did righteous deeds, so for them (is) their reward with their Lord and no fear on them and nor do they will grieve."

These verses however, are abrogated by the verse that declares that the only acceptable religion is Islam.

Surah Ali-Imran 3:85,

"And whoever seeks other than Islam (as) religion then never will be accepted from him, and he in the Hereafter, (will be) from the losers."

b. Forgiveness replaced by fighting

At first, in Mecca, Islam was a peaceful religion, and God called the Muslims to forgive and overlook any conflict. In Medina things changed and Muslims were called upon to fight the non-Muslims until they were subdued and either paid the reparation, the *jizya* tax, or were killed.

Surah Al Baqarah 2:109,

"Quite a number of the People of the Book wish they could turn you (people) back to infidelity after ye have believed, from selfish envy, after the truth hath become manifest unto them: But forgive and overlook, till Allah accomplish His purpose; for Allah hath power over all things".

Surah At Tawbah 9:29,

"Fight those who (do) not believe in Allah and not in the Day the Last, and not they make unlawful what has made unlawful Allah and His Messenger, and not they acknowledge (the) religion (of) the truth, from those who were given the Scripture, until they pay the reparation (from) willingly, while they (are) subdued."

The verses called the Verses of the Sword, the general command to fight polytheists (often referred to as *Surah At-Tawbah 9:5 or 9:36*), abolished many earlier verses that commanded patience, avoidance of confrontation, or turning away from disbelievers.

Surah At Tawbah 9:5,

"Then when have passed the months sacred, then kill the polytheists wherever you find them and seize them and besiege them and sit (in wait) for them (at) every place of ambush. But if they repent and establish the prayer and give the zakah then leave their way. Indeed, Allah (is) Oft-Forgiving, Most Merciful."

Surah At Tawbah 9:36,

"And fight the polytheists all together, as they fight you all together. And know that Allah (is) with the righteous."

c. Permission to drink alcohol replaced by prohibition

Surah Al Baqarah 2:219,

They ask you about intoxicants and games of chance Say, "In both of them (is) a sin great, and (some) benefits for people. But sin of both of them (is) greater than (the) benefit of (the) two." And they ask you what they (should) spend. Say, "The surplus." Thus makes clear Allah to you [the] Verses so that you may ponder."

Surah Al Maidah 5:90,

"O you who believe! Verily the intoxicants and games of chance and (sacrifices at) altars and divining arrows (are an) abomination from (the) work (of) the Shaitaan, so avoid it so that you may (be) successful."

d. Punishment for adultery by life imprisonment replaced with flogging

The Qur'anic verse that defines the punishment for illegal sexual intercourse (*zināh*) which covers both adultery and fornication is:

Surah An Nisa 4:15-16,

"If any of your women are guilty of lewdness, Take the evidence of four (Reliable) witnesses from amongst you against them; and if they testify, confine them to houses until death do claim them, or Allah ordain for them some (other) way And those who commit [the] immorality from your women then call to witness against them four among you. And if they testify then confine them in their houses until comes to them [the] death or makes Allah for them a way."

This verse was replaced by:

Surah An Nur 24:2,

"The fornicatress and the fornicator, [then] flog each one of them (with) one hundred lash(es). And (let) not withhold you for them pity concerning (the) religion (of) Allah if you believe in Allah and the Last Day. And let witness their punishment a group of the believers."

Abrogation therefore poses a dilemma. It shows that some words of the Qur'an have been replaced. It creates uncertainty about which words to believe. It undermines the confidence in the authority of the verses. It allows for "cherry picking" of verses which suit the readers' doctrines and allows them to ignore or negate others. It allows for the misapplication of verses.

9. The Dilemma of the Confirmation of the Bible

We have already discussed this in the previous chapter. The Qur'an mentions that it is written as a confirmation of the Law and the Gospels in many verses.

Ali Imran 3:3-4,

"It is He Who sent down to thee (step by step), in truth, the Book, confirming what went before it (i.e. the Bible); and He sent down the Law (of Moses) and the Gospel (of Jesus) before this, as a guide to mankind."

Al Baqarah 2:136,

"Say, "We believe in Allah and that which has been sent down to us and that which has been sent down to Abraham, Ishmael, Isaac, Jacob, and to the twelve sons of Jacob, and that which has been given to Moses and Jesus, and that which has been given to the Prophets from their Lord. We make no distinction between any of them, and to Him we submit."

So, Allah declared that the Law, the Gospel and the message from all the Bible Prophets must be obeyed! The dilemma arises, why do Muslims not read and study the Bible?

10. The Dilemma of the Unquestionable Nature of the Qur'an

Surah Al-Maidah (5):101-102,

"O ye who believe! Ask not questions about things which, if made plain to you, may cause you trouble.... Some people before you did ask such questions, and on that account lost their faith."

If we cannot ask questions, or to seek to verify the truth, how can we know the truth for sure?

Conclusion

The Qur'an gives the challenge to test the validity of the Qur'an. It declared:

Al Hijr 15:9,

"We have, without doubt, sent down the Message; and We will assuredly guard it from corruption."

"inna nahnu nazzalna thikra, wa inna lahu lahaa fithuun".

Has it been guarded from corruption?

If God could not guard the Law and the Gospels and the Psalms from corruption, how could he guard the Qur'an?

The Bible also gives the challenge.

Isaiah 8:20,

"To the law and to the testimony: if they speak not according to this word, it is because there is no light in them."

Questions to discuss:

1. Does the Qur'an speak the same message as in the Law and the Gospel?
2. Does the Qur'an confirm the word of God in the Law and the Gospel? If not, how can there be any light in the Qur'an?
3. If the Qur'an has experienced thousands of alterations, and there are over 30 different versions of Islamic Qur'ans today, which one is perfect, unaltered, protected and authentic?
4. How does the doctrine of "abrogation" affect your understanding of divine revelation and accuracy of the Qur'an?

DILEMMA 4

THE TRINITY OR TAUHID DILEMMA

Understanding the Islamic and Christian Concepts of God

The essence of this dilemma is to understand the nature of God. Is God just one individual deity as Islam states or is God Three Divine Persons in One Deity as is believed in the Christian world?

In Islam, the word used is TAUHID which means ONENESS. Islam claims it is a blasphemous and unforgiveable sin to declare that God is a Trinity. Furthermore, Islam declares that the prophets of the Bible all declared that God was ONE and not THREE and they quote from Moses and Jesus in the Bible. How do we answer this challenge? How do we solve this dilemma?

In Islam it is taught that the doctrine of the Trinity is an invention of the Council of Nicea in 325 AD. Is that true? In that Council we learn of the Arian controversy. Arius claimed that Jesus was not fully divine but rather a created being. In history, this view adopted by Arab Christians who rejected the decision of the Council of Nicea that Jesus was of one essence with the Father, eventually leading to the deviation of that Christian sect bringing about the birth of Islam which is based on that Arian heresy. This is discussed in detail in books examining the historical and archeological evidence of the origins of Islam and Muhammad, such as: *The Hidden Origins of Islam, by Karl-Heinz Ohlig and Gerd-R. Puin* in 2010, as well as in *Muhammad, A Critical Biography, by Robert Spencer* in 2024.

Tauhid, the Islamic term for the Oneness of God

In Islam, "God", or the Arabic word, "Allah", is just One *'Entity'*

Surah An-Nisaa 4:48,

"Allah forgives not that partners should be set up with Him; but He forgives anything else, to whom He pleases; to set up partners with Allah is to devise a sin most heinous indeed."

The unforgiveable sin in Islam is called *"shirk"*. While *"tauhid"* means the *"oneness"* of God, the word *"shirk"* is the direct opposite and means associating others as being equal with God. This is why the Qur'an declares that there is no god except the ONE Allah and to say otherwise is blasphemy and the unforgiveable sin.

Surah Al-Maida 5:73,

"Laqad kafara addeen qaalu inna allah thalithu thalathatin"

"They do blaspheme who say: Allah is one of three: for there is no god except One Allah."

Al-Ikhlas 112:1-4,

"Say: He is Allah, the One! Allah, the eternally besought of all! He begetteth not nor was begotten. And there is none comparable (equal) unto Him."

Jews and Christians emphatically declare that there is only ONE GOD. The Christian faith declares that the ONE GOD is revealed in THREE PERSONS but not GOD plus two other GODS. Absolutely not! Christians only believe in ONE GOD. We need to understand this truth theologically, practically and spiritually so that we can explain it clearly to those of other faiths. Islam, while declaring their faith in ONE GOD named "Allah", also declare their rejection of the doctrine of the Trinity. The Qur'an states in *Surah Al-Maida (5):116,* that Christians believe in a Trinity where there is ALLAH plus two other GODS i.e. Mary and Jesus, but this not a Christian belief.

Where does the Islamic understanding of the Trinity come from?

The Mariamite Sect

Wikipedia describes the Mariamite Sect as "a specific religious order within the **Maronite Church**—an Eastern Catholic Church in full communion with Rome. It is distinct from the general Maronite ethnoreligious group, although closely tied to its tradition.

The *Mariamites* were influenced by a heathen Egyptian belief concerning three gods. In that belief system *Osiris,* the god of goodness married the goddess *Isis* and gave birth to a son, the god *Horus.* The *Mariamite doctrine of the Trinity* only replaced the names with **Allah** who married **Maryam** and gave birth to **Jesus (Isa).** Islam rejected that doctrine, as can be read in the Qur'an.

Surah Al-Maida 5:116,

"Behold! Allah will say: "O Jesus the son of Mary! Did you say unto men, worship me and my mother as two gods besides Allah?" He will say: "Glory to You! Never could I say what I had no right (to say)."

The Ebionite Sect

Another Christian sect that grew in the first century and expanded into Arabia were the Ebionites. They began to disappear in the 4th Century after the Council of Nicea where their beliefs were destroyed by the adoption of teachings accepted and confirmed with the rise of Nicene orthodoxy. The Ebionites supported the views of Arius and were considered heretical by the Church Fathers. Their major beliefs were:

- Jesus was not divine but was adopted as the Messiah, the Son of God at His baptism.
- They rejected Paul as an apostate
- They rejected the concept of the Trinity of Moses
- They strictly obeyed the Law of Moses

The Ebionites began to decline in prominence by the 4th Century as mainstream Christianity emerged and became more defined, particularly with the rise of Nicene orthodoxy. The beliefs of the Mariamites and the Ebionites and other sects were increasingly marginalized and eventually faded from historical records.

Along with the Mariamites and the Ebionites there were possibly other sects which over the next three centuries significantly influenced the views of the Arabic tribes which eventually led to the rise of the Islamic religion and the concepts adopted by Islam today.

Islamic belief as seen in Surah Al-Maidah 5:116,

- Islam rejects that Allah is 1 of 3 i.e. Allah plus two other Gods
- Islam rejects a Trinity of Allah plus Jesus plus Mary
- Islam also rejects the need of a Saviour or Redeemer and every person must save themselves by their own good deeds.

Christians also reject the concept of the Trinity as taught by the Mariamites! Why do we reject that concept? Because the Christian concept of the Trinity is not the same as what is rejected by the Qur'an. We believe in the Three-in-One God and not 1 God + 2 others! We believe that there are Three Divine Persons in ONE GOD, *Deuteronomy 6:4; Mark 12:29.*

We will compare the declaration in the Qur'an with the Bible, both Old and New Testaments, in the next section.

The Qur'an declares that God is ONE:

Surah Al-Ikhlas 112:1,

"Say, He is ONE GOD"
"qul huwa allah rabb wahidun"

The Bible also declares that God is ONE:

Deuteronomy 6:4,

"Hear, O Israel: The LORD our God, the LORD is ONE."
"isma ya israeel: arrabb ilhuna rabbun wahidun"

Deuteronomy 6:4,

(Hebrew): "shema yisrael elohenu yahweh echad"

Islam also highlights that Jesus Himself quoted this verse and declared it as an absolute truth, not just for the Jews but also to all who follow Him.

Matthew 12:29, *(Greek):* 'Ιησους: Ἄκουε, Ισραηλ· κύριος ὁ θεὸς ἡμῶν κύριος εἷς ἐστιν·

Jesus: "Hear, O Israel: The LORD our God, the LORD is ONE."

Mark 12:29, "Jesus answered him, "The first of all the commandments is: *'HEAR, O ISRAEL, THE LORD OUR GOD, THE LORD IS ONE."*

Muslims challenge Christians asking, "How can 1 + 1 + 1 = 1? This a major point for Muslims, and for many Christians it is a dilemma that needs to be solved. Can God be 3 and yet 1 at the same time?

The word Trinity isn't in the Bible. It's a term that was developed later to summarize the biblical reality.

Theophilles of Antioch was one of the first known writers to use the word "trinity" back in the second century. Thinkers like **Tertullian, Origin, and Irenaeus** in the second and third centuries worked to articulate this biblical truth, not to invent it. They were simply creating a vocabulary to describe the relational God they met in the pages of both the Old and New Testaments. They saw that the Bible presents one God, yet it also presents three distinct persons who are each called God:

- **The Father is God,** *1 Peter 1:2.*
- **The Son is God,** *John 1:1, Romans 9:5.*
- **The Holy Spirit is God,** *Acts 5:3-4.*

They are not three parts of God. Each is fully 100% God. They are one in essence, nature, and purpose, yet distinct in person and role. Some call it a mystery and to many it is, but the statements in the Bible are clear. There is only ONE GOD, yet in that one God there are THREE DISTINCT DIVINE PERSONS.

Is there such a thing as a plural "one" or a composite "one"?

We can always check on definitions given by Google, or in various dictionaries and we will discover that religious definitions usually dominate. Undeniably, we are affected by our religious beliefs and what we have been taught by our religious leaders. However, this is such an important subject that we need to investigate for ourselves what we believe and what the Bible teaches us about this vital subject. As you research this topic we are sure you will find some exciting and inspiring revelations that will solve this dilemma.

Some General Definitions

In the Bible, the Hebrew word *echad* (אֶחָד) frequently denotes a compound, composite or collective unity—a "one" composed of multiple parts or individuals—rather than an absolute singular (*yachid*). Key examples include the union of marriage, the gathering of people, and the joining of objects.

Ahad (أحد) in Arabic represents the same concept as echad (אֶחָד) in the Hebrew. It's a profound, indivisible unity, often signifying a "unique one" rather than just a numerical "1". It can be one as an individual unit, or one as a composite unit consisting of multiple parts, for example, one family. The family is a singular unique unit yet it consists of multiple persons like a father, a mother, and children. Likewise, one nation is a unique singular unit, yet consists of multiple towns, cities, races, languages and geographical areas. God is described with the same term *ahad* (أحد) in the Arabic and is the word used to denote a collective, absolute oneness. The Arabic word *wahid* is a singular number, like the Hebrew *yachid.* God is absolutely a "unique one". There are not two or three Gods. There is only one God in a unique composite unity of three divine Persons, the Father, the Son, and the Holy Spirit.

Examples of *Echad/Ahad* as Collective Unity:

In the Hebrew Bible the word ***echad*** is used. In the same verses in the Arabic Bible, the word ***ahad*** is used in its various forms:

- **Genesis 2:24 (One Flesh):** A man and his wife become "***one*** flesh" (*basar* ***echad***), representing two distinct individuals united in one union.
- **Ezra 2:64 (One Assembly):** The entire assembly together (*kahal* ***echad***) is described as "***one***" yet it consisted of 42,360 people.
- **Exodus 36:12-13 (One Tabernacle):** The many different parts of the tabernacle are joined together to become "***one*** tabernacle".

"Fifty loops he made on one curtain, and fifty loops he made on the edge of the curtain on the end of the second set; the loops held ***one*** curtain to ***another (echad el echad)*** And he made fifty clasps of gold, and coupled the curtains to one another with the clasps, that it might be ***one*** tabernacle (ha mishkan ***echad***). It was one (echad) tabernacle that consisted of multiple parts.

- **Deuteronomy 6:4 (The Shema):** "Hear, O Israel: The LORD our God, the LORD is ***one*** *(echad).*"

Wikipedia states that the Shema is the central declaration of the Jewish faith affirming their belief in the Oneness of God. It is recited twice daily and taught to their children as a foundational element of their faith.

Linguistically, the Three Divine Persons in the Bible, together, are the ONE GOD. The word for ONE in Hebrew is ***echad*** and ***ahad*** in Arabic and can mean either a literal, numeric one or a composite one.

Theologians agree the consistent use of the term ***echad*** (Hebrew) and ***ahad*** (Arabic) indicates an often-used compound unity and that this use applies to the Shema and supports the understanding of the Trinity within the Godhead. We will see that this is also well supported from the use of these terms throughout both Hebrew and Arabic writings as well as direct examples in both the Old and New Testaments.

The Authority of the Bible

The Qur'an CONFIRMS the Scriptures given to the Jews and the Christians, i.e. the Old and New Testaments, or the Law, the Psalms, the Prophets and the Gospel. It is important to know that God, in the Qur'an, acknowledges the Bible as 100% authentic! The Bible reveals that God is Triune (Three in One). Muslims, therefore, should believe in the triune God as revealed in the Scriptures. There are over 20 references in the Qur'an directly stating that the purpose of the Qur'an was to confirm the Scriptures given to Moses and Jesus. Every true Muslim should, therefore, believe in the Torah, the Psalms, all the revelations given to all of Israel's prophets, and of course the New Testament referred to as the Gospel of Jesus Christ!

Surah Al-Maidah 5:46,

"We sent Jesus... confirming that which was revealed before him in the Torah, and We bestowed on him the Gospel wherein is guidance and light..."

Surah Al-Baqarah 2:41,

"And believe in what I (i.e. GOD) reveal, *confirming* the revelation (i.e. the BIBLE) which is with you."

Surah Ali 'Imran 3:3,

"He sent down to you this scripture, truthfully, *confirming* ALL previous scriptures, and He sent down the Law (of Moses) and the Gospel (of Jesus) before this, as a guide to mankind."

Surah Al-Baqarah 2:136,

"Say: "We believe in Allah, and the revelation given to us, and to Abraham, Isma'il, Isaac, Jacob, and the Tribes, and that given to Moses and Jesus, and that given to (all) the prophets from their Lord: We make no difference between any of them: and unto Him we submit."

Significantly, early Muslim commentators (eg. Bukhari and al-Razi) all agreed that the Bible could not be changed since it was God's Word. Several centuries passed before Muslims began to claim that the Bible had been changed after they realized that the stories in the Qur'an were different from those in the Bible. This loving God, i.e. the Father, Son and Holy Spirit, now invites all mankind to join His eternal and glorious fellowship. Our role is to be His witnesses and to introduce God to our friends that they too might know Him.

The Bible is the FOUNDATION of Divine Revelation, the highest authority for understanding and interpreting Truth. This loving, merciful God now invites all of mankind to believe in Him and to join His eternal fellowship by faith through Jesus the Messiah, the Saviour of all mankind.

The Name of God/Allah in History and Linguistics

In history, for more than 3500 years, the word *Allah* has been the Arabic word for God, like *Theos* is in the Greek and *Elohim* in the Hebrew. From the time Muhammad began preaching Islam (610-632), the word *"Allah"* became more than the generic word for God, it became the name of the God they worshipped. Outside of Islam in the Middle East, the word *"Allah"* continued to be a generic noun for the one worshipped as the Creator and not as a personal name.

In the Jewish faith, *Allah* is known by the Hebrew word *Elohim* with the name Yahweh. In the early Christian faith, God was *Theos* in the Greek with the name *Kurios*, and in English He is *God* with the name *Lord*. The Jews of Yemen, in their Bible (Old Testament) which was in the Arabic language did not have a problem using the word *Allah* as the word for God and that's the word for God throughout their Bible.

Understanding the Arabic word "Allah"

Many countries have the word "Allah" in their languages as the normal word for "God", as has been the case in Arabic for over 3500 years. The word *"Allah"* is used by Arabic Christians in their Bible and they have used the word *"Allah"* since the birth of the church in 30AD. This is recorded in *Acts 2*, on the Day of Pentecost, 592 years before the birth of Islam in 622AD.

In history, 3 major groups have used the word *Allah*

i. ***Polytheist Idolators*** - For 3500 years polytheists worshipped many idols in the Middle East. The word *Allah* has been used in various dialectic forms as 'god' the object of worship and not as a name. Each *Allah (or ilah)* was given a name according to its nature.

ii. ***Judeo-Christian*** - The revelation of the Bible, supported by archaeology and history, reveal that Monotheists in the Middle East have commonly used the word *Allah* or its variants, *ilah, el, eloh, eloah, elohim, alaha,* as an object of worship since *Genesis 1:1.* The word *Allah* has been used in 40 countries and 20 languages as a generic word for God. In the same way, the word 'God' has existed in many European languages, Dutch, German, Danish etc as a generic noun for an object of worship and not as a personal name. In the Scriptures of the Judeo-Christian faiths, God (Allah/Theos/God) has a personal name which is not Allah but YHWH/Kurios/Lord.

iii. ***Islam*** – The religion of Islam originates in the collision of the Polytheists (idol worshippers) with the Monotheists (Judeo-Christian) 1400 years ago in Arabia. In Islam the word *ilah, allah* was changed by Muhammad from being just an object of worship, a generic noun to become the personal name of the one they worship. So the name of their *ilah/allah* (God/Theos) is also the word Allah composed of *al+ilah* to become Allah, meaning "The God."

Aramaic in the Hebrew Bible

The Semitic language group of Hebrew, Arabic, Syriac, Aramaic, is unique in that each word consists of a basic three consonants as its foundation. A small part of the Old Testament was originally written in Aramaic (e.g. parts of Daniel and Ezra) and like the Hebrew and Arabic used the same three consonant root *A-L-H* for God. In Aramaic it produced the form *elah.* The same root A-L-H is in Arabic and Hebrew as these are all from the same root of Semitic languages.

Daniel 2:47, "your God is a God of gods." Aramaic: "di **elah**ekon hu **elah elah**in"

Ezra 5:1, "in the name of the God of Israel." Aramaic: "be shum **elah** yisra'el" *elah* (Aramaic) = *ilah* (Arabic) = *eloh*/*eloah* (Hebrew).

From Wikipedia article on Allah:

The term Allāh is derived from a contraction of the Arabic definite article **al-** "the" and **ilāh** "deity, god" to become **al-lāh** meaning "the [sole] deity, God" (or in the Greek: ὁ θεὸς μόνος, ho theos monos). Cognates of the name "Allāh" exist in other Semitic languages, including Hebrew and Aramaic. Biblical Hebrew mostly uses the plural form **Elohim**. The corresponding Aramaic plural form is **'Ĕlāhā in Biblical Aramaic** and **'Alâhâ, in Syriac** as used by the Assyrian Church, **both meaning simply 'God'.**

The word *Allah* in the History of the Church

Acts 2:8-11 – people from 16 languages said: "we do hear them speak in our languages the wonderful works of God." The word for ***God*** was heard in 16 languages – What word for 'God' did they hear?

The Greeks heard the word **THEOS**. The Romans heard the word **DEO**. The Hebrews heard the word **ELOHIM**. The Syriacs heard the word **ELAHA.** The Aramaics heard th word **ALAHA**, while the Arabs heard the word **ALLAH**.

So the word *Allah* has been used by Christian Arabs since the Day of Pentecost in 30AD, some 600 years before the birth of Islam. The word *Allah* **does not** originate in Islam!

Use of the word *Allah* in Christian History

a. The words, "Bismillah Al-Rahman Al-Raheem" in Arabic Church History

On more than 20 Church buildings in Madaba near Mt. Nebo, Jordan, and many Christian homes in Syria, Lebanon, Iraq and Palestine since the C4th can be found the words: *Bismillah al-Rahman al-Raheem.* This phrase is commonly used by Muslims and in the Qur'an. It means *"In the Name of God, the Merciful, the Compassionate."*

b. Ancient Christian Arabic inscriptions pre-Islam

Inscriptions found in Christian tombs and in Church buildings including in Umm al-Jimāl, Jordan. *Enno Littmann, Arabic Inscriptions (Leiden, 1949)*

c. Council of Nicea – 325AD

Church leaders from all over the world gathered including from Arabia with names like Bishop Abdallah i.e. Servant of Allah. *(Enno Littmann, Arabic Inscriptions (Leiden, 1949).* The word "Allah" was understood to be the Arabic equivalent for the word "God" and had been in common usage for centuries.

d. Oldest complete Bible in Arabic script - 867AD.

Codex 151 found in St. Catherines in Egypt and earlier Arabic fragments dating to pre-Islam.

(The Early Versions of the New Testament: Their Origin, Transmission, and Limitations Oxford University Press, USA (September 15, 1977), p. 261). The word *Allah,* throughout history, has been a common word for the object of worship, as an idol and as the Creator. This usage is evident in history for over 3500 years, especially by Israelites, pagans and Christians. Later, in Islam, the word Allah was introduced as a name for the Lord of Mecca.

Evidence of the Trinity throughout the Bible

The evidence in the Bible, both Old and New Testaments, written between 1500 BC and 100 AD, totally reject the Islamic claim that the doctrine

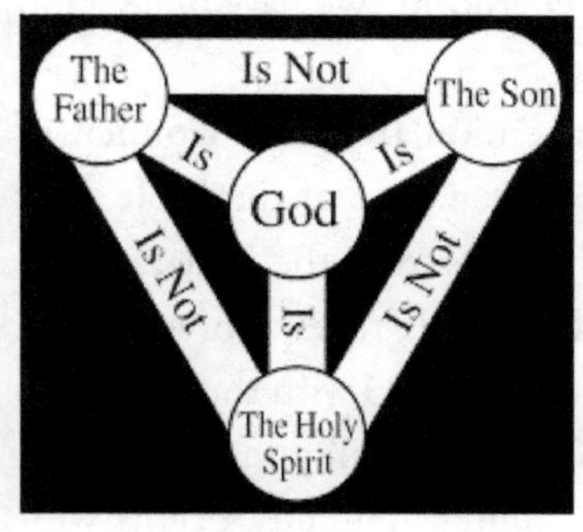

of the Trinity was invented at the Council of Nicea in 325 AD. There are literally hundreds of evidences that indicate the concept of the Trinity throughout the Bible. This can be seen in direct statements of the Three Divine Persons as ONE GOD as well as multitudes of grammatical evidence indicating a composite plurality or unity in the divine characteristics. There can be no doubt that the doctrine of the Trinity is 100% Biblical and it begins with the very first verse in the Bible.

Genesis 1:1,

"In the beginning God (Elohim)."

From the very first words in the Bible, the Trinity is indicated, and that can be expanded to the first three verses of *Genesis 1* as we can see the roles of the Father God, God the Son, the Word, and God the Holy Spirit are all at work in the foundation of Biblical and human history.

ELOH**IM** is a plural word. Sometimes it is used to express the state of the compound unity of the Trinity, that God is a COMPOSITE UNITY (i.e. PLURALITY IN ONE or THREE IN ONE). It is obvious from the use of PLURAL words used to speak about God. Note the key words or phrases in the following verses that indicate this element of plurality within the ONE Lord God.

Genesis 1:26,

"Then God (Eloh**im**) said, "Let **US** make man in **OUR** image, according to **OUR** likeness."

This was not God plus the angels. No, it's just God! Note also the word used for God is plural. In Semitic languages plurality begins with THREE, not two as in English. The **IM** in Eloh**IM** shows that there had to be THREE. We have one cherub but many cherub**im**. We have one seraph but many seraph**im**.

The truth of the Trinity was not an invention from the Council of Nicea, it was God's revelation from the very first verse of the Bible. The word Trinity is a theological term, although not used in the Bible, is used to summarize the clear statements in the Bible that reveal Three Divine Persons in the ONE GOD. This is clear in *Genesis 1:26* with the use of the terms ELOHIM, and US and OUR showing the plurality in unity. Each of those terms are plural and in Hebrew grammar, plurality begins with THREE.

Genesis 3:22,

"Then the LORD God said, "Behold, the man has become like **one of US**, to know good and evil."

The phrase "one of US" shows that God is PLURALITY in ONE.

Genesis 11:7,

"Come, let **US** go down and there confuse their language, that they may not understand one another's speech."

God is plurality in unity – 3 in 1. He is a Trinity. He is Triune.

The passages in Genesis are planting a seed of divine plurality in perfect unity that becomes the foundation of our understanding throughout the whole of the Bible.

Numbers 13:33,

"Then they came to the Valley of Eshcol, and there cut down a branch with **one cluster** of grapes; they carried it between two of them on a pole."

The word for one is ***echad***. Just one, yet it was a cluster, or a bunch consisting of many grapes. It was PLURALITY in ONE. It carries the concept of unity in diversity. This is intrinsic in the Arabic word *ahad* and the Hebrew word *echad*.

Appearances of Angels demonstrate the same principle

There are several examples that illustrate that references to Angels or the Angel of the LORD specifically reveal God appearing in a form that humans can see, for no man can yet see God in His full Deity and live.

Exodus 33:20,

"No man shall see Me, and live."

1Timothy 6:14-16,

"Keep this commandment without spot, blameless until our Lord Jesus Christ's appearing, which He will manifest in His own time, He who is the blessed and only Potentate, the King of kings and Lord of lords, who alone has immortality, dwelling in unapproachable light, **whom no man has seen or can see**, to whom be honour and everlasting power."

Who is Paul talking about? Who is this one dwelling in unapproachable light? Who is the one whom no man has seen or can see? Who is this one who is called the King of kings and Lord of lords? It is none other than Jesus in the fulness of His Divine glory. The same glory possessed by the Father and the Holy Spirit. It is the same glory that we will inherit as co-heirs with Christ. All that He has, we will have! Absolutely awesome!

Revelation 19:16,

"He has on His robe and on His thigh a name written: King of kings and Lord of lords."

Romans 8:17,

"heirs of God and joint heirs with Christ"

2Corinthians 3:18,

"We all, with unveiled face, beholding as in a mirror the glory of the Lord, are being transformed into the same image from glory to glory, just as by the Spirit of the Lord."

And yes! We will see God in the fullness of His glory because we will have sinless, immortal, glorified bodies just like Jesus.

Matthew 5:8,

"Blessed are the pure in heart, for **they shall see God**."

Job 19:25-27,

"I know that my Redeemer lives, and He shall stand at last on the earth; And after my skin is destroyed, this I know, That in my flesh **I shall see God**, Whom I shall see for myself, and my eyes shall behold, and not another. How my heart yearns within me!"

1John 3:2,

"Beloved, now we are children of God; and it has not yet been revealed what we shall be, but we know that when He is revealed, we shall be like Him, for **we shall see Him as He is**."

1Corinthians 15:51-53,

"Behold, I tell you a mystery: We shall not all sleep, but we shall all be changed— in a moment, in the twinkling of an eye, at the last trumpet. For the trumpet will sound, and the dead will be raised incorruptible, and we shall be changed. For this corruptible must put on incorruption, and this mortal must put on immortality."

The Men – the Angels – the LORD that appeared to Abraham in Mamre

Genesis 18:1-2,

"Then **THE LORD** appeared to him by the terebinth trees of Mamre, as he (Abraham) was sitting in the tent door in the heat of the day. So he lifted his eyes and looked, and behold, **THREE MEN** were standing by him; and when he saw **THEM**, he ran from the tent door to meet **THEM**, and bowed himself to the ground,"

Abraham saw the LORD in THREE PERSONS.

This is an amazing revelation of the Trinity. The LORD appears as three men. It had to be this way as no sinful man could look on God in His Holiness and Glory and live. This is called a theophany, God revealing Himself in a human form. This is not an incarnation. Incarnation is when God becomes a human being. This was God showing Himself in a form that Abraham could see, i.e. in human appearance.

This account continues with the LORD saying He would personally go down to Sodom and Gomorrah, and then the LORD also stayed personally with Abraham. This is only possible because God is Triune. The LORD stayed and the LORD left for Sodom and Gomorrah.

Genesis 18:20-22,

"And **the LORD said,** "Because the outcry against Sodom and Gomorrah is great, and because their sin is very grave, **I WILL GO DOWN now and see whether they have done altogether according to the outcry against it that has come to Me**; and if not, I will know." Then the men turned away from there and went toward Sodom, **but Abraham still stood before the LORD**."

Who left for Sodom and Gomorrah? The LORD.

Who stayed with Abraham? The LORD.

Well, who arrived in Sodom and Gomorrah? The two men who departed from Abraham now appear as Angels. Who were these Angels?

Genesis 19:1,

"Now the two angels came to Sodom in the evening, and Lot was sitting in the gate of Sodom."

In ***Genesis 19:1-30*** we gain further insight into this event. These "two angels" had the authority and power of the LORD (YHWH):

19:11 – "they struck the men who were at the doorway of the house with blindness."

19:12-13 – The angels said, "take them (Lot's family) out of this place! For **WE will destroy this place.**"

19:14 – "So Lot went out and spoke to his sons-in-law, who had married his daughters, and said, "Get up, get out of this place; for **the LORD will destroy this city**!"

Who will destroy Sodom? The two angels! See verse 13. Then in verse 14, the LORD will destroy the city. Conclusion? The two angels are the LORD!

This next verse is amazing, so grasp it and understand it!

19:24 – "Then **the LORD** rained brimstone and fire on Sodom and Gomorrah, **from the LORD** out of the heavens."

Note the reference to TWO LORDS!

Yet we know that Abraham, at this same time was with **the LORD** in Mamre! That makes three LORDS!

Observe closely that the LORD **(#1)** was reigning down fire and brimstone on Sodom and Gomorrah from the LORD **(#2)** in heaven, while at the same time the LORD **(#3)** was with Abraham!

There are THREE who are called YAHWEH. This event points to a Divine Plurality within the ONE GOD.

Is it any surprise then that Jesus could say to the Pharisees that He had been with Abraham?

John 8:56-59,

"Your father Abraham rejoiced to see My day, and he saw it and was glad." Then the Jews said to Him, "You are not yet fifty years old, and have You seen Abraham?" Jesus said to them, "Most assuredly, I say to you, before Abraham was, I AM." Then they took up stones to throw at Him." Why? Because Jesus declared Himself to be the "I AM".

Other Angelic appearances of the LORD GOD

In the Bible, God often appears in the form of an angel:

Genesis 16 7-13,

"When Sarai dealt harshly with Hagar, she fled from her presence. Now the Angel of the LORD found her by a spring of water in the wilderness, by the spring on the way to Shur. And He said, "Hagar, Sarai's maid, where have you come from, and where are you going?" She said, "I am fleeing from the presence of my mistress Sarai." The Angel of the LORD said to her, "Return to your mistress, and submit yourself under her hand." Then the Angel of the LORD said to her, "**I will multiply your descendants exceedingly**, so that they shall not be counted for multitude." And the Angel of the LORD said to her: "Behold, **you are with child, and you shall bear a son. You shall call his name Ishmael**, because the LORD has heard your affliction. He shall be a wild man; His hand shall be against every man, and every man's hand against him. And he shall dwell in the presence of all his brethren." Then **she called the name of the LORD who spoke to her, *You-Are- the-God-Who-Sees;*** for she said, "Have I also here seen Him who sees me?"

This indeed is the LORD. He prophesies over her the blessing of multiplying her descendants through Ishmael. He even names Ishmael and foretells his fighting character likened to a donkey.

This account of the Angel of the LORD coming to Hagar is prophetically important. It not only had to do with preserving Hagar's life but also preserving Ishmael. As we have seen, this is prophetic of that part of Islam that cries out to God, and his name, Ishmael, means, "God hears."

The Angel of the LORD comes in a visible form like a human being but Hagar recognizes that the Angel is not human. He is Divine. So she "called **the name of the LORD who spoke to her, *You-Are- the-God-Who-Sees;*** for she said, "Have I also here seen Him who sees me?"

Then in ***Genesis 22:1-18*** the same Angel who ministered to Hagar, now stops Abraham from sacrificing Isaac and says you haven't withheld your son from Me again speaking as if He is God, for indeed He is God. Initially it refers to the Angel of the LORD, but then He says the LORD.

Genesis 22:15-18,

"Then ***the Angel of the LORD*** called to Abraham a second time out of heaven, and said: "***By Myself I have sworn, says the LORD***, because you have done this thing, and have not withheld your son, your only son— blessing I will bless you, and multiplying I will multiply your descendants as the stars of the heaven and as the sand which is on the seashore; and your descendants shall possess the gate of their enemies. In your seed all the nations of the earth shall be blessed, because ***you have obeyed My voice.***"

The terms "Angel of the LORD" and "the LORD" are used interchangeably. Similarly in the next example where Jacob is wrestling with a "Man" who clearly is identified as God.

Genesis 32:24-30,

"Then Jacob was left alone; and **a Man** wrestled with him until the breaking of day. Now when He saw that He did not prevail against him, He touched the socket of his hip; and the socket of Jacob's hip was out of joint as He wrestled with him. And He said, "Let Me go, for the day breaks." But he said, "I will not let You go unless You bless me!" So He said to him, "What is your name?" He said, "Jacob." And He said, "Your name shall no longer be called Jacob, but Israel; for **you have struggled with God** and with men, and have prevailed." Then Jacob asked, saying, "Tell me Your name, I pray." And He said, "Why is it that you ask about My name?" And He blessed him there. So Jacob called the name of the place Peniel: "For **I have seen God face to face, and my life is preserved**."

When the time came for Jacob to bless his children and he came to Joseph we see he too uses the Angel and God interchangeably.

Genesis 48:15-16,

"And he blessed Joseph, and said: "**God**, before whom my fathers Abraham and Isaac walked, **the God** who has fed me all my life long to this day, **the Angel** who has redeemed me from all evil, bless the lads; Let my name be named upon them, and the name of my fathers Abraham and Isaac; and let them grow into a multitude in the midst of the earth."

Exodus 3:1-5,

"Now Moses was tending the flock of Jethro his father-in-law, the priest of Midian. And he led the flock to the back of the desert, and came to Horeb, the mountain of God. And **the Angel of the LORD** appeared to him in a flame of fire from the midst of a bush. So he looked, and behold, the bush was burning with fire, but the bush was not consumed. Then Moses said, "I will now turn aside and see this great sight, why the bush does not burn." So when **the LORD** saw that he turned aside to look, **God called to him** from the midst of the bush and said, "Moses, Moses!" And he said, "Here I am." Then He said, "Do not draw near this place. Take your sandals off your feet, for the place where you stand is holy ground." Moreover He said, "**I am the God of your father—the God of Abraham, the God of Isaac, and the God of Jacob**." And Moses hid his face, for he was afraid to look upon God."

The Angel of the LORD appears to Moses in the burning bush and interchangeably uses the terms Angel, the LORD and God who appeared to Moses and spoke directly to him.

Judges 6:11-14,

"Now the **Angel of the LORD** came and sat under the terebinth tree which was in Ophrah, which belonged to Joash the Abiezrite, while his son Gideon threshed wheat in the winepress, in order to hide it from the Midianites. And the **Angel of the LORD** appeared to him, and said to him, "The LORD is with you, you mighty man of valour!" Gideon said to Him, "O my lord, if the LORD is with us, why then has all this happened to us? And where are all His miracles which our fathers told us about, saying, "Did not the LORD bring us up from Egypt?" But now the LORD has forsaken us and delivered us into the hands of the Midianites." **Then**

the LORD turned to him and said, "Go in this might of yours, and you shall save Israel from the hand of the Midianites. Have I not sent you?"

The LORD appeared to Gideon as the Angel of the LORD and Gideon questioned, "where are all His miracles?" Then the LORD turned to him and commissioned him to win the battle. Were the Angel of the LORD and the LORD the same person or was it two persons with each one speaking? In the passage it is clear that the Angel of the LORD is indeed the LORD.

In ***Judges 13:1-25*** we have the intriguing encounter of Manoah and his wife with the LORD. They were from the tribe of Dan and had no children. Manoah's wife was barren so they had no children. The Angel of the Lord appeared to her and confirmed that she was barren and then prophesied over her that she would bear a son and told her how she should raise the boy because he would be a Nazirite to God and would deliver Israel out of the hand of the Philistines. She raced to her husband and excitedly told him that a Man of God who had the countenance of the Angel of God had come to her with this fantastic news.

Manoah believed his wife and prayed to the LORD that the Man of God would come again. He did. Manoah asked the Man for His name, and the Angel replied with an awesome revelation:

Judges 13:17-18,

"What is Your name, that when Your words come to pass we may honour You?" And **the Angel of the LORD** said to him, **"Why do you ask My name, seeing it is wonderful?"**

This was an amazing answer. Who's name is called Wonderful?

Isaiah 9:6,

"For unto us a Child is born, Unto us a Son is given; And the government will be upon His shoulder. And His name will be called **Wonderful,** Counselor, **Mighty God**, Everlasting Father, Prince of Peace."

This heavenly visitor who came as **the Angel of the LORD**, and as **the Man of God**, was none other than Jesus, the Mighty God, the Prince of Peace.

When Manoah made an offering to the LORD and in front of their eyes **the Man, the Angel of the LORD** ascended in the flames. Manoah and his wife fell on their faces then Manoah knew that He was the Angel of the LORD. Manoah said to his wife, "We shall surely die, because we have seen God!"

Theologically this is called a theophany – God appearing in a visible, human form, to bring a message from the LORD.

This is very real to Jeff as he had such an amazing experience when the Lord appeared to him in 1968 confirming his call to Indonesia and giving him the vision and the message that he was to proclaim.

Isaiah 63:7-10

"I will mention the lovingkindnesses of **the LORD** and the praises of the LORD, according to all that the LORD has bestowed on us, and the great goodness toward the house of Israel, which He has bestowed on them according to His mercies, according to the multitude of His loving-kindnesses. For He said, "Surely they are My people, Children who will not lie." So He became their Saviour. In all their affliction He was afflicted, and **the Angel of His Presence** saved them; In His love and in His pity He redeemed them; And He bore them and carried them All the days of old. But they rebelled and **grieved His Holy Spirit**; So He turned Himself against them as an enemy, And He fought against them."

Isaiah presents us with Three Divine Persons, multiple times, in this passage:

1. The LORD
2. The Angel of His Presence – the Saviour and Redeemer
3. The Holy Spirit

We see this elsewhere in Isaiah as well. When you read these verses, how could you possibly deny the Trinity in the Old Testament? This message in Isaiah is so powerful and so clear.

Isaiah 43:13-17,

"Indeed My hand has laid the foundation of the earth (JESUS – the Word of God), And My right hand has stretched out the heavens; When I call to them, They stand up together. "All of you, assemble yourselves, and hear! Who among them has declared these things? The LORD (The FATHER) loves him; He shall do His pleasure on Babylon, and His arm shall be against the Chaldeans. I (JESUS – the Word of God), even I, have spoken; Yes, I have called him, I have brought him, and his way will prosper. "Come near to Me, hear this: I have not spoken in secret from the beginning; From the time that it was, I was there. And now the Lord GOD (the FATHER) and His Spirit (the HOLY SPIRIT) have sent Me (JESUS, the Word of God)." Thus says the LORD, your Redeemer, the Holy One of Israel: "I am the LORD your God, Who teaches you to profit, ***Who leads you by the way you should go."***

Here is an answer for my Muslim friends who are wanting to solve this dilemma. Yes, there is a Straight Path, it is Jesus, and we need to follow Him. And Yes, there is a Three-in-One-God. It is God the Father, God the Son, and God the Holy Spirit. So we can shout together:

ENGLISH: "Hear O Israel: The Lord our God is ONE"
HEBREW: "shema yisrael: yahweh elohenu yahweh echad"
ARABIC: "isma' ya isra'eel: arrabb ilahuna rabbun wahidun"

Semitic Grammar confirms Divine Plurality in the Old Testament

We have discussed briefly the concepts of plurality in unity or composite oneness. We have looked at the Semitic plural which begins with THREE and not TWO as in English and almost every other language. But it would be helpful to look at a few examples which indicate plurality in unity. Some of these examples may surprise you.

Gary Rendsburg (July 1982) wrote *"Dual Personal Pronouns and Dual Verbs in Hebrew". The Jewish Quarterly Review: New Series. 73 (1): 38–58. Doi:10.2307/1454459:*

"In Biblical, Mishnaic, and Medieval Hebrew, like Arabic and other Semitic languages, all nouns can have singular, plural or dual forms." Plurality begins with three.

Many Jewish Rabbis observe that God, in the Old Testament, is referred to in terms of tri-unity and acknowledge the possibility of a Trinity of Three Divine Persons. This is drawn from the Hebrew Grammar. We will note a few examples.

1. How many Creators do we have?

In ***Ecclesiastes 12:1*** it states:

"Remember now your Creator in the days of your youth."

Our English Bible writes the word in the singular, but in the Hebrew it is plural, and plurality in Semitic languages begins with THREE! The word "Creator" ***(bor^{e}ekha)*** here is plural. So, who is our Creator?

Answer: The FATHER, the SON and the HOLY SPIRIT.

2. If God's people are His Bride, how many Husbands do we have?

Isaiah 54:5,

"For your **Maker** is your **husband**, The LORD of hosts is His name"

Maker (plural *osayik* – from singular *asah*) is your **husband** (plural *boalayik* - from singular *baal*).

Answer: We have ONE HUSBAND – "the LORD (YHWH) is His name.

Who is the LORD? He is Elohim, the Triune God - Father, Son, and Holy Spirit.

This, and much more, is just the Old Testament – the Law, the Psalms and the Prophets.

IS THE TRINITY ALSO IN THE NEW TESTAMENT?

After showing the abundant evidence in the Old Testament, what about the New Testament? Does it also teach the Doctrine of the Trinity, that God is Three Divine Persons in ONE GOD? If it is true, what is the evidence?

We will share a few key verses which clearly show that even in the New Testament the Three Divine Persons of the Trinity – the Father, the Son and the Holy Spirit – are the same ONE GOD declared by Moses in the Old Testament and Jesus in the New Testament.

Jesus laid the foundation of our faith in God in **Mark 12:29,**

"The first of all the commandments is*: 'HEAR, O ISRAEL, THE LORD OUR GOD, THE LORD IS ONE'."*

This was the foundation of faith in God declared by Jesus, and as we have seen in the Old Testament, it was a declaration that could only be fulfilled in a Triune God. This is also crystal clear in the New Testament with Jesus being the main expositor of this reality. There are numerous verses where Jesus is talking with His Father, and verses where Jesus refers to the Holy Spirit, but the whole Three are not mentioned in that verse. We have not included these verses but rather have concentrated on the verses where all Three are mentioned.

Matthew 3:16-17,

"When He had been baptized, **Jesus** came up immediately from the water; and behold, the heavens were opened to Him, and He saw **the Spirit of God** descending like a dove and alighting upon Him. And suddenly a voice came from heaven, saying, "This is **My (the Father** speaking) **beloved Son,** in whom I am well pleased."

All three persons of the Godhead are present and active in the same moment, yet clearly distinct:

- **Jesus the Son** is in the water being baptized.
- **The Holy Spirit** descends upon him in the form of a dove.
- **The Father's voice** speaks from heaven.

Matthew 28:19,

"Go therefore and make disciples of all the nations, baptizing them in the name of **the Father** and of **the Son** and of **the Holy Spirit**."

Pay close attention to the language here. **He doesn't say in the "names" plural. He says in the "name" singular,** one name, one divine essence and authority. **Yet that one name encompasses three distinct persons,** the Father, the Son, and the Holy Spirit. This is the composite unity of **echad** fully expressed. It's the plural reality of Elohim fully revealed.

John Chrysostom, a native Greek speaker from the 4th century, argued that the Apostle John masterfully shows in ***John 1:1*** both the Word's distinction from God the Father as a separate Divine Being yet is identical in nature with the Father.

John 1:1,

"In the beginning was the Word, and the Word was with God, and the Word was God."

'Εν ἀρχῇ ἦν ὁ Λόγος, καὶ ὁ Λόγος ἦν πρὸς τὸν Θεόν (**ton theon**), καὶ Θεὸς (**theos**) ἦν ὁ Λόγος.

Scholars of Greek grammar, like **Daniel Wallace** (Professor of New Testament Studies at *Dallas Theological Seminary*), note that when a noun like ***theos*** comes before the verb, the absence of the article is meant to emphasize the quality or nature of the noun. John isn't saying the Word was "a god". He's saying that whatever the essence of God is, whatever makes God God, the Word shares that essence completely. He, 100%, has the very nature of God.

The Word is fully God. And yet He is also personally distinct from the Father.

Then just a few verses later in ***John 1:14,*** the Word became flesh and dwelt among us. The eternal divine person who existed face to face with the Father, who shared the very essence of God, entered into human history as Jesus of Nazareth. This is the foundation. Without this, the Trinity can feel like an abstract formula. But with it, you realize the entire Christian faith is built on this truth."

Luke 3:21-22,

"When all the people were baptized, it came to pass that **Jesus** also was baptized; and while He prayed, the heaven was opened. And **the Holy Spirit** descended in bodily form like a dove upon Him, and a voice came from heaven which said, "You are **My** (**the Father** speaking) **beloved Son**; in You I am well pleased."

John 14:16-17,

"**I (Jesus)** will pray **the Father**, and He will give you **another Helper, that He may abide with you forever— the Spirit of truth,** whom the world cannot receive, because it neither sees Him nor knows Him."

Romans 14:17-18,

"The kingdom of God is not eating and drinking, but righteousness and peace and joy in **the Holy Spirit**. For he who serves **Christ** in these things is acceptable to **God (the Father)** and approved by men."

1Corinthians 12:4-6,

"There are diversities of gifts, but **the same Spirit (Holy Spirit)**. There are differences of ministries, but **the same Lord (Jesus)**. And there are diversities of activities, but it is **the same God (the Father)** who works all in all."

2Corinthians 1:21-22,

"Now He who establishes us with you in **Christ** and has anointed us is **God (the Father)**, who also has sealed us and given us **the Spirit** in our hearts as a guarantee."

2Corinthians 13:14,

"The grace of **the Lord Jesus Christ**, and **the love of God (the Father)**, and **the communion of the Holy Spirit** be with you all. Amen."

Ephesians 2:18,

"For through **Him (Jesus)** we both have access by **one Spirit (the Holy Spirit)** to **the Father**."

Ephesians 4:4-6,

"There is one body and **one Spirit**, just as you were called in one hope of your calling; **one Lord (Jesus)**, one faith, one baptism; **one God and Father of all,** who is above all, and through all, and in you all.

Colossians 2:9,

"For in **Him (Jesus)** dwells all **the fullness of the Godhead bodily (the Father, the Son and the Holy Spirit)**."

1Peter 1:1-2,

"Peter, an apostle of Jesus Christ, to the pilgrims of the Dispersion in Pontus, Galatia, Cappadocia, Asia, and Bithynia, elect according to the *foreknowledge of* **God the Father**, in *sanctification of* **the Spirit**, for obedience and sprinkling of *the blood of* **Jesus Christ**: Grace to you and peace be multiplied."

1John 5:7-8 (Greek New Testament Byzantine),

"οτι τρεις εισιν οι μαρτυρουντες **το πνευμα (the Holy Spirit)** και **το υδωρ (the Father)** και **το αιμα (the Son)** και οι τρεις εις το εν εισιν"

"There are three that bear witness: the **Spirit (the Holy Spirit)**, and the **water (the Father)**, and the **blood (the Son)**; and these three are one."

This last one with the Greek is a little more complicated. This is because it is the corrected Greek text after the interpolation in the King James text has been removed. However, it does not remove the revelation of the Trinity in these verses. The next verse tells us that the testimony of God is greater that the testimony of man.

Muslims are commanded by God in the Qur'an to believe the "Law and the Gospel".

Both the "Law and the Gospel" teach that God is Triune. In the Old Testament (the Law) God (Elohim) is Triune. It's the same in the New Testament! The following is a short summary of key characteristics found within each Divine Person in the Trinity that are easily discoverable in the Bible.

The Triune God

TRIUNE GOD IS:	FATHER	SON	HOLY SPIRIT
God	Philippians 1:2	John 1:1	Acts 5:3-4
Creator	Isaiah 64:8	John 1:3	Job 33:4
Omnipresent	1Kings 8:27	Matthew 28:20	Psalm 139:7-8
Omniscient	1John 3:20	John 16:30	1Corinthians 2:10-11
Eternal	Psalm 90:2	John 17:5	Hebrews 9:14
Life Giver	Genesis 2:7	John 5:21	2Corinthians 3:6,8

The Triune Creator has stamped His Creation with the nature of Triunity

The Creator is Triune as we have seen throughout the whole Bible. It is not surprising therefore that throughout the creation this triune nature is displayed. We see it everywhere. This does not prove the Trinity but it shows the nature of the Creator in a magnificent display of His glory.

Here are a few examples that are evident everywhere in creation. Learn them and use them as illustrations of triunity in the creation from a Triune God:

1. A Trinity of Trinities in the first verse of the Bible
   Genesis 1:1, "In the beginning (TIME – past, present, future) God created the heavens (SPACE – length, width, height) and the earth (MATTER – protons, electrons, neutrons).
2. Colour pigments (eg. Paint): Blue, Yellow, Red
3. Earth: Crust, Mantel, Core
4. Sources of Light: Sun, Moon, Stars
5. Family: Father, Mother, Child
6. Colours of Light: Red, Green, Blue
7. Man is triune: Body, Soul, Spirit - *1 Thessalonians 5:23*
8. Egg: Shell, White, Yoke
9. Fruit: Skin, Flesh, Seed

These are imperfect analogies, of course, because God is unlike anything else. But they help us grasp at the edges of a truth that is ultimately a mystery, a reality so deep and vast it can be known but never fully contained by our finite minds. Nevertheless, these examples from nature reflect that a Triune God, created the universe and the solar system and everything in it as a reflection of His Divine Triune nature and being. It is therefore no surprise that everywhere we look, we find reflections of this triune pattern.

Conclusion:

1. There is only ONE GOD and He is manifested in THREE DIVINE PERSONS. This theological concept is known as the TRINITY.
2. The word ONE, *echad* in Hebrew and *ahad* in Arabic, can be an individual singularity or it can be a composite unity. In reference to the nature of God, the Scriptures clearly revealed that the ONE GOD, *Elohim*, is a PLURALITY in perfect ONENESS, THREE DIVINE PERSONS IN ONE GOD.
3. The Father, Son and Holy Spirit lived in an eternal fellowship that was so glorious with perfect love, joy, peace, light, glory, holiness etc. that God decided to multiply that fellowship by creating man. That makes manvery special, the most glorious of God's creation. He loves us so much that this Triune God was willing to go through the pain and humiliation of the Cross so that we might be saved and fulfill His masterplan for all eternity. From the beginning God – the Father, the Son and the Holy Spirit revealed this amazing plan:

   Genesis 1:26-27, "God said, Let US (the Father, Son and Holy Spirit) make MAN in OUR image according to OUR likeness … So God created mankind in his OWN image, in the image of GOD He created them; MALE and FEMALE He created them."

The truth of the Trinity reveals that true spiritual life can't be lived in isolation. It's lived in a loving, self-giving community with others, mirroring in our own imperfect way the perfect community that exists within God Himself. It is into that eternal community of fellowship that God now invites us through accepting Jesus as our Lord and Saviour.

The dilemma of the Trinity has a solution. We now need to understand it and learn how to share it with others who maybe struggling to accept it or comprehend it. Sit down with your friends, discuss it and share it.

For more information watch a few videos on this subject where we also found helpful material and discussions as we investigated this important dilemma:

www.youtube.com/watch?v=7GZ-tMeVvUk
www.youtube.com/watch?v=Xj4HrwSEcss
www.youtube.com/shorts/wq6RcK78SFM
www.youtube.com/watch?v=-WQmpZCQ7oM
www.youtube.com/watch?v=Xj4HrwSEcss&t=10s
www.youtube.com/watch?v=qH4gF_9qv9Y

Questions for Discussion:

1. Can you give an example from the both the Old and New Testaments that prove that God is Triune?
2. If you are told that the Qur'an rejects the Trinity, how can you answer that rejection?
3. Does the Qur'an deny that the Father, the Son and the Holy Spirit are the ones Christians refer to as the Trinity?
4. What verse in the Qur'an names the three persons it is said the Christians call the Trinity?

DILEMMA 5

THE JESUS DILEMMA

Is Jesus only one of many prophets?

The Qur'an recognizes twenty-five prophets, most of them from the Bible. Among them all, one stands out above all the other human prophets. It is Jesus. In the Arabic His name is "*Isa*." His nature, character and power differ from all others.

How does Jesus compare to all the other prophets? Is Jesus greater than the prophet Muhammad?

Who is Jesus in the Qur'an? Where do the stories about Him in the Qur'an come from? Why is He so prominent in the Qur'an? Many Muslims ignore these questions. They believe He is just a prophet. They believe in Him. But… Muslims say that He's just a prophet, a man like all other prophets, a man with a message, but a message only for Christians, a man who is honoured, but who is not as great as the final prophet, the prophet Muhammad. Is that true? Is that what the Qur'an really says?

The appearance of Jesus in the Qur'an raises many dilemmas for Muslims. If they must believe in Him, should they not also read and believe in the books about Him, the books of the Christians? If they have questions about Him, should they not ask "the People of the Book (*Ahl-Kitab*)?

For Christians it all raises a dilemma. If Muslims believe in Jesus, do we still have to proclaim the Gospel to them? Do they really know who Jesus is?

Prophets in the Qur'an

Muslims believe that Jesus is just one of the prophets. There are 25 prophets mentioned by name in the Qur'an, most of them are in the Bible.

The most frequently mentioned of the prophets by name, are Adam (*Adam*) who is mentioned 25 times, Noah (*Nuh*) 45 times, Abraham (*Ibrahim*) 69 times, Lot (*Lut*) 27 times, Joseph (Yusuf) 27 times, Aaron (*Harun*) 27 times, Moses (*Musa*) 136 times and Jesus (*Isa*) who is mentioned 25 times.

The other prophets mentioned are *Idris*, who is considered to be Enoch, *Salih* who was either Methusaleh or an unknown Arabian prophet, *Hud* who some scholars think was Heber, Ishmael, Isaac, Jacob, *Shuaib* either an Arabian prophet or Jethro, Job (*Ayub*), Solomon (*Sulaiman*), Ezekiel (*Dhulkifl*), David (*Dawud*), Elijah (*Ilyas*), Elisha (*Elias/Al-Yasa)*, Jonah (*Yunus*), Zechariah (Zakariya), John the Baptist (*Yahya*). Together with Muhammad who is only mentioned by name 4 times in the Qur'an, these are the 25 official prophets of Islam.

Another man, sometimes identified as a prophet, *Dhu al-Qarnayn*, who is mentioned in the Qur'an and is identified as Alexander the Great. (*Surah al-Kahf 18:83–101).*

Note that the name of Jesus is mentioned 25 times, but "Muhammad" is mentioned by name only 4 times. For Muslims Muhammad is the most important of the prophets. The reason he is the most important is because he is considered to be the last prophet and because it was to him that the Qur'an was revealed.

This raises many questions. Why is his name only mentioned four times? Why is one third of the Qur'an a retelling of the stories of these other prophets? Why are Moses and Abraham and Jesus so prominent? Why are the stories that are retold so similar, yet so significantly different from what is recorded in the Old and the New Testaments? Why are there no direct quotes? The New Testament directly quotes the Old Testament about 300 times. The Qur'an has no direct quotes and only one indirect parallelism. (*Psalm 37:29* says, "The righteous will inherit the land" while the Qur'an says in *Surah Al-Anbiya 21:105,* "My righteous servants shall inherit the earth."

All these stories that Muhammad said he received from God and were to be included in the Qur'an concerning these prophets, were revealed a thousand years after the Old Testament had been written and 600 years after Jesus lived on earth and the Gospels were written down.

Among all these prophets, Jesus was revealed in the Qur'an as just one of them, a human being sent from God with a revelation and a book called the Gospel (*Injil*). Is this true? What does the Qur'an say about this prophet Jesus?

What Muslims Believe about Jesus

The Qur'an declares that Muslims must believe in Jesus.

One of the most renowned modern promulgators of Islam, ***Dr Zakir Naik***, said, "No Muslim is a Muslim if he does not believe in Jesus."

Another famous Islamic author and orator, **Ahmad Deedat (1918-2005)**, said, "We believe that Jesus Christ was one of the mightiest messengers of God. We believe that he was the Messiah. We believe in his miraculous birth, which many modern-day Christians reject today. We Muslims happen to be of the only non-Christian faith, which makes it an article of faith for its followers to believe in Jesus. No Muslim is a Muslim if he does not believe in Jesus."

But... what does "believing in Jesus" mean for a Muslim?

What Muslims reject about Jesus

Muslims must believe in Jesus, nevertheless it appears that they do not believe in:

- **The Deity of Jesus**: That Jesus is God *(An Nisa 4:171; Al Maedah 5.17; Al Anaam 6:101)*
- **The Trinity**: that God is Father, Son and Holy Spirit *(An Nisa 4:171; Al Maedah 5.73)*
- **The Incarnation**: That Jesus is the Son of God *(Maryam 19:89-92)*
- **The Crucifixion**: That Jesus died. *(An Nisa 4:157)*
- **The Atonement**: That Jesus is the sacrifice for our redemption
- **The Lordship of Christ**

These are all basic doctrines and considered fundamental truths for Christians. What is the truth and who has the truth about Jesus? Christians or Muslims? Who is the true Jesus, the one depicted in the Bible or the one depicted in the Qur'an?

The Christian view of Jesus is very different to that of the Qur'an. However, there are many verses in the Qur'an that mention Jesus and tell the story of his birth and his life, verses that we can use to bridge gaps in understanding and to challenge Muslims to face the dilemma of His identity.

Christian understanding of Jesus comes from what is written in the New Testament by eyewitnesses. The New Testament was completed before the second century, within 60 years of Jesus' lifetime. Islamic understanding of Jesus comes from what was written in the Qur'an about 600 years after He lived on earth. Furthermore, the Hadith, which has reports about what Muhammad said about Him, was only collected 750 to 800 years after Jesus had lived on earth.

The Qur'an indeed teaches that Muslims must believe in Jesus and the revelation given to Him.

Surah Al Baqarah 2:136,

"Say ye: "We believe in Allah, and the revelation given to us, and to Abraham, Ismail, Isaac, Jacob, and the Tribes, and that given to Moses and Jesus, and that given to (all) Prophets from their Lord: We make no difference between one and another of them: And we bow to Him."

Surah Ali Imran 3:84.

"Say: "We believe in Allah, and in what has been revealed to us and what was revealed to Abraham, Ismail, Isaac, Jacob, and the Tribes, and in (the Books) given to Moses, Jesus, and the Prophets from their Lord."

Muslims are told that they must say that they believe in all the prophets of the Bible and the writings in their books and they must believe in Jesus. Why don't they read the original books? Why don't they go to the source of so much of what is written in the Qur'an?

What Muslims accept about Jesus

The Qur'an commands obedience to Jesus (*Isa*) by establishing him as a messenger of Allah, specifically in this verse, where Jesus says, "I have come to you with a sign... So fear Allah, and obey me."

Surah Ali-Imran 3:50,

"Isa: "(I have come to you), to attest the Law which was before me. And to make lawful to you part of what was forbidden to you; I have come to you with a Sign from your Lord. So fear Allah, and obey me."

The Qur'an commands to have no doubt, but to follow Jesus. It says that "This is the Straight Way." Indeed, Jesus said in the Gospels, "I am the Way," ***John 14:6.***

Surah Az-Zukhruf 43:61-62,

"And (Jesus) shall be a Sign (for the coming of) the Hour (of Judgment): Therefore, have no doubt, but follow ye Me: This is a Straight Way."

The Qur'an says that God sent Jesus and gave Him the Gospel with "guidance and light." Surely the guidance and light of the Gospel must be obeyed and followed! Jesus said, "I am the light of the world" ***John 8:12; 9:5.*** In Him was life and the life was the light of men. *(John 1:4).* He was prophesied by Isaiah to be a light to the nations, *Isaiah 49:6.*

Surah Al-Maidah 5:46,

"And We sent Jesus…and We gave him the Gospel, in it (was) Guidance and light"

Another verse in the Qur'an describes Jesus as a "Messenger of Allah" and gives a clear command to believe in God and His messengers. Jesus is also described in this verse as "His Word." In what capacity Jesus is the Word of God is not elaborated on in the Qur'an and Muslims reject the Biblical teaching of who Jesus is. This is a great problem for Islam. How can they believe in Jesus, when they reject His teaching? How can they reject the man who is called "The Word of God?"

Surah An-Nisa 4:171,

"Christ Jesus the son of Mary was (no more than) a messenger of Allah, and His Word, which He bestowed on Mary, and a spirit proceeding from Him: so believe in Allah and His messengers."

The Hadith also talk about Jesus

Al-Bukhari 3435,

"Whoever believes there is no god but Allah, alone without partner, that Muhammad is His messenger, that Jesus is a servant and messenger of God, His word breathed into Mary and a spirit emanating from Him, and that Paradise and Hell are true, shall be received by God into Heaven."

Can a Muslim enter Paradise without believing in Jesus? According to what Muhammad said in the Hadith, no Muslim can go to heaven if he does not believe in Jesus.

There are many verses in the Qur'an that speak about Jesus. He is spoken of in over 90 verses in 12 different Surahs. The name of Jesus, is mentioned about 25 times.

Jesus is called:

Ibn Maryam – Son of Mary (23 times)
Al Masih – Messiah / Christ (11 times)
Abdullah – Servant/Slave of God
Rasulullah – Apostle of God.

Thus it is, that all Muslims accept that there was a man called Jesus (*Isa*) who was a prophet of God, the son of a virgin who is called the Messiah and like Muhammad was also a servant and an apostle of God.

The Confirmation of Jesus' Ministry and Message

1. Jesus Himself speaks and declares His ministry and mission

Surah Ali-Imran 3:45,

"I have come to you, with a Sign from your Lord, in that I make for you out of clay, as it were, the figure of a bird, and breathe into it, and it becomes a bird by Allah's leave: And I heal those born blind, and the lepers, and I quicken the dead, by Allah's leave; and I declare to you what ye eat, and what ye store in your houses. Surely therein is a Sign for you if ye did believe."

Jesus brings a sign, creates a living bird, heals the blind and lepers, raises the dead, tells them unseen things and declares that in all these things they are a sign from their Lord.

2. God speaks and His testimony confirms the ministry and mission of Jesus

Surah Al-Maedah 5:110,

"Then will Allah say....Oh Jesus ... behold! You make out of clay, as it were, the figure of a bird, by My leave, and you breathe into it and it becomes a bird by My leave, and you heal those born blind, and the lepers, by My leave. And behold! You bring forth the dead by My leave."

In *Ali Imran 3:45* it is Jesus speaking. In *Al Maedah 5:110,* it is God speaking to Jesus. God affirms everything that Jesus had spoken.

Here in the Qur'an, is a double confirmation of the work and power of Jesus. They are both the words of Jesus and the words of God. They are the foundational verses for understanding Jesus in the Qur'an. Jesus comes with a sign. Muhammad came with no signs. The Qur'an records many of the Meccans asking for physical signs but Muhammad only replied that the prerogative of working signs belongings to God alone. Jesus brought many signs. The only sign Muhammad brought, according to the Qur'an, was the Qur'an.

God confirmed Jesus with many signs and miracles. This is also stated in the Bible.

Acts 2:22,

"Fellow Israelites, listen to this: Jesus of Nazareth was a man accredited by God to you by miracles, wonders and signs, which God did among you through him, as you yourselves know."

Acts 10:38,

"God anointed Jesus of Nazareth with the Holy Spirit and power, and how he went around doing good and healing all who were under the power of the devil, because God was with him."

The only sign given to confirm Muhammad as a prophet is the Qur'an.

Surah Al-Ankabut 29:50-51,

"And they say, 'Why are not signs sent down to [Muhammad] from his Lord?' Say, 'The signs are only with Allah, and I am only a plain warner.' Is it not sufficient for them that We have sent down to you the Book [the Qur'an] which is recited to them?."

The Uniqueness and Preeminence of Jesus in The Qur'an

The Unique Birth of Jesus

His mother, Mary, is the only woman named in the Qur'an

Jesus' mother, Mary, is the only woman named in the Qur'an and she also gives her name to one of the 114 Surah (chapters or books) in the Qur'an. The Qur'an names no other woman, yet it mentions the name of Mary the mother of Jesus 34 times. Indeed, her life is referred to or featured up to 70 times. Why is Mary the only woman named? Could it be that the mother of Jesus is more important than the mothers of all other prophets, including the mother of Muhammad himself? If so, why? This is a dilemma.

In the Qur'an, Jesus' birth is described as unique and miraculous.

Jesus' birth was announced by the angel Gabriel

Jesus was born righteous from the womb.

Surah Maryam 19:19,

"He (Gabriel) said: "I am only a messenger from your Lord, to give you the gift of a righteous (sinless) son."

Surah Ali-Imran 3:46,

"The angel says to Mary, "He will be one of the righteous."

Mary, his mother, was a virgin

In the Old Testament God promised that a virgin would give birth to a son whose name would be called Immanuel, which means God with us. *Isaiah 7:4.* In the New Testament, a baby is born of a virgin and His name is Immanuel. *Matthew 1:23.*

In the Qur'an also, it records that Jesus was born of a virgin.

Surah Maryam 19:20,

"How can I have a son, when no man has touched me, nor am I unchaste!"

Mary was honoured above all women on earth.

Surah Ali-Imran 3:42,

"And remember when the angels said, "O Mary! Surely Allah has selected you, purified you, and chosen you over all women of the world."

His birth was decreed by God as part of His plan. It was a deeply intentional, ordained miracle. The Qur'an states that Mary's pregnancy was a decreed event designed to act as a sign of God's power and mercy to humanity.

Surah Ali Imran 3:47,

"She said: "O my Lord! How shall I have a son when no man hath touched me?" He said: "Even so: Allah createth what He willeth: When He hath decreed a plan, He but saith to it, 'Be,' and it is."

So, Jesus' birth was:

- A "matter already decreed"
- A creation by Divine command
- The Miracle of a Virgin Birth
- A new creation, similar to that of Adam
- A Word and Spirit from God

Jesus' birth is unique. No other man is like Him. Christianity declares it! Islam declares it! History declares it! There is one thing that cannot be denied: there has never been any other man who walked on this earth who is like Jesus!

Jesus Purpose: He was born as a sign for the worlds

Jesus was a sign and a mercy ***to all mankind.*** Nowhere does the Qur'an say that Jesus was sent only to the Jews, or only to the Christians. ***He is a sign for ALL mankind.*** He is a sign for the worlds. In fact, God said that it was a matter decreed, determined and ordained by Himself.

Surah Maryam 19:21,

"We have made him ***a sign for mankind*** and ***a mercy from Us***; and it is ***a matter decreed.***"

Surah Al-Anbiya 21:91,

"We breathed into her Our spirit, and we made her and her son ***a sign for the worlds.***"

Muslims often say that He was only sent to the Jews or the Christians.

Yes, Jesus was sent as a messenger to the Israelites.

Surah Ali-Imran 3:49 *makes this explicit:*

"And [make him] a messenger to the Children of Israel."

Jesus was sent to confirm to the children of Israel that the Torah was the true, authentic word of God. His message was for the Jews.

Surah Al Maidah 5:46,

"And in their footsteps We sent Jesus, the Son of Mary, confirming the Law [Torah] that had come before him."

His message was to confirm that the Book the Jews had received was the truth. His message was not only for Jews. It was also for Christians. The Qur'an says Jesus was given a Book, the Gospel. However, the only

Book of the Christians was the Bible that teaches the Gospel message that Jesus brought and that His disciples and apostles wrote down as they were inspired by the Holy Spirit. The "Gospel" referred to in the Qur'an, can mean no other than the whole Bible. There is no other "Book" that the Christians held. If Islam insists it was a Book that came down to Jesus, and was given to Him and written by Him, they face a significant dilemma. There is no such book that existed in Jesus' day, nor in the times of the apostles, nor in history before Muhammad and certainly not ever since then. This "Gospel" mentioned in the Qur'an can only mean the whole Bible, which of course includes the four Gospels that speak of His life and ministry, and also includes the whole of the New Testament. The Gospels, the Acts, the Epistles and the Revelation are all part of the Book that Christians held in their hands, the Book that all Christians believed, that was read and distributed in the days of Muhammad and which is the same Book that we have today.

Surah Al-Maidah 5:47,

"Let the people of the Gospel judge by what God has revealed in it."

The Gospel is true and authoritative! The Qur'an commands Christians to judge by what is revealed in it. This Gospel is the full counsel of God revealed in the 66 books of the Bible from Genesis to Revelation. It is the final authority for Christians. The Qur'an commands us to believe in it, stand upon it and judge all things by its message.

Jesus Birth is Glad Tidings

The Qur'an says that Jesus' birth is glad tidings. It is good news. It is not just for Jews and Christians. It is good news for Muslims. It is good news for the whole world.

Surah Ali-Imran 3:45,

"O Mary, God gives you glad tidings of a Word from Him."

This is also the message written in the Gospel.

Luke 2:10-11,

"Then the angel said to them, "Do not be afraid, for behold, I bring you good tidings of great joy which will be to all people. For there is born to you this day in the city of David a Saviour, who is Christ the Lord."

This is the glad tidings, the joyful news for all people! Christians have been spreading the news and singing the joyful tidings ever since.

We've got a story to tell to the nations!
Let the song go round the earth!
Spread the tidings all around, Jesus saves! Jesus saves!

Go, tell it on the mountains,
Over the hills and everywhere.
Go, tell it on the mountains,
That Jesus Christ is born.

Jesus Birth was Holy

The Qur'an and the Hadith say that Jesus was born sinless, in fact it says that He is the only man on earth, in history, who was born without Satan's touch. Satan's touch imparts sin and Jesus was the only man, the only prophet that Satan could not touch!

Sahih Al-Bukhari, Hadith 506,

"When any human being is born, Satan pinches the body with his two fingers, except 'Isa, the son of Maryam, whom Satan tried to pinch but failed, for he touched the placenta instead."

Sahih Al-Bukhari, Hadith 641,

"Abu Huraira said, "I heard Allah's Apostle saying, 'There is none born among the off-spring of Adam, but Satan touches it. A child therefore, cries loudly at the time of birth because of the touch of Satan, except Mary and her child." Then Abu Huraira recited: "And I seek refuge with You for her and for her offspring from the outcast Satan."

The birth of Jesus was different to the birth of every man born on earth down through the whole of human history. There is not one person who was born like Jesus. He was born of a virgin. What does that mean? Does not that signify that He is preeminent among men? If Satan couldn't touch Him, who is He? Why couldn't Satan touch Jesus?

Why don't Muslims join us at Christmas celebrating this greatest of births? It is celebrated in their own scriptures, the Qur'an and the Hadith. They acknowledge Jesus' miraculous birth, announced by the angel Gabriel, the virgin birth, from the most famous mother of all times which is good tidings and a sign to all peoples.

The Unique Miracles of Jesus

The Qur'an says that Jesus performed many miracles.

Surah Al-Baqarah 2:87,

"We gave Jesus the son of Mary CLEAR (SIGNS) and strengthened him with the holy spirit"

Surah Ali-Imran 3:49,

"And (appoint him) a messenger to the Children of Israel, (with this message): "I have come to you, with a SIGN from your Lord, in that I make for you out of clay, as it were, the figure of a bird, and breathe into it, and it becomes a bird by Allah's leave: And I heal those born blind, and the lepers, and I quicken the dead, by Allah's leave; and I declare to you what ye eat, and what ye store in your houses. Surely therein is a SIGN for you if ye did believe."

Surah Al-Maedah 5:111,

"Then will Allah say: "O Jesus the son of Mary! Recount My favour to thee and to thy mother. Behold! I strengthened thee with the holy spirit, so that thou didst speak to the people in childhood and in maturity. Behold! I taught thee the Book and Wisdom, the Law and the Gospel and behold! Thou makest out of clay, as it were, the figure of a bird, by My leave, and thou breathest into it and it becometh a bird by My leave, and thou healest those born blind, and the lepers, by My leave. And behold! thou bringest forth the dead by My leave. And behold! I did restrain the Children of Israel from (violence to) thee when thou didst show them the CLEAR SIGNS, and the unbelievers among them said: "This is nothing but evident magic."

He miraculously provided food

Thus, according to the Qur'an: Jesus prays to Allah to send down a table of food from heaven to satisfy his disciples and serve as a sign of his prophethood. The disciples of Jesus asked if his Lord could send down a table spread with food from the sky.

Al-Ma'idah 5:114,

"Jesus, son of Mary, said: O Allah, Lord of us! Send down for us a table spread with food from heaven."

Allah promised to send it down but warned that anyone who disbelieved afterward would face a severe punishment. According to Muslim commentators, the table arrived with food—often described as bread and fish—to strengthen the faith of the disciples and as a witness.

This story may have been confused with the New Testament narratives. It could be a retelling of Jesus' feeding of the 5000 (*Matthew 14:13-21*, the Last Supper *(Matthew 26:20-29),* the disciples' request for bread from heaven *(John 6:31-35)* or with Peter's vision of a sheet filled with animals that came down from heaven in when Peter was told to rise and eat (*Acts 10:9-16*).

It is also possible that this story could have been based on *The Gospel of the Twelve Apostles*, a little-known Syrian text. It was found in Edessa and dated late 7th to 8th century although it could have been copied from earlier texts. It tells a similar story of the disciples gathering and asking God to send down a table of food from heaven. It is another indication that the stories in the Qur'an owe much to the traditions and stories of the Syriac Christians.

Jesus spoke in the cradle

This is a miracle not mentioned in the Bible, but in the Christian apocryphal writings, especially in the *Infancy Gospel of Thomas*. The Qur'an mentions Jesus speaking as a baby to defend his mother, Mary *(Maryam 19:29-33)*. This story was being circulated in the Arabian Peninsula in the days of Muhammad through oral tradition and texts. Whether this story really happened or not, it is certain that no other newborn baby on earth is ever recorded as speaking in the cradle.

He created a bird

This is another miracle that was being circulated in the *Infancy Gospel of Thomas*. The Qur'an *(Surah Ali-Imran 3:49)* mentions Jesus forming a clay bird and breathing into it to give it life, but the *Infancy Gospel of Thomas* describes Jesus forming twelve birds from clay and making them live. It is not considered an inspired book but rather a fable told by some early Christians.

Infancy Gospel of Thomas, 2:1-4,

"When this boy, Jesus, was five years old, he was playing at the ford of a rushing stream. He then made soft clay and shaped it into twelve sparrows; Jesus simply clapped his hands and shouted to the sparrows: "Be off, fly away, and remember me, you who are now alive!" And the sparrows took off and flew away noisily."

He healed the blind and the lepers

Surah Ali-Imran 3.49,

"And I cure the blind and the leper."

Just as is recorded in the Gospels, Jesus went about performing many miracles of healing. The blind saw, the lepers were cleansed, the deaf heard, the dumb spoke, the lame walked again. Jesus also raised the dead. These miracles are all signs that Jesus was unique among the prophets. No other prophet performed as many miracles as He did. No other prophet possessed the power to heal the human body, as Jesus did.

He knew hidden things – He was Omniscient

Surah Al-'Imran 3:49,

"And I inform you of what you eat and what you store in your houses."

Jesus was able to do what no other could do. He knew hidden things. People could not hide from Jesus, not what they ate, not what they kept in their houses. He had a unique ability to know things that no other prophet possessed.

All of these things are signs. They demonstrate a supernatural power. Why was Jesus given all these signs? What do these signs mean? Why was He the only one who had all these signs? Does He still perform these signs today? Is He not preeminent among men? If this is all true, then why not believe the Gospel? Why not follow what He teaches?

The Unique Nature of Jesus

Jesus is the Word of God

What is the basic nature of Jesus according to the Qur'an?

John the Baptist (Yahya) was born and came to confirm the Word from God.

Surah Ali-Imran 3:39,

"Then the angels called him [Zachariah], … "Allah gives you glad tidings of Yahya, confirming the Word from Allah."

We are then told that the Word from Allah is a man whose name is Jesus the Christ (*Isa Almasih*).

***Surah Ali-Imran* 3:45,**

"The angels said: "Oh Mary, Verily, Allah gives you the glad tidings of a Word from Him, his name will be Christ Jesus, the son of Mary held in honour in this world and the Hereafter and of (the company of) those nearest to Allah."

Surah Maryam 19:34,

"Such is Jesus, son of Mary -- a statement of truth about which they dispute."

In the Qur'an, John the Baptist came to confirm the Word of God. In the Qur'an Jesus is said to be the Word from God. Jesus is unique as the Word from God. No other man is described like that!

Jesus is the Spirit from God

Christ Jesus the son of Mary was a messenger of Allah, and His Word, which He bestowed on Mary, and a spirit proceeding from Him: so believe in Allah and His messengers.

The Qur'an clearly says that Jesus is a Spirit from God breathed into Mary.

Surah An -Nisa' 4:171,

"O People (of) the Book! (Do) not commit excess in your religion and (do) not say about Allah except the truth. Only the Messiah, Isa, son (of) Maryam, (was) a Messenger (of) Allah and His word which He conveyed to Maryam and **a spirit from Him**. So believe in Allah and His Messengers."

The Qur'an also states that God Himself breathed His Spirit into Mary.

Surah Al-Anbiya 21:91,

"We breathed into her of Our spirit and we made her and her son a sign for the worlds."

The Bible says that Mary was found with child of the Holy Spirit, *Matthew 1:18.* The angel of the Lord declared to Joseph that what was conceived in her was of the Holy Spirit, *Matthew 1:20.* The angel Gabriel said to Mary,

Luke 1:35,

"The Holy Spirit will come upon you and power of the Highest will overshadow you, therefore, also, that Holy One who is to be born will be called the Son of God."

Jesus was born of the Spirit of God. The Qur'an also declares that Jesus' birth was unlike any other human conception in history. Only one baby was ever born on earth, directly by the breath of God, by the Spirit of God. Only one baby in the whole of history of mankind was born without a human father. That was Jesus.

The Dilemma

Muslims try to refute that Jesus is the Word of God and the Spirit from God.

Muslims will argue that the conception of Jesus is just like the creation of Adam. The Qur'an describes how Adam was created. They will say that Adam and Jesus are compared to show that both of them were created by God's word without a human father. This, they believe highlights and emphasizes their humanity rather than divinity.

Surah Ali-Imran 3:59,

"Indeed, the example of Jesus to Allah is like that of Adam. He created him from dust; then He said to him, 'Be,' and he was."

However, the difference between Adam and Jesus is clear.

Adam was created by the Word of God. Jesus is the Word of God.

Adam had the spirit breathed into him. Jesus is the Spirit from God.

Do Muslims really accept that Jesus is the Word and Spirit from God? Are not the Word and the Spirit part of the Creator, not part of the creation? How can God be separate from His Word and His Spirit? Was any other man born this way? Was any other prophet born this way? To believe what the Qur'an says about Jesus, is to believe that Jesus is unique among the prophets and preeminent in His conception and birth, in His nature and being.

Jesus is the Messiah

The Qur'an repeatedly claims that Jesus is the Messiah. However, the title "Messiah" is not explained in the Qur'an. The Arabic word, *"Al-Masih"*, similar to the Hebrew word, means "anointed one." Only Jesus is given this title.

Surah Ali 'Imran 3:45,

"[And mention] when the angels said, "O Mary, indeed Allah gives you good tidings of the word from Him, whose name will be the Messiah, Jesus, the son of Mary - distinguished in this world and the Hereafter and among those brought near [to Allah]."

Surah An-Nisa 4:157,

Refers to him as "the Messiah, Jesus, the son of Mary, the messenger of Allah."

Surah An-Nisa 4:171,

"The Messiah, Jesus, the son of Mary, was but a messenger of Allah."

Surah Al-Ma'idah 5:17, 72, 75,

Mentions "The Messiah, Mary's son."

Surah At-Tawbah 9:31,

Explicitly uses the term . "the Messiah, son of Mary."

What does the Messiah mean for Muslims? For Jews and Christians, we know it means the Anointed One, the Christ. For Muslims it just means that Jesus is a special human prophet.

The Unique Message of Jesus

Jesus came to bring the Gospel

Muslims believe that Jesus was sent by God Himself. He came with the Gospel (*Injil*). His Gospel confirms that the Torah is true. God gave Jesus the Gospel, which was guidance and light and instruction, together with the Torah, for the righteous.

Surah Al Maidah 5:46,

"And We sent, following in their footsteps, Jesus, the son of Mary, confirming that which came before him in the Torah; and We gave him the Gospel, in which was guidance and light and confirming that which preceded it of the Torah as guidance and instruction for the righteous."

Surah Al Hadid 57:27,

"Then, We sent after them, Our Messengers, and We sent 'Isa (Jesus) - son of Maryam (Mary), and gave him the Injil (Gospel)."

Muslims will say that the Gospel, in Arabic, the *Injil*, was a special book revealed and given to Jesus. However, as has been said, there is no evidence whatsoever that Jesus ever wrote a book. The Gospel He came with is revealed in the New Testament, especially in the four gospels of Matthew, Mark, Luke and John.

Followers of Jesus, Christians, in the Qur'an are called, "The People of the Book." What was that Book? The Book was a book that they held "between their hands" *(bayna yadihi)* in the days of Muhammad. The only "Book" that the Christians held between their hands in the seventh century was the Bible, that is, the Old and New Testaments, the Law and the Gospels, in Arabic, the *Torah* and the *Injil.* The Gospel is affirmed as "the Book" *(al-kitab)* that the Qur'an says was given by God Himself, that confirms the Torah, that is a light and guidance and instruction for the righteous.

Surah Ali Imran 3:187,

"And remember Allah took a Covenant from the People of the Book, to make it known and clear to mankind, and not to hide it."

Interesting! In this verse the People of the Book (*ahl kitab*) are the Jews and the Christians. This verse says that God has made a covenant with us to make the Book known, to make it clear to mankind and not to hide it. What a challenge!

Jesus indeed gave us a commission to preach the Gospel of the Kingdom to the ends of the earth. This is part of the New Covenant. We dare not throw it away behind our backs and purchase with it some miserable gain! We need to be obedient to the Lord Jesus Christ and make the Book known! Tell the story of Jesus! Preach the Gospel to the ends of the earth! Declare the word of the Lord in our homes, in our streets, in our towns, in our cities!

Jesus was taught directly by God Himself

While Muhammad received all his revelations from an angel called Gabriel, not from God Himself directly, the Qur'an says that Jesus was taught by God. In the Qur'an, God Himself says that He is the one who taught Jesus - the Book, the Wisdom, the Law and the Gospel.

Surah Ali Imran 3:48,

"And He will teach him the Book, Wisdom, the Law and the Gospel."

Jesus had a direct relationship with God. He was taught by God Himself. God spoke to Jesus In the Qur'an God directly addresses Jesus.

Surah Al-Maidah 5.110,

"Behold! I taught thee the Book and Wisdom, the Law and the Gospel."

Surah Ali Imran 3:55.

God tells Jesus, "O Jesus, I will take you and raise you to Myself...."

Surah Al-Ma'idah 5:116-117,

"O Jesus, Son of Mary, did you say to the people, 'Take me and my mother as deities besides Allah?'"

Of course, Jesus never said that He and His mother were deities. This is totally contrary to the teaching of the Bible. No Christians say that. This is a complete twisting of who Mary is and of who Jesus is.

Jesus came with clear signs and wisdom

Az-Zukhruf 43:63,

"When Jesus came with Clear Signs, he said: "Now have I come to you with Wisdom, and in order to make clear to you some of the (points) on which ye dispute: therefore fear Allah and obey me."

Jesus came with the wisdom of God. The Gospel is the power of God unto Salvation! Why not believe what God said? Why not believe the Gospel of Jesus Christ?

The Unique Righteousness and Holiness of Jesus

While all prophets are considered righteous, the Qur'an highlights Jesus righteousness and sinlessness above all others.

Surah Ali Imran 3:46,

"And he is among the righteous."

Surah Al-Baqarah 2:87,

"We gave Jesus the son of Mary Clear (Signs) and strengthened him with the holy spirit."

As we have discussed, the Hadith declare that Jesus is the only man untouched by Satan at birth.

(Ali Imran 3:36) and (Hadith, Sahih Bukhari, Volume 4, Book 60, Number 3431).

Abu Huraira said,

"I heard Allah's Apostle saying, 'There is none born amongst the offspring of Adam, but Satan touches it. A child therefore cries loudly at the time of birth because of the touch of Satan, except Mary and her child.'" Then Abu Huraira recited: "And I seek refuge with You for her and for her offspring from the outcast Satan."

The Dilemma: Jesus is the only perfect human being. All mankind, including all the other prophets, sinned. Only Jesus is sinless. Only Jesus, could not be touched by Satan. Why is this so? Is He not unique? Is He not different to all other men? Yes He is! He is God come in the flesh. He is Immanuel – ***Matthew 1:23.***

The Unique Greatness of Jesus

According to the Qur'an, Jesus was just a slave of Allah, not a son. Muhammad also was only described as a slave of Allah. He never knew God as Father. Muhammad, the Qur'an and the religion of Islam portray Jesus as just another human prophet. Yet, in their portrayal is hidden the description of the Son of God.

Nevertheless, the Qur'an reveals that Jesus is both unique and greater than all the other prophets. Several individuals and groups are distinguished as having been brought near to God. They were especially close to God. The most prominent among them is Jesus, son of Mary. He is explicitly described as "distinguished in this world and the Hereafter, and among those brought near [to Allah]."

Surah Ali Imran 3:45

"And mention when the angels said, "O Mary, indeed Allah gives you good tidings of the word from Him, whose name will be the Messiah, Jesus, the son of Mary - distinguished in this world and the Hereafter and among those brought near (to Allah)."

The Qur'an describes the unique greatness and power of Jesus … and then defies it.

Surah Al-Maidah 5:19,

"Say "Who then hath the least power against Allah, if His Will were to destroy Christ the son of Mary, his mother, and all--every one that is on the earth?"

Why would God tell Muhammad to say, that if God willed, He could destroy Jesus and Mary and everyone on earth?

Is Muhammad the greatest prophet or is it Jesus?

Recently it has been brought to light through historical and archaeological evidence that it was common for Christians in the 6th to 8th centuries, to use the term "Muhammad" (the praised one) as a messianic title for Jesus. It was so used before the arrival of the religion of Islam. Researchers have also shown that the term "Muhammad" (*the praised one*) used in the Qur'an was originally used as a descriptive title for Jesus, as the Messiah. This was based on the work of scholars like Oleg Grabar who suggested that in the 7th century, *"mmed"* and *"mhmd"* was originally a title referring to Jesus. This title was found on coins togethernwith crosses and on early Islamic inscriptions pointing to Jesus. It seems incongruous that Islamic coins would have a cross inscribed upon them. Islam acknowledges Jesus as the distinguished one. The word Muhammad means "the praised one." Could the name "Muhammad" which is used only four times in the Qur'an, have been given as a title to Jesus, instead of the prophet who founded Islam? This will be investigated further later in this book.

The Challenge: Is Jesus more than a prophet?

We are left with the challenge. Was Jesus just another prophet, was he the greatest among all the prophets, or was he more than a prophet? In the Gospels, Jesus' disciples faced the same challenge, the same dilemma. Who were they following? Jesus confronted his disciples with this question, "Who do men say, that I, the Son of man am?

Matthew 16:13-17,

"When Jesus came into the coasts of Caesarea Philippi, he asked his disciples, saying, Whom do men say that I, the Son of man, am? And they said, Some say that thou art John the Baptist: some, Elias; and others, Jeremias, or one of the prophets. He said unto them, But whom say ye that I am? And Simon Peter answered and said, You are the Christ, the Son of the living God. And Jesus answered and said unto him, Blessed art thou, Simon Barjona: for flesh and blood hath not revealed it unto thee, but my Father which is in heaven."

Peter received a revelation of who Jesus was. Not everyone did. In fact, many of the most religious Jews believed that Jesus was not a prophet. Some believed he was of the Devil. Many believed he was just a man. Peter had a revelation that he was the Christ, the Son of the living God.

Muslims face the same challenge. They follow the prophet Muhammad. A dilemma arises when they compare Jesus and Muhammad. All Muslims must believe in Jesus. But who is Jesus? Do they believe in the Jesus who is revealed in the Qur'an? Do they believe in the Jesus who is revealed in the Gospel? Can they answer the question, "Who is Jesus?" They face a great dilemma in understanding Jesus.

As ***Samuel Zwemer***, a missionary to the Muslims, said, "Islam is the only one of the great non-Christian religions which gives a place to Christ in its book and yet it is also the only one of the non-Christian religions which denies His deity, His atonement and His supreme place as Lord of all in its sacred literature."

Although intellectual answers may not convince Muslims, we can plant a seed in their hearts and minds by praying for them to receive a revelation, showing them verses from their Qur'an about Jesus and sharing the message of the Gospel from the Bible with them. They need to receive a revelation of the Son of God from the Father, who is in heaven. Let us pray and work to that end!

A List of Qur'an Verses mentioning Jesus:

Al Baqarah 2:87; 2:136; 2:253
An Nisa 4:156-175
Al Maedah 5:46-47; 5:110-120
Al Anam 6:85
Maryam 19:16-40
An Nabiya 21:91
Al Muminuun 23:50
Ash Shura 42:13
Az Zukhruf 43:57-64
Al Hadid 57:27
As Saff 61:6,14.

Important questions we can ask and discuss with our Muslim friends:

1. Why can't Allah have a son without a wife but Mary could have a son without a husband? Is anything impossible for God?
2. Why is Mary, Jesus mother, highlighted in the Qur'an while Muhammad's mother is never named?
3. Why are Moses, Abraham and Jesus mentioned by name far more than Muhammad?

4. What did Jesus do, that no other prophets could do?
5. Why not read the Gospels for yourself and discover who Jesus really is?

DILEMMA 6

....

THE CRUCIFIXION DILEMMA

The Crucifixion is a major dilemma for Muslims. The crucifixion of Jesus and His death, burial and resurrection is central to the Christian faith. This becomes **a major dilemma for Muslims** since they deny that Jesus died, was buried and raised from the dead. If He actually was crucified, was buried and rose from the dead, then this destroys Islamic beliefs. However, if He escaped being crucified but was taken alive to heaven then there is also no resurrection. **This creates a huge dilemma for Christians.**

The apostle Paul declared:

1Corinthians 15:3-4,

"I delivered to you first of all that which I also received: that Christ died for our sins according to the Scriptures, and that He was buried, and that He rose again the third day.

1Corinthians 15:14-17,

"If Christ is not risen, then our preaching is in vain and your faith is also in vain. Yes, and we are found false witnesses of God, because we have testified of God that He raised up Christ, whom He did not raise up—if in fact the dead do not rise. For if the dead do not rise, then Christ is not risen. And if Christ is not risen, your faith is futile; you are still in your sins!"

This issue is so important that the truth of the Bible stands or falls on the whether Jesus was really crucified, died, buried and raised from the dead.

Islamic theology states that Jesus did not die on the cross, but someone else died in His place and was made to look like Jesus so that it appeared to the onlookers that Jesus was actually crucified. Some Islamic scholars suggest that God (Allah) made Judas look like Jesus to punish him for his betrayal, and that it was he who died on the cross. Other Islamic scholars have suggested that another, unnamed disciple, offered himself to die instead of Jesus with the promised reward of guaranteed eternal life in the Islamic heaven.

It is very important that we understand the importance of this dilemma and how it affects the certainty of our salvation as well as the opportunity to share the Gospel of Jesus with our Muslim friends.

If Allah made someone else to look like Jesus and that one died on the Cross, does that make Allah a deceiver trying to make us think that Jesus died when in fact He didn't die?

Does it also make Jesus a deceiver if He was part of Allah's conspiracy as when He appeared to the disciples, including Thomas, and showed them the wounds from the Cross, when in fact it was all a lying conspiracy because He wasn't really crucified at all.

It would seem that the angels at the tomb also conspired in this conspiracy telling the Marys that Jesus was risen from the dead when in fact He hadn't even died!

What sort of God would create such a lying conspiracy to deceive the Jews and the Christians that Jesus was killed by crucifixion when, according to the Qur'an, He was not?

Islam rejects the crucifixion of Jesus or that He died

In the **Qur'an p.914,** published by the *King Fahd Glorious Qur'an Complex, Madinah, Kingdom of Saudi Arabia,* it gives a very important declaration:

"Muslims believe that Jesus was not crucified by the Jews as revealed in the Holy Qur'an by Allah in a crystal clear manner (Q.4:157,158). If the story of the Cross is disproved then the very foundation on which Christianity is based will be demolished."

The dilemma for Christians is that if this Allah creates such a lying conspiracy to deceive Jews and Christians how could anyone put their trust in such a God?

The basis of Islam's rejection of the Biblical account of the Cross needs to be thoroughly examined and understood. We must look at the evidence that is presented, evaluate it and come to a conclusion as to what the Qur'an is actually telling us. They declare that it has being revealed "in a crystal clear manner (Q.4:157,158)". Is that true? The whole message of the Bible and the Qur'an depends on this message. The truth of Islam and Christianity hangs on the message of the Cross with the death and resurrection of Jesus. Note one translation that makes this declaration very clear.

***Surah An-Nisa 4:157* Translated by Hilali and Khan (Official Saudi Arabian Qur'an),**

"And because of their saying (in boast), "We killed Messiah Iesa (Jesus), son of Maryam (Mary), the Messenger of Allah," - but they killed him not, nor crucified him, **but the resemblance of Isa (Jesus) was put over another man (and they killed that man),** and those who differ therein are full of doubts."

Surah An-Nisa 4:157 (Yusuf Ali Translation),

"They (the Jews) said, "We killed Christ Jesus the son of Mary, the Messenger of Allah"; but they killed him not, nor crucified him, but **so it was made to appear to them**."

This verse in the Qur'an is used to justify the belief that Jesus was not crucified and that He did not die. This verse is also used to support the substitution theory that someone else was made to look like Jesus and that person died instead of Jesus. Is this what that verse actually says?

It is so important that we understand this verse and that we discuss it with our Muslim friends. It is vital for both their salvation as well as our own. Let's dig into this verse and examine what it clearly says.

The Jews claim that they Killed and Crucified Jesus

Surah An-Nisa 4:157 declares that the Jews claimed that they had killed and crucified Jesus. God's response was to reject that claim, saying, "they killed him not, nor crucified him, but so it was made to appear to them."

So, we have a contradiction here. The Jews saying they killed and crucified Jesus, and God saying, "No, you didn't." Who is right?

Read the verse again, carefully. Inspect what it is actually saying. Does it say Jesus was not crucified and that He did not die? No! It is just saying that it wasn't the Jews who killed Him.

The contention in this verse is that Allah rejects the Jewish claim that they killed Jesus. Allah says, "No, it wasn't you that killed Him, it only appeared to you as if you had killed him." This is extremely important.

Understand what it clearly says, and what it clearly does not say. The verse is emphatic in saying that the Jews claimed to have killed and crucified Jesus, but equally emphatic is Allah saying that the Jews did not kill or crucify Jesus. What we need to see in the clear statements in this verse is that it does not say that Jesus was not crucified nor that He did not die. It just states that it was not the Jews who killed and crucified Him.

However, another statement in this verse is also important and will be elaborated on further when we discuss the Muslims destroying the Meccans at the Battle of Badr. The important statement is "but so it was made to appear to them." This statement has multiple interpretations which we will also discuss. So, the question we need to ask is: If it wasn't the Jews who killed and crucified Jesus, then who did?

The Prophetic Witnesses from the Old Testament going back to 4000 BC

From the earliest chapters of the *Book of Genesis* we begin to read of God's amazing plan to redeem mankind from their sin. Let's look at a few of these prophetic witnesses.

(i) In the Garden of Eden, the First Prophecy

Despite mankind's disobedience and sinfulness, God still loved us and did not want us to be damned to an eternity in hell. Absolutely not! God wanted to save us.

2Peter 3:9,

"The Lord is not slack concerning His promise, as some count slackness, but is longsuffering toward us, not willing that any should perish but that all should come to repentance."

1Timothy 2:3-4,

"For this is good and acceptable in the sight of God our Savior, who desires all men to be saved and to come to the knowledge of the truth."

From the beginning, 4000 years before Christ, in the Garden of Eden, after the Fall and the disobedience of Adam and Eve, God revealed His intention to provide a Saviour. That Saviour would come as a human, "the seed of the woman", who would destroy the power of Satan.

Genesis 3:14-15,

"So the LORD God said to the serpent: "Because you have done this, You are cursed more than all cattle, and more than every beast of the field; On your belly you shall go, and you shall eat dust all the days of your life.

And I will put enmity between you and the woman, and between your seed and her Seed; He shall bruise your head, and you shall bruise His heel."

(ii) There had to be the Shedding of Blood for Redemption

The Book of Hebrews clearly describes the necessity for the shedding of blood to bring atonement for sin and salvation to those who believe in the necessity of the crucifixion of Jesus.

Hebrews 9:11-22,

"Christ came as High Priest of the good things to come, with the greater and more perfect tabernacle not made with hands, that is, not of this creation. Not with the blood of goats and calves, but with **His own blood** He entered the Most Holy Place once for all, having obtained eternal redemption. For if the blood of bulls and goats and the ashes of a heifer, sprinkling the unclean, sanctifies for the purifying of the flesh, **how much more shall the blood of Christ,** who through the eternal Spirit offered Himself without spot to God, cleanse your conscience from dead works to serve the living God? And for this reason **He is the Mediator of the new covenant, by means of death, for the redemption of the transgressions** under the first covenant, that those who are called may receive the promise of the eternal inheritance. For where there is a testament, there must also of necessity be the death of the testator. For a testament is in force after men are dead, since it has no power at all while the testator lives. Therefore not even the first covenant was dedicated without blood. For when Moses had spoken every precept to all the people according to the law, he took the blood of calves and goats, with water, scarlet wool, and hyssop, and sprinkled both the book itself and all the people, saying, **"THIS IS THE BLOOD OF THE COVENANT WHICH GOD HAS COMMANDED YOU."** Then likewise he sprinkled with blood both the tabernacle and all the vessels of the ministry. And according to the law almost all things are purified with blood, and **without shedding of blood there is no remission."**

The Law, which the Qur'an declares was given by God and its words cannot be changed, and must be believed and obeyed.

Surah Al-Baqarah 2:136,

"Say: We believe in Allah and (in) that which has been revealed to us, and (in) that which was revealed to Abraham, and Ishmael and Isaac and Jacob and the tribes, and (in) **that which was given to Moses** and Jesus, and (in) that which was given to the prophets from their Lord, we do not make any distinction between any of them and to Him do we submit."

Surah Al-Maida 5:44,

"It was We who revealed the law (to Moses): therein was guidance and light."

(iii) The Messiah would come and be the Redeeming Sacrifice

800 years before Jesus came the prophet Isaiah prophesied that Jesus would be our Saviour, the Messiah and that He would die and be raised from the dead to redeem us and bring salvation to mankind. Scholars have recorded some 351 prophecies in the Old Testament of the coming Messiah that were fulfilled in Jesus. Among them are the prophecies that were fulfilled in the death, crucifixion and resurrection of Jesus. The prophecy in Isaiah is remarkable in the detail that is provided.

Isaiah 53:4-11,

"Surely He has borne our griefs and carried our sorrows; Yet we esteemed Him stricken, **Smitten by God**, and afflicted. But He was wounded for our transgressions, He was bruised for our iniquities; The chastisement for our peace was upon Him, and by His stripes we are healed. All we like sheep have gone astray; We have turned, every one, to his own way; And **the LORD has laid on Him the iniquity of us all.** He was oppressed and He was afflicted, Yet He opened not His mouth; **He was led as a lamb to the slaughter,** And as a sheep before its shearers is silent, So He opened not

His mouth. He was taken from prison and from judgment, and who will declare His generation? For **He was cut off from the land of the living; For the transgressions of My people He was stricken.** (He was crucified for us) And they made His grave with the wicked (He was buried) —But with the rich at His death, Because He had done no violence, Nor was any deceit in His mouth. Yet it pleased the LORD to bruise Him; He has put Him to grief. When You make His soul an offering for sin, **He shall see His seed, He shall prolong His days** (He will be raised from the dead). And the pleasure of the LORD shall prosper in His hand. He shall see the labour of His soul, and be satisfied. By His knowledge My righteous Servant shall justify many, For **He shall bear their iniquities** (The Messiah would bear our sins)."

Compare the details in *Psalm 22* and the message is clear.

Even the prophet Yahya (John the Baptist) declared that the Messiah, this lamb referred to by Isaiah, would be God's sacrifice to take away the sin of the world.

John 1:29,

"The next day John (Yahya) saw Jesus coming toward him, and said, "Behold! The Lamb of God who takes away the sin of the world!"

How can 4000 years of prophetic history be disregarded and ignored when it declared that there had to be the shedding of blood of a sacrifice for the atonement, redemption and salvation of mankind. And the Qur'an declared that we had to believe this message.

Surah Al-Anaam 6:115,

"The word of thy Lord doth find its fulfilment in truth and in justice: **None can change His words:** for He is the one who heareth and knoweth all."

Surah Yunus 10:64,

"There is no changing the Words of Allah - that is the Supreme Triumph."

In *Surah Al-Baqarah 2:136,* quoted above, it declares that Allah sent His word to ALL the Bible prophets, therefore those words cannot be changed. This message was declared to be irrevocable and unchangeable, sent down by Allah, and the words cannot be changed. yet today Islamic interpreters would try to deny the necessity of this blood atonement for our sins. Is Allah so weak that He cannot preserve His own Word? This indeed is a huge dilemma facing our Muslim friends!

Is there evidence in the Qur'an that Jesus did actually die?

After reading the absolute rejection of the Cross in the Saudi Qur'an, it may surprise you that there are a number of witnesses in the Qur'an and in the Hadith, that make it very clear that Jesus did in fact die. He indeed was crucified and then three days later was raised from the dead. 40 days later, He ascended to heaven.

Firstly, we will examine key Islamic sources.

1. The Prophets or Messengers before Jesus and Muhammad all Died

Al Maeda 5:75,

"The Messiah, son of Mary, was only a messenger; messengers before him had indeed passed away."

Since Jesus was also declared by the Qur'an to be a prophet, and since all prophets before Him had died, and all the prophets before Muhammad had died, then that means that Jesus also died.

Surah Ali Imran 3:143,

"And Muhammad is only a messenger — messengers have already passed away before him."

This Surah uses the same words that are used to state that all prophets before Muhammad died. Since no prophet arose between Jesus and Muhammad, the second verse shows that Jesus also died. Also, the Qur'an says in other verses that no mortal or prophet from the times before Muhammad, escaped death.

Surah Maryam 21:34, "And We made no mortal before thee to live on forever."

Surah Maryam 21:8, "Nor did they (the prophets) live on forever."

2. Muhammad on his death bed confirmed that Jesus had died

- Before he died Muhammad said: "O people! I have heard that you fear the death of your Prophet. Did any prophet before me live on so that I should be expected to live on amongst you? Listen! I am about to meet my Lord, and so will you. ..." *(Al-anwar ul-Muhammadiyya min al-Muwahib al-Ladinya, Egypt, p. 317).*
- Aisha reported Muhammad had said that Jesus died:
  "Aisha (God be pleased with her) said that, in his illness in which he died, the Holy Prophet said: 'Every year Gabriel used to repeat the Holy Qur'an with me once, but this year he has done it twice. He has informed me that there is no prophet but he lives half as long as the one who preceded him. And he has told me that Jesus lived a hundred and twenty years, and I see that I am about to leave this world at sixty'." *(Hujjaj al-Kiramah, p.428; Kanz al-Ummal, vol.6, p.160, from Hazrat Fatima; and Mawahib al-Ladinya, vol.1, p.42)*
- "A Christian delegation asked Muhammad who Jesus' father was. He said: 'Do you not know that a son resembles his father?' They replied: 'Yes'. Muhammad said: "Do you not know that our Lord lives forever while Jesus perished." *(Asbab an-nuzul, by Imam*

Abu-l-Hasan Ali ibn Ahmad al-Wahidi of Neshapur, published in Egypt, p. 53).

This report shows that Muhammad told the Christian delegation that he believed that Jesus had died.

3. Jesus testified that it was God who put Him to death

The Qur'an states that Jesus, while still a baby in the cradle, told the visitors about His birth, death and resurrection. He said He would die! The same language is used a few verses earlier in describing the birth, death and resurrection of John the Baptist (the prophet Yahya) and we know he was born and died. The same phrase is used regarding Jesus.

Surah Maryam 19:33,

"Peace is on me the day I was born, the day that I die, and the day that I shall be raised up to life again!"

"Wa salam alaya yaum wulidtu, wa yaum amutu, wa yaum aba'thu haya."

Now see the same 3 things were said about John the Baptist in verse 15,

"And peace be upon him the day he was born and the day he dies and the day he is raised alive."

Surah Al-Maidah 5.117,

"And I (Jesus) was a witness of them (my disciples) so long as I was among them, but when Thou (God/Allah) didst cause me to die (*tawafaitani*), Thou wast the Watcher over them. And Thou art Witness of all things'."

4. Allah said that He would cause Jesus to die

The Quranic word "mutawaffika" of verse 3:55 (also see 5:116-117)

إِذْ قَالَ اللَّهُ يَاعِيسَى إِنِّي مُتَوَفِّيكَ وَرَافِعُكَ إِلَيَّ

Noble Qur'an explains itself

No any man-made sectarian mutually conflicting Tafsirs of old or new Mullahs or Mullahs-forged contexts or Persians' forged 2.3 millions so labelled hadiths that thy forged 250-400 years after the death of prophet & attached that lies with the name of our beloved Prophet; can explain BOOK of Allah except Allah himself. Allah has designed Quran in such a way that Quran is the best Tafsir for Quran. Yet we find explanation of word Wafat (natural death) used in verse 3:55; 5:116-117 for Eisa (Jesus) PBUH in Quran.

The Quranic word 'mutawaffika' in 3:55, 5:116-117 and its derivation are found in over 25 times in the Noble Quran (see 2:234,240; 3:55,193; 4:15,97; 5:117; 6:61; 8:50; 10;46,104; 12:101; 13:40; 16:28,32,70; 22:5; 40:67,77; 47:27). In all places they imply death.

When word WAFAT comes in other verses & 10:46, Criminal Jahil Fanatics translate it as Death but when the same word WAFAT appears in 3:55, 5:116-117, these Stubborn Mad Jahils translate it "To take up with human body" in order to validate fiction of ascension & return of Eisa (Jesus) PBUH. No doubt, Mirza Qadiani was an impostor but Majority of our evil-Mullahs & and their brainless Jahil perts are also disciples of Iblees (Satan). Be curse of Allah on these Twister of Noble Quran.

Surah Ali Imran 3:55,

"God said: O Jesus! Verily, I shall cause thee to die ***(mutawaffiika),*** and shall exalt thee ***(rafiuka)*** unto Me."

This verse will be discussed more fully in the next chapter due to the controversy of the translation of the word ***mutawaffiika.***

5. Muhammad verified Jesus' Testimony in Surah Al-Maida 5:117

Muhammad says the same things about himself using the words Jesus is said to have said: "I was a witness of them so long as I was among them, but when You caused me to die, You were the Watcher over them." ***(Sahih Bukhari 60:8).***

Islam today says that Jesus did not die but this is not in line with the clear statements of Muhammad, Jesus, the Hadith and the Qur'an!

Why is there such contradiction? Does modern Islam believe the same as Muhammad did in 632 AD? Is there a deception and if so, who is being deceived?

6. Bukhari, the most trusted Hadith writer confirms the Cross

Sahih al-Bukhari 6929,

"As if I am looking at the Prophet, while he was speaking about one of the prophets whose people have beaten and wounded him and he was wiping the blood off his face and saying, O Lord! Forgive my people as they do not know."

Compare Luke 23:34,

"Jesus said, Father, forgive them, for they do not know what they do."

This is exactly and exclusively what happened on the Cross. Even the most famous of the Hadith writers confirms the crucifixion of Jesus.

Standard Muslim Beliefs are based on Surah An-Nisa 4:157-159

- The Jews believe they killed Jesus.
- God reveals they definitely did not. Jesus was not killed or crucified by the Jews.
- There was someone else (unnamed) who was to look like Jesus who died in his place, maybe Judas.
- God instead took Jesus up to heaven without having died.

Why the Deception? Who was being deceived? Who was the deceiver?

Surah Ali Imran 3:54,

"And they deceived and Allah deceived and Allah is the best of deceivers."

"Wa makaruu wa makara allah wa allahu khair ulmakariin."

- The Jews were deceived by saying they crucified Jesus when it was someone else
- Allah deceived them, so that the Jews only *thought* that they killed Jesus
- Allah is the greatest of deceivers
- If Jesus was a true prophet, but did not die on the Cross and was substituted by someone else made to look like Him, how could He come to the disciples in the upper room and deceive them into thinking that He had truly died and truly risen from the dead? What sort of a prophet would do that?

Why the Deception? Because IF Jesus did not die on the cross:

- There is NO sacrifice for sin
- There is NO redemption
- There is NO salvation for mankind

It really tells us something about the source of that deception. It denies grace and demands that everyone must try to earn their own salvation!

Compare the Battle of Badr – 624 AD

A powerful testimony of Islamic conquest occurred at the Battle of Badr in 624AD. The idol-worshippers in Mecca hated Muhammad and his teachings on Islam. They wanted to kill him. For this reason Muhammad had fled Mecca and went to the city of Yathrib. This was a majority Jewish and Christian city and they gave protection to Muhammad. After Muhammad took over the city, the name Yathrib was changed to Medina. Many of Muhammad's disciples also fled but they went to Ethiopia pursued by the pagans of Mecca who also wanted to kill them. The Christian King of

Ethiopia, Najashi, gave them protection because they were monotheists and said they believed in Jesus.

The Meccans later pursued Muhammad to Yathrib/Medina and a battle between Muhammad's army of 318 and the Meccans with over 1000 was a defining battle in Islam's history. The Muslims crushed the Meccan army and the Muslims boasted on how they slaughtered the Meccans. However, Muhammad received a revelation that it was not the Muslims who killed the Meccans. It was God Himself. It only appeared to the Muslims that they had killed the Meccans.

Surah Anfal 8:17,

"And you did not kill them, but it was Allah who killed them. And you threw not, when you threw, but it was Allah who threw that He might test the believers with a good test. Indeed, Allah is Hearing and Knowing."

The account of the crucifixion has similarities to the Battle of Badr. The ones appearing to be the "killers" were not the real killers! 318 Muslims claimed to have defeated 1000 Meccans but it only appeared that way to them as the one who really killed them was Allah. Likewise the Jews thought they killed Jesus, but actually it was Allah who put Jesus to death.

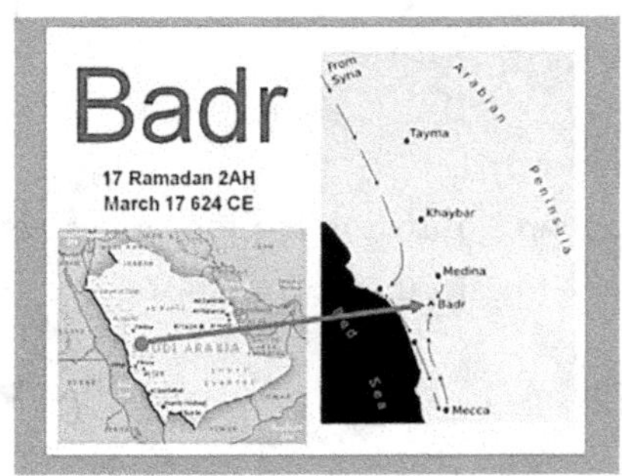

The Biblical evidence of the crucifixion of Jesus?

There is abundant evidence in the Bible for the crucifixion and resurrection of Jesus. There are many eye-witnesses who directly saw Jesus being crucified and/or saw Him after His resurrection from the dead three days later. Many Muslims will not accept these witnesses as they believe the story is fabricated and the Bible has been altered and corrupted to promote the teaching of the Cross and the Resurrection. Nevertheless, we give you a list of the Bible witnesses and the verses you can read to verify their testimonies.

1. Eye Witnesses

a. **Several women eye-witnesses**

i. Crucifixion: *John 19:25-27*
ii. Resurrection: *John 20:11-18*

Mark 16:9, The first witness of the resurrection was a woman.

b. Disciples of Jesus:

i. Crucifixion – *Acts 10:39*
ii. Resurrection - *John 20:19-20*

c. A large group of people

i. Crucifixion - *Luke 23:26-27*
ii. Resurrection – *1Corinthians 15:4-6*

d. Roman soldiers

i. Crucifixion – *Luke 23:36-37*
ii. Resurrection – *Matthew 27:51-54*

e. Jewish Leaders:

i. Crucifixion – *Matthew 27:41-43*
ii. Resurrection – *Matthew 27:65-66; Matthew 28:2-4, 11-15*

f. Paul met the Resurrected Jesus

i. Crucifixion – It seems that Paul did not witness the crucifixion.
ii. Resurrection – *Acts 9:1-6; 1Corinthians 15:8-22*

2. Jesus Prophesied His own Death and Resurrection

Matthew 17:22-23; Mark 9:31; Luke 9:22; John 12:32-33,

"And He began to teach them that the Son of Man must suffer many things, and be rejected by the elders and chief priests and scribes, and be killed, and after three days rise again."

Why did Jesus prophesy His own death and resurrection, if He wasn't going to die?

They were not wrong! The one who rose from the dead is the same person who was crucified! Only one who dies can rise from the dead – and that was not Judas!

There were many eye-witnesses to the Crucifixion and Resurrection of Jesus. They all knew that it was really Jesus on the cross that died and not someone else. The things that Jesus did on the cross proved that it was He Himself.

If, for example, it was Judas Iscariot, or some other disciple, suffering the excruciating agony of the whippings, the nailing of his hands and feet, he would have been shouting out, "I am not Jesus. I'm Judas. Get me down from here!" There's no way that someone could calmly accept such torture.

On the Cross there were amazing things that happened because the one being crucified was Jesus Himself. He was the Son of God. And He was the son of Mary. He nodded to John and then to His mother, Mary, and said to him, "Behold your mother!" Then he looked at Mary and nodded to John and said to her, "Behold your son." He was taking care of Mary's future. Only Jesus would have done this. A counterfeit being crucified instead of Jesus wouldn't be doing such a loving act as to care for Mary, His mother!

A counterfeit would not talk the way Jesus did on the Cross speaking to the thieves on the Cross and the one who believed in Him. Jesus said to him, "Today, you will be with Me in paradise." For three hours the sky darkened and Jesus cried out, "My God, My God, why have you forsaken Me?" Never before had Jesus been separated from the Father, but Jesus was now carrying the sin, sickness, rebellion and judgement of the whole world, the whole of humanity from the time of Adam until the time He returns again at His 2nd Coming.

No other could have borne all of this. Jesus cried out with a loud voice, "Father forgive them, they don't know what they are doing." No-one else could have done that, and then He cried out, "Father, into Your hands, I commit My spirit", and He died. This was an amazing death witnessed by His disciples, His family, the Jewish crowds, the Romaan soldiers and the Jewish priests who wanted Him dead.

The one who died was Jesus. No other. And the one who rose from the dead was certainly not Judas, or some other anonymous man. It was Jesus and no other!

3. Historical Evidence of Non-Christian witnesses from around the world

a. Amazing signs around the world at the time of the Crucifixion of Jesus

In every continent around the globe there were amazing accounts of people groups and countries that witnessed the signs of the event happening that day in Jerusalem. They witnessed the three hours of darkness and experienced the terror of that day. There are many accounts in their historical records of what happened. They were not Jews or Christians, but they were representatives of many races and languages like the Australian Aborigines, the Chinese, the American Indians, the Europeans and others.

Here are some Catholic sourced Youtube videos you can watch to learn about these accounts. All accounts must be evaluated in the light of Scripture and history.

Youtube videos documenting these accounts:

China - *www.youtube.com/watch?v=-p1MBhTwJ-o*

Australia - *www.youtube.com/watch?v=e1OVtAnPlZ0*

Egypt, Greece, Rome - *www.youtube.com/watch?v=RtIoUF6Y_MY&t=222s*

India - *www.youtube.com/watch?v=yyaoO-IwxZE*

America - *www.youtube.com/watch?v=z_4eITbRVZY&t=56s*

Russia - *www.youtube.com/watch?v=rE3PF1cFNcE*

b. Thallus – a Samaritan historian who wrote a 3 Volume history of the Mediterranean region around 52AD. He was the first secular writer to write about Jesus:

"At that time there was a fearful darkness that fell on the whole world; rocks were split by the great earthquake and many places in Judea and other districts too were destroyed."

c. **Publius Cornelius Tacitus – 56-120 AD. An Official Roman historian and politician, known for his critical and insightful writings on the Roman Empireduring the first century AD.**

"Nero accused … the hated citizens … who are called Christians by the people. That name came from the Christ who is their source, a person sentenced to death in the reign of Tiberius who was executed by… Pontius Pilate and for a short time the movement was stopped, but after a short time it became a great movement again not only in Judea, the place of the origins of this evil, but indeed it has also reached the city of Rome."

d. **Mara Bar-Serapion – 70AD, a Syrian philosopher known for his letter to his son, which contains one of the earliest non-Christian references to Jesus Christ.**

Bar-Serapion wrote to his son about the destruction of Jerusalem and about Jesus, the wise King. "… also about the Jews who killed their wise king … After they had killed him their kingdom was destroyed. Truly God has taken revenge for their actions. However, their king still lives through his teachings which they practice."

e. Talmud written by Jewish refugees in Babylon, 70-200M

These Jewish refugees hated the Christians and Jesus and gave him a name, "Yeshu" which was an acronym for "may his name be wiped from our memories forever." Nevertheless, even their testimony is evidence of the fact that Jesus was indeed crucified.

"At the beginning of Passover **Yeshu** was hung [on a cross]. For 40 days beforehand, the messengers cried out, "He will be stoned to death for sorcery and for seducing Israel into apostacy."

f. Josephus – 94AD, Jewish Roman historian

Contracted by the Roman Empire to write the history of the Jews and the Romans in Palestine. His book is called *Jewish Antiquities.*

In the section called Testimonium Flavianum, it is written: "In those days there was a man named Jesus, a wise man, if it is appropriate to call him a man. For he performed many miracles. … He was the Christ. When Pilate sentenced him to be crucified, those who had begun to love him, did not leave their love. On the third day he rose from the dead and was seen … alive again. … And those Christian groups persist among us even until today."

g. Pliny the Younger– 61-113AD – Governor in Bithynia, Asia Minor

Letters from Pliny the Younger written to Ceasar Trajan. In his letters he asked for advice on the best ways to handle the sect called Christians. He wrote that the Christians "usually gathered on certain days very early in the morning while it was still dark then they sang back and forth to Christ as if he was God, and they make commitments not to commit evil, to steal, to deceive, to commit adultery, to lie or to be traitors. They often gather to eat together – and they just eat common foods."

h. Suetonius (69-122AD) - A Roman historian who wrote *Lives of the Caesars* (AD120) mentioning "constant disturbances" among Roman Jews and Christians instigated by Chrestus (Christ).

Conclusion

1. ALL the prophetic witnesses from the Old Testament going back to 4000 BC revealed that the Messiah would come, be killed, rise from the dead, and be the Saviour of humanity.
2. ALL eye-witnesses say it was Jesus who was crucified.
3. ALL historians conclude that it was Jesus who was crucified.
4. ALL the enemies of Jesus say it was Jesus who was crucified.

So, what does the Qur'an and the Hadith say? Did Jesus really die? Is there any historical justification to deny the crucifixion of Jesus? None whatsoever. It is a verified, historical event.

The Apostle Paul declared the crucifixion and resurrection of Christ as the central belief and essential essence of the Christian faith. If Jesus was not crucified, buried and raised from the dead, then indeed the Christian faith is useless and futile. However, if Jesus was really crucified, buried and raised from the dead then this message is the most powerful and important message for all of humanity.

1Corinthians 15:3-26,

"I delivered to you first of all that which I also received: that **Christ died for our sins** according to the Scriptures, and that **He was buried,** and that **He rose again** the third day according to the Scriptures, and that He was seen by Cephas, then by the twelve. After that He was seen by over five hundred brethren at once, of whom the greater part remain to the present, but some have fallen asleep. After that He was seen by James, then by all the apostles. Then last of all He was seen by me also, as by one born out of due time. For I am the least of the apostles, who am not worthy to be called an apostle, because I persecuted the church of God. But by the grace of God I am what I am, and His grace toward me was not in vain; but I laboured more abundantly than they all, yet not I, but the grace of God which was with me. Therefore, whether it was I or they, so we preach and so you believed. Now **if Christ is preached that He has been raised from the dead, how do some among you say that there is no resurrection of the dead? But if there is no resurrection of the dead, then Christ is not risen. And if Christ is not risen, then our preaching is empty and your faith is also empty.** Yes, and we are found false witnesses of God, because we have testified of God that He raised up Christ, whom He did not raise up—if in fact the dead do not rise. For **if the dead do not rise, then Christ is not risen. And if Christ is not risen, your faith is futile; you are still in your sins!** Then also those who have fallen asleep in Christ have perished. If in this life only we have hope in Christ, we are of all men the most pitiable. **But now Christ is risen from the dead,** and has become the firstfruits of those who have fallen asleep. For since by man came death, by Man also came the resurrection of the dead. For as in Adam all die, even so **in Christ all shall be made alive.** But each one in his own order: Christ the firstfruits, afterward those who are Christ's at His coming. Then comes the end, when He delivers the kingdom to God the Father, when He puts an end to all rule and all authority and power. For He must reign till He has put all enemies under His feet. The last enemy that will be destroyed is death."

Discussion Questions:

1. How strong do you believe is the evidence for the death of Christ?
2. Who do you think had Jesus executed and why?
3. What do you think are the implications of the substitute theory that someone else died in the place of Jesus?

DILEMMA 7

WHO KILLED JESUS DILEMMA

Previously we saw that most Muslims believe that Jesus was not crucified or was killed by the Jews. Many also believe that Jesus was replaced by someone else, Judas Iscariot. Others think it was an unidentified disciple who was crucified in His place in turn to receive the guaranteed salvation in the Islamic heaven.

It is also said that Jesus fled the scene and hid and then some 30 days later Allah took him up to heaven, alive where He now lives waiting the time for His return when Jesus will then kill all the pigs and the Christians who have not accepted Muhammad as the final prophet.

They base their belief on two main things:

1. The Gospel of Barnabas, which was written by an Italian Catholic who converted to Islam in the 11th Century and wrote a book to promote the cause of Islam. The book has so many errors that contradict both the Qur'an and the Bible, as well as displaying a total lack of knowledge of the geography of Israel that it is a totally discredited and false document.
2. The second method to support this doctrine is to bring an interpretation to a verse that denies that the Jews killed or crucified

> Christ, and to say it means Jesus wasn't crucified at all and that someone else was substituted in his place. This is based on ***Surah An-Nisa 4:157,*** which we also discussed in the previous chapter, which denies the Jews claim that they killed and crucified Jesus.

We were able to establish that the evidence recorded in the Qur'an, in the Bible and in history proved conclusively that it was Jesus who was crucified, was buried and He did rise from the dead after three days.

After solving that dilemma, there is new dilemma facing both Christians and Muslims relating to who was responsible for the crucifixion of Jesus. If it was not the Jews, was it the Romans? We know that Pontius Pilate reluctantly gave the order for Jesus to be crucified. So was it Pilate that crucified Jesus? Jesus was handed over to the Roman soldiers to carry out the order, so it could be said that they were the executioners. It could also be claimed that it was humanity who killed Jesus because He died to pay the penalty for our sins.

Is there clear evidence that conclusively proves who was ultimately responsible for killing Jesus? There is an answer where both the Bible and the Qur'an seem to conclusively agree on this issue.

Who killed Jesus and why?

There are two matters here and we need to examine them separately. Firstly, we will look at who killed Jesus because here we will see that the case can be made both from the Bible and the Qur'an that it was God Himself who put Jesus to death. There are clear statements on this issue.

Look at the following statements in the Qur'an where God clearly states that He put Jesus to death, and this is also confirmed by the Islamic Jesus in the Qur'an.

We know that Muslim preachers world-wide proclaim that Jesus did not die nor was crucified, but they are mis-interpreting ***Surah An-Nisa 4:157-158.*** This is strange because the Qur'an does not say that Jesus was not crucified. It does say that Jesus was not crucified by the Jews. We can agree with that because those verses do not say that Jesus did not die nor was He crucified. It only says that it was not the Jews who killed and crucified Him. This is important as if Jesus was not crucified at all or was not killed at all, then it creates a massive contradiction with other statements in the Qur'an which show that Jesus did die. If Jesus indeed did die then who is responsible for His death? The answer may surprise you but the answer can be demonstrated in both the Bible and in the Qur'an.

The Qur'an reveals that it was God who put Jesus to death

Is that true? Does the Qur'an clearly state that Jesus did die and that He was put to death by God! Many Muslims are confused by this. Ahmadiyya Muslims, a minor sect within Islam, says that Jesus did die. Sunni and Shi'a Muslims say Jesus didn't die but was taken alive to heaven. But what does the Qur'an itself say? What does Allah say? And what does Muhammad say? Let's look at the confession of the one claiming to have put Jesus to death.

Surah Ali-Imran 3:55,

"O Jesus, truly **it was I (God) who put you to death** and raised you up to Myself."

Arabic: "ith qaala Allah, ya Isa, inni ***mutawaffika*** wa rafiuka ilayya."

The Arabic word used in the Qur'an is "***mutawaffika***". This word comes from the word **"wafat"** which means **"dead."** The same word is used in the Malay and Indonesian languages and is commonly used in Death Notices in the local newspapers. This verse in the Qur'an is so important because God is directly saying that He put Jesus to death. This contradicts what most Muslims preach and believe. This verse becomes embarrassing to them so that they try to hide the true meaning of the Arabic original texts in the various translations, whether into English, Malay, Indonesian and other languages. Let's look at some of these variant translations.

Different translations of *Surah Ali-Imran 3:55* to hide that it says that Allah put Jesus to death:

All of these following quotes are translations of exactly the same Arabic words in the Qur'an but are translated very differently to try and hide what the verse is actually saying in its original language:

(1) *Khan Translation:* "Allah said, "O Jesus, indeed ***I will take you*** and raise you to Myself."
(2) *Sarwar Translation:* "He told Jesus, "***I will save you from your enemies***, raise you to Myself."
(3) *Sherali Translation:* "ALLAH said, "O Jesus, ***I will cause thee to die a natural death*** and will raise thee to Myself."
(4) *Maulana Translation:* "Allah said: O Jesus, ***I will cause thee to die*** and exalt thee in My presence."
(5) *Rashad Translation:* "GOD said, "O Jesus, ***I am terminating your life***, raising you to Me."
(6) *Shakir Translation:* "Allah said: O Isa, ***I am going to terminate the period of your stay (on earth)*** and cause you to ascend unto Me."
(7) *Yusuf Ali Translation:* "Allah said: "O Jesus! ***I will take thee*** and raise thee to Myself."

Only some translations accurately translate the Arabic, most change it. They do not want English readers to know what the Arabic language actually says. The Indonesian Qur'an published in 1978 gives an accurate translation faithful to the original Arabic. It was translated by a prestigious group of Islamic leaders, in accordance with the original Arabic, i.e.

- MUI (Council of Islamic Clergy),
- Minister of Religious Affairs,

- Minister of Internal Affairs
- Chairman of the Council of National Religious Literature

Surah Ali Imran 3:55,

"Allah said, "Truly it was I who put you to death and raised you to Myself."

The Islamic Jesus declares that it was God who put Him to death

We see the same issue surfacing in another very important verse where Islamists who do not want us to know what the Qur'an says in the original Arabic, attempt to cover up what is clearly stated, that is that it was God who put Jesus to death.

In this following verse, it is Jesus talking with God and testifying that while He was alive, He looked after His disciples but after God put Him to death, then God looked after the disciples.

Surah Al-Maeda 5:117,

"I (Jesus) was a witness over them as long as I remained among them, but since ***Thou (God) didst cause me to die,*** Thou, hast been the Watcher over them, and Thou art Witness over all things."

The Arabic word used in this verse is *"tawaffaytani"* and also comes from the word "wafat" which means dead just like *"mutawaffika"* above.

Observe the different translations of *Surah Al-Maeda 5:117.* Some try to hide that it says that God put Jesus to death:

As we have seen in ***Surah Al-Imran 3:55,*** there is a concerted effort by some translators to mislead us into not knowing that these verses tell us of the fact that it was God who killed Jesus.

(1) *Khan Translation:* "I (Jesus) was a witness over them (the disciples) while I dwelt amongst them, ***but when You took me up,*** You were the Watcher over them."

(2) *Maulana Translation:* "I (Jesus) was a witness of them (the disciples) so long as I was among them, but ***when Thou didst cause me to die*** Thou wast the Watcher over them."

(3) *Rashad Translation:* "I (Jesus) was a witness among them (the disciples) for as long as I lived with them. ***When You terminated my life on earth,*** You became the Watcher over them."

(4) *Sarwar Translation:* "I (Jesus) watched them as long as I was among them (the disciples) until ***You raised me to Yourself and You Yourself*** had also watched over them."

(5) *Shakir Translation:* "I (Jesus) was a witness over them (the disciples) as long as I remained among them, but since ***You did cause me to die,*** You, have been the Watcher over them."

(6) *Sherali Translation:* "I (Jesus) was a witness over them (the disciples) as long as I remained among them, but since ***Thou didst cause me to die,*** Thou, hast been the Watcher over them."

(7) *Yusuf Ali Translation:* "I (Jesus) was a witness over them (the disciples) whilst I dwelt amongst them; ***when Thou didst take me up*** Thou wast the Watcher over them."

This Key Qur'anic Verse was quoted by Muhammad and recorded by Bukhari the most authoritative writer of the Hadith

Muhammad stated that just as Jesus watched over his disciples before he was killed and then God looked after his disciples, likewise Muhammad would look after his disciples until his death and then God would look after them. Based on his own testimony, Mohammad believed that Jesus really did die!

Here is the Hadith about the day of judgment, collected by Al-Bukhari as proof that Jesus died. It should be noted that in Islam the collection of Hadiths, the recorded statements and actions of Muhammad are considered of the highest authority in Islam and regarded as the most authentic sayings for accurate interpretation of the Qur'an.

Sahih Bukhari - Kitab Bhavan, 1984, vol. 3, no. 3263. See also vol. 4, no. 4349, 4463.)

"On the authority of Ibn Abbas: The Prophet of Allah said, '...Then I will say as the pious slave Jesus, son of Mary, said: 'And I was a witness over them while I dwelt amongst them. When you caused me to die *('tawaffay-tani')* you were the watcher over them, and you are a witness to all things."

(See, Bukhari, Muhammad Ibn Ismail. Sahih al-Buhari, trans. Muhammad Muhsin Khan, New Delhi.)

Since Muhammad referred to himself with the same phrase *('tawaffay-tani')* that Jesus used in ***Surah Al Ma'idah, 5:117*** it becomes clear that the prophet of Islam, who died, confirms that Jesus also died! A further confirmation is found in ***Surah Yunus 10:46, Surah Al Ra'd 13: 40,*** and ***Surah Ghafir 40:77,*** where basically the same term that is used for Jesus' last moments, '*natawaffayannaka*' meaning, "we indeed cause you to die" is applied also to Muhammad.

The Qur'an therefore confirms that Jesus did die just as Muhammad also died. This solves one dilemma that has faced Christians who have heard their Muslim friends say that they don't believe Jesus died. This then becomes a huge dilemma for them as the Qur'an and the Hadith strongly declare that Jesus did die, and it was on the Cross in Jerusalem.

Some Muslims have come to agree that Jesus was truly crucified and died on the Cross

The famous C9th Islamic scholar, **Abu Ja'far Muhammad b. Jarir al-Tabari (839-923),** held the position that Jesus was crucified and raised into heaven.

C20th Muslim Scholar, **Yusuf Ali,** wrote in the footnote number 2485 of his translation of the Holy Qur'an (1975): "those who believe that he (Jesus) never died should ponder over this verse." These remarks made by this highly respected Muslim scholar were quickly expunged and replaced with the explanatory words "Jesus was not crucified *(Surah 4:157)*" by the editorial board of the new edition of "The Meaning of the Holy Qur'an!" (Amana Publications, Beltsville, U.S.A., 1989). This is the dilemma that many of our Muslim friends now face.

In the Bible, it was God who put Jesus to death. Jesus was the one eternal sacrifice for sin and it involved the whole Triune Godhead

This is the story of amazing grace. The Jews and the Romans couldn't kill Jesus. They couldn't even catch Him until the time came when He offered Himself to be the sacrificial lamb at that Passover nearly 2000 years ago. Jesus had been chosen to be the sacrificial lamb from before the foundation of the world.

1Peter 1:18-20,

We were redeemed "with the precious blood of Christ, as of a lamb without blemish and without spot. He indeed was foreordained before the foundation of the world".

No-one could kill Jesus, He laid down His own life, and He was given as the perfect sacrifice by God the Father.

John 10:15-18,

"I lay down My life for the sheep. And other sheep I have which are not of this fold; them also I must bring, and they will hear My voice; and there will be one flock and one shepherd. "Therefore My Father loves Me, because I lay down My life that I may take it again. **No one takes it from Me, but I lay it down of Myself. I have power to lay it down, and I have power to take it again.** This command I have received from My Father."

It was only when His time had come that He allowed them to arrest Him and take Him to be tried and crucified. It was not the nails that held Him to the Cross, it was His love for us that held Him to that Cross.

GOD THE FATHER offered Jesus as a perfect sacrifice

This was prophesied in the offering of Abraham's "only begotten son". There were only two "only-begotten" sons in the Bible, Isaac and Jesus – *Genesis 22:2; John 3:16, Hebrews 11:17.*

Isaiah 53 is an amazing prophecy of the coming Messiah and how He shall become the sacrificial lamb bearing the sins, diseases and rebellions of the whole world. It is the Father, like Abraham, who puts His Son on the altar to be sacrificed. We see His anguish and love as He bears the greatest suffering in the whole of eternity, and He cries out in the deepest agony:

Mark 15:34,

"Jesus cried out with a loud voice, saying, "Eloi, Eloi, lama sabachthani?" which is translated, "My God, My God, why have you forsaken me?"

He was bearing the sin, suffering, shame, rejection, humiliation, diseases for the whole of humanity. It was an eternal anguish and because of His great love for us, He endured it. Likewise the love of God the Father knew there was only one way to save mankind. There had to be a perfect sinless sacrifice, so God the Father, gave His Son to bear the agony of the Cross.

John 3:16,

"For **God so loved the world** that He gave (sacrificed) His only begotten Son, that whoever believes in Him should not perish but have everlasting life."

A glorious Divine Exchange occurred as Jesus took our death and exchanged it for His life. He took our curse so that we might have His blessing. He took our hell to give us His heaven. He took our diseases that we might gain His eternal health. He took our defeats to give us His victories. He took our humiliation so that we might experience His glory. He took our sorrows that we might have His joy. He took our hatred that we might have His love. What a fantastic bargain! That's a Divine Exchange worth talking about!

2Corinthians 5:21,

"For He made Him who knew no sin to be sin for us, that we might become the righteousness of God in Him."

GOD THE SON gave Himself as a sacrifice to be our Saviour

Not only did the Father give Jesus to be sacrificed, Jesus Himself gave His own life and was willing to face the horror of the Cross as He knew that there was no other way by which humanity could find salvation. Hallelujah! What a Saviour!

This was God, the Creator of Heaven and Earth, who, because of His love for us, was willing to suffer the humiliation of leaving Heaven, leaving His Divine rights, and becoming a mortal human being willing to suffer the most excruciating pain and rejection so that you and I could be saved. This is how great His love is for you and I.

Philippians 2:5-11,

"Let this mind be in you which was also in Christ Jesus, who, being in the form of God, did not consider it robbery to be equal with God, but made Himself of no reputation, taking the form of a bondservant, and coming in the likeness of men. And being found in appearance as a man, **He humbled Himself and became obedient to the point of death, even the death of the cross.** Therefore God also has highly exalted Him and given Him the name which is above every name, that at the name of Jesus every knee should bow, of those in heaven, and of those on earth, and of those under the earth, and that every tongue should confess that Jesus Christ is Lord, to the glory of God the Father."

John 10:10-11,

"The thief does not come except to steal, and to kill, and to destroy. I have come that they may have life, and that they may have it more abundantly. I am the good shepherd. The good shepherd gives His life for the sheep."

Jesus gave His own life, they did not take it from Him.

1John 3:16,

"By this we know love, because He laid down His life for us."

GOD THE HOLY SPIRIT enabled Jesus to offer Himself as the sacrifice

The Holy Spirit is the spiritual engine room of dynamic power that enabled the Father and the Son to act. Without the Holy Spirit's active participation, Jesus could not have been crucified, and He could not have been raised from the dead.

Hebrews 9:14,

"How much more, then, will the blood of Christ, who **through the eternal Spirit** offered himself unblemished to God, cleanse our consciences from acts that lead to death, so that we may serve the living God!"

Romans 8:11,

"But if the Spirit of Him who raised Jesus from the dead dwells in you, He who raised Christ from the dead will also give life to your mortal bodies through His Spirit who dwells in you."

This action by the Holy Spirit opened a new and living way into fellowship with God and into the fellowship of the Body of Christ where the fulfillment of the eternal plan of God is being processed, and transforming us into the image of Christ. That's why we have been born of the Holy Spirit *(John 3:1-8),* filled with the Holy Spirit *(Acts 2:4),* pray in the Holy

Spirit *(Romans 8:26; 1Corinthians 14:15),* and walk in the Holy Spirit *(Galatians 5:16).*

2Corinthians 3:18,

"But we all, with unveiled face, beholding as in a mirror the glory of the Lord, are being transformed into the same image from glory to glory, just as by the Spirit of the Lord."

Without the Cross and without the power of the Holy Spirit, this would have been impossible.

Both the Bible and the Qur'an concur that the death of Jesus cannot be fully attributed to the Jews or to the Romans, nor to sinful humanity. It was an act of amazing grace and abounding love from God that leaves us in awe and showing us the reason why God had to put Jesus to death.

Why did God have to kill Jesus? Couldn't we save ourselves?

From the time of Adam and Eve *(Genesis 3)* and then Cain and Abel *(Genesis 4),* God revealed that man could not save themselves. Sin demands death, a principle seen in both the Old and New Testaments:

Genesis 2:16-17,

"And the LORD God commanded the man, saying, "Of every tree of the garden you may freely eat; but of the tree of the knowledge of good and evil you shall not eat, for in the day that you eat of it you shall surely die."

Ezekiel 18:20,

"The soul who sins shall die."

Romans 6:23,

"The wages of sin is death, but the gift of God is eternal life in Christ Jesus our Lord."

Our efforts to save ourselves are futile for even our most righteous deeds are as filthy rags before God.

Isaiah 64:5-6,

"You are indeed angry, for we have sinned—In these ways we continue; And ***we need to be saved.*** But we are all like an unclean thing, And all our righteousnesses are like filthy rags."

Sin has totally overtaken humanity and none of our good deeds can ever be good enough to save us. Mankind had become totally evil and incapable of saving himself. No-one deserves to be saved!

Genesis 6:5,

"The LORD saw that the wickedness of man was great in the earth, and that every intent of the thoughts of his heart was only evil continually."

It does not matter what human opinions we have about how good people can be. The only opinion that counts is the verdict of God. No sinfulness, or unrighteousness can ever enter the eternal Kingdom of God.

Romans 3:10,

"There is none righteous, no not one."

1. **God's verdict was that there was no other way. There had to be a perfect, sinless sacrifice, for mankind to be saved**

Everything testifies against us. Human nature and the law tell us that no matter how hard we try, we will always fall into sin, and if we break one law then we have violated them all.

James 2:10,

"For whoever shall keep the whole law, and yet stumble in one point, **he is guilty of all.**"

Revelation 20:12-15,

"And I saw the dead, small and great, standing before God, and books were opened. And another book was opened, which is the Book of Life. And the dead were judged according to their works, by the things which were written in the books. The sea gave up the dead who were in it, and Death and Hades delivered up the dead who were in them. And they were judged, each one according to his works. Then Death and Hades were cast into the lake of fire. This is the second death. And anyone not found written in the Book of Life was cast into the lake of fire."

Revelation 21:7-8,

"He who overcomes shall inherit all things, and I will be his God and he shall be My son. But the cowardly, unbelieving, abominable, murderers, sexually immoral, sorcerers, idolaters, and all liars shall have their part in the lake which burns with fire and brimstone, which is the second death."

Revelation 21:24-27,

"And the nations of those who are saved shall walk in its light, and the kings of the earth bring their glory and honour into it. Its gates shall not be shut at all by day (there shall be no night there). And they shall bring the glory and the honour of the nations into it. But there shall by no means enter it anything that defiles, or causes an abomination or a lie, but only those who are written in the Lamb's Book of Life."

The only way to enter heaven is by believing in the power of the Cross and the Resurrection of Jesus Christ. He alone is the Way, the Truth and the Life.

John 14:6,

"I am the way, the truth, and the life. No one comes to the Father except through Me."

"qaala lahu yasua: ana huwat tariq, walhak, walhayat. laysa ahadun ya'ti ilal ab ila bi"

As Peter also proclaimed:

Acts 4:12,

"Nor is there salvation in any other, for there is no other name under heaven given among men by which we must be saved."

Jesus is called the light of the world. He is the only one that destroys darkness and brings us into the joy, truth, love and pure relationship found in His light, and nowhere else.

John 8:12,

"Jesus spoke to them again, saying, "I am the light of the world. He who follows Me shall not walk in darkness, but have the light of life."

1John 1:5-7,

"This is the message which we have heard from Him and declare to you, that God is light and in Him is no darkness at all. If we say that we have fellowship with Him, and walk in darkness, we lie and do not practice the truth. But if we walk in the light as He is in the light, we have fellowship with one another, and **the blood of Jesus Christ His Son cleanses us from all sin."**

There had to be the shedding of blood and death and the Cross

Many of our Muslim friends desire to be clean from their sins. They are afraid of eternal punishment in hell. They want to be saved. Their inability to cleanse themselves by their good works, or their trips to Mecca leaves them frustrated. They see evil in many of their fellow Muslims and they worry about spending eternity in the fires of hell. This a terrible dilemma for them. Our dilemma is how to best help them find the Straight Path, Jesus, the only one who can forgive them and set them free.

We have seen that in the Bible all our sins are recorded and we will be judged and condemned by them. The same message is conveyed in the Qur'an, which means Muslims have the same problem as Christians. That's why there is an urgent need to get saved and to find a Redeemer-Saviour now. By God's grace, love, compassion and mercy we h
in Jesus Christ – the only way to salvation.

Our Muslim friends are still struggling with this dilemma and they live in fear of the eternal consequences of never being good enough. They believe that on the Day of Judgement all our good and evil deeds will be placed on the scales of justice and if we are found guilty then eternal punishment in the fires of hell is waiting for us.

Surah Al Mu'minun 23:102-104,

"And those whose scales are heavy [with good deeds] - it is they who are the successful. But those whose scales are light - those are the ones who have lost their souls, [being] in Hell, abiding eternally. The Fire will sear their faces, and they therein will have distorted smiles."

The one book in the Bible not mentioned in the Qur'an is the Book of Life. Why is this book important? Because every person who comes to Jesus in repentance and faith, has all their sins (all the bad deeds written against them) wiped away and their name is written in the Book of Life.

Paul and Jesus talk about their friends having their names in the Book of Life:

Philippians 4:3,

"my fellow workers, whose names are in the Book of Life."

Revelation 3:5,

"He who overcomes shall be clothed in white garments, and I will not blot out his name from the Book of Life; but I will confess his name before My Father and before His angels."

These all have their sins blotted out. They are cleansed, forgiven and saved.

Colossians 2:12-14,

We are "buried with Him in baptism, in which you also were raised with Him through faith in the working of God, who raised Him from the dead. And you, being dead in your trespasses and the uncircumcision of your flesh, **He has made alive together with Him, having forgiven you all trespasses, having wiped out the handwriting of requirements that**

was against us, which was contrary to us. And He has taken it out of the way, having nailed it to the cross."

The great danger is if a persons name has not been written in the Book of Life. It means that they would have rejected the Straight Path, the only Way of Salvation. They would have rejected Jesus as the Son of God and only Saviour of mankind, and because of that, their names will not be found in the Book of Life.

Revelation 13:5-8,

"And he (the Antichrist) was given a mouth speaking great things and blasphemies, and he was given authority to continue for forty-two months. Then he opened his mouth in blasphemy against God, to blaspheme His name, His tabernacle, and those who dwell in heaven. It was granted to him to make war with the saints and to overcome them. And authority was given him over every tribe, tongue, and nation. All who dwell on the earth will worship him, whose names have not been written in the Book of Life of the Lamb slain from the foundation of the world."

Those who reject Jesus and do not have their names in the Book of Life, have a fearful and horrible fate. This is the dilemma that our Muslim friends fear. If they reject the Messiah, Jesus, the only sinless prophet, the only Way to eternal salvation, the one declared to be the Mercy of God *(rahmatullah)* then what is left is an unthinkable, eternal torment.

Revelation 16:2-10,

"So the first went and poured out his bowl upon the earth, and ***a foul and loathsome sore*** came upon the men who had the mark of the beast and those who worshiped his image. … Then the fourth angel poured out his bowl on the sun, and power was given to him **to scorch men with fire.** And men were **scorched with great heat,** and they blasphemed the name of God who has power over these plagues; and they did not repent and give Him glory. Then the fifth angel poured out his bowl on the throne of the beast, and his kingdom became full of darkness; and **they gnawed their tongues because of the pain**."

Revelation 17:8,

"The beast (Antichrist) that you saw was, and is not, and will ascend out of the bottomless pit and go to perdition (eternal hell-fire punishment). And those who dwell on the earth will marvel, **whose names are not written in the Book of Life** from the foundation of the world, when they see the beast."

They marvel because they had rejected Jesus to follow this beast, and are now doomed to the same eternal punishment as the Antichrist.

Consider carefully this following question: Is your name in the Book of Life? Only friends of Jesus get their name in that Book, and they are the ones who go to heaven.

2. We are not able to save ourselves. We need a Saviour.

The Bible makes it abundantly clear, that all have sinned and that everyone must pay the consequences of their sins. Our good works all fall short so none of us can save our loved ones nor be saved by another as everyone is accountable for their own sins. We cannot even save ourselves. It is impossible to save ourselves by our own righteous deeds, for the penalty of sin is death and even our most righteous deeds are like filthy rags before God, as we have seen.

Psalm 14:2-3,

"The LORD looks down from heaven upon the children of men, to see if there are any who understand, who seek God. They have all turned aside, They have together become corrupt; There is none who does good, No, not one."

Look into your heart. You know that there is sin in your life. You know the bad intentions that are in your mind. You know the unholy thoughts that disturb you that let you know you are not sinless, not perfect and that you need a Saviour. You know that you can never be good enough by your own efforts to escape eternal judgement, that's why we all need to come to Jesus. He's the one that God has sent to save us. We all need Him. I need Him. You need Him.

What's the difference between Jesus and any other?

The difference is that Jesus is the one and only sinless person in the whole of humanity. He's the only one that could be our Saviour. We can't save ourselves, yet God still loves us and wants to save us. That's why Jesus came. We needed a perfect, sinless sacrifice who could be our Saviour, conquer death and hell and bring eternal forgiveness to all who follow Him and believe in Him.

In ***Surah Maryam 19:19***, the translators use various words to describe the sinlessness of Jesus:

Maulana, Rashad, Sarwar and Shakir say Jesus is "a pure boy"
Pickthal says Jesus is "a faultless son"
Sherali says Jesus is "a righteous son" and
Yusuf Ali says Jesus is "a holy son"

The Arabic in ***Surah Maryam 19:19*** is **zakiyya** زَكِيًّا meaning "pure, blameless, sinless."

Islamic commentaries refer to Jesus as having no sin. Likewise in the Bible we see that Jesus is declared to be without sin.

Hebrews 4:14-16,

"Seeing then that we have a great High Priest who has passed through the heavens, Jesus the Son of God, let us hold fast our confession. For we do not have a High Priest who cannot sympathize with our weaknesses, but was in all points tempted as we are, **yet without sin.** Let us therefore come boldly to the throne of grace, that we may obtain mercy and find grace to help in time of need."

The Trauma of the Garden of Gethsemane

As Jesus prayed in the Garden of Gethsemane He experienced the greatest trauma of His life. Only Jesus knew the full extent of the agony He was about to experience. We sing a chorus which says:

"I'll never know how much it cost
To see my sin upon that cross"

That may be true here, but in eternity we probably will know and be able to fully comprehend. The trauma He faced was the eternal punishment, agony, rejection, humiliation, pain, suffering, separation and loneliness of the totality of the sin of all humanity, the billions and billions of souls, from Adam down to the last human being born. He was about to bear it all. Only He could know and understand. That's why He was in so much pain that He was sweating drops of blood from His forehead. His blood vessels were bursting with the strain and agony of the burden He was bearing.

Matthew 26:39; Luke 22:42-44,

"O My Father, if it is possible, let this cup pass from Me; nevertheless, not as I will, but as You will." … "And being in agony, He prayed more earnestly. Then His sweat became like great drops of blood falling down to the ground."

Jesus knew it was not possible to avoid the Cross because there was no other way for mankind to be saved. It didn't make it any easier because He was about to experience hell, separation from God the Father and God the Holy Spirit. This had never ever happened before, yet Jesus, though sinless, chose to obey the will of the Father. Look how great the love of the Father was for you and me:

John 3:16,

"For God so loved the world that He gave (sacrificed) His only Son."

There was no other way. This was the only way. No human could save themselves or cleanse themselves from sin and Jesus loved us enough to be willing to suffer hell so that you and I could be saved.

Because He Himself never sinned, Satan, death and hell could not hold Him. He destroyed the power of death and hell for all who believe in Him and we are given new, sinless, perfect and glorious bodies to be able to live with Him in His eternal glory.

1Corinthians 15:50-57,

"Now this I say, brethren, that flesh and blood cannot inherit the kingdom of God; nor does corruption inherit incorruption. Behold, I tell you a mystery: We shall not all sleep, but we shall all be changed— in a moment, in the twinkling of an eye, at the last trumpet. For the trumpet will sound, and the dead will be raised incorruptible, and we shall be changed. For this corruptible must put on incorruption, and this mortal must put on immortality. So when this corruptible has put on incorruption, and this mortal has put on immortality, then shall be brought to pass the saying that is written: "death is swallowed up in victory." "O death, where is your sting? O hades, where is your victory?" The sting of death is sin, and the strength of sin is the law. But thanks be to God, who gives us the victory through our Lord Jesus Christ."

3. The Miracle of the Incarnation

The incarnation is the response of God's love to the impossibility of our saving ourselves. The only way was for God Himself to become a Man and to make our salvation possible. The incarnation solves a dilemma facing

Muslims. They ask, "How can God die? If Jesus is God, how could He die?" God can never die, but human flesh can. To be the perfect mediator, equally representing God and man, Jesus had to have both. That is the miracle of the incarnation. The Law of the Old Testament did not have this and that's why the Law could never bring salvation or a perfect redemption as *Hebrews 10* explains.

Hebrews 10:1,

"For the law, having a shadow of the good things to come, and not the very image of the things, can never with these same sacrifices, which they offer continually year by year, make those who approach perfect."

Hebrews 10:11-14,

"And every priest stands ministering daily and offering repeatedly the same sacrifices, which ***can never take away sins***. But this Man, after He had offered one sacrifice for sins forever, sat down at the right hand of God … For ***by one offering He has perfected forever*** those who are being sanctified."

The principle of priesthood in the Bible demands that as a mediator, a priest must evenly and fairly represent both parties. The Old Testament Melchizedek could only represent God. We needed a New Testament Melchizedek. Under the Law, Jesus was banned from being a Levitical Priest as He was not born of the Tribe of Levi, but the Tribe of Judah,

Hebrew 7:11-19,

"Therefore, if perfection were through the Levitical priesthood (for under it the people received the law), what further need was there that another priest should rise according to the order of Melchizedek, and not be called according to the order of Aaron? For the priesthood being changed, of necessity there is also a change of the law. … For on the one hand there is an ***annulling of the former commandment because of its weakness and unprofitableness, for the law made nothing perfect***; on the other hand, there is the bringing in of a better hope, through which we draw near to God."

Hebrews 7:22-28,

"Jesus has become a surety of ***a better covenant***. Also there were many priests, because they were prevented by death from continuing. But He, because He continues forever, has an unchangeable priesthood. Therefore He is also ***able to save to the uttermost*** those who come to God through Him, since He always lives to make intercession for them. For such a High Priest was fitting for us, who is holy, harmless, undefiled, separate from sinners, and has become higher than the heavens; who does not need daily, as those high priests, to offer up sacrifices, first for His own sins and then for the people's, for this He did once for all when He offered up Himself. For the law appoints as high priests men who have weakness, but the word of the oath, which came after the law, appoints the Son who has been perfected forever."

Jesus could only be an effective Priest according to the order of Melchizedek, where, as the Son of God and the Son of Man He could be our great High Priest, *Hebrews 3:1.* He is the only one who can be both a priest for God and man at the same time – *1Timothy 2:5; Hebrews 8:6; 9:15; 12:24.* That's why God had to become a Man and be our Saviour. No-one can ever save themselves, and no-one else would be able to save another. It would take a perfect, sinless priest and a perfect, sinless sacrifice. Jesus was both! It took the intervention of God's Mercy, and in fact, in the Qur'an, it states that Jesus was given to us, as the Mercy of God."

Hebrews 4:14-16,

"Seeing then that we have a great High Priest who has passed through the heavens, Jesus the Son of God, let us hold fast our confession. For we do not have a High Priest who cannot sympathize with our weaknesses, but was in all points tempted as we are, yet without sin. Let us therefore come boldly to the throne of grace, that we may obtain mercy and find grace to help in time of need."

Surah Maryam 19:19-21,

"The angel said: "Nay, I am only a messenger from thy Lord, (to announce) to thee the gift of **A HOLY (sinless) SON**. Allah had destined her to be the mother of the Prophet Jesus Christ and now had come the time when this should be announced to her. She said: "How shall I have a son, seeing that no man has touched me, and I am not unchaste?" He said: "So (it will be): Thy Lord saith, 'that is easy for Me: and (We wish) to appoint him as a Sign unto men and a Mercy from Us': It is a matter (so) decreed."

Even in Islam, Jesus is the ONLY SINLESS PROPHET and is therefore the ONLY ONE who qualifies to be a Redeemer or Saviour!

The Qur'an states several times that Muhammad is a sinner, *(Surah 40:55; 47:19; 48:2)*. This is why Allah, the angels and the Muslims pray for Muhammad's salvation daily, *Surah Al-Ahzab 33:56*. Even Muhammad doesn't know himself if he will be saved, *Surah Al-Ahqaf 46:9*.

Surah Al-Ahzab 33:56,

"***Truly Allah and His angels (the jinn) pray for the Prophet.*** O believers, you also, pray for the Prophet and salute him with a worthy salutation."

Allah also prays for Muhammad's salvation. Not even Allah knows for sure if Muhammad will make it to heaven. An interesting question: Who does Allah pray to?

Surah Al-Ahqaf 46:9,

"Say: "I am no bringer of new-fangled doctrine among the messengers, **nor do I know what will be done with me or with you.** I follow but that which is revealed to me by inspiration; I am but a Warner open and clear."

Since Muhammad even needs Allah and the angels and all the Muslim world to pray for him, it means that Muhammad's salvation is in real doubt. He's not sure about his own eternal fate, nor is he sure of the fate of those who follow him. However, Jesus is 100% sure.

John 5:24,

"Most assuredly, I say to you, he who hears My word and believes in Him who sent Me has everlasting life, and shall not come into judgment, but has passed from death into life."

John 11:25-26,

"I am the resurrection and the life. He who believes in Me, though he may die, he shall live. And whoever lives and believes in Me shall never die."

There is only one sinless prophet who qualifies to be a mediator, a High Priest and a Saviour, and that is Jesus. He guarantees forgiveness and salvation. He gives eternal life. No-one else can offer this. He is truly the Straight Path, the Way, the Truth and the Life.

He is the Son of God who became the Son of Man in the miracle of the incarnation, the Word that came down, became a human being and lived among us. He did this so that we could be saved. There is no other way and there is no other Saviour!

John 1:1-3,

"In the beginning was the Word, and the Word was with God, and the Word was God. He was in the beginning with God. All things were made through Him, and without Him nothing was made that was made."

This reveals that Jesus is the Word. He is eternal. He is the creator!

Even the Qur'an acknowledges that Jesus is the Word of God. In the Qur'an. Jesus is called the ***kalimatullah – the Word of God!***

The miracle of the incarnation is declared to us:

John 1:14,

"The Word became flesh and dwelt among us, and we beheld His glory, the glory as of the only begotten of the Father, full of grace and truth."

Philippians 2:5-11,

"Let this mind be in you which was also in Christ Jesus, who, being in the form of God, did not consider it robbery to be equal with God, but made Himself of no reputation, taking the form of a bondservant, and coming in the likeness of men. And being found in appearance as a man, He humbled Himself and became obedient to the point of death, even the death of the cross. Therefore God also has highly exalted Him and given Him the name which is above every name, that at the name of Jesus every knee should bow, of those in heaven, and of those on earth, and of those under the earth, and that every tongue should confess that Jesus Christ is Lord, to the glory of God the Father."

Hebrews 2:14-18 (NIV),

"Since the children have flesh and blood, he too shared in their humanity so that by his death he might break the power of him who holds the power of death—that is, the devil—and free those who all their lives were held in slavery by their fear of death. For surely it is not angels he helps, but Abraham's descendants. For this reason he had to be made like them, fully human in every way, in order that he might become a merciful and faithful high priest in service to God, and that he might make atonement for the sins of the people. Because he himself suffered when he was tempted, he is able to help those who are being tempted."

If you have lived as a slave, Jesus wants to make you a son. In Islam, God has no sons, He only has slaves! Receive Jesus and follow Him and you will be free from slavery and you will become a son of God.

John 1:12-13,

"To all who did receive him, to those who believed in his name, he gave the right to become children of God— children born not of natural descent, nor of human decision or a husband's will, but born of God."

Wow! This is His offer to all of us. No longer slaves to sin or Satan, but sons and daughters of the living God!

The Mystery of the Meaning of Melchizedek's name – *Hebrews 7:1-3*

Take careful note that Melchizedek (*melek* = King and *tsedek* = Righteousness) must seek the total destruction and elimination of sin. Melchizedek is also King of Jerusalem and therefore King of Peace. He cannot tolerate war and violence in His Kingdom. His nature of peace and love demands reconciliation. Destroy the sin but save the sinner!

The Levitical Priesthood could not do this, that's why the priesthood had to be changed, *Hebrews 7:11-17*, and bring in Christ's Priesthood after the order of Melchizedek. As the Great High Priest, Jesus stands perfectly between the two aspects of righteousness (judgement) and peace (forgiveness and reconciliation). He is the only one that can fulfil the outpouring of the wrath of God against sin and the forgiveness and love of God bringing reconciliation and salvation to the sinner. Only on the CROSS could this happen.

It is these two doctrines that Islam tries to deny – the INCARNATION – that God became a Man and the CROSS where sin is destroyed but the sinner is saved! Hallelujah! Amazing Grace!

Observe these 3 critical elements of Melchizedek:

1. Jesus is the Great High Priest
2. Jesus is the King of Righteousness
3. Jesus is the King of Peace

Jesus had to be:

1. The Perfect High Priest
2. The Perfect Sacrifice

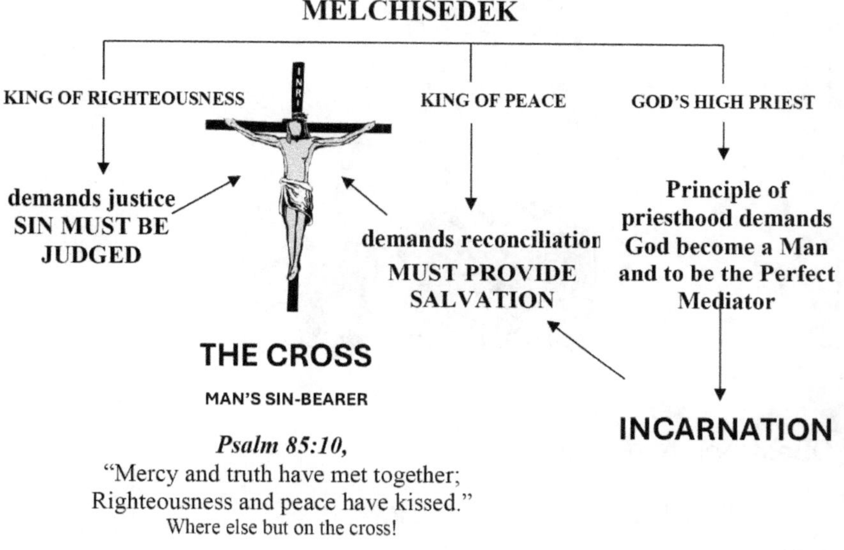

Psalm 85:10,
"Mercy and truth have met together;
Righteousness and peace have kissed."
Where else but on the cross!

No wonder Paul said in ***Galatians 6:14,***

"God forbid that I should glory, save in the cross of our Lord Jesus Christ,"

What does this revelation of Melchizedek reveal?

1. No-one is able to save themselves because all have sinned.
2. Man needs help – a Saviour, a Redeemer, that is Jesus. Only He qualifies!
3. The Incarnation and the Cross provide God's amazing answer for all and any who want to be saved and are willing to accept Christ as their Lord and Saviour. Jesus is the Son of God who became the Son of Man, so that we the sons and daughters of men could become the sons and daughters of God.

Questions to discuss:

1. Who do you think killed Jesus?
2. Why did Jesus have to die?
3. Are you worried that your good works are not good enough to save you? What will you do about it?
4. Do you feel like you have been a slave to sin and want to be set free? Who can help you?

DILEMMA 8

THE STRAIGHT PATH DILEMMA

Every day, Muslims in their five compulsory prayer times have to pray the first Surah in the Qur'an, Al-Fatiha, a minimum of seventeen times. The central part of that prayer is: **"Show us the straight way."** Some translations call it **"the straight path."** This prayer request about the Straight Path creates a dilemma requiring a clear answer. Is the Straight Way or Straight Path a religion or a person? The dilemma is apparent from the very first Surah of the Qur'an, which is titled "Al-Fatiha" meaning "The Opening".

The breakdown of the five compulsory prayer times and praying the Al Fatiha 17 times are:

- Fajr (Dawn): 2 times.
- Dhuhr (Noon): 4 times.
- Asr (Mid-Afternoon): 4 times.
- Maghrib (Sunset): 3 times.
- Isha (Evening): 4 times.

In Islam, the Straight Path, is claimed by a majority of Muslims to be the religion of Islam. Other Muslims are not so sure what it is and that's why it's a central prayer request every day. If it was clear,

Muslims would not have to ask. In Christianity, the Straight Path, or the Straight Way, is not a religion, it's a person. That person is Jesus Christ. The dilemma comes into focus when we read how the Qur'an defines the Straight Path as we will discuss in this Chapter.

Every day, Muslims in their five compulsory prayer times have to pray this Surah a minimum of seventeen times. Every Muslim has memorized the Al Fatiha. One way to test if a person is a Muslim or not is to get them to recite the Al Fatiha. Similarly, ask a Christian to recite the Lord's Prayer from *Matthew 6:9-13.* Most Christians can.

The central part of the Al Fatiha prayer is: "Show us the straight way." It is a prayer or request to God by Muslims to show them the true path to eternal life. This request indicates that there is doubt. A Muslim could be asking, "Do we know what the term "Straight Way" really means? Have we found it or are we still seeking to find it? Is it our religion, our faith that is the Straight Way, or is it a Person, Jesus Christ, as the Christians and even verses in the Qur'an claim?" In this Chapter, we will seek to resolve this dilemma as we dig deeper into this very important topic.

Surah Al-Fatiha (The 1st Surah) is a compulsory prayer that must be prayed, in Arabic, at least 17 times every day.

This opening prayer reveals a number of truths that are important to understanding Islam and our understanding of the message of the Qur'an. Let's read this opening prayer of the Qur'an.

[1] In the name of God, Most Gracious, Most Merciful

[2] Praise be to God, the Cherisher and Sustainer of the worlds;

[3] Most Gracious, Most Merciful;

[4] Master of the Day of Judgment.

[5] Thee do we worship, and Thine aid we seek.

[6] **Show us the straight way,** (Arabic: **ihdinas siraat al mustaqeem**)

[7] The way of those on whom Thou hast bestowed Thy Grace (the Muslims), not those whose (portion) is wrath (the Jews), and not those who go astray (the Christians).

Who or What in the Qur'an is called the Straight Path?

The answer is clear. The only one fulfilling all the criteria to be the Straight Path is Jesus and Jesus Himself reveals in the Qur'an that He is indeed the Straight Path.

Surah Ali Imran 3:50-51,

Jesus said: "(I have come to you), to attest the Law which was before me. And to make lawful to you part of what was (before) forbidden to you; I have come to you with a Sign from your Lord. So, fear God, and obey me. It is God who is my Lord and your Lord; then worship Him." ***This is the Straight Path.***"

How does it define the Straight Path? There are three elements mentioned:

1. Fear God
2. Obey Jesus
3. Worship God

Surah Az-Zukruf 43:63-64.

"When Jesus came with Clear Signs, he said: "Now have I come to you with Wisdom, and in order to make clear to you some of the (points) on which ye dispute: therefore, fear God and obey me. For God, He is my Lord and your Lord: so, worship ye Him: **this is a Straight Way**."

These three parts of the Straight Path are repeated:

a. Fear God
b. Obey Jesus
c. Worship God

Muslims repeatedly state that they honour Jesus, and that Jesus was given the Gospel as a guidance to all mankind. This gives rise to an interesting question:

How can we follow the Straight Path if we don't read the Gospel of Jesus?

John 8:46,

Jesus said, "If I am telling the truth, why don't you believe me?"

Arabic: "in kuntu aquulu ulhaqq falimatha lastum tu'minuna bi?

If Jesus and the Gospel are truly from God, as the Qur'an says, then they must acknowledge that Jesus is the Straight Path. Jesus also revealed in the Gospel that He is the ONLY way to heaven for all people who will believe in Him – Jews, Christians, Muslims and anyone else.

John 14:6,

Jesus answered, "I am the Way and the Truth and the Life. No one comes to the Father except through me."

Other Qur'anic Verses on the Straight Path

What is commonly found is that the Straight Path leads to God. One must follow it, walk justly and walk in His mercy so as not to be led astray. It all points to Jesus as the central element of the Straight Path.

Surah An-Nisaa 4:175,

"So, as for those who believed in God and held fast to Him, He will admit them to His Mercy and Grace, and guide them to Himself ***by a Straight Path.***"

Both the "Mercy" of God and the Straight Path indicate Jesus is the Way

Jesus was given to be the Mercy of God and a Sign from God.

Surah Maryam 19:21,

"Thy Lord saith (to Mary), 'That is easy for Me: and (We wish) to appoint him (Jesus) as a **Sign** unto men and a **Mercy** from Us.'"

Grasp the impact of this - Jesus was given to be both a Sign and a Mercy from God! In this study its meaning will become clearer to us.

Surah Al-Anaam 6:39,

"Those who reject Our Signs are deaf and dumb in darkness. God sends astray whom He wills and ***He guides on the Straight Path*** whom He wills."

It could be argued that to reject Jesus is to reject God's Sign since Jesus was given as a Sign to mankind. See *Surah Maryam 19:21 above.*

The Qur'an states that the Straight Path was the Religion of Abraham

Surah Al-Anaam 6:82-89,

"It is those who believe and confuse not their beliefs with wrong - that are (truly) in security, for they are on (right) guidance. … We gave to Abraham … We gave him Isaac and Jacob: all (three) guided: and before him, We guided Noah, and among his progeny, David, Solomon, Job, Joseph, Moses, and Aaron: thus do We reward those who do good. And Zakariya and Yahya, and Jesus and Elijah: all in the ranks of the righteous: And Ishmael and Elisha, and Jonah, and Lot: and to all We gave favour above the nations: And also some of their fathers and their progeny and their brethren, We chose them, and ***We guided them to a Straight Path.*** … Those are the ones to whom We gave the Scripture and authority and prophethood."

So, Old Testament believers were already on the Straight Path! It began in the Garden of Eden and leads all the way to the Cross of Calvary.

Surah Al-Anaam 6:161,

"Say: As for me, my Lord has ***guided me to the straight path***, a right religion, the faith of Abraham, the upright one, and he was not of the polytheists."

What did Jesus say about Abraham?

John 8:56-58,

"Your father Abraham rejoiced to see My day, and he saw it and was glad." Then the Jews said to Him, "You are not yet fifty years old, and have You seen Abraham?" Jesus said to them, "Most assuredly, I say to you, before Abraham was, I AM."

In these verses Jesus claimed to be YHWH, the Lord God, the great I AM. Jesus is more than a Prophet. He is Eternal, He is God and Abraham had already met Jesus 2000 years before the Cross! What an amazing story! No wonder the Jews wanted to stone Jesus.

Surah Al-Maida 5:12,

"Indeed, God took the covenant from the Children of Israel (Jews), and We appointed twelve leaders among them. And God said: … But if any of you after this, disbelieved, he has indeed gone astray from ***the Straight Path***."

So, it was God who blessed Israel and gave them the Covenant and the land of Palestine. How much do we, or Muslims, understand the significance of these Covenants given to Adam, Noah, Abraham, Moses, David etc which could only ever be fulfilled in the Messiah at the Cross. It is clear that the Jews, were already on ***the Straight Path*** in following the revelation of the faith of Abraham and Moses!

Surah Al-Anaam 6:125-126,

"Those whom God (in His plan) willeth to guide, He openeth their breast to Islam; those whom He willeth to leave straying, He maketh their breast close and constricted, as if they had to climb up to the skies: thus, doth God (heap) the penalty on those who refuse to believe. ***This is the straight path*** of thy Lord: We have detailed the signs for those who receive admonition."

Surah Yunus 10:87-89,

"We inspired Moses and his brother with this Message: "Provide dwellings for your people in Egypt, make your dwellings into places of worship, and establish regular prayers: and give glad tidings to those who believe! And Moses said: "Our Lord, surely Thou has given Pharaoh and his chiefs finery and riches in this worlds' life, our Lord, ***that they may lead (people) astray from Thy way.*** O Lord, destroy their riches and harden their hearts, so that they believe not till they see the painful chastisement. God said: "Accepted is your prayer (O Moses and Aaron)! so ***continue in the straight path*** and follow not the path of those who know not."

Israel was already in the Straight Path and were warned against straying into a wrong Path. This is the clear message in both the Qur'an and the Bible.

The Qur'an tells us that the Bible Prophets were in the Straight Path

Surah Al-Anaam 6:82-87,

"It is those who believe and confuse not their beliefs with wrong - that are (truly) in security, for they are on (right) guidance. ... We gave to Abraham ... We gave him Isaac and Jacob: all (three) guided: and before him, We guided Noah, and among his progeny, David, Solomon, Job, Joseph, Moses, and Aaron: thus do We reward those who do good."

Other prophets from the Bible mentioned in the Qur'an as prophets of Islam: Adam, Jesus, Jonah, Elijah and Elisha are recognized as prophets following the Straight Path.

A Major Problem - Muhammad's Salvation is in Doubt

Because Muhammad's salvation is still in question, he too needed to be shown the Straight Path. How clearly did the Gospel message come to him? Were divisions in the Christian faith and the failure to fulfill the Great Commission effectively, causes for Muhammad to reject Christ as the Son of God. What confusion did Satan put into his mind. Muhammad accepted Jesus as Messiah but not as Saviour. He accepted Jesus as the miracle-working, creating and all-knowing Prophet but could not accept Him as God.

Muhammad was left without certainty and in doubt, with no guaranteed salvation. What an awful condition to live in! Sadly, many Muslims live in the same doubt and fear. God wanted to show Muhammad the pathway to salvation and the forgiveness of his sins. He would only be able to find it if he was to walk in the Straight Path. With this great doubt, God, the angels and all Muslims pray daily for Muhammad's salvation.

How do we get to Heaven? In ***Sahih Al-Bukhari*** we are told: "None of you can get into heaven without God's Mercy." Who is God's Mercy? It's Jesus, ***Surah Maryam 19:21.***

"The Prophet (pbuh) said: "Not one of you will enter Paradise by his deeds alone." They asked, "Not even you, O Messenger of God?" He said, "Not even me, unless God covers me with His Grace and Mercy." ***(Bukhari, Riqaq, 18; Muslim, Munafiq, 71-73).***

Surah Al-Fath 48:2,

"That God may forgive thee (Muhammad) of thy sin that which is past and that which is to come, and may perfect His favour unto thee, and may guide thee on a straight path."

Surah Al-Anaam 6:153

"Truly, ***this is My straight path:*** follow it: follow not other paths: they will scatter you about from His path: in this way He commands you so that you may be righteous."

So, Islam teaches that there is ONLY ONE WAY and it is the Straight Path. It is Jesus!

Many Muslims are confused about the understanding of "the Straight Path". Some of their scholars say that it is Muhammad, some say it is submission, some say it is the religion of Islam. They look for any other explanation than that which is clearly before them in the Qur'an, i.e. that Jesus is the Straight Path, the Mercy of God, the Sign sent from God and that He, therefore, is **the one and only way** to escape eternal judgement, obtain salvation and gain entrance into eternal paradise.

The Straight Path is also a major theme of the Bible – the Law and the Gospel

In the Old Testament, God prophesies the coming of the Straight Path. John the Baptist, who is called the Prophet Yahya in the Qur'an was sent to prepare the coming of the Straight Path.

Isaiah 40:3,

"The voice of one crying in the wilderness: "Prepare the way of the LORD; ***Make straight in the desert a highway for our God."***

The Straight Path in the 4 Gospels:

Who is coming – his name and nature are revealed in these verses:

Matthew 3:1-3,

"In those days John the Baptist came, preaching in the wilderness of Judea and saying, "Repent, for the kingdom of heaven has come near." This is he who was spoken of through the prophet Isaiah: "A voice of one calling in the wilderness, ***'Prepare the way for the Lord (YHWH - Yahweh), make straight paths for him.'"***

This message is repeated in Mark 1:1-3, Luke 3:2-6 and John 1:23. The One coming is the LORD (YHWH). It is the LORD God – Yahweh Elohim who is coming. He is Jesus!

See the message of the Straight Path throughout the Bible

The names of many believers in the Old Testament are mentioned to show that they were walking in the Straight Path. The Straight Path is nothing new. It was revealed from the time Adam and Eve were in the Garden of Eden. Because of their sin, they were put out of the Garden of Eden. God knew that if Adam and Eve were to eat from the Tree of Life in that sinful state they would have eternalized their sin and there would have been no hope for their salvation.

To protect the Straight Path, Adam and Eve were banished from the Garden. This would protect the Straight Path that God had prepared. Indeed, it was the only Path that could bring mankind to salvation.

To open the access to the Straight Path, it was going to take a perfect sacrifice and for this reason God was preparing the Cross from before the creation of the world. God knows all things. He is Omniscient.

1Peter 2:18-20 (NIV),

"For you know that it was not with perishable things such as silver or gold that you were redeemed from the empty way of life handed down to you from your ancestors, but with the precious blood of Christ, a lamb without blemish or defect. **He was chosen before the creation of the world.**"

God knew that man would sin, so before the Fall, God had prepared the only Way possible for the redemption of mankind. That's why Jesus was chosen to be the perfect, sinless Lamb who would be the Only Way, the Straight Path for mankind to be saved. He was chosen from before creation, and activated the moment that Adam and Eve sinned. From that moment, in 4000 BC, Jesus was activated as the Lamb of God, appointed to die for the sins of mankind. This indeed is the Mercy of God, the *Rahmatullah*, declared by the Qur'an as the only way that we can be saved and Jesus is declared to be a Sign from God and a Mercy from God.

Surah Maryam 19:21,

"We will make him a sign to the people and a mercy from Us (**rahmatam minnaa**)."

An Islamic scholar, Sheikh Mohammed al-Ghazali *(www.aboutislam.net/reading-islam/understanding-islam/if-not-for-his-mercy/)* wrote:

> "The interpretation of the words of the Prophet Muhammad: "No one will enter Paradise by his deeds."
>
> The Companions asked: "Not even you, O Messenger of Allah?"
>
> He said: **"Not even me, unless Allah covers me with His Mercy."**

Jesus is the Mercy of God *(Rahmatullah)* given to us for our salvation. Even the founder of Islam, Muhammad, acknowledged this truth.

When Adam and Eve disobeyed God, and sinned, the plan to activate God's Mercy to save mankind began. This activation was 4000 years before Jesus was crucified. Why did we have to wait 4000 years before Jesus came as the Lamb of God. He was identified by the prophet John the Baptist, known as the prophet Yahya in the Qur'an. Yahya is a highly respected prophet in Islam and the Qur'an states that he was specifically sent to guide the Children of Israel, confirm the prophethood of Isa (Jesus), and uphold the Torah (the Law).

Surah Maryam 19:12,

"O Yahya! take hold of the Book with might": and We gave him Wisdom even as a youth."

Yahya (John the Baptist) was indeed a great prophet with amazing wisdom from God. It was he who had the wisdom from God to identify that Jesus was the Messiah, the Lamb of God, who would be the Saviour of the world.

John 1:29,

"The next day John saw Jesus coming toward him, and said, "Behold! The Lamb of God who takes away the sin of the world!"

It had been 4000 years since the Fall and sin of Adam and Eve, and it was the Prophet Yahya (John the Baptist) who had the wisdom and understanding to identify that the prophesied Saviour of the world had come. He had come as the perfect, sinless Saviour, the spotless Lamb of God. He was the only one who could bring us to the Straight Path, and that's why Jesus said,

John 14:6,

"I am the Way, the Truth and the Life. No man comes to the Father except through Me."

Later the Apostle Peter recognized this same amazing, miraculous fulfillment of prophecy that went back 4000 years when he declared that Jesus was the Redeemer from before Creation.

1Peter 1:18-23,

"knowing that ***you were not redeemed with corruptible things***, like silver or gold, from your aimless conduct received by tradition from your fathers, ***but with the precious blood of Christ, as of a lamb without blemish and without spot.*** **He (Jesus) indeed was foreordained before the foundation of the world,** but was manifest in these last times for you who through Him believe in God, who raised Him from the dead and gave Him glory, so that your faith and hope are in God. Since you have purified your souls in obeying the truth through the Spirit in sincere love of the brethren, love one another fervently with a pure heart, having been born again, not of corruptible seed but incorruptible, through the word of God which lives and abides forever."

Why did we have to wait 4000 years for the Saviour to come?

Mankind had to wait 4000 years for the Lamb, the Redeemer, the Saviour to come. And He came right on time. He did not delay. He was not late. He fulfilled all the prophecies perfectly. The Qur'an commands us to believe all the prophets in the Bible for they bring the true revelation of God.

Surah Al-Baqara 2:136,

"Say, "We believe in GOD, and in what was sent down to us, and in what was sent down to Abraham, Ismail, Isaac, Jacob, and the Patriarchs; and in what was given to Moses and Jesus, **and all the prophets from their Lord.** We make no distinction among any of them. To Him alone we are submitters."

The coming Redeemer, the Lord God Almighty, was prophesied 800 years before His miraculous birth to the virgin Mary. He would lead us to the Straight Path, the Way that we should go.

Isaiah 48:17,

"Thus says the LORD, your Redeemer, The Holy One of Israel: "I am the LORD your God, Who teaches you to profit, Who leads you by the way you should go."

Isaiah also prophesied that the coming Messiah would be killed, as a Lamb, for the sins of the world and then rise again from the dead.

Isaiah 53:4-11,

"He is despised and rejected by men, A Man of sorrows and acquainted with grief. And we hid, as it were, our faces from Him; He was despised, and we did not esteem Him. Surely **He has borne our griefs and carried our sorrows**; Yet we esteemed Him stricken, Smitten by God, and afflicted. But He was wounded for our transgressions, He was bruised for our iniquities; The chastisement for our peace was upon Him, And by His stripes we are healed. All we like sheep have gone astray; We have turned, every one, to his own way; And **the LORD has laid on Him the iniquity of us all**. He was oppressed and He was afflicted, Yet He opened not His mouth; **He was led as a lamb to the slaughter**, And as a sheep before its shearers is silent, So He opened not His mouth. He was taken from prison and from judgment, And who will declare His generation? For **He was cut off from the land of the living**; For the transgressions of My people He was stricken. And they made His grave with the wicked—But with the rich at His death, Because He had done no violence, Nor was any deceit in His mouth. Yet it pleased the LORD to bruise Him; He has put Him to grief. When You make His soul an offering for sin, **He shall see His seed, He shall prolong His days**, And the pleasure of the LORD shall prosper in His hand. **He shall see the labour of His soul, and be satisfied**. By His knowledge My righteous Servant shall justify many, For He shall bear their iniquities."

The Messiah would be our sin bearer, our Redeemer. He would suffer for all our sins, transgressions, rebellions and iniquities. The He would conquer death, rise from the dead and prolong His days. 800 years after Isaiah prophesied Jesus was born. Only divinely anointed prophets can do this.

Moses was also a powerful prophet and God gave him the revelation that the Lamb that brings redemption must be chosen and kept for **FOUR DAYS.** Why? While man's days are 24 hours, God's calendar days are 1000 year days. God revealed to Moses that He had told Adam that he would die in the same day he ate of the forbidden fruit. He died 930 years later!

(Genesis 5:5). And no man has ever lived 1000 years. Not yet anyway, but we will in the Millennium! After Christ's return there will be a Millennium of peace and glory, 1000 years of Christ reigning on the earth, called the Day of the Lord *(2Peter 3:8-13; Revelation 20:1-15; Revelation 21:1-8)* and we will live with Him and with all the believers of all time. We will live that 1000 years because there is no more sin – and then forever more!

The FOUR PROPHETIC DAYS that the Lamb was kept *(Exodus 12:1-11; 1Corinthians 5:7-8; 1Peter 1:18-20)* are fulfilled in the 4000 years from the Fall of Adam and Eve until the Cross of Christ. It was a perfect fulfillment of divine revelation – right on time.

Galatians 4:4-5,

"When the fullness of the time had come, God sent forth His Son, born of a woman, born under the law, to redeem those who were under the law."

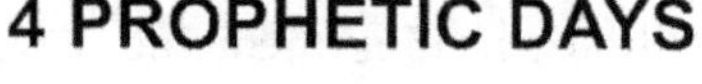

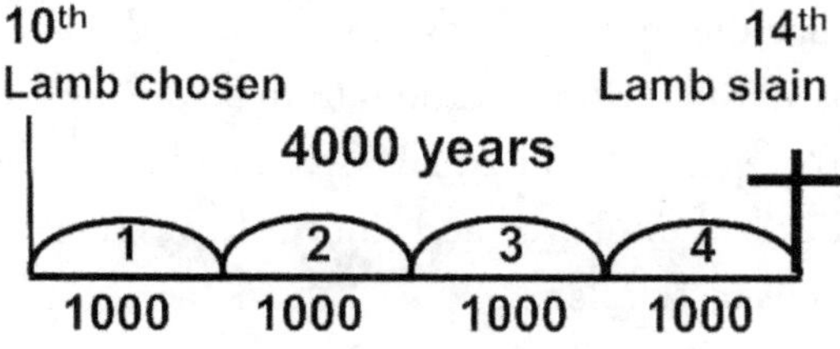

2Peter 3:8 - 1 Day = 1000 Years

What happened at the Fall of Adam and Eve?

The sin of Adam and Eve, eating from the Tree of the Knowledge of Good and Evil, broke the relationship they had with God. Until the Fall, they had a beautiful relationship with God. He would come into the Garden to have fellowship with them but something had changed. Their sin brought shame and fear and they sought to hide from God. They had no peace.

They knew they were sinners. They knew that the penalty was death. Their world had changed. Their relationship with God was damaged. They tried to cover up their nakedness but failed.

Genesis 3:7-8,

"Then the eyes of both of them were opened, and they knew that they were naked; and they sewed fig leaves together and made themselves coverings. And they heard the sound of the LORD God walking in the garden in the cool of the day, and Adam and his wife hid themselves from the presence of the LORD God among the trees of the garden."

What was God's Response?

God is omniscient. He sees and knows all things. He knew that they had sinned. He didn't come to judge them or to wipe them out as a failed experiment. No! Before man had ever sinned, God had a plan. Before there was the disease, God had the divine healing medicine. Before there was a problem, God had the answer. That's why we are told that the Messiah, the Lamb, was chosen from before Creation, from before the foundation of the world. God was prepared. He loved His Creation. He loved Adam and Eve, even though they had disobeyed and sinned. It was now time for God to begin to reveal His masterplan.

When God came into the Garden, He already knew what had taken place. He knew they had rebelled and sinned, but He wanted Adam and Eve to know how much He loved them.

Genesis 3:8-9,

"And they heard the sound of the LORD God walking in the garden in the cool of the day, and Adam and his wife hid themselves from the presence of the LORD God among the trees of the garden. Then the LORD God called to Adam and said to him, "Where are you?"

God's first act was to come with a gentle call, "Where are you?" These were not the words of anger or judgement, but the cry of God's loving heart wanting to save His Creation.

His second act was to inform them, *Genesis 3:11-20,* of the consequence of sin. God was not going to wipe them out. He had a powerful plan for redemption and He was now setting the scene of what would follow.

- **Satan would suffer the curse**

Genesis 3:14-15,

"So the LORD God said to the serpent: "Because you have done this, You are cursed more than all cattle, And more than every beast of the field; On your belly you shall go, And you shall eat dust all the days of your life. And I will put enmity between you and the woman, and between your seed and her Seed; He shall bruise your head, and you shall bruise His heel."

The beast, the serpent, Satan used would crawl on his belly all his life. There would be war between the Seed of the Woman (Jesus) and the seed of satanic deception. This would continue "all the days of your life." We see this battle today. The Apostle John heard it from Jesus.

John 16:1-3,

"These things I have spoken to you, that you should not be made to stumble. They will put you out of the synagogues; yes, the time is coming that **whoever kills you will think that he offers God service**. And these things they will do to you because they have not known the Father nor Me."

1John 2:18-25,

"Little children, it is the last hour; and as you have heard that **the Antichrist is coming**, even now **many antichrists** have come, by which we know that **it is the last hour.** They went out from us, but they were not of us; for if they had been of us, they would have continued with us; but they went out that they might be made manifest, that none of them were of us. But you have an anointing from the Holy One, and you know all things. I have not written to you because you do not know the truth, but because you know it, and that no lie is of the truth. Who is a liar but he who denies that Jesus is the Christ? **He is antichrist who denies the Father and the Son.** Whoever denies the Son does not have the Father either; he who acknowledges the Son has the Father also. Therefore let that abide in you which you heard from the beginning. If what you heard from the beginning abides in you, you also will abide in the Son and in the Father. And this is the promise that He has promised us—eternal life."

This battle will consummate in the last days and will give rise to many small antichrists, the spirit of Antichrist and then 'the' Antichrist. This all began in the Garden of Eden and is a consequence of the Fall. We will see a demonic attack against God, against the Seed of the Woman, both Christ and His church as was prophesied.

Psalm 2:1-3,

"Why do the nations rage, And the people plot a vain thing? The kings of the earth set themselves, and the rulers take counsel together, against the LORD and against His Anointed, saying, "Let us break their bonds in pieces and cast away their cords from us."

We are seeing the rise of this "Esau spirit" around the world bringing terrorism, violence, murder, immorality, deception and a rejection of the Trinity, the deity of Jesus and the saving power of the Cross.

It all goes back to the Garden of Eden.

- **Eve, and women would suffer mixed consequences**

Genesis 3:15-16,

"I will put enmity Between you and the woman, and between your seed and her Seed; He shall bruise your head, and you shall bruise His heel." To the woman He said: "I will greatly multiply your sorrow and your conception; In pain you shall bring forth children; Your desire shall be for your husband, And he shall rule over you."

God had no plans to destroy Eve, but there were consequences to her actions. In *Genesis 3:15,* God spoke directly to Satan, but it also involved the woman. Despite her sin, Eve was a chosen vessel to be the instrument that would bring forth the Messiah, the Saviour of the world, who would destroy Satan. What amazing grace! What an honour for the woman. She would be the instrument to bring forth the Saviour, the Redeemer. However, she still had to face some painful consequences to her disobedience. Yes, she would bring forth the Saviour, but childbirth would be her painful reminder of the consequences of sin. Furthermore, she would live in desire to her husband and in submission to him.

In the New Testament we see the full restoration of Eve, representing all women. Yes, she is still called to live in submission to her husband, just as the Church is to live in submission to Christ. This is actually a glorious redemption as it speaks of the wife as in intimate reflection of the Bride of Christ.

Look how her husband treats her. It gives a new picture of submission. It is not the submission of a slave, or an employee, or a citizen to government. No! It is a glorious relationship where she is so valued that her husband loves her so much, he is willing to lay down his life for her. Ladies, if you find a man like that, don't let him go. He's precious, rare and expensive. Hang on to him as he is the best thing that can happen to you in your life other than finding Christ as your Saviour and Lord! He values you and does everything possible to make you the happiest, most blessed, and beautiful wife a man could ever have. It's a pure monogamous relationship, and a friendship and partnership that reflects our relationship with our Redeemer Saviour Jesus Christ.

Ephesians 5:22-27,

"Wives, submit to your own husbands, as to the Lord. For the husband is head of the wife, as also Christ is head of the church; and He is the Savior of the body. Therefore, just as the church is subject to Christ, so let the wives be to their own husbands in everything. Husbands, love your wives, just as Christ also loved the church and gave Himself for her, that He might sanctify and cleanse her with the washing of water by the word, **that He might present her to Himself a glorious church, not having spot or wrinkle or any such thing, but that she should be holy and without blemish**."

How great is God's love that He cares so much for the women. This is a huge dilemma for many Islamic woman. They do not know what it is to be a redeemed woman like we see in this passage. Woman – learn to live the life of a redeemed woman and your testimony could be the deciding factor that brings many from the "Ishmael" type women who want this sort of a redeemed relationship with their husbands.

Men! Make sure that you treat your wives like the Bride of Christ. Be true followers of Jesus in your relationship with your wife. As they enjoy their redemption in Christ, you too will gain the full redemption of being a true Christian husband.

I love the statement: "Happy wife. Happy life!"

Men, if you want your wife to be an angel, treat her like one!

- **Adam would have to bear the responsibility for sin**

The Bible never says "the sin of Eve" even though she was the first one to eat the forbidden fruit. The Bible refers to the original sin as the sin of Adam. Eve was not yet created when God gave the command to Adam not to eat of the forbidden fruit. When Eve was tempted by Satan, Adam was standing there and said nothing. He did not protect his wife. He did not reject Satan. He totally avoided his responsibility before God and to his wife.

Genesis 3:6,

"So when the woman saw that the tree was good for food, that it was pleasant to the eyes, and a tree desirable to make one wise, she took of its fruit and ate. She also gave to her husband with her, and he ate."

Adam was right there, and did nothing!

Adam was guilty. He disobeyed while Eve had been deceived.

Romans 5:12-19,

"Therefore, just as **through one man sin entered the world**, and death through sin, and thus death spread to all men, because all sinned— (For until the law sin was in the world, but sin is not imputed when there is no law. Nevertheless death reigned from Adam to Moses … by the one man's offense many died … judgment which came from one offense resulted in condemnation … by the one man's offense death reigned … through one man's offense judgment came to all men, resulting in condemnation, … by one man's disobedience many were made sinners."

Because of this terrible responsibility, Adam and Eve now had to be put out of the Garden of Eden. Eating the forbidden fruit robbed them of innocence and placed them in danger of never being able to be saved. Not only them, but all future humanity. What a burden to carry. One stupid act of disobedience can have horrific consequences.

If after eating of the fruit of the Tree of the Knowledge of Good and Evil, they were to eat of the Tree of Life, it would bring devastating eternal consequences. No-one would ever be able to be saved. There was only one thing that God could do. He had to banish them from the Garden of Eden. He had to deny them access to the Tree of Life, for if they ate of that fruit, their sin and damnation would have been eternalized for all future humanity. Salvation would never be possible.

Because God still loved them, and had plans for their eternal redemption and for all future humanity, He had to banish them from access to the Tree of Life and put them out of the Garden. Furthermore, God put guards around the Tree of Life so that they could not access it.

Genesis 3:22-24,

"Then the LORD God said, "Behold, the man has become like one of Us, to know good and evil. And now, lest he put out his hand and take also of the Tree of Life, and eat, and live forever"— therefore the LORD God sent him out of the garden of Eden to till the ground from which he was taken. So He drove out the man; and He placed cherubim at the east of the garden of Eden, and a flaming sword which turned every way, to guard the way to the Tree of Life."

Outside the Garden of Eden, Adam also had to bear the physical burden of finding food to live. The ground was cursed and would have thorns and thistles. It would be hard labour and lots of sweat - until we die.

Genesis 3:17-19,

"Cursed is the ground for your sake; In toil you shall eat of it all the days of your life. Both thorns and thistles it shall bring forth for you, and you shall eat the herb of the field. In the sweat of your face you shall eat bread till you return to the ground, for out of it you were taken; for dust you are, and to dust you shall return."

How many paths are there to Salvation?

Psalm 1:6 (NIV),

"For the LORD watches over the way of the righteous, but the way of the wicked leads to destruction."

Matthew 7:13-14,

"Enter by the narrow gate; for wide is the gate and broad is the way that leads to destruction, and there are many who go in by it. Because narrow is the gate and difficult is the way which leads to life, and there are few who find it."

John 14:6,

"Jesus said to him, "I am the Way, the Truth, and the Life. No one comes to the Father except through Me."

How many paths to salvation has God provided? Only ONE and His name is Jesus!

That's why we must follow Him. We need to walk in His footsteps.

We have Two choices - Salvation or Destruction?

The dilemma we face is making sure we are on the right path, the Straight Path, the Straight Way. The only way to solve this dilemma is to see that Jesus is the Straight Path. This is clear in the Al-Qur'an and in the Bible. Jesus is the only Way to enter Heaven. God calls us to choose – salvation or destruction, the curse or the blessing, everlasting death in the fires of hell or the everlasting life of love, joy, peace and glory in the presence of God in Heaven.

Deuteronomy 30:19,

"I call heaven and earth as witnesses today against you, that I have set before you life and death, blessing and cursing; therefore, **choose life,** that both you and your descendants may live."

Study and know this subject well and prepare your story on how to introduce the amazing story of the Straight Path. Muslims praying at their 5 compulsory prayer times, pray, "Lord show us the Straight Path!" 17 times a day. Ishmael is crying. Ishmael is looking for the way home to the Father, so share your story of the Straight Path with a friend! Share how Jesus saved you and transformed your life! Help them to solve the dilemma in taheir life as their eternal life is dependent on following Jesus the Messiah, the Redeemer, the Saviour.

Remember to tell your friends – CHOOSE LIFE – for themselves, their family and their friends. If people want to bless their family and secure for them eternity in Heaven, then choose life, choose Jesus "that both you and your descendants may live!"

Questions to consider or discuss:

1. How can I follow the Straight Path if I don't read the Gospel of Jesus?
2. How would you interpret *Matthew 3:1-3?*
3. Why did the lamb have to be kept for four days before being sacrificed at the Passover? *Exodus 12:3-6; 1Corinthians 5:7*

DILEMMA 9

THE WOMEN'S DILEMMA

The Place of Women in Islam and the Bible

What is the position of women in Islam? Can Muslims reconcile the position of women in Islamic societies with principles of equality, freedom and dignity? Women's freedom is very restricted in all nations that are ruled by Islamic Sharia laws today. Is this indicative of what the Qur'an really teaches?

The traditional role of women in Islam is based on the Qur'an, the examples of Muhammad's teachings and actions in the Hadith, histories and the early commentaries and traditions that go back to the period of the seventh to the eleventh centuries. Muslim woman live today in the shadows of the teachings of Allah, Muhammad, the Qur'an and Hadith, that formed over a thousand years ago.

While the religious and traditional Islamic position and role of women is strictly determined by the teachings of the Qur'an and Hadith, we do see many cultural variations throughout the Islamic world. The role of women varies from nation to nation, from tribe to tribe, from big cities to remote villages, based on how closely they conform to the written form of Islam.

Indicative of the variations is in the wearing of head coverings by women, the burka (burqa), the hijab and the niqab. The **burka** conceals the whole body including the face, and sometimes with a mesh over the eyes. The **hijab** covers the hair and neck but leaves the face visible. The **niqab** covers the face but leaves the eyes exposed. In some cultures other terms are also used like the jilbab, khimar and abaya.

In Yemen, where we spent time over several years, studying Arabic, almost all Yemeni women wore the full black burka. Most women only showed their eyes, but sometimes even had a mesh veil over their eyes. Yemen is a nation under strict Sharia law.

In Indonesia however, when we first arrived there in 1974, very few women wore a head scarf. The wearing of head scarves was banned in all government schools and offices. The situation changed quite remarkably after 11th September 2001. The destruction of the Twin Towers in New York by Muslim terrorists, changed the situation dramatically. Islam achieved a new prominence. Islam became an ideology to be proud of and to identify with. Since that time head scarves gradually appeared more and more on the streets and now they are worn everywhere, including in the government schools and by women officials in government offices.

During our travels, we also found the same change occurring in Egypt and in Turkey. Whereas the women in these countries rarely wore the head-scarf before the beginning of the twenty first century, today most Muslim women in these countries cover their heads, and some also cover their faces.

We have also read of the very major changes that took place in Iran after 1979 when the Shah was ousted and the Ayatollah came to power. As Islam was enforced by the mullahs, there a was dramatic change in women's costumes, and an enforcement of wearing the full burka.

How do Muslim leaders justify the treatment of women in Islamic societies?

The typical response of Islamic leaders is that in Islam, women are considered spiritually equal to men and are granted distinct rights regarding property, education, and marriage. They claim that women are ensured of dignity, honour, respect and autonomy under Islam. They tell us that Islam raised the status of women from pre-Islamic times by granting specific rights in education, property, marriage, and financial independence. They say that it is patriarchal traditions and cultural practices in some Muslim-majority countries that often restrict rights,

However, when we look at the reality, we easily see how women are treated in Islamic societies today.

How are women treated in Afghanistan?

"Since the Taliban's 2021 return, Afghan women live under severe, systemic restrictions described as "gender apartheid." They are forbidden from education beyond sixth grade, banned from most employment, and restricted from public spaces like parks and salons. Women must cover their faces and bodies, require male chaperones, and face public punishments like flogging." Afghanistan is the worst country in the world for women's rights.

How are women treated in Iran?

"Women in Iran face significant legal, social, and systemic discrimination, ranking low on global gender equality indices. Iranian law places heavy restrictions on women, including mandatory hijab laws, requiring male permission to travel or work, unequal rights in marriage, divorce, and child custody, and legal validation of child marriage."

How are women treated in Yemen?

"Yemen currently ranks as the lowest performing country in the Middle East and North African region and the second worst overall according to Georgetown Institute for Women, Peace and Security (GIWPS) 2025 Women, Peace and Security Index, which ranks 181 countries on 13 indicators of women's inclusion, justice, and security."

Islamic societies are patriarchal societies. A woman's chief role in life is her duty to her husband because that is what Muhammad said will determine Paradise or Hell for her.

Muhammad indicated that a woman's entrance to heaven or hell is dependent on her husband's pleasure. The Hadith state that Muhammad asked a woman, "Do you have a husband?" and when she told him she did, he said to her, "Look to how you are with respect to him, for he is your Heaven or Hell." *(Sunan an Nasai 3367 and Ahmad 3.156).*

A woman's righteousness is measured and determined by her kindness to her children and how she looks after her husband and his property. "Abu Huraira narrated The Prophet (saw) said, "The righteous among the women of Quraish are those who are kind to their young ones and who look after their husband's property." *(Sahih al-Bukhari (5365) and Sahih Muslim (2527).*

The ultimate guide to understanding the Islamic position and role of all Muslim women is based on the foundational teachings in the original sources. Teaching about women is highlighted in the fourth Surah in the Qur'an, called An-Nisa meaning "Women." Are the teachings of the Qur'an and the Hadith consistent with equality, freedom and dignity as women?

Muslim Claims

Muslims claim that Islam has lifted the status of women. Yet, as we look around the world, what do we see? Islam is the ideology in power in Saudi

Arabia, Yemen, Iran, Afghanistan, the Sudan, Algeria, Palestine and Egypt. In all these countries women are oppressed and suffering.

Dr. Jamal A. Badawi is a Muslim scholar and propagandist. In an article first printed in 1971, he claims that Islam and the Qur'an lifted women's status. He said: "The Holy Book affirms tht men and women are created from one soul to be partners to each other, that males and females have the same religious responsibilities, and that both genders will receive like rewards on the day of judgment." Yet, what does the Qur'an really say? Does Islam really teach that man and women are equal?

The Qur'an and the Equality of Women

Equality of works and reward

It is true that there are a number of verses that speak of common rewards for both male and female. They both can do good and receive rewards.

Surah An-Nahl 16:97,

"Whoever does good, whether male or female, and is a believer, We shall certainly make him live a good life, and We shall certainly give them their reward for the best of what they did."

Surah Ali-Imran 3:195,

"I will not suffer the work of any worker among you to be lost whether male or female, the one of you being from the other."

However, there are two key verses in the Qur'an that state that the man and the woman are not equal.

One states that men have been created by God as "superior" to the woman or as other translations say, God has "preferred" or "made to excel" ("*faddala*") the one over the other."

Surah An Nisa 4:34,

"Men have authority over women because God has made the one superior (the Arabic word "*faddala*" means preferred) to the other."

The other verse states that men are "a degree" or a "rank" or "status" (Arabic – "*darajah*") above women.

Surah Al Baqarah 2:228,

"And they (women) have rights similar to those (of men) over them in kindness, and men are a degree (*darajah*) above them. Allah is Mighty, Wise."

Thus, it is a clear teaching in the Qur'an by Allah that men and women are not on the same level. Men were created by God to be over and above women. The evidence is all around us. This is particularly so in the Sharia-based areas like Saudi Arabia, Iran, Gaza, Yemen etc.

From birth to death, the Saudi Muslim woman is under the control of a man. Every Saudi woman must have a male guardian, normally a father or husband, but in some cases a brother or even a son, who has the power to make a range of critical decisions on her behalf. Until 2017, when laws began to be changed, a Saudi woman was not permitted to drive a car. She was not permitted to leave the house without the permission of her husband. She was not allowed to travel anywhere without a responsible male relative with her. Every woman had to have a man who had authority over her. Adult women were legal minors who could not make key decisions for themselves. This is the traditional place of women in Islamic societies. This is clearly based on what the Qur'an and the Hadith teach.

The creation of woman: Crooked

Muslims often say that the Qur'an teaches man and women were created equally from one soul and therefore were created equal. In the creation account of the Qur'an, woman was created from Adam.

Surah An-Nisa 4:1,

"O mankind, fear your Lord, who created you from one soul and created from it its mate."

Adam was the "one soul" that was created by God. Woman was "its mate" that was created from the man. The Qur'an tells us the name of the first man, Adam, but never mentions the name of the woman. God tells them to descend to earth as enemies to one another.

Al-Araf 7:19-27,

"Allah said, "Descend as enemies to each other. You will find in the earth a residence and provision for your appointed stay."

In the Hadith accounts, woman was created from a crooked rib. "Narrated Abu Huraira: Allah's Apostle said, "The woman is like a rib; if you try to straighten her, she will break. So, if you want to get benefit from her, do so while she still has some crookedness." (*Sahih Bukhari 7:62:113.)*

Moreover, woman was not only created by God from a crooked rib, but a woman also cannot be straightened and remains forever crooked.

Sahih Muslim 8:3466-3468,

"When you attempt to straighten it, you would break it. And if you leave her alone you would benefit by her, and crookedness will remain in her. Woman has been created from a rib and will in no way be straightened for you; so, if you wish to benefit by her, benefit by her while crookedness remains in her. And if you attempt to straighten her, you will break her, and breaking her is divorcing her. Allah's Apostle said: He who believes in Allah and the Hereafter, if he witnesses any matter he should talk in good terms about it or keep quiet. Act kindly towards woman, for woman is created from a rib, and the most crooked part of the rib is its top. If you attempt to straighten it, you will break it, and if you leave it, its crookedness will remain there. So, act kindly towards women."

Muslim men therefore must be kind towards the woman because she will inevitably have some crookedness or shortcomings in her character.

The character of women: Stupid

Although many Islamic websites say that in Islam both the man and woman sinned and Eve is not blamed, it is clear from the Hadith that Muhammad did blame Eve for sin.

Eve is blamed for women betraying their husbands.

Sahih Bukhari 4:55:547,

"The Prophet said, "But for the Israelis, meat would not decay and but for Eve, wives would never betray their husbands."

Eve is blamed for menstruation, foolishness of women and difficulty in childbirth.

At-Tabari I:529,

"Were it not for the calamity that afflicted Eve (*Hawa*), the women of this world would not menstruate, would be wise, and would bear their children with ease."

Allah also claimed to have made Eve stupid after she ate the fruit from the tree.

At-Tabari I:280,

"Allah said, 'It is My obligation to make Eve bleed once every month as she made this tree bleed. I must also make Eve stupid, although I created her intelligent.'"

Because Allah afflicted Eve, all of the women of this world menstruate and are stupid.

The Role of Women in Religion: Unclean

The role of women in Islamic religion is relegated to the home. That is normally where they do their daily prayers. Although they are permitted at times to go to the mosque, they have no role there. They must pray in rows behind the men or pray in a separate area. Sometimes, as in Yemen, they have separate mosques for women.

The women in Islam cannot participate in prayers or enter a mosque if she is menstruating. However, she is not only unclean when she is menstruating, she is so unclean that even touching her can pollute a man. Having her pass close in front of a man while praying, can nullify his prayers. The Qur'an teaches that menstruation makes a woman unclean.

Surah Al-Baqarah 2:222,

"They ask thee concerning women's courses. Say: They are a hurt and a pollution: So, keep away from women in their courses, and do not approach them until they are clean."

Contact with women makes a man unclean. This is the reason why many Muslim men will not shake hands with a woman. When we were studying at an Islamic language college in Yemen, at the graduation ceremony, the principal shook the hands of all our team, except for the hands of the women. Doing that would have made him unclean.

Surah An-Nisa 4:43,

"Muslims, draw not near unto prayer…(if) ye have touched women… then go to high clean soil and rub your face and your hands."

Surah Al-Maidah 5:6,

"If ye have had contact with women, and ye find not water, then go to clean, high ground and rub your faces and your hands with some of it."

Our principal in Yemen was following the command and the example of the prophet Muhammad.

Sahih Al-Bukhari 7214,

"And the hand of Allah's Messenger did not touch any woman's hand except the hand of that woman his right hand possessed. (that is, his captives or his lady slaves)."

Also, there is a Hadith from Ma'qil ibn Yasar, saying; "The Prophet (Peace and blessings be upon him) said, "It is better for you to be stabbed in the head with an iron needle than to touch the hand of a woman who is not permissible to you."

Sunan Abî Dâwûd 232, Sunan Ibn Mâjah 644,

Women are not allowed into the mosque when menstruating. In the Hadith, "Âishah relates that the Prophet said: "I do not permit a woman in her menses or a person in a state of major ritual impurity into the mosque."

Sahih al-Bukhari 351,

"Menstruating women were told to stay away from the actual place of prayer."

Islam teaches that a woman in a state of menstruation cannot touch the copy of the Qur'an. Allah says about the Qur'an:

Surah Al-Waqi'ah 56:79,

"Only the clean ones touch it."

The Hadith also reinforce the command that menstruating women cannot recite the Qur'an.

Al-Tirmidhi (131), Ibn Majah (595),

"The menstruating woman and the one who is in a state of major ritual impurity *(janabah)* should not recite anything of the Qur'an."

This has recently caused problems in an Australian Islamic school. In February 2026, it was reported that girls have to be excused from praying the Islamic prayers during their periods. They have had to report when they were having their periods and were sent to period rooms or "rag rooms" while the other students were doing their ritual prayers.

https://www.news.com.au/lifestyle/parenting/school-life/serious-breach-of-human-rights-experts-condemn-islamic-schools-tracking-girls-periods/news-story/0bc27dbf62c4b86b70d378fdc2cd0dd5

Women are likened to animals

Because of the uncleanness of women, the woman defiles a man's prayer just like a dog, an ass or a pig.

Abu Dawud 2:704,

"The Apostle of Allah said: When one of you prays without a sutrah, a dog, an ass, a pig, a Jew, a Magian, and a woman cut off his prayer, but it will suffice if they pass in front of him at a distance of over a stone's throw."

Aisha, the young wife of Muhammad complained to him that God had reduced her to the status of a dog or an ass.

Sahih Muslim: Book 4: Hadith 1039,

"Al-Aswad reported that 'A'isha said: You have made us equal to the dogs and the asses, whereas I lay on the bedstead and the Messenger of Allah came there and stood in the middle of the bedstead and said prayer. I did not like to take off the quilt from me (in that state), so I moved away quietly from the front legs of the bedstead and thus came out of the quilt."

Sahih Al-Bukhari 1: 9: Hadith 490, 493, 511,

Narrated 'Aisha: "The things which annul the prayers were mentioned before me. They said, "Prayer is annulled by a dog, a donkey and a woman (if they pass in front of the praying people)." I said, "You have made us (i.e. women) dogs. I saw the Prophet praying while I used to lie in my bed between him and the Qibla. Whenever I was in need of something, I would slip away. for I disliked to face him."

Sahih Al-Bukhari: Hadith 498,

"Narrated 'Aisha: It is not good that you people have made us (women) equal to dogs and donkeys. No doubt I saw Allah's Apostle praying while I used to lie between him and the Qibla and when he wanted to prostrate, he pushed my legs and I withdrew them."

Women are also likened to camels.

Sunan Abu Dawud Book 11, Number 2155,

"Narrated Abdullah ibn Amr ibn al-'As: The Prophet said: If one of you marries a woman or buys a slave, he should say: "O Allah, I ask Thee for the good in her, and in the disposition Thou hast given her; I take refuge in Thee from the evil in her, and in the disposition Thou hast given her." When he buys a camel, he should take hold of the top of its hump and say the same kind of thing."

Women are an evil omen

Sahih Al-Bukhari, 7.62.30, 31; 4.52.110, 111. Sahih Muslim 36.6603. 6604,

"I heard the Prophet saying. 'Evil omen is in three things: The horse, the woman and the house."

The Hadiths call on men to fear the company of women as they bring bad luck.

Compare the attitude of Jesus to women

A woman touched Him and made Him unclean according to the law, *Leviticus 15:19.* Jesus turned around and said, "Who touched me?" He then did not condemn her but instead praised her for her faith, *Luke 8:43-48.*

In Islam Women are Irreligious and Half Witted

Women are also irreligious and stupid, according to Muhammad.

Sahih Al-Bukhari, 6:304; Sahih Muslim 1:6:301,

"Oh ye women I have yet to find anyone swifter to the heart of a resolute man than one of you half-witted and irreligious lot! They asked: 'How are we irreligious and half-witted, oh Apostle of God' He replied: Isn't the testimony of the woman equal to half that of the man? They said: 'Yes.' He countered: That is due to her inferior mind; adding isn't it true that during her period she neither prays nor fasts? They said: 'True' Then he said: That is due to her lack of religion!"

Note how different the reaction of Jesus was to women. He commended the Canaanite woman for her faith, even though she was a foreigner, *Matthew 15:21–28.* He praised the woman with the issue of blood who touched the hem of His garment, even though she was ritually impure and technically defiled Him by her touch, *Matthew 9:22.* He forgave the many sins of the sinful woman, who washed his feet with tears, *Luke 7:36–50.* When in Bethany, the woman anointed His feet with oil, Jesus declared that her deed would be declared as a memorial, wherever the Gospel was preached, *Mark 14:3-9.*

The Position of the Woman under Islamic Law

Inheritance rights

Women's rights in inheritance are half that of a man's rights.

Surah An-Nisa 4:11,

"God charges you, concerning your children: To the male the like portion of two females and if they be women above two, then for them two-thirds of what the deceased leaves. But if she be one, she shall have one-half thereof."

Islamic law, the Sharia, is based on the Qur'an and the Hadith and enforces the inheritance rights of women as being half that of the male.

Testimony in courts of law

The woman's testimony is only half the value of that of a man. The Qur'an states that one man's witness is equal to the witness of two women.

Surah Al-Baqarah 2:282,

"And let two men from among you bear witness to all such documents [contracts of loans without interest]. But if two men be not available, there should be one man and two women to bear witness so that if one of the women forgets (anything), the other may remind her."

The Hadith confirm this.

Sahih Al-Bukhari 3:48:826,

"The Prophet said, "Isn't the witness of a woman equal to half of that of a man?" The women said, "Yes." He said, "This is because of the deficiency of a woman's mind."

Role as Leaders

Women are not permitted roles as leaders in society under Islam. Although there are a few Islamic nations that have been led by Muslim women, for example in Pakistan and Indonesia. This is despite Islam, not because of it. There have been no Islamic women leaders in the Middle East. This is because of the words of Muhammad in the Hadith.

Sahih Al-Bukhari 7099,

"The Prophet said, "A people that choose a woman as their leader will not succeed."

The Qur'an also discourages women from being leaders in the society and the nation and recommends that women stay in their homes.

Surah Al-Ahzab 33:33

"And stay in your houses, and do not display yourselves like that of the times of ignorance."

Prophethood and kingship are usually confined to men in Islam because as the Qur'an states, Allah says: "But men have a degree over them," *Surah Al-Baqarah 2:228*. The word "degree" indicates position.

Also, the Qur'an says men are protectors, of women, *Surah An-Nisa 4:34*). As such men have a special responsibility over women. Many classical scholars interpret "protectors" (Arabic, *qawwamun*) as "leaders," "guardians" or "those in authority", meaning that men are not just leaders in the family, but also in social and political positions.

Rights as Prisoners of War captured by the Islamic forces

During a war, any women captured belong to the Muslim fighters. In Muhammad's day they were divided up among his army and that practice continues until today. Woman are considered booty that become the property of the jihadis. Muhammad set the example and took women who were captured as his wives and his concubines. Sometimes after use he would then give them to his soldiers to enjoy.

Surah An-Nisa 4:24,

"And forbidden to you are wedded wives of other people except those who have fallen in your hands [as prisoners of war]."

Sexual slavery and rape are sanctioned in the Qur'an where female captives aren't even referred to as "people" but as "possessions" of Muslim males. Slaves are referred to as "those whom your right hand possesses."

Surah Al-Muminuun 23:5-7,

"Who abstain from sex, except with those joined to them in the marriage bond, or (the captives) whom their right hands possess,- for (in their case) they are free from blame."

The right of Islamic Jihadists to rape captive women right in front of their vanquished husbands is established in both the Qur'an and the Hadith.

Sunaan Abu Dawud 8.77.598,

"Abu Sa'id al-Khudri (Allah her pleased with him) reported that at the Battle of Hanain Allah's Messenger sent an army to Autas and encountered the enemy and fought with them. Having overcome them and taken them captives, the Companions of Allah's Messenger seemed to refrain from having intercourse with captive women because of their husbands being polytheists. Then Allah, Most High, sent down regarding that: "And women already married, except those whom your right hands possess, *Surah An-Nisa 24*)" (i.e. they were lawful for them when their 'Idda period came to an end)."

Muhammad set the example by taking a women captive and sleeping with her on the same night that he and his army had killed their husbands.

Sahih Bukhari 8:12:372,

"We conquered Khaibar, took the captives, and the booty was collected. Dihya came and said, 'O Allah's Prophet! Give me a slave girl from the captives.' The Prophet said, "Go and take any slave girl." He took Safiya bint Huyai. A man came to the Prophet and said, "O Allah's Messengers! You gave Safiya bint Huyai to Dihya and she is the chief mistress of the tribes of Quraidha and An-Nadir and she befits none but you." So the Prophet said, "Bring him along with her." So Dihya came with her and when the Prophet saw her, he said to Dihya, "Take any slave girl other than her from the captives." Anas added: The Prophet then manumitted (released from slavery) her and married her." Thabit asked Anas, "O Abu Hamza! What did the Prophet pay her (as Mahr = mandatory gift)?" He said, "Herself was her Mahr for he manumitted her and then married her." Anas added, "While on the way, Um Sulaim dressed her for marriage (ceremony) and at night she sent her as a bride to the Prophet. So the Prophet was a bridegroom and he said, 'Whoever has anything (food) should bring it.' He spread out a leather sheet (for the food) and some brought dates and others cooking butter. (I think he (Anas) mentioned As-Sawaq). So they prepared a dish of Hais (a kind of meal). And that was Walima (the marriage banquet) of Allah's Messenger."

In Indonesia during the jihad wars in North Maluku, Adel, a married Christian woman was captured by the jihadists. She was given as booty to the jihadi who killed her mother, mother-in-law and six-year-old son. After giving birth to a little girl, eventually, after about 18 months captivity, she was able to escape and return to her own husband. She is a friend of ours and lived with us until the jihad discovered her whereabouts and we had to escape to the Philippines. The practice Muhammad taught, continues till today. Part of Adel's story can be read and viewed online in the Youtube video, *Island Jihad.*

Escaping Radical Islam: A Story of Martyrdom and Survival
https://www.youtube.com/watch?v=QiBioSN6mYI /methu062405.aspx

Rights of Women as Wives

The Qur'an teaches that women are created as mates for the men and that women must be created kindly. However, there are many limitations that are put on women as wives.

The Qur'an does say that women were created in pairs, with mates.

Surah An-Naba 78:9,

"And We created you in pairs."

Surah Al-Araf 7:189,

"He (God) it is who did create you from a single soul and therefrom did create his mate, that he might dwell with her."

Surah An-Nahl 16:72.

"And Allah has given you mates of your own nature, and has given you from your mates, children and grandchildren, and has made provision of good things for you. Is it then in vanity that they believe and in the grace of God that they disbelieve?"

Surah Ash-Shura 42:11,

"The Creator of heavens and earth: He has made for you pairs from among yourselves."

Surah Adz-Dzariyaat 51:49.

"Allah has created every living being in pairs, male and female."

The Qur'an also says that there should be love and compassion between the husband and wife. This is a positive message from the Qur'an. The concept of being "a mate" is also linked to the creation of all animals, and implies a relationship that links the male and female in reproduction.

Husbands to be kind

The Qur'an also includes a verse exhorting men to be kind to their wives.

Surah An-Nisa 4:19,

"Dwell with your wives in kindness for even if you hate them, you might be hating someone in whom God has placed so much good."

Another verse says that God puts love and compassion between husbands and wives.

Surah Ar-Rum 30:21,

"And one of His signs is that He created mates for you from yourselves that you may find rest in them, and He put between you love and compassion; most surely there are signs in this for a people who reflect."

Husbands must be Muslims

Muslim women are only permitted to marry Muslim men. They are forbidden to marry men of any other religion. Originally all Muslims could only marry Muslims. Later on Allah permitted Muslim men to also marry women from the People of the Book, Christians and Jews.

Muslim women can marry only one man. Muslim men can marry four wives at one time, plus have as many slaves or concubines as he wishes. King Saud (1902-1953) of Saudi Arabia had 25-30 wives and many concubines. He had 108 children. He was reported to be a good Muslim who only ever had four wives at a time, divorcing many times to keep the Islamic rules.

Duties of women as wives

Islam claims the woman has the right to kind and proper treatment, marital relations, not to be beaten, privacy, justice between multiple wives, to be taught her religion and defense of her honour.

Wives are like Fields to be Harvested

Al Baqarah 2:223.

"Your women are your fields, so go into your fields whichever way you like."

Wives are like Garments

Surah Al-Baqarah 2:187.

"They (your wives) are your garment and you are a garment for them."

Wives must be Obedient

Surah An-Nisa 4:34

"Righteous women are devoutly obedient."

Duties of wives

According to Islamic teaching, a wife's duties are to be fulfilled in the home. Below is a list of duties from different Islamic Hadiths and traditions.

- *To welcome her husband:* "The Holy Prophet stated: 'The duty of a woman is to answer the call at the door and welcome her husband'".
- *To wash his hands:* "The Holy Prophet stated: 'A wife is duty-bound to arrange for a basin and towel to wash her husband's hands'." From a Shiite Hadith collected by *Mustadrak Al-Wasa'il* who died in 1320.

- To take care of him well: "Imam Ali (a.s) stated: 'The Jihad of a woman is to take care of her husband well'." ***Bihar al-Anwar, vol 103, p 254.***
- To do her duty: The Holy Prophet also stated: "If a woman does not perform her duty as a spouse, she has not done her duty to Allah'." ***Mustadrak, vol 2, p 552.***
- To satisfy him: The prophet of Allah said: "When a man calls his wife to satisfy his desire, let her come to him though she is occupied at the oven." (*Mishkat al-Masabih Book I, Section 'Duties of husband and wife', Hadith No. 61.)*
- To sleep with him, whenever he wishes: Narrated Abu Huraira: The Prophet said, "If a man invites his wife to sleep with him and she refuses to come to him, then the angels send their curses on her till morning," *Sahih Bukhari 7:62:121 Also Sahih Muslim 8:3366.*
- To not allow anyone into the house that her husband dislikes." "And beware of Allah concerning women. You have taken them as a trust from Allah and have made their bodies lawful to you by the word of Allah. You have the right upon them that they not allow anyone in your house that you dislike. If they do that, you may hit them in a way which does no harm. They have a right over you for sustenance and clothing according to what is right."

  Mu'awiyah asked: "Messenger of Allah, what is the right of the wife of one of us over him? He replied: That you should give her food when you eat, clothe her when you clothe yourself, do not strike her on the face, do not revile her or separate yourself from her except in the house," *Sunan Abi Dawud 2142.*
- To not perform fasts without permission of her husband, as it can violate his rights.

Sahih Bukhari 519

"Allah's Messenger said, "It is not lawful for a lady to fast (nawafil = optional prayers) without the permission of her husband when he is at home; and she should not allow anyone to enter his house except with his permission; and if she spends of his wealth (on charitable purposes) without being ordered by him, he will get half of the reward."

A woman should not go out without her husband's permission. Another Hadith says: The woman believer in Allah is not allowed to leave the house against the wishes of her husband." The Qur'an advises women to stay in their houses, *Surah Al-Ahzab 33:33*. In Yemen, women are not allowed out of their houses without their husband's permission. Only rarely did we see women in restaurants, which were usually packed with men, and even if they were there, it was in a special room with their husband and children.

- The wife is to preserve and protect her husband's property in his absence. She is not allowed to give something if she knows that her husband would be against it. It was narrated from Abu Hurayrah that the Messenger of Allah was asked: "What is the best wife?" He replied, the one who pleases him when he looks at her, obeys him when he tells something to her and is not contrary to her husband if he does not like that – that in herself or in how she spends his property.
- ***Sahih al-Bukhari (Volume 3, Book 46, Hadith 730 and Sahih Muslim 1829***. A woman should do housework, washing, cleaning the house. The Prophet says: "A woman is responsible for her husband's home, and she will be asked about it."

Women have the right keep their dowry

Surah An-Nisa 4:4,

"And give women their dowries as a gift. Then, if they are pleased to give some of it to you, consume it with good health and enjoyment."

Women have the right to be fed and clothed

Ahmad, Abu Dawud and Ibn Majah transmitted it. (Mishkat Al-Masabih: vol. 2, p. 691) "Hakim b. Mu`awiya al-Qushairi quoted his father as telling that he asked, "Messenger of God, what right can any wife demand of her husband?" He replied, "That you should give her food to eat, clothe her when you clothe yourself, not strike her on the face, and do not revile her or separate from her except in the house."

'A few beatings won't kill you': judge rejects divorce request of woman abused by husband in Afghanistan | Afghanistan | The Guardian

The Submission of Women

Who are the Best Women?

According to the Hadith, "The Prophet said: "The best among women are the ones who pleases you when you look at her, obeys you when you give her an order and guards herself and your wealth during your absence." Then the Prophet recited: "Men are the protectors and maintainers of women."

At-Tirmidhi 1159,

"The Hadith further explains what a good woman is responsible to do: "Ibn Abbas narrated that he said, [Men] are commanders and [the woman] has to obey him in all that God commands her to obey him. Obedience to man is being good to his family." The prophet said, "Had it been permissible that a person may prostrate himself before another I would have ordered that a wife should prostrate herself before her husband."

At-Tirmidhi 3255,

"The Prophet Muhammad: "But if I had to command, that one man leaned over the other in prostration, then I would, of course, ordered the woman to bow down in front of her husband."

Rights of Husbands

The husband also has rights over his wife.

Ibn Ishaq's "Sirat Rasulallah", Guillaume's translation [11], page 651.

"You have rights over your wives, and they have rights over you. You have the right that they should not defile your bed and that they should not behave with open unseemliness. If they do, God allows you to put them in separate rooms and to beat them, but not with severity. If they refrain from these things and obey you, they have right to their food and clothing with kindness. Lay injunctions on women kindly, for they are your wards having no control of their persons."

The husband has the following rights according to Islam:

- Being head of the household
- To be obeyed in all that is not disobedience to Allah
- Marital relations
- That she not allow anyone into the house of whom he disapproves
- That she not leave the house without his permission
- That she cook for him and keep his house
- To be thanked for his efforts

Sunan Ibn Majah 1851 (Book 9, Hadith 1851,

"If they do that [commit clear obscenity/*nushuz*], then forsake them in their beds and hit them, but without causing injury or leaving a mark."

Sahih al-Bukhari 5193,

"If a wife refuses to respond to her husband's request for intercourse, she has done something forbidden (Arabic, *haram)* and has committed a major sin, unless she has a valid Sharia excuse such as menses, obligatory fasting or sickness."

Marriage as a Contract or Covenant?

Surah An-Nisa 4:21.

"How could you take it once you have entered unto one another and they (the women) have taken from you an awesome covenant."

Bukhari 62:81,

"Narrated 'Uqba: The Prophet said: "The stipulations most entitled to be abided by are those with which you are given the right to enjoy the (women's) private parts (i.e. the stipulations of the marriage contract)."

Compare the Bible concept of the marriage covenant. It began in the Garden and was confirmed by Jesus and by Paul. Malachi talks of "your wife by covenant," *Malachi 2:14.* The Islamic marriage is a contract, confirmed by a payment of the dowry and with the option of divorce on any grounds. The Christian marriage is based on the relationship of Christ and the Church. The husband is called to love his wife as he loves himself and to lay down his life for her. The wife is called to honour her husband and submit to him as her head. The concept of marriage is that of one body, a unity where two people with different roles walk together as one, *Ephesians 5:22-33.* This concept does not exist in the Qur'an or the teaching of Muhammad.

Equal Divorce?

Divorce is simple for the man and permitted for any reason. He simply has to say, "I divorce thee" three times even without her knowing, and the divorce is valid. Multiple marriages and divorces are permitted, even between the same couple. If however, the same couple have been divorced and wish to remarry again, the wife must first consummate a marriage with another man, before she will be allowed to return to the first husband.

Surah Al Baqarah 2:230,

"And if the husband divorces his wife (for the third time), she shall not remain his lawful wife after this (absolute) divorce, unless she marries another husband and the second husband divorces her. [In that case] there is no harm if they [the first couple] remarry."

'Sunan at-Tirmidhi, Hadith 360,

Women are considered in Islam to be somewhere in between a slave and a free person. The Hadiths record: "The Messenger of Allah said: "The prayer of two people hardly rise above their heads, it is a runaway slave and a disobedient wife."

Sunan al-Tirmidhi, Hadith 1174,

"The Holy Prophet also stated: 'The women of Paradise (houris) say to those women who abuse their husbands in this way: 'May Allah kill you. Do not misbehave with your husband. This man (the husband) is not yours, and you do not deserve him. Soon he will leave you and come towards us'."

Sunan Ibn Mājah 971 and Jami` at-Tirmidhi 360,

"The Prophet of Islam stated: 'The prayers of a woman who teases her husband with her tongue, are not accepted (by Allah) even though she fasts every day, gets up for the acts of worship every night, sets free a few slaves and donates her wealth in the way of Allah. A bad-tongue woman who hurts her husband in this way, is the first person who enters hell'."

Wasa 'il al Shiah, vol 14, p 3,

"The Prophet of Allah stated: 'Whoever chooses to follow my tradition must get married and produce offspring through marriage (and increase the population of Muslims) so that on the day of resurrection I shall confront other Ummah (nations) with the (great) numbers of my Ummah'.'"

Sunan Abī Dāwūd (1050),

"Marry the loving and fertile, for I will boast of your great numbers before the other nations."

For a discussion of rights of divorce in Australia, see *https://www.abc.net.au/news/2018-04-18/abused-muslim-women-denied-right-to-divorce/9632772*

Polygamous Marriages

Polygamy is an option. A Muslim man can have four wives at one time. The Qur'an does state that a man must be able to support the wives he takes.

Surah An-Nisa 4:2,

"If you fear that you will not act justly towards the orphans, marry such women as seem good to you, two, three, four; but if you fear you will not be equitable, then only one, or what your right hands own; so it is likelier you will not be partial."

There was only one man who was exempt from the four wives' rule. It was Muhammad. Muhammad as a prophet, was given a special exemption from the laws for normal men. He was given specific permission to marry as many as he wished and whatever women wanted to be his wives. He took between 11 to 13 wives, plus slave girls and concubines. When he died he left behind 9 wives.

A list of his wives includes Khadijah, Sawdah, Aisha, Hafsah, Zaynab bint Khuzayma, Umm Salamah, Zaynab bint Jahsh, Juwayriyah, Umm Habibah, Safiyyah, and Maymunah. His concubines who were captured in war, included, Maria al-Qibtiyya (mother of his son Ibrahim) Rayhana bint Zayd, a "beautiful slave woman", and a slave woman given to him by Zaynab bint Jahsh.

Surah Al-Azhab 33:50,

"O Prophet! We have made lawful to thee thy wives to whom thou hast paid their dowers; and those whom thy right hand possesses out of the prisoners of war whom Allah has assigned to thee; and daughters of thy paternal uncles and aunts, and daughters of thy maternal uncles and aunts, who migrated (from Makka) with thee; and any believing woman who dedicates her soul to the Prophet if the Prophet wishes to wed her;- this only for thee, and not for the Believers (at large); We know what We have appointed for them as to their wives and the captives whom their right hands possess;- in order that there should be no difficulty for thee. And Allah is Oft-Forgiving, Most Merciful."

Muhammad also received special permission to marry his adopted son's wife. This story is told in *Surah Al-Ahzab.* Muhammad had an adopted son, Zaid. One day he saw her and his heart desired her. God then rebuked Muhammad for hiding his feelings because he was afraid of what people might think. God commanded Muhammad to marry her. It was to show that adopted sons are not considered biological sons and to establish a legal precedent, ending a cultural taboo on men marrying their adopted son's wives.

Surah Al-Ahzab 33:37,

"And when you said to him to whom Allah had shown favor and to whom you had shown a favor: Keep your wife to yourself and be careful of (your duty to) Allah; and you concealed in your soul what Allah would bring to light, and you feared men, and Allah had a greater right that you should fear Him. But when Zaid had accomplished his want of her, We gave her to you as a wife, so that there should be no difficulty for the believers in respect of the wives of their adopted sons, when they have accomplished their want of them; and Allah's command shall be performed."

Temporary Marriages - Mut'ah

The husband also has the right to engage in extra sexual activity (some call it "Islamic prostitution") through temporary (*Mut'ah)* marriage. On a journey, a man may take a temporary wife for a fixed time and a fixed fee. At the expiry of the set time period, the temporary wife is automatically divorced. He can conduct this "marriage" without the knowledge or consent of his wife or wives. *An Nisa 4:24; Sahih Bukhari – 8.3246, 3247, 3248. Sahih Muslim – 8:3252, 8:3253, 8:3258.*

Although Sunni Muslims claim that this type of marriage was abrogated or revoked, Shia Muslims continue to regard it as a legitimate part of Islam and Sharia and continue to practice it today, as in fact do many Sunni Muslims.

One of our Yemeni teachers came and spent two months with us in Jakarta and teaching Arabic in our church. He was surprised how little Arabic the local Muslim mosque leaders knew. He was also very surprised and rather shocked when he was offered a temporary wife by the local imams when we visited the city of Surabaya. Our teacher had only one wife and seemed to love and respect her. He was one of the Muslims who took the advice of Muhammad to dwell with one's wife with kindness. Hopefully there are many such Muslims. After many discussions and attending church with us, he eventually confessed having faith in Jesus and loving Him.

Equal Penalties for sexual immorality?

Surah An Nisa 4:15,

"If any of your women are guilty of lewdness, Take the evidence of four (Reliable) witnesses from amongst you against them; and if they testify, confine them to houses until death do claim them, or Allah ordain for them some (other) way."

Some say this means starve them to death. Furthermore, the term "lewdness" can be and has been construed throughout Islamic history to mean many things, even to walk out the front door of one's home without permission.

Compare this to the punishment for the same act for men.

Surah An-Nisa 4:16,

"If two men among you are guilty of lewdness, punish them both. If they repent and amend, Leave them alone; for Allah is Oft-returning, Most Merciful."

These verses were both abrogated, that is, changed for a better verses which calls for both parties to be beaten.

Surah An-Nur 24:2

"The fornicatress and the fornicator, [then] flog each one of them (with) hundred lash(es). And (let) not withhold you for them pity concerning (the) religion (of) Allah if you believe in Allah and the Day the Last. And let witness their punishment a group of the believers."

Beating of Wives

Allah states in the Qur'an that if a man fears that his wife will be disobedient, he has a right to beat her. The Arabic word used is *daraba* which means "to beat." It does not say lightly!

Surah An-Nisa 4:34,

"If you fear highhandedness (other translations – ill-will, disloyalty ill-conduct) from your wives, remind them [of the teaching of God], then ignore them when you go to bed, then hit (*daraba*) them. If they obey you, you have no right to act against them. God is most high and great."

Muhammad gave permission to men to beat their wives, even if it was only because they fear ill conduct from them.

Abu Dawud 11:2141,

This right of a man to beat his wife is confirmed by the teaching and examples of the Hadith. "Iyas b. Abdullah reported God's messenger as saying, "Do not beat God's handmaidens;" but when Umar came to God's messenger and said, "The women have become emboldened towards their husbands," he gave license to beat them. Then many women went round God's messenger's family complaining of their husbands, and he said, "Many women have gone around complaining of their husbands. Those are not the best among you."

Al-Tirmidhi Hadith:104,

"Narrated Amr ibn al-Ahwas al-Jushami: Amr heard the Prophet say in his farewell address on the eve of his Last Pilgrimage, after he had glorified and praised Allah, he cautioned his followers: "Listen! Treat women kindly; they are like prisoners in your hands. Beyond this you do not owe anything from them. Should they be guilty of flagrant misbehaviour, you may remove them from your beds, and beat them but do not inflict upon them any severe punishment."

According to Muhammad a wife can be beaten without any need to justify it to anybody else.

Abu Dawud 11:2142,

"Narrated Umar ibn al-Khattab: The Prophet said: "A man will not be asked as to why he beat his wife."

However, a woman shouldn't be disfigured or beaten excessively.

Sahih Bukari 7.62.77,

"Avoid disfiguring her or beating her excessively or abandoning her except at home."

And a woman shouldn't be beaten and then slept with on the same day.

Sahih Bukhari 7:62:132,

"Narrated 'Abdullah bin Zam'a: The Prophet said, "None of you should flog his wife as he flogs a slave and then have sexual intercourse with her in the last part of the day."

There are also examples in the Hadith of men beating their wives.

Razi's 'At-Tafsir al-Kabir' on 4:34. Razi is one of the greatest Muslim scholars.

"A woman complained to Muhammad that her husband slapped her on the face, (which was still marked by the slap). At first the prophet said to her: "Get even with him" but then added: "Wait until I think about it." Later on, Allah supposedly revealed *Surah 4:34* to Muhammad, after which the prophet said: "We wanted one thing but Allah wanted another, and what Allah wanted is best." (i.e. To beat your wife is best.)

Hadith from *Sahih Bukhari Book 8, vol. 7, no 715*, supports the case for beating wives:

"Narrated Ikrima: 'Rifaa divorced his wife whereupon Abdur-Rahman married her. Aisha said that the lady came wearing a green veil and complained to her (Aisha) and showed her a green spot on her skin caused by beating. It was the habit of ladies to support each other, so when Allah's messenger came, Aisha said, "I have not seen any woman suffering as much as the believing women. Look! Her skin is greener than her clothes!" Muhammad's companion also beat his wives and other women. "(Umar) found the Prophet sitting sad and silent with his wives around him. ... (Umar) decided to say something which would make the Prophet laugh, so he said, "Messenger of God, I wish you had seen the daughter of Kharija when she asked me for extra money and I got up and slapped her on the neck." God's messenger laughed and said, "They are around me as you see asking for extra money." Abu Bakr then got up, went to A'isha and slapped her on the neck, and Umar did the same to Hafsa." ***Mishkat Al-Masabih: vol. 2, p. 690; Muslim: bk. 9, no. 3506, Siddiqui.***

Bukhari: vol. 6, bk. 60, no. 132, Khan,

"Aisha, Muhammad's young wife also testified how her father hit her violently. "Narrated Aisha: A necklace of mine was lost at Al-Baida' and we were on our way to Medina. The Prophet made his camel kneel down and dismounted and laid his head on my lap and slept. Abu Bakr came to me and hit me violently on the chest and said, "You have detained the people because of a necklace."

Sahih Muslim: Book. 4, no. 2127,

"Muhammad himself also hit Aisha. She said, "He (Muhammad) struck me (Aisha) on the chest which caused me pain." 'A'isha said: "Should I not narrate to you about myself and about the Messenger of Allah? We said: Yes. She said: When it was my turn for Allah's Messenger to spend the night with me, he turned his side, put on his mantle and took off his shoes and placed them near his feet, and spread the corner of his shawl on his bed and then lay down till he thought that I had gone to sleep. He took hold of his mantle slowly and put on the shoes slowly, and opened the door and went out and then closed it lightly. I covered my head, put on my veil and tightened my waist wrapper, and then went out following his steps till he reached Baqi'. He stood there and he stood for a long time. He then lifted his hands three times, and then returned and I also returned. He hastened his steps and I also hastened my steps. He ran and I too ran. He came (to the house) and I also came (to the house). I, however, preceded him and I entered (the house), and as I lay down in the bed, he (the Holy Prophet) entered the (house), and said: Why is it, O 'A'isha, that you are out of breath? I said: There is nothing. He said: Tell me, or the Subtle and the Aware would inform me. I said: Messenger of Allah, may my father and mother be ransom for you, and then I told him (the whole story). He said: Was it the darkness (of your shadow) that I saw in front of me? I said: Yes. He struck me on the chest, which caused me pain, and then said: Did you think that Allah and His Apostle would deal unjustly with you?"

This Hadith shows that Muhammad hit his wife, Aisha, daughter of Abu Bakr, his right-hand companion.

Muslim women are subordinate to their husbands. Around the world we can see the impact of Qur'anic teaching and the permission to beat their wives.

In a heated debate on wife-beating in Arab-Islamic Society, **Islamic scholar Walid Ismail told researcher Dr. Afaf Al-Sayyed** that women like her who interrupt men should be beaten "from the start" and says that if a husband warns his rebellious wife, his beatings will not harm her. *https://www.instagram.com/reel/DUV7ppAgq3e/*

Mauritanian scholar **Sheikh Muhammad Ould Dedew** explained wife beating in Islam: "Three Blows with the Hand on the Back. He said that the beating should be a man's last resort, and he must avoid hitting his wife's face or beating her in a fit of anger." **Sheikh Dedew** explained that the man should beat his wife three times with his hand on her back and not use a whip. *https://www.facebook.com/watch/?v=10154422363584717*

The beating of wives, continues to occur in Muslim countries today. Studies in various regions, including Egypt, Palestine, Tunisia, and Israel, have shown that a significant number of Muslim women report being beaten by their husbands. Some studies suggest at least one in three women may experience this. A 2022 report highlighted that around 5 million Egyptian women are victims of domestic violence annually, while a 2013 United Nations report found that 99.3% of Egyptian women had experienced some form of sexual harassment.

https://euromedrights.org/publication/egypt-report-violence-women/

In Afghanistan under the rule of the Taliban, men have the right to beat their wives:

'A few beatings won't kill you': judge rejects divorce request of woman abused by husband in Afghanistan | Afghanistan | The Guardian

For women being beaten in Australia, see:

https://www.abc.net.au/news/2018-08-29/koran-434-islam-domestic-violence/10112916

Child Marriages

Muhammad married Aisha when she was six years old and consummated the marriage when she was nine and he was fifty-two. Muhammad is the perfect example for Muslims to follow. Some Muslims deny that Aisha was so young but the Hadith is very clear.

Sahih Al Bukhari: volume 5, book 58, number 236,

"Narrated Hisham's father: Khadija died three years before the Prophet departed to Medina. He stayed there for two years or so and then he married 'Aisha when she was a girl of six years of age, and he consummated that marriage when she was nine years old."

Furthermore, she was still playing with her dolls when Muhammad came for her.

Sahih Muslim, Book 008, Number 3311,

"'A'isha reported that Allah's Apostle married her when she was six or seven years old, and he was taken to his house as a bride when she was nine, and her dolls were with her; and when he (the Holy Prophet) died she was eighteen years old."

Another Hadith also states that Aisha played with dolls.

Sahih al-Bukhari 6130; similarly in Sahih Muslim 2440 and Abu Dawud 4932,

"Aisha narrated: "I used to play with the dolls in the presence of the Prophet, and my girl friends also used to play with me."

Muhammad stated that it was Allah who revealed and justified this relationship.

Sahih Al-Bukhari volume 5, book 58, number 235,

"Narrated 'Aisha: That the Prophet said to her, "You have been shown to me twice in my dream. I saw you pictured on a piece of silk and someone said (to me). 'This is your wife.' When I uncovered the picture, I saw that it was yours. I said, "If this is from Allah, it will be done."

Also, according to the Qur'an, marriage is permitted with young girls who have not yet had their periods. The Qur'an declares that a man can divorce his wife, but for her there has to be a waiting period *(iddah)* to make sure that the girl or woman is not pregnant. This is because the baby would belong to the man as his child. That waiting period is three months, for all women including the ones who have not yet had a period and those who have reached menopause. This verse shows that divorced women must wait three months for it to be final. In that time a man can take them back if they are pregnant.

Surah Al-Baqarah 2:228,

"Divorced women remain in waiting for three periods, and it is not lawful for them to conceal what Allah has created in their wombs if they believe in Allah and the Last Day. And their husbands have more right to take them back in this [period] if they want reconciliation. And due to the wives is similar to what is expected of them, according to what is reasonable. But the men have a degree over them [in responsibility and authority]. And Allah is Exalted in Might and Wise."

Surah At-Talaq (the Divorce) 65:4,

"And those who no longer expect menstruation among your women - if you doubt, then their period is three months, and [also for] those who have not menstruated. And for those who are pregnant, their term is until they give birth. And whoever fears Allah - He will make for him of his matter ease."

These verses show that both wives who have not yet had a period (that is, under-aged girls) and also menopausal women who have finished having periods but who could possibly get pregnant, must wait the three months, just to make sure they are not pregnant.

Sahih Al-Bukhari, Chapter 68: Book of Tafsir,

"Mujahid said that "if you have any doubt" means if you do not know whether she menstruates or not. Those who do not longer menstruate and those who have not yet menstruated, their 'idda is three months."

The most esteemed interpreter of the Qur'an, *Al Tabari, (839–923 AD)* also explains:

Tafsir Al-Tabari, 14/142,

"The interpretation of the verse "And those of your women as have passed the age of monthly courses, for them the 'Iddah (prescribed period), if you have doubt (about their periods), is three months; and for those who have no courses (i.e. they are still immature) their 'Iddah (prescribed period) is three months likewise." He said: The same applies to the 'iddah for girls who do not menstruate because they are too young, if their husbands divorce them after consummating the marriage with them."

Therefore, there is no doubt that the Qur'an and the Hadith both explicitly permit the marriage of men with young girls who have not yet menstruated. It is an example provided by Muhammad for Muslim men. This is the reason that in countries like Yemen, it is impossible to ban child marriages. It is deeply entrenched in Islam through the texts of the Qur'an and the Hadith and the example of the prophet Muhammad himself.

Head Covering for Muslim women

The Qur'an teaches that women must cover themselves up. The covering symbolizes women's inferior position in Islam and their sexual segregation. The woman wears the veil, to show herself as a modest and religious woman as well as to protect the man from temptation to lust. In Islamic society the veil is justified and considered necessary to maintain a pure and moral society.

The dress code for Muslim women is revealed in the following verse from the Qur'an:

Surah An-Nur 24:31,

"And tell the believing women to subdue their eyes and maintain their chastity. They shall not reveal any parts of their bodies, except that which is necessary. They shall cover their chests, and shall not relax this code in the presence of other than their husbands, their fathers, the fathers of their husbands, their sons, the sons of their husbands, their brothers, the sons of their brothers, the sons of their sisters, other women, the male servants or employees whose sexual drive has been nullified, or the children who have not reached puberty. They shall not strike their feet when they walk in order to shake and reveal certain details of their bodies. All of you shall repent to God, O you believers, that you may succeed."

The Hadith records that after Muhammad issued this command for women to cover themselves, the women responded by tearing up sheets to cover their faces, *Sahih Bukhari 60:282.*

Other verses from the Qur'an also call on women to cover themselves up.

Surah Al-Azhab, 33:59,

"O Prophet! Tell your wives and your daughters and the women of the believers that they should cast their outer garments over them (when abroad); this is more proper, that they should be known (recognized as such) and not molested. And Allah is ever Forgiving, Merciful."

There were special rules written into the Qur'an for the wives of the prophet Muhammad.

Surah Al-Azhab 33:32-33,

"O Consorts of the Prophet! ... stay quietly in your houses, and make not a dazzling display, like that of the former Times of Ignorance."

Surah Al-Azhab 33:53,

"And when ye ask (Muhammad's wives) for anything ye want, ask them from before a screen: that makes for greater purity for your hearts and for theirs. Nor is it right for you that ye should... marry his [Muhammad's] widows after him at any time. Truly such a thing is in God's sight an enormity."

There is an exception clause for old women. It's an escape clause Annette used to justify not wearing the veil in Yemen. As a foreigner and non-Muslim, Annette was not forced to wear a veil, although on occasion she was berated for it. Annette was told that women must wear a veil to prevent men seeing a woman's hair and being tempted to sin.

Surah An-Nur 24:60,

"Such elderly women as are past the prospect of marriage, there is no blame on them if they lay aside their (outer) garments, provided they make not a wanton display of their beauty: but it is best for them to be modest: and God is One Who sees and knows all things."

According to the Hadith unless a woman wears a veil, her prayer will not be accepted.

Abu Dawud 2:641,

"Narrated Safiya bint Shaiba: 'Aisha used to say: "When (the Verse): "They should draw their veils over their necks and bosoms," was revealed, (the ladies) cut their waist sheets at the edges and covered their faces with the cut pieces." The Prophet said: "Allah does not accept the prayer of a woman who has reached puberty unless she wears a veil."

Honour killings

Male relatives have the duty to protect a female's chastity. Alleged or suspected sexual transgression, the desire of women to choose a marriage partner of their own, or to seek divorce, wearing immodest dress, living an unacceptable lifestyle, changing their religion or even being raped, so disgraces the honour of the family that a man will kill his daughter or sister. This is happening in Saudi Arabia, Jordan, Syria, Yemen, Lebanon, Egypt, Sudan, the Gaza strip and the West Bank (Palestine), Jordan, Pakistan, Indonesia, Malaysia, Nigeria, Somalia, Turkey, Iran and is now taking place around the world. In 2000, the United Nations estimated that 5,000 honour killings were committed worldwide annually.

Some examples of honour killings - Recent Cases and Examples (2020s):

- **Bethany Israel** (USA, 2024): In May 2024, Jack Ball pleaded guilty to the premeditated murder and dismemberment of his pregnant older sister, Bethany Israel, in Lakeville, Minnesota, after claiming in his journal that she was "impure."
- **Saman Abbas** (Italy, 2021): The 18-year-old was murdered by her uncle and family members in Novellara, Italy, after refusing an arranged marriage.
- **Mona Heydari** (Iran, 2022): The 17-year-old was beheaded by her husband (often supported by male relatives in such cases) in Ahvaz, Iran, after seeking a divorce. Images of the killing circulated widely.
- **Tiba al-Ali** (Iraq, 2023): The YouTube star was strangled by her father in Diwaniya, Iraq, who stated he was "saving the family's honour."

- **Maryam H.** (Germany, 2021): The 34-year-old Afghan mother of two was strangled and had her throat slit by her two younger brothers in Berlin because she gave up strict Islamic practices.
- **Jennifer and Gretl Petelczyc** (Australia, 2024): In a May 2024 domestic violence case, a man killed a mother and daughter in their home.

Prevalence: Globally, about 47,000 women and girls are killed annually by intimate partners or family members—averaging one woman killed every 11 minutes.

Honour-Based Violence: This violence is frequently premeditated, often to punish women for choosing their own partners, refusing arranged marriages, or behaving in ways perceived as "too Westernized."

Role of Female Relatives: In some cases, mothers or sisters may participate in the pressure or abuse that leads to the killing, or help the male perpetrators.

Rising Concerns in Australia: In 2024, the ABC reported a high number of female deaths by violence, with 90 per cent of deaths involving a male perpetrator known to the victim, including brothers, sons, and fathers.

On the 29th September 2016 after a Muslim woman in Australia rejected Islam, Muhammad and Allah, her husband got so enraged that he stabbed her to death. Ms Abek had been stabbed multiple times by her husband, Amir Darbanou, 42.

Read more at *http://www.9news.com.au/national/2016/09/29/11/58/police-find-body-of-woman-in-potts-point-home#fC3w3mtkpcymWVUt.99 and http://www.dailymail.co.uk/news/article-3815124/Hairdresser-35-stabbed-death-Iranian-husband-Potts-Point-apartment-angry-converted-CHRISTIANITY.html*

A woman was brutally stabbed to death by her own brother for daring to leave her house alone, police in Jordan said. Her throat was slit and she was knifed more than 20 times in the horrific "honour killing" reportedly carried out "to cleanse the family honour." Cops say the victim, 20, was murdered at her Duleil home on Sunday before being dumped on waste ground some 500 yards away. The alleged 25 y.o killer, who has not been named, reportedly flew into a rage because his sister spent "too little time at home."

http://www.nydailynews.com/news/world/honour-killing-victim-killed-brother-cops-article-1.1332901

Article 340 of the Jordan penal code states: "He who discovers his wife, or one of his female ascendants or descendants or sisters with another in an unlawful bed and he kills, wounds or injures one or both of them, benefits from a penalty reduction." *http://www.al-monitor.com/pulse/culture/2012/08/jordans-dishonourable-honour-killings.html#ixzz4M2PjbJ5i*

Honour killings in Jordan occur regularly and may get only a six-month sentence. These offenses average 23 cases per year. These crimes are frequently planned by family councils, with pressure to uphold "honour." Methods include stoning, stabbing, beating, burning, beheading, hanging, throat slashing, lethal acid attacks, shooting, and strangulation.

Earthly Destiny for Muslim Women

The following issues are supported by the teachings of the Qur'an and the Hadith and enshrined in Sharia, Islamic law. They are enforced in nations like Saudi Arabia. Because of large scale Muslim immigration, these aspects of Muslim life are being introduced into Western nations. There is a lot of pressure to make them not only culturally acceptable, but even to allow them to be introduced into laws of the land.

- Enforced wearing of the veil
- Forced marriages
- Polygamy
- Underage marriage. Girls as young as ten being forced to marry.
- The authority of a man to force his wife to obey his will

- The right of a man to beat his wife
- Female Genital Mutilation (FGM)
- Women's testimony to be only worth half of a man's testimony in court
- Exclusion from public life, confining the woman to the home
- Honour killings
- Lack of rights to child custody
- Lack of rights to divorce

From our own experience we have seen some of the frustration and oppression experienced by Muslim women.

Annette's testimony of what she experienced

I remember sitting with a group of women on the floor in an Islamic boarding school in Java, being the only one not wearing a veil. Suddenly one of the women exclaimed that it was so hot, she wished she could take her veil off.

Another time we were in the Jakarta airport at the luggage carousel after arriving from the Middle East, when one of the Indonesian maids arriving on the same plane and collecting her luggage after a two-year stint of working there, threw her veil off and cried out, "Freedom!"

I remember being invited with Jeff, to have dinner with our Arabic teacher in Yemen. We sat in the lounge room together with a few male family members. Our teacher served us up the meal and ate with us. After we had finished, I was given permission to go into a bedroom to meet his wife in private. Jeff as a male guest, was not even allowed to see her.

Another time we were invited to a wedding in Yemen. Jeff went to one place with the male members of our team to celebrate with the men, the actual wedding. I and our female team members went to a different place to wait with the bride for the bridegroom to come after the ceremony and collect her. All the Yemeni women arrived clothed from head to toe in black.

However, upon entering the wedding hall, all of them threw off their black robe and presented a dazzling display of beautiful costumes. There were about two hundred women present. we sat on the floor, drank the bottles of water and ate the biscuits provided while we listened to music over the loudspeaker system and some of the women danced together. When on one occasion, two men came in to fix up a problem in the sound system, all the women giggled, dived for their black robes and covered up until the men had finished and left. The bride sat patiently for about two hours waiting for the bridegroom to appear, at which point, we all shook hands with her and went home. The actual "wedding ceremony" happened where Jeff was. The Bride was not there. She didn't get to attend her own wedding!

As a foreigner I had little contact in general with the women in Yemen, but I found the few I met, gentle and kind. I would smile at them as we passed on the streets and through the slit in the face veil for their eyes, I could see the smiling response. Visiting the zoo one day, a Yemeni woman in a burka walked quickly towards me and said in English, "Welcome to Yemen. If you need anything, just let me know." She disappeared back into the crowds, but it touched my heart.

Further information on the rights of women in Islam:

https://www.youtube.com/watch?v=D65DRXbpf1c

1 in 3 Women Face This Horrific Truth! -Women's Rights in Islam

Eternal Destiny of Muslim Women

What about the eternal destiny Muslim women face? A Muslim woman's eternal destiny is dependent on her faith and good deeds, and also on her relationship with her husband.

The Qur'an states that both men and women can go to heaven.

Surah An-Nahl 16:97,

"To whoever, male or female, does good deeds and has faith, We shall give a good life and reward them according to the best of their actions."

The Qur'an also says that women can enter heaven with their husbands.

Surah Az-Zukhruf 43:70,

"Enter into Paradise, you and your wives, with delight."

However, the Hadith says that it is only the woman whose husband dies, while satisfied with her, who will be taken to Paradise to join her husband.

Jami` at-Tirmidhi: Hadith 1161. Sunan Ibn Majah: Hadith 1854,

"Any woman who dies while her husband is pleased with her, she will enter Jannah (Paradise)."

If not, she will be sent to hell.

What rewards will a woman receive in heaven?

One response from an unidentified Islamic leader was: "Women should not preoccupy themselves with inquiring about the details of their entering Paradise, what they will be doing there, where they will go, and so on. It is enough for every Muslim woman to know that once she enters Paradise, she will forget all the misery and hardships she ever faced, because her life in Paradise will be one of endless happiness."

Listen to Annette's testimony on what she was taught in the Islamic College.

When I asked our Muslim teacher, Sheik Abdul Hafith, in Yemen, what a woman would receive in Paradise, he told me that I would spend all my days in a huge mansion by myself and I would wait with longing desire all day for my husband, Jeff, to return home and have sex with me. He also mentioned that Jeff could have sex with 100 houris evertday before coming home. That was the vision of heaven he could offer me! But when I complained that I would not be happy if Jeff was spending the rest of the time with the multitude of houris that he had promised him, he told me not to worry. He said God would wipe all that out of my memory and I would just experience endless happiness without any knowledge that would hurt me, just endless bliss! I was shocked, and wept. Jeff had to calm me down as I was so angry. I said to the Sheik, "Your God is a deceiver!" Jeff held my arm to calm me down and whispered, "We want to get out of here alive!"

The Majority of Hell Dwellers are Women

What about Hell? What is it like for women in Hell? The Hadith say that the majority of people in Hell are women. Muhammad said that he saw into Hell and the majority of hell dwellers were women.

Sahih Al-Bukhari 1:6:301,

"Narrated Abu Said Al-Khudri: Once Allah's Apostle went out to the Musalla (to offer the prayer) o 'Id-al-Adha or Al-Fitr prayer. Then he passed by the women and said, "O women! Give alms, as I have seen that the majority of the dwellers of Hell-fire were you (women)." They asked, "Why is it so, O Allah's Apostle?" He replied, "You curse frequently and are ungrateful to your husbands. I have not seen anyone more deficient in intelligence and religion than you. A cautious sensible man could be led astray by some of you." The women asked, "O Allah's Apostle! What is deficient in our intelligence and religion?" He said, "Is not the evidence of two women equal to the witness of one man?" They replied in the affirmative. He said, "This is the deficiency in her intelligence. Isn't it true that a woman can neither pray nor fast during her menses?" The women replied in the affirmative. He said, "This is the deficiency in her religion."

Mohammed the Prophet said, "I looked at Paradise and found poor people forming the majority of its inhabitants; and I looked at Hell and saw that the majority of its inhabitants were women."

The significance of this Hadith can be seen in the numerous times it was recorded in all of the Hadith literature. This Hadith can be found in: *Sahih al-Bukhari: 29, 304, 1052, 1462, 3241, 5197, 5198, 6449, 6546; Muslim: 80, 885, 907, 2737, 2738; Al-Tirmithi: 635, 2602, 2603, 2613; Al-Nasa'i: 1493, 1575; Ibn Majah: 4003.* It can also be found multiple times in *Musnad Ahmad, and in Muwata' Malik: 445; Sunan Al-Darimi: 1007. Sahih al-Bukhari 304, 3241, & 6449.*

Entrance into Paradise is dependent on her husband and her obedience to him.

At-Tirmidhi, Hadith 1161, and Sunan Ibn Majah, Hadith 1854),

"In the Hadith, Muhammad stated: "Any woman who dies while her husband is pleased with her, enters Paradise'."

Ṣaḥīḥ Ibn Ḥibbān 4163,

"The Messenger of Allah said: "If a woman prays five times, fasts during Ramadan, preserves her chastity and obeys her husband, she will be told, "Enter Paradise through those gates that you want!"

While the chief rewards of heaven for men, are the virgins of Paradise, there are no specific rewards for women. Moreover, a woman's chance of getting into Paradise is rather limited.

Thus, on earth, women's role in Islam is mainly confined to the home and that is where she will spend eternity. The Qur'an mainly mentions the woman in connection with her husband and discusses issues of marriage, divorce, the dowry, inheritance, her dress and her submission. In the afterlife, her chances of going to hell are far greater than going to Paradise, a Paradise designed especially for men.

What impact has this teaching on Muslims? Below are a few testimonies of women who are no longer Muslims and who are answering the question of why they left Islam.

Testimonies of Women who have left Islam

Nazzia Momina,

"I had some questions about status of women, and at the same time I realized I was always in denial about true status of non-Muslims in Islam. I couldn't find any satisfactory answers, so I started re reading Qur'an and Hadiths. That was that."

CanadianExMuslim,

"Allah allows sex slavery, child marriage, and wife beating. He commands Muslims to hate Christians and Jews and kill non-Muslims. That's why I left Islam."

Anna

"I left Islam because my ex-husband used Islam to justify domestic abuse. Local imams agreed. His family agreed. Police got me and my kids to safety. I thought I'd study more Qur'an because they must have been wrong. … Indeed, they must have been wrong. There's no way the Qur'an says, "Oh, wait. Here it is in *Surah An-Nisa 4:34*."

Aliya PBUHer,

"I left because it's a toxic ideology that stands against girls/women, freedom, critical thinking, personal choice and overall human rights. I'm a *#ChildMarriageSurvivor* because of Islam. Many won't want to hear it, but it's my lived truth. You're free to speak yours, and I'm free to speak mine."

Sara Ghorbani,

"Because I am considered half a man in Islam.

Because I have a male legal guardian who decides whether I can get a job, a passport, or even an education.

Because I was forced into hijab at age 6.

Because I was told over and over again I am responsible for the honour of the family. Because I was sexually assaulted at age 11 but I was told I was responsible for all men's sexual desires.

Because I inherit half my brother.

Because my witness in court is half.

Because my father, brother, uncle, grandfather, any man in the family could kill me to restore the honour of the family if they feared my rebellion and dishonouring the family name and would never be punished.

Because I am worth half a man if I get killed.

Because I was told my whole life I was going to burn in hell for my hair showing and my improper hijab.

Because I knew if my husband wanted to have a second or third or fourth wife, I could not object.

Because he could divorce me whenever he pleased and take my children if I ever gave birth. Because he could beat me black and blue and I still couldn't get a divorce.

Because I was tired of not being human enough for Islam to be afforded dignity and safety and autonomy."

(These testimonies, and many more, are from ***Adam the Apostate's post on X*** and recorded by David Wood on You Tube.)

https://x.com/The1Apostate/status/2034888706121670732)

www.youtube.com/watch?v=U7spANQhxS4

What does the Bible Teach about Women?

Are the teachings of the Bible consistent with equality, freedom and dignity for women? Does the Gospel really offer hope of a better life on earth and a better eternal destiny?

The Biblical teaching about women begins in the ***Book of Genesis***. Women are created in the image of God, created to rule and to have dominion together with the man. Adam was shown all the creatures over whom he was to have dominion, and the woman was not among them.

Then God took a rib out of Adam's body and formed a woman and brought her to him to become one with him, *Genesis 2:21-25*. This was where the headship of the husband was instituted. His headship was over one body. It was a sign of the two becoming one flesh, integrated, interconnected, interdependent, mutually connected in a true unity. God joined the husband and the wife together as one.,

After the fall, this unity was broken. The woman was subjected to the rule of the man. "He shall rule over you." *Genesis 3:16.* After that, conflict and misunderstandings plagued the marriage of a men and women. The coming of Jesus brought hope for women.

When Jesus came, things changed. We read in the Gospels how Jesus treated women. He sat at the well and spent time with the Samaritan woman, teaching her about the living water that He came to give her, *John 4:1-42.* He healed women, talked with them, taught them and forgave them. Women travelled with Him and ministered to Him, *Luke 8:1-3.* He told Martha, who was busy serving, that Mary had chosen the better part, that is, to sit at His feet and be taught by Him, *Luke 10:38-42.* Women walked with Him on the road to the Cross, *Matthew 27:55-56.* Many stood with Him at the Cross, some watching from afar and others standing close by, *Matthew 27:55-56; John 19:25–27.* Women were the first to witness the resurrection and take the news of it to His apostles, *Luke 24:9–10.*

Jesus, through His work in redemption, by His death and resurrection, restored not only men, but also women, so that they together could be children of God, members of the Body of Christ, *Galatians 3:28,* and co-heirs together with Christ, *1Peter 3:7.* Jesus came to bring restoration, not only in the relationship between God and man, but also in the relationship between a husband and his wife. Jesus calls us back to real marriage relationships as it was in the beginning, *Matthew 19:4-8.*

After Jesus ascended to heaven, the women gathered together with the men in the Upper Room, *Acts 1:14.* They were present with the men on the Day of Pentecost and were filled with the Spirit in the same way as the men, *Acts 2:1-4.* Both the Old Testament and the New Testament state that the Holy Spirit is poured out on both men and women, *Joel 2:28-32; Acts 2:16-18.*

In the New Testament church, we read that women prayed and prophesied, *1Corinthians 11:5.* The evangelist, Phillip, had four daughters that prophesied, *Acts 21:8-9.* Women were prominent in the Church. Dorcas, also called Tabitha, was so prominent in her ministry of serving the church and sewing clothes for widows and orphans that she was raised from the dead, *Acts 9:36-42*. Lydia was the first convert when Paul's ministry began in Europe and the church in Philippi met in her home, *Acts 16:13-15,40*.

Women were laborers in the Gospel, fellow workers, members of the apostolic teams with Paul in the Gospel, deaconesses and leaders in the churches in homes. Phoebe was a deaconess and a patron of many and with her Paul sent the letter to the Romans *(Romans 16:1-2)*. Priscilla ministered and taught with her husband, Apollos, and with him led in the church at Rome and Corinth *(Acts 18:2-3,18-26; Romans 16:3-5; 1Corinthians 16:19; 2Timothy 4:19*. Junia was mentioned as a prominent apostle together with her husband, Andronicus, *Romans 16:7*. Tryphena, Tryphosa, and Persis were women who "labored" or "worked very hard" in the Lord, *Romans 16:12*. Mary was in the church in Rome and was commended for working very hard there, *Romans 16:6*. Euodia and Syntyche were laborers together with Paul in the Gospel, *Philippians 4:2-3*. See how many women are mentioned and the prominent roles they are given. Compare this with the Qur'an where only one woman's name is mentioned at all, that is, Mary the mother of Jesus.

We read in the epistles how Paul holds up marriage as a picture of the relationship between Christ and His Church. A man, as a husband will love his wife as Christ loved the Church and willing to give his life for her. A woman as a wife, with such a husband, will joyfully live in submission to her husband, becoming one with him, as a body becomes one with a head, just as it was in the beginning, *Ephesians 5:21-33*. This powerful unity born out of the love of Christ between the two of them, not only shows the equality of the husband and the wife but reflects in the role of women in the Church where there is no distinction between male and female in Christ Jesus, *Galatians 3:28*. Both men and women serve the Lord together, *Romans 16:1-16*. Their roles and gifts may be different, there is no difference in the value of their giftings and there is no difference in the eternal destiny of a man or a women. Each will find salvation, their calling in life, and an eternal destiny through the love and faith they have in Jesus Christ.

The Gospel offers a Muslim women hope for this life and for the next. The Gospel offers her a Saviour to forgive her of her sins, and a Heavenly Father who loves and cares for her, as well as brothers and sisters in Christ that will give her dignity and a loving family. The Gospel calls her out of the shadows, out of the darkness and into the glorious light and liberty of our Lord Jesus Christ.

THE DILEMMA:

Who will women trust to be their God?
Which book will they believe?
Who will they follow, Muhammad or Jesus?
Will they live in fear and oppression or the freedom God offers?
Where will they spend eternity, in Heaven or Hell?
How can Christians show and demonstrate to
Muslim women the love and freedom
that can only be found in the Gospel?
Who will help them to solve the dilemma?

QUESTIONS FOR DISCUSSION

1. Do you know some Muslim women? Or women of other backgrounds?
2. Have you ever discussed with them the challenges of married life? How did they respond?
3. Have you found women to be open to talk about their dreams and aspirations in life?
4. Are the women you know free to talk about faith and eternity?

5. Discuss among yourselves steps you could take, either alone or in groups, to befriend another woman and walk with them in a journey of discovery to find the Straight Path that brings eternal salvation.
6. Could inviting a friend to Alpha or an Alpha-like course be a useful step?

DILEMMA 10

THE HEAVEN & HELL DILEMMA

The great dilemma for all mankind, including Christians and Muslims, is where will our destination be after we die. Will we go to heaven, or will we end up in hell?

We were attending a debate held in a Muslims university near Surabaya, Indonesia. There were three speakers. Towards the conclusion of the debate, in Jeff's final challenge, he stated that we all want to go to heaven. The Muslim professor nodded his head vigorously in strong agreement. Jeff continued and said that we all needed to find the solution to the dilemma of which pathway to choose. One led to heaven, and others led to hell. The wrong choice would be eternally fatal. Jeff explained why he believed in the crucifixion and resurrection of Jesus then asked the question, "But what if I'm wrong?" He then said that the Muslim Professor believed that following Muhammad was the true pathway, then added, "But what if he's wrong?" The moment created an unexpected challenge among the 300 Islamic leaders that afterward had them buzzing. They wanted to hear more and invited Jeff to speak with their leaders in Surabaya, Jember, Sidoardjo, Situbondo, Madura and Jakarta. The largest gathering had 15,000 attending in a large outdoor event.

Both Muslims and Christians believe in heaven and hell. Both the Qur'an and the Bible provide teaching about and descriptions of heaven and hell. Their visions are similar in some ways and radically different in others.

Both teach about the way to heaven. Both claim to be the only way. Which way should we take? Our eternal destination is of vital importance to both Christians and Muslims. It is a dilemma which every individual must face. We knew that in speaking to these large Islamic audiences that there were radicals who put a contract out to eliminate Jeff. Boldness also requires sacrifice, wisdom and the promise that Jesus will always be with us. There were many that were hungry and seeking the truth. We knew there were "Esau" types as well as "Ishmael" types and the Lord protected us in the midst of several dangerous situations. We wanted to make sure that the "Ishmael" types would have a clear opportunity to hear how Jesus loved them and wanted to save them.

Heaven in the Bible

What does Heaven mean for Christians?

For Christians, Heaven is the place where God dwells. It is the place of the Father. Jesus taught us to pray "Our Father in heaven" (13 verses). He spoke about "My Father in heaven" (8 verses). Heaven is also described as the place where God reigns in His kingdom. Jesus constantly referred to the Kingdom of heaven (34 verses) and the Kingdom of God (68 verses). In Revelation, we read of heaven described as the New Jerusalem. *(Revelation 21-22)*. Heaven is primarily the place of relationship and fellowship where all the righteous will live together with God forever.

What will we do in Heaven?

Heaven will be a place of glory. We cannot truly understand yet what it will be like because it is still a mystery, *1Corinthians 2:9; 2Corinthians 12:2-4.* What we do know is that in heaven, we will relate and communicate and fellowship. We will know one another and sit down together and eat and drink with Abraham, Isaac and Jacob, *Matthew 8:1).* We will love one another but there will be no sexual relationships as in marriage on earth, *Matthew 22:30.* It is where we will receive our eternal inheritance, *1Peter 1:4.* It is the place of His presence, where there is fulness of joy, *Psalm 16:11.* It is a place of praise and worship where we will rejoice and express our thankfulness and appreciation of who He is and what He has done, *Revelation 5:13.* There, we will live with God in His presence as His people forever, *Revelation 21:3.* What God has prepared is so awesome it is difficult for us to fully comprehend but we know His love, His character and that what He has prepared will be so wonderful because we know who He is. Our relationship with Him here shows us how even more amazing it will be when we are with Him there.

1Corinthians 2:9,

"As it is written: "Eye has not seen, nor ear heard, nor have entered into the heart of man the things which God has prepared for those who love Him."

How can we enter Heaven?

Because heaven is the place of relationship with God, we can only enter through relationship with Him. If we have no relationship with Him, He will say to us, "Depart from Me, I never knew you." *(Matthew 7:21-23).* The Bible clearly explains the way that we can come into that relationship.

- **Be Converted** – leave sin and follow Christ.
  Matthew 18:3,

"Be converted and become as a little child."

- **Be Born Again**
  John 3:3,5,
  "Most assuredly I say to you, unless one is born again, he cannot see the kingdom of God… Most assuredly I say to you, unless one is born of water and the Spirit, he cannot enter the kingdom of God."

- **Repent**
  Acts 2:38,
  "Repent and let every one of you be baptized in the name of Jesus Christ for the remission of sins, and you shall receive the gift of the Holy Spirit."

- **Call on the name of the Lord.**
  Acts 2:21,
  "And it shall come to pass that whoever calls on the name of the Lord shall be saved."

- **Believe on Jesus Christ.**
  Acts 16:31,
  "Believe on the Lord Jesus Christ and you will be saved, you and your household."

- **Confess Jesus as Lord.**
  Romans 10:9,
  "If you confess with your mouth the Lord Jesus and believe in your heart that God has raised Him from the dead, you will be saved."

Entrance into heaven is not based on works but on God's grace and our response of repentance and faith. We enter heaven not because of our religion but because of our relationship with the Lord Jesus Christ.

Titus 3:4-6,

"But when the kindness and the love of God our Savior toward man appeared, not by works of righteousness which we have done, but according to His mercy He saved us, through the washing of regeneration and renewing of the Holy Spirit, whom He poured out on us abundantly through Jesus Christ our Savior."

The opportunity and call to come into relationship with God is for all mankind. The good news is to be preached in all the world, to all nations. This is the Gospel of the Kingdom. Through faith in Jesus Christ, we can be transferred from the kingdom of darkness into the kingdom of light, from the kingdom of Satan into the kingdom of God, from the kingdom of this world into the kingdom of heaven.

The Christian has a strong assurance of salvation. We know that Jesus is our Saviour, that we are born again, that we have passed from darkness to light, from death to life and that if we die today, we will be with Jesus in heaven.

1John 5:20,

"And we know that the Son of God has come and has given us an understanding, that we may know Him who is true; and we are in Him who is true, in His Son Jesus Christ. This is the true God and eternal life."

But what about Muslims? What is their concept of Heaven? How do they believe they can enter heaven?

Heaven in Islam

What is Heaven like according to the Qur'an?

There are many verses in the Qur'an that describe the glories of the Islamic Paradise. The problem is that Islam only offers a worldly heaven, full of the things that satisfy the lust of the flesh and the lust of the eyes, the very things that tempted Adam and Eve in the Garden of Eden and led them to fall into sin.

Genesis 3:6,

"So when the woman saw that tree was good for food, that it was pleasant to the eyes and a tree desirable to make one wise, she took of its fruit and ate. She also gave to her husband with her and he ate."

Satan tempted Eve with the desire for food, "the lusts of the flesh." He tempted her to take something pleasant to the eyes, "the lust of the eyes." He tempted her with something desirable to make one wise, "the pride of life."

Why would God entice us into heaven with the very same temptations that Satan used to tempt Eve into sin?

It is Satan who tempts us to fulfill all our fleshly and worldly desires. We are told in the Bible not to love and desire the things of this world.

1John 2:15-17,

"Do not love the world or the things in the world. If anyone loves the world, the love of the Father is not in Him. For all that is in the world – the lust of the flesh and the lust of the eyes, and the pride of life – is not of the Father, but is of the world. And the world is passing away, and the lust of it; but he who does the will of God abides forever."

The Islamic heaven is a garden of delights for men with multiple sex partners called *houris*. There will be all kinds of worldly luxury and abundant feasting. This is the promise of Allah to those who submit to Him.

Surah Az-Zukhruf 43:68-73,

"O My servants, you have nothing to fear on that Day, nor will you grieve. Those who believed in Our revelations, and were submissive. Enter the Garden, you and your spouses, Joyfully. They will be served around with trays of gold, and cups. Therein is whatever the souls desire and delights the eyes. Therein you will stay forever. Such is the Garden you are made to inherit, because of what you used to do. Therein you will have abundant fruit, from which you eat."

This is the wonderful Heaven that is portrayed in the Qur'an and the Hadith and of which Muslims dream. The following verses show what the Islamic Paradise is like.

1. The fulfillment of all fleshly desires

Surah Al-Maedah 5:122,

Allah will say: "This is a day on which the truthful will profit from their truth: Theirs are the Gardens, with rivers flowing beneath, --their eternal home": Allah well-pleased with them, and they with Allah: That is the great Salvation, the fulfillment of all desires."

Surah Az-Zukhruf 43:71,

"There will be there all that the souls could desire, all that the eyes could delight in: And ye shall abide therein for aye."

2. Gardens

Surah Al-Baqarah 2:25

"But give glad tidings to those who believe and work righteousness, that their portion is Gardens, beneath which rivers flow."

Gardens and rivers were what was lacking in the deserts of Arabia. No wonder they longed for such a Paradise.

3. Rivers

There are rivers of water, milk and wine. In the deserts of Arabia, water is scarce, milk turns sour in the heat and wine is forbidden. All this changes in heaven.

Surah Muhammad 47:15,

"In it are rivers of water incorruptible; rivers of milk of which the taste never changes; rivers of wine, a joy to those who drink; and rivers of honey pure and clear."

In the Islamic Paradise, there are not only rivers of water, but also rivers of milk. In Arabia, in the heat of the desert milk quickly soured, wine was forbidden and honey was highly valued and highly priced as a very precious commodity. All of these were scarce and very desirable. Such a Paradise is very enticing!

4. Fruits

Surah Al-Baqarah 2:25,

"Every time they are fed with fruits therefrom, they say: "Why, this is what we were fed with before…"

The Hadith records that in heaven there will be an abundance of fruits, similar in form but different in taste, such as grapes and bananas, and when picked, they will be immediately replenished.

5. Drinks including wine

Surah As-Saffat 37:40-48,

"There will be passed to them a Cup from a clear flowing fountain, crystal white, of a taste delicious to those who drink thereof, Free from headiness; nor will they suffer intoxication therefrom."

Surah At-Tur 52.23,

"They will pass from hand to hand a cup, inspiring no idle talk, no sinful urge."

Surah Al-Waqiah 56:18,

"There shall wait on them immortal youths with bowls and ewers and a cup of purest wine (that will neither pain their heads, nor take away their reason)."

Wine is forbidden to Muslims on earth, but it is promised to them in abundance in heaven. True, it will not make them drunk in heaven, nevertheless it is still "wine." What is forbidden on earth becomes freely available in heaven without any negative side effects.

5. Meat

Surah Al-Waqiah 56:21,

"And flesh of fowls they relish."

Food and drink in heaven will be of superior quality, endless in supply, and provide pure enjoyment. According to the Hadith, the meat of any bird they desire (such as chicken or pigeon), as well as the meat of a specially fed bull, will be available. Other Hadiths state that the initial meal served to people when they enter Paradise will be the "caudate lobe of whale liver," a tender and prized portion. (*Sahih Muslim (315) and Sahih al-Bukhari (3329*). The caudate lobe is described as a special, superior portion attached to the liver, symbolizing an honourable welcoming gift. Again, we see that the Muslim Heaven is the place where all the desires of the flesh are satisfied.

5. Dishes of crystal and silver

Surah Al-Insan 75:15-18,

"Passing around them are vessels of silver, and cups of crystal. Crystal-clear, made of silver—they measured them exactly. They will be served therein with a cup whose flavor is Zanjabeel (ginger). A spring therein named Salsabeel."

6. Beautiful clothing and jewelry

Surah Al-Kahf 18.31,

"They will be adorned therein with bracelets of gold, ... they will be arrayed in fine green silk and rich brocade."

7. Comfortable Couches and Raised Thrones

Al-Kahf 18.31,

"They will recline therein on raised thrones. How good the recompense! How beautiful a couch to recline on! In it are thrones raised high."

Raised thrones or uplifted couches will be the comfortable seats in heaven promised to those who make it there. The most superior comfort and luxury will be provided. The Islamic heaven appears to be a place of eternal relaxation, an eternal holiday in Paradise.

8. Virgin Companions called Houris

There are many descriptions of the virgin companions of Paradise in the Qur'an. The English versions vary in their translations, but they all describe them as virgin maidens of paradise with dark beautiful eyes. They are pure beings with highly contrasting, beautiful eyes, intensely white and deeply black. All men will receive at least two houris. One Hadith says that each man will receive 72 wives in Paradise. *(Sunan Ibn Majah 4337).* These *houris* are not human women that come into being by the natural birth process, but are a special creation of God as a sexual reward for Muslim men. They are to be companions for them. Their virginity is restored after every sexual encounter.

As-Saffat 37:48-49,

"And besides them will be chaste women, or bashful dark eyed virgins, restraining their glances, with big eyes of wonder and beauty, as if they were hidden eggs or pristine pearls."

Surah Ad-Dukhan 44:54,

"They shall recline on couches arranged in rows. To dark eyed houris we shall wed them."

Surah At-Tur 52.20,

"And theirs shall be dark eyed houris, chaste as virgin pearls."

Surah Ar-Rahman 55:56,

"In them are [maidens] of modest gaze, whom neither human nor jinn have touched before."

Surah Ar-Rahman 55:72,

"They will be maidens with gorgeous eyes, reserved in pavilions."

Surah Al-Waqiah 56:22-24,

"We created the houris and made them virgins, loving companions for those on the right hand."

Surah An-Naba 78:33,

"And splendid companions well-matched."

These houris are what Muslim men dream about and long for. It is this vision of heaven that is their motivation for being faithful Muslims, for praying in the mosque, giving alms, fasting in Ramadhan and going on the pilgrimage (*hajj*) to Mecca. It is also their motivation for spreading Islam and for going on a jihad and fighting in the cause of Allah.

9. Young serving boys

There will not only be beautiful *houri* virgins in the Islamic Paradise, but for the men there will also be beautiful young men to serve their desires. This has controversially led to speculation about homosexuality in heaven.

Surah Al-Insan 76:19,

"There will circulate among them young boys made eternal. When you see them, you would think them (as beautiful as) scattered pearls."

Surah At-Tur 52:24,

"And there shall wait on them immortal youths."

Surah Al-Waqiah 56:17,

"And round about them will serve youths of perpetual freshness: If thou seest them, thou would think them scattered Pearls."

10. Bliss

Surah Al-Insaan 76:13-20,

"And when thou lookest, it is there thou wilt see a Bliss and a Realm Magnificent."

Surah Al Tatfif 83:22-28,

"Truly the Righteous will be in Bliss: On Thrones of Dignity will they command a sight of all things: Thou wilt recognize in their Faces the beaming brightness of Bliss. Their thirst will be slaked with Pure Wine sealed."

Thus, the heaven or paradise of the Qur'an is sensual and physical, providing for the satisfaction of all the lust and desires of the flesh. There is no sense of relationship with God or even with one another in the Qur'anic Paradise.

The dilemma for Muslims is that the ultimate in worldly wealth, luxury, comfort, indulgence becomes their motivating goal and vision.

Is this really the sort of paradise that will inspire people to draw close to God, to prepare them to live in His presence forever? Should we set our hearts on beautiful gardens with rivers, sumptuous feasts of wine and meat as we recline our comfortable couches, wearing beautiful clothing and associating with virgins with wide eyes? What impact does this have on the daily lives of those who believe that it is true? How strongly does this vision motivate them and consume their thoughts?

One of our Islamic teachers in Yemen said to us, "I lie in my bed next to my wife at night and dream of my 72 houris." We were totally shocked and appalled at this disrespectful humiliation of his wife. But, this is his vision of heaven.

Who gets to Heaven in Islam?

According to the Qur'an, admission to heaven depends on the will of Allah. No one can enter Heaven except by the will of Allah. Although the Qur'an does say that men and women will enter Paradise, only Allah will determine who they will be. Everyone is predestined by Allah to enter heaven or hell. There is no certainty for any Muslim, including Muhammad, to enter this Paradise. Muslims live in a state of balance between hope (*raja'*) in Allah's mercy and fear (*khaf*) of His punishment. God promises that Muslims who believe and do good will certainly enter heaven, but Muslims never know if they have done enough good to be approved by God. God's only binding promise is that jihadists, especially those who are martyred, will enter heaven.

1. Muslims who believe and do good deeds

The Muslim Paradise is called *Jannah*. According to the Qur'an, it is only believers and doers of good works who will enter there.

Surah Al-Baqarah 2:277,

"Those who believe, perform good deeds, establish prayer, and give charity, their reward is with their Lord. They will neither fear nor grieve."

Surah An Nisa 4.57,

"But those who believe and do deeds of righteousness, We shall soon admit to Gardens, with rivers flowing beneath,- their eternal home: Therein shall they have companions pure and holy: We shall admit them to shades, cool and ever deepening."

Surah An-Nisa 4:122,

:But those that believe, and do deeds of righteousness, them We shall admit to gardens underneath which rivers flow, therein dwelling for ever and ever; God's promise in truth; and who is truer in speech than God."

Surah Maryam 19:60,

"Except those who repent, believe and do righteousness; for those will enter Paradise and will not be wronged at all."

2. Christians, Jews and Sabians who believe and do good deeds

Surah Al-Baqarah 2:62,

"Indeed, those who believed and those who became Jews and the Christians and the Sabians - who believed in Allah and the Day [the] Last and did righteous deeds, so for them (is) their reward with their Lord and no fear on them and not they will grieve."

Surah Al-Maidah 5:69,

"Indeed, those who believed and those who became Jews and the Sabians and the Christians, whoever believed in Allah and the Day the Last. and did good deeds, then no fear on them and not they will grieve."

These two verses promise the same rewards to Jews, Christians and Sabians (followers of John the Baptist). The problem is that these verses are said to be abrogated by *Surah Ali-Imran 3:85,* which says that no other religion than Islam will ever be accepted by God. This is another enigma for Muslims. Which verses should they believe?

3. Jihadists, those who fight in the way of Allah

The only sure way to enter Paradise in Islam is to die in jihad. Warriors who die fighting in the cause of God are ushered immediately into God's presence. This becomes the motivating force for so many of the terrorists, who literally believe the following verses in the Qur'an. They must have good intentions and truly fight for Allah and not be hypocrites. The call to "jihad in the way of Allah" (*Jihad fi sabil Allah*) is a strong motivating force for many Muslims to become involved in fighting for the triumph of Islam.

Surah Ali Imran 3:157,

"And if ye are slain, or die, in the way of Allah, forgiveness and mercy from Allah are far better than all they could amass."

Surah Ali Imran 3.169-170,

"Think not of those who are killed in the Way of Allah as dead. Nay, they are alive, with their Lord, and they have provision."

Surah An-Nisa 4.74,

"Therefore let those who fight in the way of Allah, who sell this world's life for the hereafter; and whoever fights in the way of Allah, then be he slain or be he victorious, We shall grant him a mighty reward."

Surah As-Saff 61:11-12,

"That you believe in Allah and the Messenger and that you strive hard and fight in the cause of Allah, with your wealth and your lives, that will be better for you, if you but know! He will forgive you your sins, and admit you into Gardens under which rivers flow and pleasant dwelling in Paradise. That is indeed the great success."

Surah At Tawbah 9:111,

"Allah has purchased from the believers their lives and their properties in exchange for Paradise. They fight in Allah's way, and they kill and get killed. It is a promise binding on Him in the Torah, and the Gospel, and the Qur'an. And who is more true to his promise than Allah? So rejoice in making such an exchange—that is the supreme triumph."

The Role of Jihad in accessing Heaven

The Hadiths also say that Muslims who die in jihad, killing the enemy, will be granted access to Paradise.

Sahih Bukhari 4:53:353,

"Allah's Apostle said, "Allah guarantees him who strives in His Cause and whose motivation for going out is nothing but Jihad in His Cause and belief in His Word, that He will admit him into Paradise (if martyred) or bring him back to his dwelling place, whence he has come out, with what he gains of reward and booty."

Sahih al-Bukhari 52:54,

"The Prophet said, "By Him in Whose Hands my life is! Were it not for some men amongst the believers who dislike to be left behind me and whom I cannot provide with means of conveyance, I would certainly never remain behind any *Sariya'* (army-unit) setting out in Allah's Cause. By Him in Whose Hands my life is! I would love to be martyred in Al1ah's Cause and then get resurrected and then get martyred, and then get resurrected again and then get martyred and then get resurrected again and then get martyred."

Sahih al-Bukhari 2787,

"I heard Allah's Messenger saying, "The example of a Mujahid in Allah's Cause-- and Allah knows better who really strives in His Cause----is like a person who fasts and prays continuously. Allah guarantees that He will admit the Mujahid in His Cause into Paradise if he is killed, otherwise He will return him to his home safely with rewards and war booty."

One of the most famous Hadith is "Know that Paradise is under the shades of swords", *Sahih al-Bukhari 2818.* The way to Paradise, according to Muhammad is through taking up a sword and going on a jihad "in the way of Allah (*Jihad fi sabil Allah*)."

Both the Qur'an and the Hadith show that there is only one thing that can guarantee certain entrance to Paradise: the way of jihad. This explains why many martyr bombers (not suicide bombers) who have sacrificed their lives for the cause of Islam and Allah, kill the enemy in the hope of obtaining the virgins of Paradise. It is a powerful incentive.

The contrast with what Jesus taught, is stark. Jesus and His disciples teach that the way to follow Him and have eternal life, is to take up the cross, not the sword, and to follow Him. His way is the way of laying down one's life to save others, *Matthew 16:25; 1John 3:16.* As Franklin Graham said, "The God of the Bible gave his Son to die for us, but the god of Islam requires you to give your son to die for him." A favourite saying of Muslims is to say "the Christians love life, but we love death."

Hell in the Bible

Hell in the Bible is the place for the wicked who reject Jesus Christ as God and Saviour. It is an everlasting place of torment and fire.

The word 'hell' appears 54 times in the Bible. The original words for hell are the Hebrew *sheol* (abode of the dead) and the Greek *hades* (underworld) or *gehenna* (place of fire).

In the New Testament, Jesus uses the word *gehenna* frequently to describe a place of fire and judgment, particularly in the Gospels of Matthew and Mark. It refers to the final, eternal punishment for the devil and the wicked in *Matthew 25:41* and *2 Thessalonians 1:9.*

Another Greek word translated Hell is *tartarus*, the deep abyss or "gloomy dungeon" used specifically to imprison fallen angels (demons) who rebelled against God, acting as a holding place while they await final judgment.

2Peter 2:4,

"For if God did not spare sinning angels, but thrust them down into hell *(tartarus)*, and delivered them into chains of darkness, being reserved to judgment."

In the *Book of Revelation* we read about the Lake of Fire. This is where the beast (Antichrist) and the false prophet are cast at the end of the Great Tribulation, *Revelation 19:20*. It is where, after the Millennium Satan also is cast, *Revelation 20:10*. It is the place of eternal torment separated from the presence of God. After the last judgement all who have rejected Jesus and whose names are not in the Book of Life are also cast into this Lake of Fire, *Revelation 20:14-15*. All cowardly, abominable, murderers, sexually immoral, sorcerers, idolaters and all liars will have their part in the Lake of Fire that burns with fire and sulfur forever, *Revelation 21:8*.

It is surely a place that everyone would want to avoid! Jesus doesn't want anyone to go there. He offers them salvation and an eternal place with Him in a glorious heaven, but if they refuse to come into His eternal home, the only other alternative is an eternal home in the Lake of Fire. It's your choice. It's my our choice. Make sure you make the right choice.

Hell in Islam

Muslims have a similar vision of hell as the place of eternal fire. Hell is mentioned about 500 times in the Qur'an. The Arabic word for hell is *Jahanam*. The Islamic concept of hell is a place of punishment for disbelievers, hypocrites and wrongdoers. It is described as a real, blazing fire that has been created by God as an eternal abode for some, but a temporary purification place for believers who still have sin in their lives. As a vision of Heaven serves as an enticement to live a good, moral life, Hell serves as a stark warning not to live a sinful, wicked life. The Qur'an is much more descriptive of hell than the Bible and also describes what Satan and his demons do to people in hell for all eternity. It is truly a dreadful place.

The Qur'an gives several names to describe hell:

1. *Al-Naar* means "the Fire" referring to the fire of hell.
2. *Al-Jahiim* means "the Blazing Fire."
3. *Al-Hatamah* is translated "That which breaks to pieces" or "the crushing disaster." *Al Humazah 104:5.*
4. *Al-Haawiyah* means "The Abyss" *Al Qariah 101:9.*
5. *As-Sa'e*er is "the blaze" or "the burning" *Al Mulk 67:5.*

"*Azab*" (sometimes spelled *azaab* or *adhab*) primarily refers to severe punishment, torment, or torture, particularly when it is mentioning Divine judgment that God inflicts on the unbelievers and the wicked. It can also mean intense pain, suffering, or a painful, difficult situation. *Azab* in its various grammatical forms is mentioned 373 times in the Qur'an. It is often paired with fire and hell fire.

Purgatory - *Barzakh*

Like Catholics, Muslims also believe in a purgatory where people must undergo a period of time in hell in order to be purified from their sins. The place is called *Barzakh*, a partition, bar or barrier. It is the intermediate time between a person's death and the Day of Judgement, a place where souls are questioned and face torment for their sins.

Surah Al Mu'minuun 23:99-100,

"Until when death overtakes one of them, he says: My Lord, send me back, That I may do good in that which I have left. By no means! It is but a word that he speaks. And before them is a barrier (*barzakh*) until the day they are raised."

Although not yet in hell, it is believed that the sinners and unbelievers destined for it will suffer during this time. Muslims can also experience the punishment of the grave (*'adhab al-qabr*) based on their actions.

The Sirat: the narrow bridge over hell

The *Sirat* is a bridge over which every person must pass on the Day of Resurrection. To enter Paradise, it is reported in the Hadith they must tread across a bridge that is thinner than a strand of hair and as sharp as the sharpest knife or sword.

Sahih Muslim 183b,

"Abu Sa'id said: I have come to know that the bridge *(the Sirat)* would be thinner even than the hair and sharper than the sword."

The fires of Hell burn below this bridge. All sinners will fall into it's flames.

Surah Maryam 19:71-72,

"There is not one of you but shall come to it, this is an unavoidable decree of your Lord. And we will deliver those who guarded (against evil), and we will leave the unjust therein on their knees."

In Hadith Muslim 183, it records,

"Thou art our Lord. Then the bridge (Sirat) would be set up over the Hell and intercession would be allowed and they will say: O Allah, keep safe, keep safe. It was asked: Messenger of Allah, what is this bridge? He said: The void in which one is likely to slip. There would be hooks, tongs, spits like the thorn that is found in Najd and is known as Sa'dan. The believers would then pass over within the twinkling of an eye, like lightning, like wind, like a bird, like the finest horses and camels. Some will escape and be safe, some will be lacerated and let go, and some will be pushed into the fire of Hell till the believers will find rescue from the Fire."

According to Islamic tradition, there are massive iron hooks along the Sirat bridge meant to snatch people based on their earthly deeds, *Sahih al-Bukhari (No. 7439/806) and Sahih Muslim (No. 183).* These hooks are suspended along the sides of the bridge, commanded to snatch and pull down those whom they are ordered to seize, based on their deeds. Another similar, often-quoted narration is in *Sahih Muslim,* which reinforces that the hooks are "hanging ready to catch anyone whom they are commanded (to catch)."

Description of Hell in the Qur'an

The description of Hell occupies much of the Qur'an. Punishment, torture, fire or Hell are mentioned on almost every page.

Hell has seven doors and seven levels. *Surah Al Zumar 39:71; Surah Al Hijr 15:44.* The level of hell depends on the degree of offenses. Suffering is both physical and spiritual.

Surah Al-Imran 3:56,

"As to those who reject faith, I will punish them with terrible agony in this world and in the Hereafter, nor will they have anyone to help."

Surah Ali-Imran 3:176-178,

"And do not be saddened by those who rush into disbelief. They will not harm Allah in the least. Allah desires to give them no share in the Hereafter. A terrible torment awaits them. Those who exchange blasphemy for faith will not harm Allah in the least. A painful torment awaits them. Those who disbelieve should not assume that We respite them for their own good. In fact, We only respite them so that they may increase in sinfulness. A humiliating torment awaits them."

Hell is a place of terrible torment. Below is a list of graphic details mentioned in the Qur'an that describe the horror and the terror that awaits mankind in Hell.

1. Fresh roasted skins

Surah An-Nisa 4:55-56,

"And enough is Hell for a burning fire. Those who reject Our Signs, We shall soon cast into the Fire: As often as their skins are roasted through, We shall change them for fresh skins, that they may taste the Penalty: For Allah is Exalted in Power, Wise."

2. Boiling Fluids

Surah Yunus 10:4,

"To Him will be your return--of all of you. The promise of Allah is true and sure. It is He Who beginneth the process of creation, and repeateth it, that He may reward with justice those who believe and work righteousness; but those who reject Him will have draughts of boiling fluids, and a penalty grievous, because they did reject Him."

3. Death from every quarter

Surah Ibrahim 14:16-17,

"In front of such a one is Hell, and he is given, for drink, boiling fetid water (Indonesian translation: blood and pus). In gulps will he sip it, but never will he be near swallowing it down his throat: Death will come to him from every quarter, yet will he not die: And in front of him will be a chastisement unrelenting."

4. Tent of Fire

Surah Al-Khaf 18:29,

"Say, "The Truth is from your Lord": Let him who will, believe, and let him who will, reject (it): For the wrong-doers We have prepared a Fire whose (smoke and flames), like the walls and roof of a tent, will hem them in."

5. Layers of Fire

Surah Az-Zumar 39:16,

"They shall have Layers of Fire above them, and Layers (of Fire) below them": With this doth Allah warn off His Servants! "O My Servants! Then fear ye Me!"

6. Entertainment

Surah Al-Kahf 18:102,

"Do the Unbelievers think that they can take My servants as protectors besides Me? Verily We have prepared Hell for the Unbelievers for (their) entertainment."

7. Dragging through Fire

Surah Al-Qamar 54:48,

"The Day they will be dragged through the Fire on their faces, (they will hear:) "Taste ye the touch of Hell!"

8. *Surah Maryam 19:68-70,*

"So, by thy Lord, without doubt, We shall gather them together, and (also) the Evil Ones (with them); then shall We bring them forth on their knees round about Hell, Then shall We certainly drag out from every sect all those who were worst in obstinate rebellion against (Allah) Most

Gracious. And certainly We know best those who are most worthy of being burned therein."

Surah Al Dukhan 44:47,

"Seize him and then drag him in to the midst of hell."

9. Garments of Fire

Surah Al Hajj 22:18-20,

"But those who deny (their Lord), --for them will be cut out a garment of Fire: Over their heads will be poured out boiling water. With it will be scalded what is within their bodies, as well as (their) skins."

10. The Tree of Zaqqum

Surah As Saffat 37:62-68,

"For the like of this let all strive, who wish to strive. Is that the better entertainment or the Tree of Zaqqum? For We have truly made it (as) a trial for the wrong-doers. For it is a tree that springs out of the bottom of Hell fire: The shoots of its fruit stalks are like the heads of devils: Truly they will eat thereof and fill their bellies therewith."

11. Boiling and Intensely Cold Drinks and Fluids

Surah Sad 38:57,

"Yea, such! --Then shall they taste it, --a boiling fluid, and a fluid dark, murky, intensely cold!"

Surah Muhammad 47:15,

"(Can those in such Bliss) be compared to such as shall dwell forever in the Fire, and be given, to drink, boiling water, so that it cuts up their bowels (to pieces)?"

Surah Ar-Rahman 55:4,

"In its midst and in the midst of boiling hot water will they wander round!"

Surah Al-Waqiah 56:42,

"(They will be) in the midst of a fierce Blast of Fire and in Boiling Water."

Thus, hell is a place of terrible torture. What does Allah do in Hell? We note that Allah is very active in the Islamic hell. It is He who created hell. It is He who enforces punishments designed for unbelievers and hypocrites. It is He who changes burned skins for new skins to ensure continuous torment. It is He who enforces punishments like boiling water and fire garments and who rejects pleas for mercy. It is He who forces people back into the fire, whenever they try to escape.

Surah Ali-Imran 3:181,

"Certainly, heard Allah (the) saying (of) those who said, "Indeed Allah (is) poor while we (are) rich." We will record what they said and their killing the Prophets without (any) right, and We will say, "Taste (the) punishment (of) the Burning Fire."

Surah Al-Hajj 22:22,

"Every time they wish to get away therefrom, from anguish, they will be forced back therein, and (it will be said), "Taste ye the Penalty of Burning!"

This is also a dilemma for Muslims. Who is the God they are worshipping? Can they ever be good enough for Him? How can they have a relationship with Him? Will He guarantee that they will not spend eternity in the fires of hell?

Hell Dwellers in Islam

Who are the inhabitants of the Islamic Hell?

Everyone will enter hell! The Qur'an says that all mankind will be brought to hell and then God will leave the wicked there and will deliver the believers out of it, if He wills.

Surah Maryam 19:68-72,

"So by your Lord! We shall certainly gather them together and the devils, then shall We bring them around hell (*jahanam*) on their knees. Then We shall draw forth from every group those most rebellious against the Beneficent. Again, We certainly know best those who deserve most to be burned in it. And there is not one of you but shall come to it. This is an unavoidable decree of your Lord. And We shall deliver those who guard against evil, and leave the wrongdoers in it on their knees."

According to this Qur'anic verse, no one can escape Hell.

Allah says,

"We shall certainly gather them and the devils...

We shall bring them around hell...

We shall draw forth the most rebellious...

We certainly know best...

Not one of you but shall come into it...

This is an unavoidable decree...

We shall deliver those who guard against evil...

We shall leave the wrongdoers in it..."

Everyone will go there.

Who is working in Hell?

It is Allah Himself who will take all men and devils to the hell He made for them. In fact, in the Qur'an Allah says, He has created many men for hell.

Surah Al Araf 7:179,

"And certainly, we have created for hell, many of the jinn and men."

Surah Hud 11:119,

"And will be fulfilled (the) Word (of) your Lord, "Surely I will fill Hell with the Jinn and the men all together."

Surah Sad 38:77–85,

"Then I shall fill Hell with you [Iblis] and with all those that follow you, together."

God will put all men in Hell and then God will take some out of Hell and admit them to Paradise. The rest of humanity will remain there forever.

Surah Al-Baqarah 2:161-162,

"Verily, those who disbelieve, and die while they are disbelievers, it is they on whom is the Curse of Allah and of the angels and of mankind, combined. They will abide therein forever. Their punishment will neither be lightened nor will they be reprieved."

The unbelievers, the hypocrites, all who are not Muslims are sentenced to Hell.

The Qur'an states that sinners and the wicked will enter hell. The most wicked sinners are the unbelievers who reject and oppose God, Muhammad and Islam. God will forgive the little sins. The only unforgiveable sin is "shirk," which is believing that God has a son or worshipping idols.

The Qur'an describes in detail those who will enter Hell

1. Those who resist Allah

Surah Al-Anfal 8:13-14,

"For those who resist Allah, is the penalty of the Fire."

2. Those who oppose Muhammad

Surah At-Tawbah 9:63,

"Know they not that for those who oppose Allah and His Apostle, is the Fire of Hell? -Wherein they shall dwell. That is the supreme disgrace."

Surah Al-Jinn 72:23,

"Unless I proclaim what I receive from God and His Messages: for any that disobey God and His Apostle, - for them is Hell: they shall dwell therein forever."

3. Those who refuse to fight in jihad or those who turn back from jihad

Surah At-Tawbah 9:49,

Among them is a man who says: "Grant me exception and draw me not into trial." Have they not fallen into trial already? And indeed Hell surrounds the Unbelievers on all sides."

4. *Surah Al-Anfal 8:16,*

"If any do turn his back to them on such a day--unless it be in a stratagem of war, or to retreat to a troop (of his own) --he draws on himself the wrath of Allah, and his abode is Hell, --an evil refuge!"

5. Those who are sinners

Surah Ta Ha 20:74,

"Verily he who comes to his Lord as a sinner, --for him is Hell: Therein shall he neither die nor live."

Surah Al-Haqqah 69:25-31,

These verses describe how all sins are written down in books. The record of these deeds will be read out on the day of Resurrection, and the sinners will be seized and fettered and cast into the burning Fire.

6. Those who oppose Allah

Surah Al-Hajj 22:51,

"But those who strive against Our Signs, to frustrate them, --they will be Companions of the Fire."

7. Unbelievers in Allah and Muhammad

Surah Al-Hajj 22:72,

"When Our Clear Signs are rehearsed to them, thou wilt notice a denial on the faces of the Unbelievers! … It is the Fire (of Hell)! Allah has promised it to the Unbelievers! And evil is that destination!"

Surah Al- Fath 48:13-14,

"And if any believe not in Allah and His Apostle, We have prepared, for those who reject Allah, a Blazing Fire!"

Surah At-Tahriim 66:9,

"O Prophet! Strive hard against the Unbelievers and the Hypocrites, and be firm against them. Their abode is Hell, - an evil refuge (indeed)."

8. Hypocrites

Surah An-Nisa 4:145,

"The Hypocrites will be in the lowest depths of the Fire."

The Qur'an strongly condemns Hypocrisy. Muslims who pretend to believe are considered worse than the unbelievers (*al-kafiruun*). They are marked as "most abominable" to God, and destined for the lowest, most painful depths of Hellfire. They are the ones who tell lies, break their promises and their actions do not align with their professions of faith.

To study what the Qur'an says about hypocrites, read: *Qur'an Verses on Hypocrites (30 Ayat) - My Islam*

9. Non-Muslims, including Christians and Jews

Surah Al-Bayyinah 98:6,

"Surely those who disbelieve from among the followers of the Book and the polytheists shall be in the fire of hell, abiding therein; they are the worst of men."

These verses clearly show that according to the teachings of the Qur'an, all non-Muslims, every person who does not believe in Allah and his prophet, Muhammad, are the very worst of men and their destiny is the blazing fires of Hell. This Hell has been specifically prepared those who reject Allah and his prophet. The Hadith also describe Christians in Hell. According to Islamic theology, If a Jew or a Christian does not embrace Islam, does not believe in Prophet Muhammad until he dies as a Jew or a Christian, being a non-Muslim, he will go to Hell.

10. Those whose balance is light

Surah Al-Mu'minuun 23:103-104,

"But those whose balance is light, will be those who have lost their souls; in Hell will they abide. The Fire will burn their faces, and they will therein grin, with their lips displaced."

Surah Al-Araf 7:8-9,

"All sins are weighed in the scales. Those whose good deeds are light will be cast in the Fire."

Muslims believe in two angels sitting on their shoulders recording every deed, the one on the right recording good deeds and the one on the left recording bad deeds. All these deeds will be put onto the scales. Whichever scale is heavier will determine their final destination. If their bad deeds outweigh the good deeds their destination will be Hell Fire.

11. Those who are rebellious and wicked

Surah As-Sajdah 32:20.

"As to those who are rebellious and wicked, their abode will be the Fire: Every time they wish to get away therefrom, they will be forced thereinto, and it will be said to them: "Taste ye the Penalty of the Fire, the which ye were wont to reject as false."

Rebellion and wickedness and failure to believe, will surely lead to Hell.

12. Scandalmongers and Backbiters

Surah Al-Haumazah 104:1-8,

"Woe to every (kind of) scandal monger and backbiter, Who pileth up wealth and layeth it by, Thinking that his wealth would make him last forever. By no means! He will be sure to be thrown into that which Breaks to Pieces. And what will explain to thee That which Breaks to Pieces? (It is) the Fire of (the Wrath of) Allah kindled (to a blaze), the which doth mount (right) to the Hearts: It shall be made into a vault over them."

13. Those on the left hand

Surah Al-Waqiah 56:41-46.

"And those on the Left Hand – how (unfortunate) will be those on the Left Hand? In fierce hot wind and boiling water, and shadow of black smoke, neither cool nor pleasant. Verily before that they indulged in luxury, and were persisting in great sin."

Those on the Left Hand are those who will enter Hell. The Qur'an states that all sinners and all the wicked will enter Hell. The main sin is unbelief and opposition to Islam, Allah and his prophet, Muhammad. In fact, the only unforgiveable sin and the chief cause of entering hell is in believing that God has a son or the worshipping of idols. This is the sin of unbelief and in Arabic is called "*shirk*."

The Hadith also claim that most people will enter hell. One Hadith states that, out of every one thousand people entering into the afterlife, nine hundred and ninety-nine of them will end up in the fire, *Al-Bukhari, 4:55:567.*

The Hadith claim that women make up the majority of the population of Hell, *Sahih Muslim. 036:6596.* The position of women in hell is discussed in Dilemma 9.

The Fear of Hell

The very first time we read the Qur'an we were struck by the constant theme of hell fire, torture, punishment, the day of judgment. It seemed to be a message appearing on almost every page. We also observed that Muhammad was frequently described as "a warner." He was constantly warning of the flames of hell. This is one of the main messages in the Qur'an. This provides a powerful incentive to the Muslim to be a good Muslim, pray the five daily prayers, give alms, fast in Ramadhan and if possible, make a pilgrimage to Mecca. This they do with the hope of escaping the fires of Hell. Fear of hell is a highly motivating force in Islam.

The Uncertainty of Salvation

The quandary for Muslims is the fear and uncertainty of whether they will end up in heaven or hell! There is no certainty for a Muslim to be saved. No matter what a Muslim does, he can never be certain. Everything depends on the will and predestination of Allah. Even if he does go to heaven or hell there is still no certainty that he will stay there forever. It all depends on the will of God because people can be thrown out of heaven and into hell. Not the word EXCEPT in the next quotation from the Qur'an.

Surah Hud 11:106-108,

"Then as for those who are unhappy, they will be in the Fire; for them therein will be sighing and groaning. Abiding therein so long as the heavens and the earth endure, except as thy Lord please. Surely thy Lord is the Doer of what He intends. As for those who are made happy they will be in the Garden abiding therein so long as the heavens and earth endure, EXCEPT as thy Lord please, a gift never to be cut off."

Muhammad himself had no certainty about whether his destination was heaven or hell.

God told Muhammad to tell the people that he did not know what God would do with him.

Surah Al-Ahqaf 46:9,

"Say, 'I am not a new thing among the messengers, nor do I know what will be done with me or with you'."

Muhammad was also told to say that he did not know what God would do with his followers.

This is the ultimate uncertainty. It haunts every Muslim today. Their prophet didn't know what God would do to him. Their prophet did not know what would happen with his followers.

Every time Muslims mention the prophet Muhammad, they add the words, "Peace be upon him" which is often written as "*pbuh*." In Arabic they say, "*Sallallahu alayhi wa sallam*", often abbreviated as "*saw*".

Muslims say it means "Blessings of Allah be upon him as well as peace." It more literally means "Prayers of God be upon him and peace."

The verse that gives the command to say this, is written in the Qur'an:

Surah Al-Ahzab 33:56,

"Indeed, Allah and His Angels SEND BLESSINGS upon the Prophet. O you who believe! SEND BLESSINGS on him and greet him (with) greetings."

In the phrase, "*Sallallahu alayhi wa sallam*", the word "*sallah*" is interpreted to mean "to pray," "to perform *salah*," or "to invoke blessings." "*Salah*" (prayer) and "*Musalla*" (a place for prayer) are derived from the same Arabic root word. *Sallallahu* literally means "Allah prays." In other contexts it does not mean "send blessings", it means "pray."

Here are some differing translations of *Surah Al-Ahzab 33:56*. They translate "salah" with different words.

- "God and His angels ACCEPT PRAYERS for the Prophet. You who believe, PRAY for him (too) and greet him properly." *(T.B. Irving.)*
- "Surely Allah and His Angels SHOWER SERENITY (Literally: shower prayers) on the Prophet. O you who have believed, PRAY for (benediction on) him, and submit in full submission." *(Muhammad Mahmoud Ghali)*
- "Allah sends His SALAH (Graces, Honours, Blessings, Mercy, etc.) on the Prophet (Muhammad SAW) and also His angels too (ask Allah to bless and forgive him). O you who believe! Send your SALAT on (ask Allah to bless) him (Muhammad SAW), and (you should) greet (salute) him with the Islamic way of greeting (salutation i.e. AsSalamu Alaikum." *(Hilali – Khan)*
- "Verily, God and His angels PRAY for the prophet. O ye who believe! PRAY for him and salute him with a salutation." (*Edward Henry Palmer*).

Why do God and the angels and all Muslims pray continuously for the Prophet? It is because there is no certainty of his salvation. Muhammad also said in the Hadith:

Sahih al-Bukhari 7003 (Volume 9, Book 93, Hadith 502/7405,

"By Allah, though I am the Messenger of Allah, I do not know what Allah will do with me." Muhammad died without any certainty of salvation. That is why millions of Muslims around the world are sending their prayers upon Muhammad.

Another problem for Muslims is predestination. They believe in predestination as one of their six articles of faith. That means, God predetermines a person's life and chooses whom He wills to enter heaven or hell. This is clear from the Qur'an.

The God of Islam invites whom He wills to the straight path and to heaven. It's not your choice. It's His.

Surah Yunus 10:25,

"Allah invites to the Home of Peace and guides whom He wills to a straight path."

He opens the heart of whoever He wills to guide. This means, that if God does not wish you to become a Muslim, then your heart will remain closed.

Surah Al-An'am 6:125,

"Whoever Allah wills to guide, He opens their heart to Islam."

Forgiveness or punishment is also totally dependent on the will of God.

Surah Al-Baqarah 2:284,

"He will forgive whom He wills and punish whom He wills."

Mercy is only given to those whom He chooses to show mercy.

Surah Al-Baqarah 2:105,

"Allah chooses for His mercy whom He wills."

Compare this with what Jesus said about Himself.

Jesus knew where He was going.

- ➢ He said, "I go to the Father." *(John 14:28).*
- ➢ He knew the way. He said, "I am the way, the truth and the life." *(John 14:6).*
- ➢ He knew what would happen to those who believed in Him and followed Him.
- ➢ He said, "Because I live, you will live also." *(John 14:19).*

It is the Gospel of our Lord Jesus Christ that is the only way out of the predicament that faces all mankind. Jesus came to provide certainty of salvation for all those who repent of their sin and believe in Him as the Saviour. He alone provides the certainty of eternal life.

John 5:24,

"Whoever hears my word and believes him who sent me has eternal life. He does not come into judgment but has passed from death to life."

Luke 23:43,

Jesus is the one who said to the dying thief, "Today you will be in Paradise with Me."

Romans 8:15–16,

"The Holy Spirit bears witness with our spirit that we are the children of God."

1John 5:13,

John, the apostle wrote: "I write these things to you who believe in the name of the Son of God so that you may know that you have eternal life."

Christians have the certainty of salvation. This is based on the promises of God in the Bible. We know the Father loved us and gave His only Son for us. We know the Son, our Lord Jesus Christ died for us on the Cross. His death and resurrection has justified us and has made us righteous in His sight. Through the grace of God, His free and unearned gift, we receive salvation by trusting in Him. We know the Holy Spirit has given us the assurance that we are the sons and daughters of the living God.

Christians know that the Lord God is faithful and true and always keeps His promises. We know we have eternal life. We made a choice to believe Him and we know He will accept us. We look forward to living with Him forever in His presence.

The Muslim has no certainty. Their prophet had no certainty of salvation or of being in Paradise. The Qur'an offers no confidence that Muslims will be saved. Their God offers no assurance. There is no freedom. It is not we who choose, but it is God who chooses who will or will not be saved.

This leads to one of the most common sayings among Muslims, **"Insha-allah!"** That means, "If God wills!" It is all up to God. Life or death is in His hands. Heaven or Hell is dependent on His choosing. According to Islam we can do our best, but we can never have certainty!

In facing an eternal destiny, Islam only offers a Heaven filled with never ending sensual pleasures. In the Muslim Heaven, the Muslim never relates to or has fellowship with Allah. Jesus offers an eternity with so much more and the center-piece is to fellowship with God Himself. Islam offers fear and uncertainty, but Jesus offers peace and security. People have a choice whom they will follow.

A Dilemma For Muslims

Where will they spend eternity?
What about those of us who are Christians?
What do we desire for our family and friends, our neighbors.
our community, the people we meet whether Christian, Muslim,
Hindu, Buddhist or any other religion or no religion?
Are we willing to go down to the enemy's camp
and take back what he has stolen?

Are we prepared to involve ourselves in the mission of "plundering hell to populate heaven"?

Discussion Questions:

1. How important is it to you and your family to have the certainty of salvation?
2. What do you look forward to the most about going to heaven?
3. How do you think you can help your friends understand the dangers of hell and the amazing wonders and joys of heaven?

DILEMMA 11

MUHAMMAD IN THE BIBLE DILEMMA

A friend of ours named Muhammad Rasul, grew up in Iran but was educated in Dubai. In his youth he was taught that the Bible, both the Old and New Testaments named the Prophet Muhammad as the prophesied final messenger of God. This excited Muhammad Rasul as it meant his name was mentioned in the Qur'an and in the Bible. There was only one problem that troubled him. He was forbidden from having access to the Bible or even to read it himself. The Bible is an illegal book in many Islamic countries, and Muhammad Rasul was told by the scholars that the Jews and the Christians had corrupted the Bible and therefore to protect Muslims from its errors, the Bible had been banned.

However, Muhammad Rasul could not find any verses in the Qur'an to say that the Bible was corrupted. In fact, the opposite was the case. He read that God said in the Qur'an that the Bible was given as a light and guidance and must be obeyed.

He also read that no-one could change the words of the Scriptures as God had promised to protect them and that no-one could change their words.

Surah Al-Anaam 6:115,

"The word of thy Lord doth find its fulfilment in truth and in justice: **None can change His words:** for He is the one who heareth and knoweth all."

Surah Al-Kahf 18:27,

"And recite (and teach) what has been revealed to thee of the Book of thy Lord: **none can change His Words,** and none wilt thou find as a refuge other than Him."

This also specifically applies to the Bible as the Qur'an asserts that the Law and the Gospel were given by God and must be obeyed.

Surah Al Maidah 5:46-47,

"And in their footsteps We sent Jesus the son of Mary, confirming the Law that had come before him: We sent him the Gospel: therein was guidance and light, and confirmation of the Law that had come before him: a guidance and an admonition to those who fear Allah. Let the people of the Gospel judge by what Allah hath revealed therein. If any do fail to judge by (the light of) what Allah hath revealed, they are (no better than) those who rebel."

This frustrated Muhammad Rasul as he desperately wanted to see for himself if his name was written in the Bible. This lack of access to the Bible created a dilemma for Muhammad Rasul on two accounts:

a. If Islamic teaching was correct then surely seeing the name Muhammad in the Bible would prove that the Qur'an was correct and that the Christians who denied that Muhammad was prophesied in the Bible, would be proved to be false.
b. If the Qur'an justified the Bible as being a true revelation from God then seeing Muhammad's name in the Bible would justify the Qur'an, but if Muhammad's name was not there,

then this would prove that the Qur'an was false and that the Islamic scholars had lied to him.

This is the dilemma Muhammad Rasul and many millions of Muslims world-wide have faced. It is important that we investigate this dilemma to determine the truth. If Muhammad was prophesied to be the Final Messenger of God to humanity then all of humanity must submit to the message he declared. If Muhammad is not declared to be the Final Messenger then we need to understand who he really is.

Modern Islamic Scholars claim that Muhammad is clearly prophesied in the Bible

Modern Islamic scholars quote from both the Old and New Testament scriptures in their efforts to prove that Muhammad was truly prophesied in the Bible. Some also claim that the name Muhammad was originally clearly recorded in both the Old and New Testaments but now has been deleted from the Bible. This conspiracy from both Jewish scholars and Christian theologians was designed to hide the truth about the prophecies concerning Muhammad. We will examine these claims and seek to solve this important dilemma.

Several key verses in the Qur'an declare that Muhammad is mentioned in both the Law and the Gospel, or in other words, in the Old and New Testaments.

Surah Al Araaf 7:157,

"Those who follow the Messenger, the Prophet who can neither read nor write (i.e.Muhammad SAW) whom they find written with them in the Taurat (Torah) (Deut, xviii, 15) and the Injil (Gospel) (John xiv, 16)."

(Yusuf Ali Translation),

"Those who follow the messenger, the unlettered Prophet (Muhammad), whom they find mentioned in their own (scriptures), in the law and the Gospel."

These references in the Qur'an state the belief that Muhammad is clearly mentioned in the Bible, both the Old Testament (Torah) and the New Testament (Gospel).

It should be noted that whenever you read the Qur'an and see words in brackets, that these are added words that do not appear in the original Arabic Qur'an. Do not be deceived. The word "Muhammad" is only mentioned four times in the whole of the Qur'an but in the various translations into other languages, like English, Indonesian, Malay, French, German, Chinese etc the word "Muhammad" is recorded many hundreds of times and can be found on almost every page. The clear intent is to give the impression that the contents were directed towards this man who is said to be the final prophet. Elsewhere, in the historical records, the word "Muhammad", meaning "the praised one" was used for hundreds of years before Islam to refer to Jesus. Jesus was the "Muhammad, i.e. the praised one. This is clear in the ancient manuscripts and archeological evidence.

During the 7th to 10th centuries in Arabia and Persia, the use of the word ***"Muhammad"*** transitioned to become the prophet of Islam. You can read

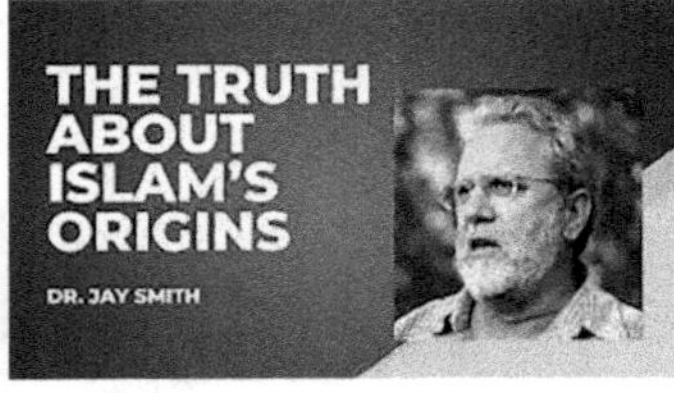

more on this subject in *"Muhammad, A Critical Biography"* by Dr. Robert Spencer, and *"The Hidden Origins of Islam"* by Karl-Heinz Ohlig and Gerd-R. Puin. You can also investigate research on the internet and Youtube, particularly by Abdul Fadi, from CIRA International. a former fundamentalist Muslim follower of Osama Bin Laden, from Saudi

Arabia, and Dr. Jay Smith on *www.youtube.com/watch?v=drRXueGNPGU* that discuss this important subject concerning the real Muhammad.

Who is the Original Muhammad in History?

This is a very interesting and important question which creates a serious dilemma for our Muslim friends. What if the original Muhammad in history is actually Jesus? Would this affect the way that Muslims look at who Jesus really is?

I asked Google a serious question concerning the Prophet Muhammad

"Before Islam, was Jesus called "the praised one" or was it "Muhammad"?

I was surprised by the answer, and I quote it here in full, unedited:

"In early 7th-century, pre-Islamic, and early Islamic contexts, the term "Muhammad" (meaning "the praised one") appeared as an honourific title, often applied to Jesus in Christian, Arab, and early Muslim contexts rather than only as a proper name.

Some scholars argue that early coins and inscriptions referring to "Muhammad" (or *Mmed*) were originally used for Jesus to denote "the praised one" or "Messiah," only later becoming associated with the prophet of Islam.

Key details:

- **"Muhammad" as a Title:** The word *Muhammad* itself translates to "the praised one" or "praiseworthy." It was used as a title for the Messiah, which is why it appeared alongside Christian symbols like the cross on coins from the 7th-century Levant.
- **Theological Shifts:** Some scholars, like Günter Lüling, argue that the Qur'anic usage of "Muhammad" originally referred to a

Christian understanding of Jesus as the praised one, and this was only later adopted in the 8th/9th centuries for the Islamic prophet.

- **Jesus in Islam:** In the Qur'an, Jesus is known as *Isa al-Masih* (Jesus the Messiah) and is described as a "word from God."
- **Ahmad vs. Muhammad:** The Qur'an *in Surah As-Saff (61:6)* mentions a messenger coming after Jesus named *Ahmad* (the most praised one), which Muslims widely interpret as referring to the Prophet Muhammad, not Jesus.

Therefore, while the name "Muhammad" was not used to *identify* Jesus in the Bible, "the praised one" (often written as *Mmed* or *Mhmd*) it was used as an epithet for Jesus in early Arabic Christian contexts." ***End of Google quote.***

Muslims claim that Bible verses predict the coming of Muhammad

Islamic preachers often cite verses from the Qur'an and compare them with the Bible to argue that this coming prophet refers exclusively to Muhammad. Christians reject that interpretation stating these verses refer specifically to the coming Messiah, Jesus. We need to examine these claims and analyse the meaning of each of the references. A key prophecy by Moses is the major reference for inferring that Muhammad is the prophesied prophet who is yet to come.

The Main Old Testament Prophecy

Deuteronomy 18:18,

"I will raise up for them a Prophet like you from among their brethren, and will put My words in His mouth, and He shall speak to them all that I command Him."

This is a frequently quoted Bible verse which Muslims say prophesies the future coming of the prophet Muhammad. When we look at each phrase it becomes obvious that the prophecy is clearly referring to Jesus. We will see that there is no similarity between Muhammad and Moses, but there are many similarities between Jesus and Moses.

a. **The First element of this Prophecy: "A prophet like you (Moses)" – In what ways was Jesus like Moses?**
   i. After their birth, the lives of Moses and Jesus were under threat of death by the command of the ruling Authority. Pharoah of Egypt wanted to kill all the newborn males, which included Moses *(Exodus 1:22).* Moses survived. Herod of Israel wanted to kill Jesus so he had all the children under two years old killed by his soldiers *(Matthew 2:16).* Jesus escaped and survived.
   ii. Moses brought the Law and Jesus came to fulfil it *(John 1:17; Matthew 5:17).*
   iii. Both Moses *(Deuteronomy 34:5-7; Jude 1:9; Matthew 17:1-8)* and Jesus died and rose again *(Matthew 27:45–28:10).* We know that Moses was raised to life as Satan disputed with Michael about the whereabouts of Moses' body as if he was dead where was his body *(Jude 1:9)?* Furthermore, Moses was very much alive and with Elijah and Jesus on the Mount of Transfiguration *(Matthew 17:3; Mark 9:4; Luke 9:30).* In the end-times, before Christ's return, Moses and Elijah, His two witnesses will bring judgement against the kingdom of Antichrist for 3½ years *(Revelation 11:3-6).*

b. **The second element of this prophecy: "from among their brethren" – what evidence is there that this referred to Jesus?**

The Apostle Peter clearly declared that Jesus was the fulfillment of the prophecy in *Deuteronomy 18:18,*

Acts 3:19-23,

"Repent therefore and be converted, that your sins may be blotted out, so that times of refreshing may come from the presence of the Lord, and **that He may send Jesus Christ, who was preached to you before,** whom heaven must receive until the times of restoration of all things, **which God has spoken by the mouth of all His holy prophets since the world began. For Moses truly said to the fathers, "the Lord your God will raise up for you a prophet like me from your brethren.** Him you shall hear in all things, whatever he says to you. And it shall be that every soul who will not hear that prophet shall be utterly destroyed from among the people." Yes, and all the prophets, from Samuel and those who follow, as many as have spoken, have also foretold these days."

Only Jesus fulfilled that prophecy and no-one else. The coming prophet had to be a close relative, an Israelite, "from among their brethren" not from some distant relative. According to Islamic tradition, Muhammad was 40 to 60 generations after Abraham and Moses in a separate lineage, hardly close enough to be called "from among their brethren" thus disqualifying the possibility that this prophecy could refer to the Islamic Muhammad. On the other hand the genealogy of Jesus has Him as a direct descendant, *Matthew 1:1-17; Luke 3:23-38.*

c. A third element of this prophecy: I "will put My words in His mouth, and He shall speak to them all that I command Him" – Is this what Jesus did in His ministry?

John 12:49-50,

"For I have not spoken on My own authority; but the Father who sent Me gave Me a command, what I should say and what I should speak. And I know that His command is everlasting life. Therefore, whatever I speak, just as the Father has told Me, so I speak."

It is very clear that only Jesus fulfilled exactly what the prophecy declared.

A Secondary Prophetic Reference: Muhammad in the Song of Solomon

Song of Solomon 5:16,

"His mouth is most sweet, yes, **he is altogether lovely**. This is my beloved, and this is my friend, O daughters of Jerusalem!"

The Hebrew word used for "altogether lovely" is *machmad (m**ch**md)*, which Islamic preachers identify as Muhammad due to the similarities of the base letters with *muhammad (m**h**md).*

This passage refers to the relationship Solomon had with the Queen of Sheba, a descendant of Kedar the son of Ishmael, the son of Abraham to Hagar, *(Song of Solomon 1:5).* Therefore, some Muslims interpret it to be a prophecy about Muhammad.

The Bible clearly shows that the coming Prophet is the Messiah and the Messiah is Jesus

Listen to the declaration made by John the Baptist, who is mentioned as a great prophet in the Qur'an, named Yahya.

Surah Maryam 19:12,

"O Yahya! take hold of the Book with might": and We gave him Wisdom even as a youth."

John 1:19-23,

"Now this is the testimony of John, when the Jews sent priests and Levites from Jerusalem to ask him, "Who are you?" He confessed, and did not deny, but confessed, "I am not the Christ." And they asked him, "What then? Are you Elijah?" He said, "I am not." "Are you the Prophet?" And he answered, "No." Then they said to him, "Who are you, that we may give an answer to those who sent us? What do you say about yourself?" He said: "I am "the Voice of one crying in the wilderness: "Make straight the Way of the LORD (YHWH)," "as the prophet Isaiah said."

Isaiah 4:3,

"The voice of one crying in the wilderness: "Prepare the way of the LORD (YHWH); Make straight in the desert a highway for our God."

This declaration by the prophet Yahya (John the Baptist) is in all of the Gospel records, *(Matthew 3:3; Mark 1:3; Luke 3:6)* and declares that the one coming has the STRAIGHT PATH and He is the LORD GOD YAHWEH! This could never be Muhammad. The only one fulfilling this prophecy is Jesus, the Messiah, for He is the LORD GOD YAHWEH, the Creator of heaven and earth who has come down to earth to bring us the Straight Path, the only way of salvation.

Muslim expositors have claimed that the foretold prophet was not Jesus Christ, nor any other Israelite prophet, because none of them ever claimed to be the prophet promised here. We see the falsehood in this claim:

(a) Because a prophet that Islam acknowledges and praises as being truthful, John the Baptist (Yahya), declared that the prophet referred to was Jesus, *John 1:19-23.*

(b) Because the Apostle Peter confirmed that the prophesied prophet was Jesus, *Acts 3:19-23.*

(c) Because the three key elements in the prophecy in *Deuteronomy, 18:18*, as seen above, were only fulfilled by Jesus, and none were fulfilled by Muhammad.

The most quoted New Testament Prophecy that is claimed by Islam to be Muhammad, the coming Comforter, is found in the Gospel of John 14-16

God says in the Qur'an that Muhammad is mentioned in both the Old and New Testaments as can be seen in the following verses.

Surah Al-Araf 7:157,

"Those who follow the Messenger, the Prophet who can neither read nor write (i.e.Muhammad SAW) whom they find written with them in the Taurat (Torah) (Deuteronomy 18:15) and the Injil (Gospel) (John 14:16)."

Surah Al-Baqarah 2:136,

"Say: We believe in Allah and (in) that which has been revealed to us, and (in) that which was revealed to Abraham, and Ishmael and Isaac and Jacob and the tribes, and (in) that which was given to Moses and Jesus, and (in) that which was given to the prophets from their Lord, we do not make any distinction between any of them and to Him do we submit."

The Islamic assertion is that Muhammad is referred to in these Bible passages, especially concerning the coming Helper. In some translations, the Helper is referred to as the Comforter or the Advocate. The Bible makes it clear that the one that Jesus and the Father will send is the Holy Spirit. However, Islamic scholars state that this is not the Holy Spirit, it is Muhammad.

John 14:16-17,

"And I will pray the Father, and He will give you another Helper, that He may abide with you forever— the Spirit of truth, whom the world cannot receive, because it neither sees Him nor knows Him; but you know Him, for He dwells with you and will be in you."

Furthermore, Jesus expands on this prophetic message describing His role amongst us.

John 16:7-15,

"It is to your advantage that I go away; for if I do not go away, the Helper will not come to you; but if I depart, **I will send Him to you.** And when He has come, He will convict the world of sin, and of righteousness, and of judgment: of sin, because they do not believe in Me; of righteousness, because **I go to My Father** and you see Me no more; of judgment, because the ruler of this world is judged. "I still have many things to say to you, but you cannot bear them now. However, when He, the Spirit of truth, has come, He will guide you into all truth; for He will not speak on His own authority, but whatever He hears He will speak; and **He will tell you things to come.** He will glorify Me, for **He will take of what is Mine and declare it to you. All things that the Father has are Mine.** Therefore I said that He will take of Mine and declare it to you."

When we analyse the contents of these verses, it is clear that the one who is coming has a Divine nature and presence.

- He will abide with you forever – *John 14:16* - Muhammad could not abide forever
- He is called the Spirit of Truth – *John 14:17* - Muhammad was never called a "spirit".
- He will be in you – *John 14:17* - Nowhere does the Qur'an ever suggest that Muhammad could dwell in the Muslims. This is purely the work of the Holy Spirit
- He will be sent by Jesus – *John 16:7* - Do Muslims really believe that Muhammad was sent by Jesus? That would make Jesus greater than Muhammad and Muhammad would be the servant of Jesus!

- He will tell you the future, the things to come – *John 16:13* - There are no future prophecies told by Muhammad. He is known as the prophet who never prophesied!
- He is a co-owner of all that God possesses – *John 16:15* - That would make Muhammad co-equal with God, possessing all that God possesses. Only Jesus and the Holy Spirit can claim co-equality with God.

An examination of the Bible, both Old Testament (the Law) and the New Testament (the Gospel) demonstrate conclusively that Muhammad is nowhere to be seen as the coming prophet claimed by Islam.

Was the coming of Islam Prophesied in the Bible?

There are references in the Bible that indicate certain characteristics of a coming religion that could be identified as the religion of Islam.

Paul warned of a False Gospel that would pervert the Gospel of Christ

1. A new pathway to salvation

Galatians 1:6-9,

"I marvel that you are turning away so soon from Him who called you in the grace of Christ, to **a different gospel**, which is not another; but there are some who trouble you and want to pervert the gospel of Christ. But even if we, or an angel from heaven, preach any other gospel to you than what we have preached to you, let him be accursed. As we have said before, so now I say again, if anyone preaches any other gospel to you than what you have received, let him be accursed."

In the 7th Century, Muhammad went into a cave and said an angel of light came to him and showed him another path to salvation! Not the pathway of the Cross of Christ! Not grace and faith! His was a pathway denying the need for a Redeemer as everyone would have to save themselves by their own good works.

2. The Apostle John prophesied that his new belief system would kill Christians in the name of their God believing they were doing God's will. This new belief does not know the Father and the Son

John 16:1-4,

"These things I have spoken to you, that you should not be made to stumble. They will put you out of the synagogues; yes, the time is coming that **whoever kills you will think that he offers God service.** And these things they will do to you because **they have not known the Father nor Me.** But these things I have told you, that when the time comes, you may remember that I told you of them. "And these things I did not say to you at the beginning, because I was with you."

3. The warning of coming Antichrists who deny the Father and the Son. This belief system would originate from apostate Christians

1John 2:18-26,

"Little children, it is the last hour; and as you have heard that **the Antichrist is coming**, even now **many antichrists** have come, by which we know that it is the last hour. They went out from us, but they were not of us; for if they had been of us, they would have continued with us; but they went out that they might be made manifest, that none of them were of us. But you have an anointing from the Holy One, and you know all things. I have not written to you because you do not know the truth, but because you know it, and that no lie is of the truth. Who is a liar but he who denies that

Jesus is the Christ? **He is antichrist who denies the Father and the Son.** Whoever denies the Son does not have the Father either; he who acknowledges the Son has the Father also. Therefore let that abide in you which you heard from the beginning. If what you heard from the beginning abides in you, you also will abide in the Son and in the Father. And this is the promise that He has promised us—eternal life. These things I have written to you concerning those who try to deceive you."

1John 4:1-4,

"Beloved, **do not believe every spirit, but test the spirits,** whether they are of God; because many false prophets have gone out into the world. By this you know the Spirit of God: Every spirit that confesses that Jesus Christ has come in the flesh is of God, and **every spirit that does not confess that Jesus Christ has come in the flesh is not of God. And this is the spirit of the Antichrist, which you have heard was coming, and is now already in the world.** You are of God, little children, and have overcome them, because He who is in you is greater than he who is in the world."

Do you not see the evidence around the world and in our own country? That's why we need to be truly filled with the anointing of the Holy Spirit, the ***dunamis power*** that Jesus promised *(Acts 1:8)* and which was poured out on the Church on the Day of Pentecost (Acts 2). We need a new boldness and a fresh anointing from the Holy Spirit, the wisdom of God the Father, and the love of Jesus Christ. God has not retired, nor have we!

4. They kill believers by beheading them

Revelation 20:4-6,

"And I saw thrones, and they sat on them, and judgment was committed to them. Then I saw the souls of **those who had been beheaded for their witness to Jesus and for the word of God,** who had not worshiped the beast or his image, and had not received his mark on their foreheads or on their hands. And they lived and reigned with Christ for a thousand years. But the rest of the dead did not live again until the thousand years were finished. This is the first resurrection. Blessed and holy is he who has part in the first resurrection. Over such the second death has no power, but they shall be priests of God and of Christ, and shall reign with Him a thousand years."

We are clearly living in the Last Days. The reign of the Antichrist is not far away and we need to be prepared. We need to finish the Great Commission of *Matthew 28:19-20.* We need to complete the Apostolic Commission of *Colossians 1:24-29.*

Three uncomfortable options to solve the Dilemma of Muhammad in the Bible

This is a huge problem. Islam faces three uncomfortable options:

1. **The Qur'an is wrong.** Muhammad isn't mentioned in the Law and the Gospel and these claims were invented.
2. **There's a global conspiracy.** Jews and Christians conspired together to erase every mention of Muhammad. If so, where is the evidence for this conspiracy?
3. **Allah did not preserve the evidence.** If these texts were corrupted or lost, Allah allowed the clearest proof of Muhammad's prophethood to disappear. That would prove that Allah lied when he said that no-one could change his words. It would also reveal that Allah was weak and incapable of protecting his revelations.

None of these options sit well with the Qur'an's claim that Muhammad is explicitly mentioned. The only solution is to accept that:

(a) Muhammad was never mentioned in the Bible

(b) The God of Islam is unable to protect his scriptures so that they get changed or disappear. Here's the challenge for Muslims. If this claim is incorrect, name the sources where Muhammad is explicitly mentioned. Prove that they existed before the time of Muhammad and show that it specifically names Muhammad. If not, we only have silence and silence is not evidence!

(c) That the God of the Bible has the true revelation and path of salvation through accepting His Son Jesus Christ as the Straight Path and the only Way to salvation and eternal life.

Questions to consider or discuss:

1. What verses have you found that *provide* indisputable evidence of the prophet Muhammad in the Bible?
2. Who do you think is the coming prophet mentioned in *Deuteronomy 18:18?*
3. How would you interpret *John 14:16-17 and John 16:7-15?*

DILEMMA 12

THE JESUS' DEITY DILEMMA

Is Jesus Man or God?

We have already seen that the Qur'an teaches that Muslims must believe in Jesus. We have already seen the uniqueness of Jesus among the prophets. Yet the dilemma remains, is he just one of the 25 prophets mentioned in the Qur'an or is He someone far greater than all the other prophets, including Muhammad?

Is Jesus really only a man or is He God?

Jeff and I were in Amman, Jordan. We were in a taxi and Jeff was chatting to the driver. He said to Jeff, "In Islam the greatest sin one can commit, is to say that God has a son." Jeff thought for a moment and replied, "In the Christian faith, the greatest sin is to deny that God has a Son because that would mean there is no possibility for us to be saved!" The taxi driver was not expecting this answer and said he would have to think about it.

For the taxi driver, to say God has a son, meant that he would be committing the sin of blasphemy, the sin of associating another with God. It is called "*shirk*" in Arabic.

For Christians, Jesus is God. He is the Creator. He is the Redeemer. He is eternal. He is omnipotent, all powerful. He is omniscient, all knowing.

In His eternal being He is omnipresent. We know these things from what the Bible teaches. Our salvation is dependent on believing that He is the Son of God, God who has come in the flesh.

This is a major dilemma for Muslims everywhere just as it was for this taxi driver.

According to the Qur'an, Jesus is only a slave, a man, a prophet like Abraham, Moses and Muhammad, but not the Son of God. When we visited Israel walking through the tourist trails of the old city of Jerusalem and through the streets of Nazareth, we were confronted by large billboards written in English saying, "Jesus said, "I am the slave of Allah."

And yet, what does the Qur'an really teach?

We asked one of our Muslim teachers in Yemen, to help us read the Bible. In our first class, we were learning to read the Gospel of Mark in Arabic. We opened up to Mark chapter 1, verse 1 and read, "The beginning of the Gospel of Jesus Christ, the Son of God." Our teacher was immediately confronted with the key message of the Gospel. "Jesus Christ, the Son of God." He was visibly affected by these words. They starkly contradict the teaching of the Qur'an that God has no sons, that God has no partner.

Which book contains the truth about Jesus? The Bible or the Qur'an? The central truth about Jesus in the Bible is that He is the Creator, the First and the Last, the Son of God who became a man, died on the cross to save us and rose again from the dead.

Jesus was born miraculously: Supernatural Birth

Jesus is the only human born on the earth who had no man who fathered him. His birth is unique. In the Qur'an, the only birth referred to mentioned or discussed, apart from that of Mary, his mother, is the birth of Jesus. Jesus was born as a human being and yet His birth was miraculous, a virgin birth.

Who was Jesus' father? According to the Qur'an, Jesus has no father. There is no reference to Joseph in the Qur'an. He only has a mother, a mother who is the only woman mentioned by name in the Qur'an, and the only one who has a whole surah named after her.

Jesus is repeatedly called "Son of Mary." Among Arabs, it is the inevitable custom to call children the sons or daughters of their father, never of their mother. Jesus is the only man called the son of a woman. In the very beginning of the Bible He is prophesied to be the "seed of the woman."

Genesis 3:15,

"And I will put enmity Between you and the woman, And between your seed and her Seed; He shall bruise your head, And you shall bruise His heel."

The New Testament reveals who seed of the woman. He is the one who is bruised under Satan's heel on the cross, but who also bruises his head, destroys his power and will ultimately throw him into the lake of fire forever.

Galatians 4:4,

"But when the set time had fully come, God sent his Son, born of a woman, born under the law, to redeem those under the law."

This raises a question for Muslims. The Qur'an says that God has no consort or mate. How could God produce a Son without a mate? Does God need a wife? How can God have a Son?

Islam states that because God has no wife, it's impossible for Him to have a Son

Surah Al-Anaam 6:101,

"He is the Originator of the heavens and the earth. How can He have children when He has no wife?"

Surah Al-Jinn 72:3

"And Exalted is the Majesty of our Lord: He has taken neither a wife nor a son."

Muhammad fundamentally misunderstood the Sonship of Jesus. He only thought of it in human terms. He thought to have a son, God must have a wife. Christians also reject that concept! God never got married. He never took a wife!

The question then arises, how could Mary produce a son without a father?

If God cannot have a son without a wife, then how can Mary have a son without a husband? Could Mary do what God could not do?

This question mocks Christians. What else does this question reveal?

From Islam's earliest days, their scholars have misconstrued the Christian concept of the sonship of Christ to being the result of a physical, sexual encounter between God (Allah) and Mary. In attacking the Christian faith, Ahmad Deedat, a famous Islamic apologist and debater against the Christian doctrines of the Deity of Christ and the Trinity, stated, "He (God) does not beget because begetting is an animal act. It belongs to the lower animal act of sex. We do not attribute such an act to God," *Dr. Anis A.Shorrosh, Islam Revealed: A Christian Arab's View of Islam, 1988, cited on p.25).*

Another Islamic scholar, Abdul Dawud, concludes that from a "Muslim point of belief the Christian dogma concerning the eternal birth or generation of the Son is blasphemy." *(Abdul-Ahad Dawud, Muhammad in the Bible, 1979, p.205).*

From 300 years before the times of Muhammad, we read Christian writers condemning a heresy that was circulating, that said God had sex with a woman to produce a son. Such a concept goes back to the ancient Greeks who believed intermarriage of gods with humans was possible. Such a belief has constantly been rejected by Christians. As was stated by Lactantius in 306 AD, "He who hears the words 'Son of God' spoken must not conceive in his mind such wickedness as to fancy that God procreated through marriage and union with any female, - a thing which is not done except by an animal possessed of a body and subject to death." *(Cited on p.265, Answering Islam, Norman L. Geesler and Abdul Saleeb, 2002).*

The Islamic answer to the birth of Jesus, is that God created Jesus in Mary's womb in the same way that He created Adam. Jesus' birth is compared to that of Adam's creation.

Surah Ali-Imran 3.59 *states,*

"Indeed the example of Jesus in the sight of Allah is like that of Adam. He created him from dust, then said to him, 'Be!' and he was."

There are two problems with this verse.

- ➢ Jesus was not, like Adam, created from dust. Jesus was conceived in Mary's womb.
- ➢ Jesus was not, like Adam, created by God just speaking a word. He is the Word and the Spirit who entered Mary's womb.

Jesus was created from a human egg and a Divine seed. That marks the difference between the creation of Adam and Jesus. The breath of God was breathed into dust and created Adam. The breath of God was breathed into Mary's womb and conceived Jesus, Son of Man and Son of God. Jesus became Son of Man through His birth as a human being. Jesus is the Son of God through His eternal relationship with the Father.

Surah Al-Anbiya 21.91,

"And she who guarded her chastity, so We breathed into her of Our Spirit, and We made her and her son a sign for the worlds."

Surah At-Tahrim 66.12,

"And Maryam, (the) daughter (of) Imran who guarded her chastity, so We breathed into it of Our Spirit. And she believed (in the) Words (of) her Lord and His Books, and she was of the devoutly obedient."

Jesus is the Word and the Spirit imparted into Mary's womb. This is the mystery of the incarnation. This is the mystery of godliness.

1 Timothy 3:16,

"And without controversy great is the mystery of godliness: God was manifest in the flesh, justified in the Spirit, seen of angels, preached unto the Gentiles, believed on in the world, received up into glory."

"God was manifest in the flesh." Divinity was manifest in a mortal body. This is the great mystery of the incarnation, God being revealed in flesh.

Jesus was born holy

We have already seen how Jesus was born as a righteous child who could not be touched by the sting of Satan. The Bible also declares His holiness. The angel calls Jesus "that Holy One" from his birth. (*Luke 1:35).*

The Concept of "Birth"

It is a total misrepresentation to imply a biological, sexual relationship producing the birth of Jesus. Muhammad misunderstood the concept of "Son of God." He thought of it only in terms of sexual reproduction. He thought that God fathered a child through sexual intercourse with Mary.

Both the Qur'an and the Bible declare the birth of Jesus to be a Divine miracle where the seed of God's Word was planted by the Holy Spirit directly into the womb of Mary, a chaste virgin. Jesus' conception was miraculous and holy. In both the Qur'an and the Bible, only Jesus was born in this way.

In the Bible we read of at least five different kinds of "birth" or "sonship" and four of them are non-sexual.

a. CREATION. Adam came into being through an act of Divine creation. Adam was created (Hebrew - *bara*) from dust. God took the dust, formed the man and then breathed life into him. It was the production of a man not by human procreation but by creation.
b. GENETIC ENGINEERING. Eve also came into being through an act of Divine creation, but not from dust. She was created (Hebrew – *bara*) from the rib of Adam. God took already existing genetic material and created a woman from it. Eve also did not come into being by a human procreation but by a form of genetic engineering.
c. BIOLOGICAL BIRTH. Cain and Abel were the first humans to be born through the act of physical procreation. Every human being born on earth since then has been the result of joining a human egg and a human sperm, except for Jesus.
d. INCARNATION. Jesus' birth was unique in human history. Mary was a virgin. No sexual reproduction was involved. It was a holy, miraculous birth. Jesus was born of the Holy Spirit.
e. THE NEW BIRTH. Jesus said that we must be born again. *John 3:3-8.* Paul says we are a "new creation." *2 Corinthians 5:17.* Peter explains that we have been born again, not of a corruptible seed but incorruptible, through the word of God. *1 Peter 1:3, 23.* John notes that "Everyone who believes that Jesus is the Christ is born of God." *1 John 5:1.* James mentions that God chose to "give us birth through the word of truth." *James 1:18.* The new birth is not a physical birth, it is a spiritual birth from above, where the Word of God and the Spirit of God create within us a new life, a new heart,

> a new man and through that birth, we become the sons of God. This is the glorious message of the Gospel. Jesus, the Son of God, became the Son of Man, so that we the sons of men could become the sons of God! No wonder there is such opposition against the truth of Jesus being the Son of God!

Even today there are common idiomatic expressions of sonship that do not involve human procreation. In Arabic they talk of someone being a "son of Yemen" meaning a citizen of Yemen. No sex involved! "Son of a gun" is a common idiom, often used humorously or in frustration, which historically refers to something born at sea or under a gun. "Son of the soil" refers to a person, or metaphorically a crop, that is deeply rooted in a particular place or region. The Bible refers to "sons of the prophets" who were not biological children, but disciples of the prophets. Jesus referred to James and John as "sons of thunder."

Jesus is Son of God in a unique sense. He is God and through the incarnation became a Man.

This is a fundamental doctrine that the Qur'an opposes.

The Concept of "Fatherhood"

Whose seed or foetus is in the womb of Mary? Who is responsible for Mary's pregnancy?

In the Bible, God is the Father and He accepts full responsibility.

God sends Gabriel to inform Mary that the baby conceived in her womb will be called the Son of the Highest. (*Luke 1:31*).

God sends an angel to Joseph who informs him that Mary is the chosen virgin who will bring forth a Son who shall be called "Immanuel", God with us. (*Matthew 1:23*). This is in fulfilment of the prophecy of Isaiah that was spoken about 700 years before His birth. (*Isaiah 7:14*).

At Jesus' baptism by John in the river Jordan, God acknowledges Jesus, by declaring, "This is my beloved Son, in whom I am well pleased." (*Matthew 3:17. Luke 3:21-22),*

On the Mount of Transfiguration, while Jesus meets with Moses and Elijah who represent the Law and the Prophets, the voice of God comes out of the cloud saying, "This is My Beloved Son, in whom I am well pleased. Hear Him!" (*Matthew 17:1-5).*

This fulfills the prophecy of David in the Psalms, "You are My Son, Today I have begotten you." *Psalms 2:7.*

Paul declares that this is the "glad tidings", the promise that was made to the fathers. *Acts 13:32-33.*

To deny the Sonship of Jesus is to deny the teaching of Moses, of David, of the Prophets and of the Gospels.

The Greek term "*monogenes*" or "only-begotten" demands that this birth was unique. It stands alone as the only birth ever like this. There was no birth like it before, nor will there be after it. It was not the same as the birth of Adam and Eve. This birth was super special!

The Qur'an says that the angels spoke to Zachariah and told him that he would have a son, John (*Yahya*) the Baptist who would be a prophet, who was to bear witness to a Word of God, specifically referring to the birth and mission of Jesus. The "Word from Allah" is understood by commentators to be Jesus (*Isa*), as a few verses later, the Qur'an explicitly calls Jesus a "Word from Him" (*Kalimatun-minhu*).

Surah Ali-Imran 3:39,

"While he was standing in prayer in the chamber, the angels called unto him: "Allah doth give thee glad tidings of Yahya, witnessing the truth of a Word from Allah, and (be besides) noble, chaste, and a prophet, of the (goodly) company of the righteous.""

John's witness to the Sonship of Jesus is clearly outlined in the Gospels.

John 1:14-18,

"And the Word became flesh and dwelt among us, and we have seen his
glory, glory as of the only Son from the Father, full of grace and truth. 15
John bore witness about him, and cried out, "This was he of whom I said,
'He who comes after me ranks before me, because he was before me.' 16
For from his fullness we have all received, grace upon grace. 17 For the law
was given through Moses; grace and truth came through Jesus Christ. 18
No one has ever seen God; God the only Son, who is at the Father's side,
he has made him known."

John's testimony was that Jesus is the Word, the only begotten son of the Father, full of glory grace and truth, the one who came before him, who ranks before him, for the Son of God is eternal from the beginning.

When our Arabic teacher in Yemen read these verses together with us in class, he was very puzzled. It made him think. It made him question. Why did John say, He comes after me, was before me?" He asked us, "How could Jesus exist before John the Baptist?"

Jesus was Sinless: Supernatural Holiness

It is a common belief among Muslims that Muhammad never sinned and that prophets do not sin. When we were studying Arabic in Yemen, Jeff said to one of our teachers, "Muhammad sinned." Our teacher was horrified and said, "No! Muhammad did not sin." Jeff then read a verse from the Qur'an and our teacher conceded. "Yes, there are five instances in the Qur'an where Muhammad's sin is mentioned." In fact, all the prophets sinned. None of them were pure and holy, apart from Jesus.

MUHAMMAD sinned

The Qur'an is very clear and states that Muhammad was told by God to ask forgiveness for his sins.

Surah Ghafir 40:55,

"and ask forgiveness for thy sins (*thanb*), and extol thy Sustainer's glory and praise by night and by day...."

Surah Muhammad 47:19,

".. and ask forgiveness for thy sin (*thanb*), and for the believers, men and women. God knows your going to and fro, and your lodging."

Surah Al-Fath 48:1-2,

"That God may forgive thee thy former and thy latter sins (*thanb*), and complete His blessing upon thee, and guide thee on a straight path."

Allah also rebuked Muhammad on several occasions in the Qur'an for his mistakes.

a. Muhammad desired to please his wives.

Surah At-Tahrim 66:1,

"O Prophet! Why dost thou, out of a desire to please [one or another of] thy wives, impose [on thyself] a prohibition of something that God has made lawful to thee? But God is much-forgiving, a dispenser of grace."

This verse references a situation where God rebukes the Prophet Muhammad for holding himself from something allowed by God, leading to an admonition regarding seeking pleasure. According to classical commentary (*tafsir*) and hadith, the "lawful thing" that God had allowed to him, refers to one of two main scenarios, either it was not eating honey (*Sahih al-Bukhari (Hadith 6691 and 5267)*, or it was not having conjugal relations with Maria the Copt (*Sunan An-Nasai 3411*), both of which things, his other wives did not approve.

b. Muhammad did not behave well to a blind man.

God had to addresses Muhammad regarding his behavior. Prophet Muhammad turned away from a blind man, Abdullah ibn Umm-Maktum, while focusing on preaching to the elite of the Quraish. *(Surah Abasa 80:1-10.)*

c. Muhammad wrongly gave permission to some people to stay behind and not go on jihad.

Surah Tawbah 9:43,

"May Allah pardon you ˹O Prophet˺! Why did you give them permission ˹to stay behind˺ before those who told the truth were distinguished from those who were lying?"

d. Muhammad wrongly took captives before the victory was fully enforced.

The prophet Muhammad had Bakr's set all the captives free in return for ransom. However, God disapproved the decision as is evident from the following verse.

Surah Al-Anfal 8:67–69,

(8:67) "It behoves not a Prophet to take captives until he has sufficiently suppressed the enemies in the land. You merely seek the gains of the world whereas Allah desires (for you the good) of the Hereafter. Allah is All-Mighty, All-Wise. (8:68) Had there not been a previous decree from Allah, a stern punishment would have afflicted you for what you have taken. (8:69) So eat that which you have obtained - for it is lawful and clean--and fear Allah.49 Surely Allah is Ever-Forgiving, Most Merciful."

Muhammad said he repented more than seventy times a day.

"I heard Allah's Messenger saying." By Allah! I ask for forgiveness from Allah and turn to Him in repentance more than seventy times a day," *Sahih al-Bukhari 6307-8*

Muhammad was very aware that he was a sinner. His prayer of confession and request for forgiveness is recorded in the hadith.

"O Allah, forgive me my faults, my ignorance, my immoderation in my concerns. And Thou art better aware (of my affairs) than myself. O Allah, grant me forgiveness (of the faults which I committed) seriously or otherwise (and which I committed inadvertently and de- liberately. All these (failings) are in me. O Allah, grant me forgiveness from the fault which I did in haste or deferred, which I committed in privacy or in public and Thou art better aware of (them) than myself. Thou art the First and the Last and over all things Thou art Omnipotent," *Sahih Muslim 2719*

All of the other prophets also sinned

ADAM sinned

Adam and Eve's sin is described in several places in the Qur'an. It describes the prohibition of the tree, Satan's deception, the exposure of their shame upon tasting the fruit, and Adam and Eve's plea for forgiveness. (*Surah Al-Araf 7:19-23*). Adam's disobedience is mentioned in *(Surah Taha 20:121-122)*. Adam was ordered to reside in Paradise and not approach the forbidden tree, but Satan caused them to "slip", and Adam learnt words of repentance from his Lord (*Surah Al Baqarah 2:35-37*). The children of Adam (mankind) are warned not to be deceived by Satan just as he "tempted your parents out of Paradise, stripping them of their clothing..." (*Surah Al-A'raf 7:27*).

ABRAHAM sinned

Abraham prayed fervently that God would forgive his sin on the day of judgement. In *Surah Ash-shuara 26:82,* Abraham wrongly prayed for forgiveness for his father. When God told him that his father was an enemy of God, Abraham repented and stopped praying for him.

Surah At-Tawbah 9.114,

"Abraham asked not pardon for his father except because of a promise he had made to him; and when it became clear to him that he was an enemy of God, he declared himself quit of him; Abraham was compassionate, clement."

Again in the Qur'an, we are told that although Abraham is a good example for us to follow, we should not follow his example for praying for his father's forgiveness.

Surah Al-Muntahamah 60.4

"There is for you an excellent example (to follow) in Abraham and those with him, when they said to their people: "We are clear of you and of whatever ye worship besides Allah: we have rejected you, and there has arisen, between us and you, enmity and hatred for ever,- unless ye believe in Allah and Him alone": But not when Abraham said to his father: "I will pray for forgiveness for thee, though I have no power (to get) aught on thy behalf from Allah." (They prayed): "Our Lord! in Thee do we trust, and to Thee do we turn in repentance: to Thee is (our) Final Goal According to Islamic teaching, Abraham. "The Prophet, pbuh did not lie, except on three occasions. One time while Abraham passed by a tyrant with Sarah and he mentioned the story so he gave her Hagar as a slave." (*Sahih al Bukhari 5084).*

On one occasion, Abraham told a lie and said he was sick.

Surah As-Saffat 37:83-90,

"[And Abraham] said, 'Surely I am sick. And he said: "Verily, I am sick (with plague. He did this trick to remain in their temple of idols to destroy them and not to accompany them to the pagans feast)."

On another occasion he was told to destroy idols but failed to destroy them all and left the biggest idol intact.

Surah Al-Anbiya 21:58,

"So he broke them to pieces, (all) but the biggest of them, that they might turn (and address themselves) to it."

DAVID sinned

The story of David's sin is recorded in the Qur'an. According to that story there were two plaintiffs who climbed the wall into David's private prayer chamber to seek judgment. One claimed the other has 99 ewes, while he has only one, yet the man with 99 pressured him to give up his one ewe. David immediately ruled that the man with 99 sheep has wronged the other. After he had spoken, David realized it was a divine test, so he repented and asked for forgiveness *(Surah Sad 38:21-25).*

This seems to be a distorted account based on two stories from the Bible: the account of Nathan's condemnation of David (*2 Samuel 12:1-13*) and the parable of the ninety-nine sheep told by Jesus *(Matthew 18:10-14; Luke 15:3-7).*

NOAH sinned

The sin of Noah is recorded in *Surah Hud 11:45-47.* Noah was rebuked by God for asking to save his unbelieving son. God tells him that his son was of "unrighteous conduct" and not truly of Noah's family and warned Noah against asking for things he does not know about. Noah immediately repented, and asked for forgiveness and mercy, declaring he would be among the losers without God's grace.

MOSES sinned

The Qur'an mentions several specific instances where Moses sinned. He killed an Egyptian, recognized it was wrong and prayed for forgiveness. (*Surah Al-Qasas 28:15-16).* Pharaoh confronted him and Moses acknowledged he did it while he was astray. (*Surah Ash-Shu'ara (26:19-21*). Moses also was filled with rage and anger and threw down the tablets contained in the Torah and seized Aaron by the hair. *(Surah Al-A'raf 7:150).* There is also a story in the Qur'an of how Moses, three times, broke the promise he had made not to ask questions. *(Surah Al-Kahf 18:60-82*).

JESUS NEVER SINNED

We have already seen His birth. He was born pure. He was untouched by Satan, according to the Hadith, the only man ever born who was not touched by Satan.

We read the record of His life in the Qur'an and there is no charge brought against Him. He truly is the only sinless man.

Of all the prophets, it was only Jesus who did not sin. He was sinless from birth. Only Jesus could not be touched by Satan. He is the only holy, righteous one among the prophets, *Surah Maryam 19:19.* He was not only unique among the prophets! He was more than a man. He is God. Only God does not sin. Only God is good.

Mark 10:18,

"Why do you call me good?" Jesus answered. "No one is good—except God alone." Here Jesus asks the question. If Jesus is truly good, He is truly God.

Matthew 19:17,

"There is only One who is good. If you want to enter life, keep the commandments."

Jesus is described in the New Testament also as the only one without sin. Jesus challenged his accusers, saying, "Which of you convicts me of sin?" *(John 8:46).* He said "the ruler of this world [Satan] has no claim on me", implying that there was no sin that could give Satan entrance into or power over His life. *(John 14:30).* Even Pilate declared Jesus to be an "innocent" or "just" person. *(Matthew 27:24).*

In the epistles there are many statements of His holiness. Jesus is the one who "knew no sin." *(2 Corinthians 5:21).* He was tempted in all points like we humans are, but yet without sin." *(Hebrews 4:15).* He "committed no sin, neither was deceit found in his mouth." *(1 Peter 2:22).* "In him there is no sin," *(1 John 3:5).* He is the great high priest who is "holy, innocent, unstained, separated from sinners." *(Hebrews 7:26).*

The Qur'anic picture of Jesus and the Biblical verses demonstrate that Jesus was unique in His holiness. No human could ever be as perfect, as holy and as righteous as He is. This demonstrates His Deity. He is God.

Jesus performed Miracles: Supernatural Power

The Miracle of Creation

No other prophet created life. Even today scientists are trying to manufacture life in the laboratories and they cannot do it. The creation of life requires Divine intervention.

What Jesus said was:

Surah Ali-Imran 3.49,

"I design for you out of clay, a figure like that of a bird, and breathe into it, and it becomes a bird by Allah's leave."

What Allah said was:

Surah Al-Maidah 5.110,

"And when you made out of clay, a figure like that of a bird, by My permission, and you breathed into it and it became a bird, by My permission."

Jesus' power is qualified by the words "By Allah's leave" and "By My permission" (Arabic: *bi'idhnillah*). Muslims say this makes him simply a man who had special permission from God. However, as Jesus stated in the Gospels, He came to do the will of God. The permission from God allowed Him to work. Jesus had the ability and the power within Himself to do these things. He came to do His Father's will and that is why He did everything by the permission of God.

According to the Qur'an, Jesus created a bird in a similar way to God created Adam. In creating Adam, God formed and fashioned him from clay and then breathed into him so that he lived. In the same way, the Qur'an says Jesus formed a bird from clay and then breathed life into it and the bird flew away.

This was the same method God used in the creation of man. According to the Qur'an both God and Jesus took clay and then created a being into which they breathed life.

Surah Al-Hijr 15:28-29,

"And when thy Lord said to the angels, 'See, I am creating a mortal of a clay of mud moulded. When I have shaped him, and breathed My spirit in him, fall you down, bowing before him!"

Surah Sad 38:71-75,

⸢Remember, O Prophet⸣ when your Lord said to the angels, "I am going to create a human being from clay. So when I have fashioned him and had a spirit of My Own ⸢creation⸣ breathed into him, fall down in prostration to him."

Miracles of Healing

We have already seen how the Qur'an records Jesus as a miracle worker. He opened blind eyes and healed lepers and raised the dead.

In *Surah Ali Imran 3:49*, we have read how Jesus spoke and said,

I will create for you…

I will breathe into it…

I will heal the blind and leper…

I will give life to the dead…

In *Surah Al Maidah 5:110* we have read how God spoke and said,

You did create…

You did breathe…

You did heal the blind and the leper…

You did bring forth from the dead…

Miracles of Resurrection

Jesus raised the dead. That is only something God can do. The power to raise the dead is God's alone.

Surah Ya-Sin 36:12,

"Indeed, it is We who bring the dead to life."

Only God has the power for creating and for giving resurrection life.

Jesus raises the dead. He is the giver of life

He raised the daughter of Jairus. *Mark 5:21-43*

He raised the widow of Nain's son. *Luke 7:11-15*

He raised Lazarus from the dead. *John 11:38-44.*

Al-Anam 6:109,

"Say: "Miracles can only come from God." …

Jesus was a miracle worker and healer in the Gospels and also according to the Qur'an. He did things that no ordinary man or prophet could do. Muhammad himself did not claim to be a miracle worker. Jesus had supernatural power that no other prophet ever displayed. He performed miracles that only God can do.

Jesus knew things Unseen – Supernatural Knowledge

Jesus not only did supernatural miracles, He had supernatural knowledge. He knew things that no other man or prophet could know. He knew the unseen. He is Omniscient. The only all-knowing being is God. Only God can know the unseen.

Jesus acknowledges in the Qur'an that only God knows the unseen, the things that are hidden.

Surah Al-Maidah 5:116,

"Allah asks Jesus, "O Jesus, son of Mary! Did you ever ask the people to worship you and your mother as gods besides Allah?" Jesus responds, "Glory be to You! How could I ever say what I had no right to say? If I had said such a thing, you would have certainly known it. You know what is ˹hidden˺ within me, but I do not know what is within You. Indeed, You ˹alone˺ are the Knower of all unseen."

Muhammad also acknowledged that only God knows the unseen.

Surah An-Naml 27:65-66,

"Say (O Muhammad): None in the heavens and the earth knoweth the Unseen save Allah; and they know not when they will be raised (again). Nay, but doth their knowledge reach to the Hereafter? Nay, for they are in doubt concerning it. Nay, for they cannot see it."

Surah Yunus 10:20,

"And they say: "How is it that not a sign is sent down on him from his Lord?" Say: "The unseen belongs to Allah Alone, so wait you, verily I am with you among those who wait (for Allah's Judgement)."

The Prophet Muhammad himself, is told by God, to confess that he has no knowledge of the unseen.

Surah Al-Araf 7:188,

"Say (O Muhammad): "I possess no power of benefit or hurt to myself except as Allah wills. If I had the knowledge of the Ghaib (unseen), I should have secured for myself an abundance of wealth, and no evil should have touched me. I am but a warner, and a bringer of glad tidings unto people who believe."

On the other hand, God sent Jesus to be a Messenger to the Children of Israel revealing the unseen. He tells the people that this is a sign from the Lord. Jesus has knowledge of the unseen.

Surah Ali-Imran 3:49,

"I have come to you with a sign from your Lord. … I will inform you too of what things you eat, and what you treasure up in your houses. Surely in that is a sign for you, if you are believers."

When we look at the logic of the Qur'an we can conclude:

- Only God knows or has knowledge of the unseen.
- Jesus knows and has knowledge of the unseen.
- Therefore, Jesus is God.

Jesus has come according to the Qur'an, with many signs. These signs show that He is indeed God. Jesus has the power to know the things no human can know. He is omniscient.

Jesus reveals the future: The Supernatural Prophet

Jesus knows the unseen just as God does. He is far greater than any human being, any messenger, any apostle or prophet.

According to one hadith Jesus is depicted as the only prophet or messenger who has knowledge about what first must take place before the end comes:

Sunan Ibn Majah 4081,

"It was narrated that 'Abdullah bin Mas'ud said: "On the night on which the Messenger of Allah was taken on the Night Journey (Isra'), he met Ibrahim, Musa and 'Isa, and they discussed the Hour. They started with Ibrahim, and asked him about it, but he did not have any knowledge of it. Then they asked Musa, and he did not have any knowledge of it. Then they asked 'Isa bin Maryam, and he said: 'I have been assigned to some tasks before it happens.' As for as when it will take place, no one knows that except Allah. Then he mentioned Dajjal and said: 'I will descend and kill him, then the people will return to their own lands and will be confronted with Gog and Magog people, who will: "swoop down from every mound."[21:96] They will not pass by any water but they will drink it, (and they will not pass) by anything but they will spoil it. They (the people) will beseech Allah, and I will pray to Allah to kill them. The earth will be filled with their stench and (the people) will beseech Allah and I will pray to Allah, then the sky will send down rain that will carry them and throw them in the sea. Then the mountains will turn to dust and the earth will be stretched out like a hide. I have been promised that when that happens, the Hour will come upon the people, like a pregnant woman whose family does not know when she will suddenly give birth.'" (One of the narrators) 'Awwam said: "Confirmation of that is found in the Book of Allah, where Allah says: "Until, when Gog and Magog people are let loose (from their barrier), and they swoop down from every mound *(Surah Al Anbiya 21:96)*."

According to that Hadith, Jesus knew about the future. No other prophet did.

Jesus also was a sign. He is the only prophet of God who ascended and is alive in Heaven. He is the only prophet of God who will return.

Surah Az-Zukhruf 43.61,

"And his ⸢second⸣ coming is truly a sign for the Hour. So have no doubt about it, and follow me. This is the Straight Path."

Every day Muslims pray, "Show us the straight way." Jesus is the straight path. He said, "I am the way, the truth and the life. No man comes to the Father, except by Me." *John 14:6.*

Yusuf Roni (1946-1925) was a radical Muslim youth leader. He was busy burning down churches in Indonesia. He came to a church that had Muslim homes on both sides, so instead of burning it down, he and his group made a bonfire of all the furniture and books from the church. Yusuf Roni decided to take a Bible home to read. He had never read it before. When he read *John 14:6,* he was convinced that Jesus was "the way." He became a Christian. He was arrested in 1974 after writing a book, "Why I Chose Jesus" *(Mengapa Saya Memilih Yesus")* and spent six years in jail for apostasy and blasphemy. When he came out of jail, he became a well-known pastor and evangelist.

Jesus is the Word of God: The Supernatural Word

The Qur'anic Teaching

According to the Qur'an, all the prophets had a revelation of the Word of God and spoke the Word of God. Only Jesus is the Word of God. He is the only human referred to as the Word of God.

The Qur'an says Jesus is the Word of God but then denies that He is God. Every Muslim who believes the Qur'an must believe that Jesus is the Word of God. This is a dilemma for Muslims. How can a man who is called God's Word not be God Himself?

There are three verses where Jesus is referred to as "a Word" from God (*kalimat minhu*) or "His Word" (*kalimatuhu*). (*Surah Ali-Imran 3:39, 3:45, and 4:171).*

1. **Zechariah is told by Angels that his son will be John, who will confirm a Word from God**

Surah Ali-Imran 3:39,

"Then called him the Angels when he (was) standing - praying in the prayer chamber. "Indeed, Allah gives you glad tidings of Yahya, confirming [of] a Word from Allah (*kalimat minhu*) and a noble and chaste and a Prophet among the righteous."

Zechariah is told that he will have a son, John the Baptist (*Yahya*) who was given to confirm a Word from God. That "Word from God" has a name, and His name is Jesus. When it says in the Qur'an that John came confirming "a word from God", that word was not a specific literal word, it was not a specific message, it was not a book, it was a man and that man is the Man, Christ Jesus.

2. Mary is told by Angels that she will give birth to a Word from God

Surah Ali-Imran 3:45,

"When said the Angels, "O Maryam!" Indeed, Allah gives you glad tidings of a word from Him (*kalimat minhu*) his name (is) the Messiah, Isa, son (of) Maryam, honoured in the world and (in) the Hereafter, and of those brought near (to Allah)."

Mary is told by the angels that she will give birth to a word from God. There is a word from God that has a name. That name is Christ Jesus, the one who is honoured in the world and in eternity. That Word came into the womb of Mary, was born and lived among us on earth.

John 1:14

"And the Word became flesh and dwelt among us, and we beheld His glory, the glory as of the only begotten of the Father, full of grace and truth."

That Word has "the name" that is above every name. He has "the name" at which every knee shall bow and every tongue confess that He is Lord. He is the one who is near to God, who is exalted to the highest place.

***Philippians 2:9-11*,**

"Therefore God exalted him to the highest place and gave him the name that is above every name, that at the name of Jesus every knee should bow, in heaven and on earth and under the earth, and every tongue acknowledge that Jesus Christ is Lord, to the glory of God the Father."

This is glad tidings! We need to proclaim the glad tidings. This is good news for the whole world!

3. God declares that the Messiah, Jesus, Son of Mary, is the Word of God

***Surah An-Nisa 4.171*,**

"O People (of) the Book! (Do) not commit excess in your religion and (do) not say about Allah except the truth. Only the Messiah, Isa, son (of) Maryam, (was) a Messenger (of) Allah and His word (*kalimatuhu*) which He conveyed to Maryam and a spirit from Him. So believe in Allah and His Messengers. And (do) not say, "Three;" desist (it is) better for you. Only Allah (is) God One. Glory be to Him! That He (should) have for Him a son. To Him (belongs) whatever (is) in the heavens and whatever (is) in the earth. And sufficient (is) Allah (as) a Disposer of affairs."

Again, Jesus, son of Mary is His Word. Again, His word has a name, and that name is Jesus. This time it is not the Angels it is God Himself who declares that Jesus is His Word. God's Word has a name, and His name is the Messiah/the Christ, Jesus, Son of Mary, Messenger of God. So, believe in God and His Messenger!

The Biblical Teaching

The Bible clearly declares Jesus is the Word of God.

John 1:1,

"In the beginning was the Word and the Word was with God and the Word was God. All things were made by Him and without Him, nothing was made that was made."

Jesus is the Word. He was with God from the beginning. He is God. He is the Word who created all things. He is the Word who became flesh and dwelt among us. *(John 1:14).*

"The Word was made flesh and dwelt among us." The "Word" in the Greek New Testament is the "Logos," a term which implies not just a spoken word, but the total expression of God's thoughts. Jesus is the "Word" because he embodied the complete message of God to humanity. He is the perfect mediator and the perfect revelation of God to man. Jesus is everything that God wants to say to all mankind. All the fulness of the Godhead dwells in Him.

This Bible tells us that He is coming again and at His coming, explicitly calls Jesus by the title "The Word of God." ***Revelation 19:13.*** Jesus is the Word who was and is and is coming again!

From the first verse in Genesis until the last chapters of the book of Revelation, Jesus is the Word of God.

As Samuel Zwemer (1867-1952) an American missionary, often called the "Apostle to the Muslims", said, "Islam is the only one of the great non-Christian religions which gives a place to Christ in its book and yet it is also the only one of the non-Christian religions which denies His deity, His atonement and His supreme place as Lord of all in its sacred literature."

The Denial: The doctrine of tauhid

The central doctrine of Islam is that God is one (*tauhid*). This is a doctrine that firmly denies the deity of Jesus. For Muslims, the greatest sin that they can commit is to say that God has a Son, that Jesus Christ is the Son of God. It is the sin of idolatry, of associating another with God, in Arabic, *shirk*. It is blasphemy. It is considered worse than stealing, adultery, murder and every other sin. It is the one unforgiveable sin.

Here is a list of verses that are the foundation of the Islamic doctrine of *tauhid*, the belief that God is a singular, numerical One, who has no connection with any other being.

Surah Al Baqarah 2:116,

"They say: "God has begotten a son." Glory be to Him. No, to Him belongs all that is in the heavens and on earth: everything renders worship to Him."

Surah Al Maidah 5:19,

In blasphemy indeed are those that say that Allah is Christ the son of Mary.

Surah At Tawbah 9:30,

"The Christians say the Messiah is the Son of God, that is a saying from their mouths."

Surah Maryam 19:35-36,

"It is not befitting to (the majesty of) Allah that He should beget a son. Glory be to Him! when He determines a matter, He only says to it, "Be", and it is. Verily Allah is my Lord and your Lord: therefore, serve Him; this is the Straight Way."

Surah Al-Ikhlas 112:1-4,

"Say: He is Allah, the One and Only. Allah, the Eternal, Absolute. He begets not, nor is He begotten. And there is none comparable unto Him."

As we have discussed, Muhammad misunderstood "Son of God." He thought of it only in terms of sexual reproduction, that God fathered a child through sexual intercourse with Mary.

Surah Al-Anam 6:101,

"To Him is due the primal origin of the heavens and the earth: How can He have a son when He hath no consort (female companion)? He created all things, and He hath full knowledge of all things."

All Islamic doctrine is based on this doctrine - God is One!

The Misunderstanding

Immediately after expressing the truth of Jesus being Messiah, His Word and Spirit, there comes the qualification, the denial, "Do not say "Trinity!"

Surah An-Nisa 4:171,

"O People of the Book! Do not go to extremes regarding your faith; say nothing about Allah except the truth. The Messiah, Jesus, son of Mary, was no more than a messenger of Allah and the fulfilment of His Word through Mary and a spirit ⌜created by a command⌝ from Him. So believe in Allah and His messengers and do not say, "Trinity." Stop!—for your own good. Allah is only One God. Glory be to Him! He is far above having a son! To Him belongs whatever is in the heavens and whatever is on the earth. And Allah is sufficient as a Trustee of Affairs."

"Do not say, "Three! Desist!"

"Only Allah (is) God One. Glory be to Him! That He (should) have for Him a son."

The Qur'an denies and contradicts the fundamentals of the Bible. It claims to reject idolatry, but in doing so, it creates a God who is contrary to the God of the Bible.

1. It denies the Trinity
2. It denies the Sonship of Jesus
3. It denies the Deity of Jesus
4. It denies the Fellowship of God.

The Qur'an reveals a fundamental misunderstanding of the Trinity, the Deity, the Sonship of Jesus and the Relationship of God

The "Trinity" it denies consists of God, Mary and Jesus. Christians believe in the Father, Son and Holy Spirit.

The "Deity" it denies is the concept of their being more than one God. It denies that Jesus is a separate God from Allah. Christians don't believe in two or three Gods. They only believe in one God

The "Sonship" it denies is that a Jesus is a physical son of God, born of a sexual union. Christians do not believe that Jesus was born of a physical union.

The "Fellowship" it denies is a rejection that God is a God of relationship. The Allah of the Qur'an has no partners, no family, no relationships. Christians believe that the purpose of God in creating man from the very beginning was to have fellowship, partnership, relationship. He planned to have a family, a nation for Himself.

Thus, there is a fundamental deception in the heart of the Qur'an, in the very core of Islam, in the very most vital doctrine of Allah and who Allah is.

1. The Qur'an denies the Trinity

The Qur'an rejects the Trinity. In this verse the translated "Trinity" is the "Three" (*thalatha*). Yet the trinity it denies, consists of three persons, God, Jesus and Mary. No Christian believes that Mary is God. Muhammad fundamentally misunderstood the doctrine of the three persons in the Godhead. He rejected a false trinity.

Surah An-Nisa 4:147,

"O People of the Book! ...do not say, "Trinity." Stop!—for your own good."

We agree with Muslims here. We do not believe in a God who is a Trinity composed of Allah, Mary and Jesus. The Qur'an rejects the concept of three gods, and so do all Christians.

Surah Al-Maidah 5:73,

"Certainly disbelieved those who say, "Indeed Allah (is the) third (of) three." And (there is) no [of] god except (the) God (the) One. And if not they desist from what they are saying surely will afflict those who disbelieved among them, a punishment painful."

Surah Al-Maidah 5:116,

"And behold! Allah will say: "O Jesus the son of Mary! Didst thou say unto men, worship me and my mother as gods in derogation of Allah'?" He will say: "Glory to Thee! never could I say what I had no right (to say). Had I said such a thing, thou wouldst indeed have known it. Thou knowest what is in my heart, Thou I know not what is in Thine. For Thou knowest in full all that is hidden."

This verse speaks of a trinity of Jesus, Mary and Allah. This is not the trinity of the Bible. Jesus never said to worship Him and Mary! There is no record of Jesus ever saying this

2. The Qur'an denies Jesus is the Son of God

There are many verses in the Qur'an that deny Jesus is the Son of God. It is a fundamental doctrine of Islam that God has no sons. Those who believe Jesus is God will go into hell fire.

Surah Al-Nisa 4:172,

"People of the Book, go not beyond the bounds in your religion, and say not as to God but the truth. The Messiah, Jesus son of Mary, was only the Messenger of God, and His Word that He committed to Mary, and a Spirit from Him. So believe in God and His Messengers, and say not, 'Three.'

Refrain; better is it for you. God is only One God. Glory be to Him -- That He should have a son! To Him belongs all that is in the heavens and in the earth; God suffices for a guardian,"

Surah Al-Nisa 4:172,

"The Messiah will not disdain to be a servant of God, neither the angels who are near stationed to Him. Whosoever disdains to serve Him, and waxes proud, He will assuredly muster them to Him, all of them."

Muhammad is told by God to say, that if He had a son, he would be the first to worship Him.

Surah Az-Zukhruf 43:81,

"Say: "If (Allah) Most Gracious had a son, I would be the first to worship."

The Qur'an accuses Christians of making an inappropriate claim

Surah Maryam 19:35-36,

"It is not befitting to (the majesty of) Allah that He should beget a son. Glory be to Him! when He determines a matter, He only says to it, "Be", and it is. Verily Allah is my Lord and your Lord: therefore, serve Him; this is the Straight Way."

Key Qur'anic Verses Affirming God Has No Son:

There are numerous verses scattered throughout the Qur'an that vehemently emphasize that God has no son. This is foundational to Islam.

Surah Al-Baqarah 2:116,

"They say, 'Allah has taken a son.' Exalted is He! Rather, to Him belongs whatever is in the heavens and the earth...."

Surah Al-Anam 6:101,

"[He is] Originator of the heavens and the earth. How could He have a son when He does not have a companion [i.e., wife] and He created all things?."

Surah Yunus 10:68,

"They have said, 'Allah has taken a son.' Exalted is He! He is the [self-sufficient] Owner...."

Surah Al-Isra 17:111,

"And say, 'Praise to Allah, who has not taken a son and has had no partner in [His] dominion...'."

Surah Maryam 19:35,

"It is not [befitting] for Allah to take a son; exalted is He! When He decrees a matter, He only says to it, 'Be,' and it is."

Surah Maryam 19:88-92,

"And they say, 'The Most Merciful has taken [a son].' You have done an atrocious thing... And the Christians say He has begotten a son,... Whereby the heavens are almost torn and the earth is split asunder, and the mountains fall in ruins That they ascribe a son (or offspring or children) to the Most Gracious (Allah). But it is not appropriate for the Most Merciful that He should take a son (or offspring or children."

Surah Al-Muminun 23:91,

"Allah has not taken any son, nor has there ever been with Him any deity...."

Surah Az-Zumar (39:4):

"If Allah had intended to take a son, He could have chosen what He willed of what He creates. Exalted is He...."

Surah Al-Jinn 72:3,

"And [we believe] that exalted is the nobleness of our Lord; He has not taken a wife or a son."

Surah Al-Ikhlas 112:1-4,

"Say, 'He is Allah, [who is] One, Allah, the Eternal Refuge. He neither begets nor is born, Nor is there to Him any equivalent'."

Note again the various translations of *Surah Maryam 19:92:*

"And not is appropriate for the Most Gracious that He should take a son." *(Word for Word 2021)*

"It is inconceivable that the Most Gracious should take unto Himself a son." *(Mohammed Asad).*

"And it behoves not the All-merciful to take a son." *(Arthur John Arberry).*

"For it is not consonant with the majesty of (Allah) Most Gracious that He should beget a son." *(Yusuf Ali).*

"It does not befit ˹the majesty of˺ the Most Compassionate to have children. *(Mustafa Khattab 2018).*

"The Beneficent God is too Exalted to have a son." *(Muhammad Sarwar).*

The Qur'an claims Christians utter Blasphemy

Surah Al-Maidah 5:19,

"In blasphemy indeed are those that say that Allah is Christ the son of Mary."

The Qur'an claims Christians are Deluded

Surah At-Tawbah 9:30,

"The Jews say, "Ezra is the son of Allah"; and the Christians say, "The Messiah is the son of Allah." That is their statement from their mouths; they imitate the saying of those who disbelieved [before them]. May Allah destroy them; how are they deluded?"

The Qur'an claims Christians are deluded in calling Jesus, the Son of God. The Qur'an claims they are just copying what people said before them. The Qur'an makes clear that it is not appropriate for God to have a Son. God is too glorious and majestic to have a son.

The Qur'an claims God is not a Father and He has no sons

Surah Al-Ikhlas 112:1-4.

"Say: He is Allah, the One and Only.
Allah, the Eternal, Absolute.
He begets not, nor is He begotten.
And there is none comparable unto Him."

Muslims consider this Surah to be the core definition of Islam. They recite it multiple times in their daily prayers and sometimes before sleeping. It is recommended to recite it three times a day. A hadith says that Muhammad recited it three times a day. Muslims believe that reciting it has great rewards. Muhammad said that if a Muslim recites it ten times, God will build him a house in Paradise, *Musnad Ahmad 647*. Reciting it three times is said to be equivalent to reciting one third of the Qur'an, *Sahih al Bukhari 5013, 5014 and 6643. Sahih Muslim 811*. Scholars say that this surah represents one third of the Qur'an.

For Muslims, the doctrine of tauhid that God is One, is the core Islamic doctrine.

Is Jesus truly only a man or is He truly the Son of God?

If Jesus is not the Son of God, then the Qur'an contradicts the Bible which it says it confirms, and therefore the Qur'an is false.

If Jesus is God, then the Qur'an denies the truth, and therefore the Qur'an is false.

This is a dilemma!

3. The Qur'an denies that God is the Father

Muhammad also misunderstood the concept of fatherhood.

Surah Al Maedah 5:18.

"(Both) the Jews and the Christians say: 'We are sons of God, and his beloved.' Say: 'Why then doth He punish you for your sins?"

Muhammad's father died before his birth. He had never had a father who disciplined him. Muhammad did not understand why a father punishes and chastises his children because of love. He never understood the concept of discipline that produces maturity. He thought of discipline as only punishment for sin.

Muhammad's concept of God was not as a Father, but as a distant Being who had the power of destruction at his whim. He never knew the love of a father.

Bilquis Sheik was a prominent member of a Muslim family in Pakistan. She had a good relationship with her father. She met a Christian nun who urged her to talk to God as Father. This revolutionized her life and she had a vision of Jesus. She writes her testimony of turning from Islam to Christianity, in a book titled, *"I Dared To Call Him Father"*

Muslims deny both the Father and the Son. For them, there is only one God, a God who is not a Father and is not a Son, a God who does not beget and is not begotten.

We have already seen that the Qur'an confirms that the Gospel is true.

We have already seen that the Qur'an states that Jesus is not God, nor the Son of God.

We have already seen that the Qur'an says that God is not a Father.

This raises a a major for Muslims. Is God a Father or not?

If God is not a Father, then the Qur'an contradicts the Bible which says that He is, therefore the Qur'an is false.

If God is a Father, then the Qur'an denies the truth, and therefore the Qur'an is false.

This is a dilemma!

4. The Qur'an denies that Jesus is God

Surah Al-Maidah 5:73,

"Christ the son of Mary was no more than a messenger; many were the messengers that passed away before him. His mother was a woman of truth. They had both to eat their (daily) food. See how Allah doth make His signs clear to them; yet see in what ways they are deluded away from the truth."

Surah At-Tawbah 9:31,

"They take their priests and their anchorites to be their lords in derogation of Allah, and (they take as their Lord) Christ the son of Mary; yet they were commanded to worship but One Allah: there is no god but He. Praise and glory to Him: (Far is He) from having the partners they associate (with Him)."

The Qur'an only sees Jesus as a human prophet, just like all the other prophets. The proof it offers is that Jesus had to eat food. In the Qur'an that is said to be a clear sign and proof that Jesus was no more than a human being.

This raises a major dilemma for Muslims. Is Jesus truly only a man or is He truly the Son of God?

If Jesus is not God, then the Qur'an contradicts the Bible which it says it confirms it and therefore the Qur'an is false.

If Jesus is God, then the Qur'an denies the truth, and therefore the Qur'an is false.

This is truly a dilemma!

5. The Qur'an denies that God has any relationships

The Qur'an is clear. God has "no partners," "no equals", "no associates." God has no son, no wife, no relationships. God cannot have a son. That is something impossible for God. How can He have a son when he has no wife? He has no companion, no friend, no consort, no ally, no equal. He doesn't need anyone.

Here are some key verses from the Qur'an that emphasize that God has no associates.

Surah An-Nisa 4:36,

"Worship God, and do not associate anything with Him...."

Surah An-Nisa 4:116,

"Surely, Allah does not forgive associating partners with Him...."

Surah Al-Isra 17:42,

"If there had been with Him [other] gods, as they say, then they [each] would have sought a way to the Owner of the Throne."

Surah Saba 34:22,

"Say, 'Call upon those whom you claim besides Allah.' They do not possess an atom's weight in the heavens or on the earth...."

Surah Al-Anam 6:63,

"No partner hath He: this am I commanded, and I am the first of those who bow to His will."

Surah Ash-Shura 42:11,

"There is nothing like unto Him, and He is the All-Hearer, All-Seer."

Surah Al-Isra 17:111,

"And say: 'Praise belongs to God, who has not taken to Him a son, and who has not any associate in the Kingdom, nor any protector out of humbleness.' And magnify Him with repeated magnificats."

God has no associate, no partner, no one like Him! He needs no friend, no protector, no ally, no patron, no supporter, no guardian, no helper. These are the words used in different translations that emphasize the total singular existence and isolation of the God of the Qur'an.

In Islamic theology, Allah is considered absolutely singular, unique, and independent in existence (*tauhid*), meaning there is nothing equal to, comparable to, or sharing in the divine essence. He is totally transcendent.

This raises another dilemma for Muslims.

Does God have a relationship within Himself, a communion with the Father, Son and Holy Spirit?

Does God desire to have us become His sons and daughters?

Either the message of the Bible is true and the Qur'an is false.

Or the message of the Bible is false and the Qur'an is false for confirming a false message.

This is truly a dilemma!

6. The Qur'an denies the Eternal Nature of Jesus

Surah Ali-Imran 3.59,

"Indeed, (the) likeness (of) Isa near Allah (is) like (the) likeness (of) Adam. He created him from dust then He said to him, "Be," and he was."

This verse states that Jesus is created from dust similarly to the way Adam was created. In fact, Adam's creation was totally different. He was uniquely formed from dust and then God breathed into Him. Jesus was not created from dust. He was not formed. He was not breathed into. He is the breath that was breathed. He is the Word that entered. He was created in the womb of a woman not on the dirt of the earth. He is only from dust in the sense that he has a human body. He is only like Adam in that He was human. He is only like Adam in that He is the first of creation. Adam was the first man of human creation. Jesus was the first of a new creation. *(Romans 5:12-21).*

Adam had a beginning. Jesus existed from the beginning. He did not come into existence at His birth. He was in existence before the world began. Adam had an ending. Adam died. Jesus not only died, He rose again and was raised and is alive forevermore.

Surah Ya-Sin 36:81-82,

"He is the Creator, the Knowing. His only command, wh He intends something, is to say to it, 'Be!' and it is."

Only God is creator who creates by a word, by a command. We have seen how Jesus is the Word who created all things. Jesus also had the power to send a word. A centurion said to Jesus, "But just say the word, and my servant will be healed." (*Matthew 8:8*). Jesus sent a word and healed the sick. This fulfilled the prophetic word in the Psalms, "He sent His word and healed them." *(Psalm 107:20).*

Why do Christians believe Jesus is God?

The Revelation in the Old Testament

The Trinity, the Godhead, the Father, Son and Holy Spirit, is revealed in the Old Testament. He is present in Creation as the Elohim, the God who is three in one. God created, the Word spoke, the Spirit moved. *(Genesis 1:1-3).* God said, Let US make man in OUR image. *(Genesis 1:26-28).*

God appeared to Abraham as the Elohim, the three in one God. When Abraham was 99 years old, sitting in the tent door, suddenly God appeared to Him. The LORD appeared to Abraham as three men. The Bible describes the meeting in Genesis 18 and 19.

Then ***the LORD*** appeared to Abraham. (18:1) So, he lifted his eyes and looked and behold ***three men*** were standing by him (*18:2*). Abraham addressed them in the singular, "***My Lord.***" *(18:3*). ***They*** asked Abraham where his wife Sarah was *(18:9)*. ***He*** spoke to Abraham and Sarah. *(18:10)*. ***The LORD*** spoke to Abraham. *(18:13)*. **the men** rose and looked toward Sodom. *(18:16)*. ***The LORD*** spoke again to Abraham *(18:17)*. ***I*** will go down now and see. *(18:21)*. Then ***the men*** turned away from there and went toward Sodom, but Abraham still stood before ***the LORD.*** *(18:22)*. Abraham said," Let not the **Lord** be angry. *(18:30)* So ***the LORD*** went His way. *(18:33)*. ***Two angels*** came to Sodom. *(19:1)*. Lot addressed them as *"**my lords.**" (19:2)*. The men of Sodom said, "Where are ***the men?***" *(19:5)*. ***The men*** reached out their hands and pulled Lot into the house with them. *(19:10)*. When the morning dawned ***the angels*** urged Lot to hurry. *(19:15)*. While he lingered ***the men*** took hold of his hand…*(19:16)*. ***The LORD*** being merciful to Him. *(19:16)*. Then Lot said to ***them***, *"Please, no, **my lords.**" (19:18)*. And ***he*** said to him (Lot), ***"I have*** favored you… ***I*** will not overthrow this city…Hurry, escape there. ***I*** cannot do anything till you arrive there." *(19:21-22)*. Then ***the LORD*** rained fire and brimstone on Sodom and Gomorrah, from ***the LORD*** out of the heavens. *(19:24)*.

Who is the LORD in these verses? He is variously described as three men, two men, two angels, sometimes singular, sometimes plural. In this story is an amazing revelation of the Godhead, the three in one, each distinct and yet each totally united as the LORD God.

Manoach met the LORD. "And the angel of the LORD said to him, 'Why do you ask my name, seeing it is Wonderful? *(Judges 13:18)*. The only one mentioned in the Bible whose name is Wonderful, is the name of the Lord, the Mighty God. (*Isaiah 9:6)*. God appeared to Manoach as an angel. "The angel of the Lord" who appears in the Old Testament is often a revelation of God Himself coming in the form of an angel to speak with His servants.

Solomon asked the question, in *Proverbs 30:1-4*, "Who has ascended into heaven, or descended? Who has gathered the wind in His fists? Who has bound the waters in a garment? Who has established all the ends of the earth? What is His name, and what is His Son's name, If you know?" It is only God who has ascended into heaven, it is only God who gathers the wind in His fists, it is only God who binds the waters in a garment, it is only God who has established the ends of the earth. He is God and He has a Son. What is His name?

The Old Testament also directly prophesies of Jesus' coming as God.

Isaiah prophesied that there would be a sign. A virgin would give birth to a child, who would be called Immanuel. This was the prophecy fulfilled when Mary as a virgin gave birth to Jesus, who is "God with us." (*Isaiah 7:14).*

Isaiah prophesied of a son who would be born. His name would be called "the mighty God." This is a very clear statement that the baby born to Mary, is indeed, not only a man but He is also the mighty God. (*Isaiah 9:6-7).*

Jesus' ministry when He came to open the blind eyes, cause the deaf to hear, the lame to leap and the dumb to sing, was a fulfillment of the prophecy that says, "Your God will come and save you." (*Isaiah 33:4-6).*

Another prophecy by Isaiah was that that there would come a voice in the wilderness, crying "Prepare the way of the LORD." (*Isaiah 40:3).* The word LORD there is YHWH, Yahweh or Jehovah. The LORD is God. This prophecy was fulfilled when John the Baptist was sent ahead of Jesus to prepare the way for His coming. (*Matthew 3:3; Mark 1:2-3; Luke 3:4; John 1:23).*

John, the apostle, stated that the prophet Isaiah saw the pre-existent Messiah (*al-Masih*) in His glory. Isaiah heard the call, "Who will go for ***US***? The three-fold cry of the angels, 'Holy, Holy, Holy" signifies the nature of God who is worshipped, the three in one. (*Isaiah 6:1-3).*

The Revelation in the New Testament

Jesus warns that failure to believe in His true identity ("***I am he***") results in dying in one's sins. *(John 8:24).*

Jesus is the Son of God who was "born of woman" to redeem those under the law, *Galatians 4:4–5.*

Christ was in the "form of God," took the "form of a servant" and was "born in the likeness of men," *Philippians 2:5-8.*

In the Old Testament God spoke through the prophets in various times and ways but in these last days He has spoken to us by His Son, through whom also He made the worlds, *Hebrews 1:1-2.*

Jesus partook in flesh and blood to destroy the power of death, *Hebrews 2:14–17.*

The Challenge for Muslims: Is Jesus the Son of God?

Why do Christians believe Jesus is the Son of God? We do not accept the Islamic concept that presumes Christian believe in a marriage between God and Mary that produces Jesus as a son. We do not accept the Islamic concept that states that Christians believe in a Trinity of God and Jesus and Mary. We do not believe that Jesus was not crucified on the cross as Muslims claim.

We believe Jesus existed eternally as God from the beginning. He was in God and proceeded forth from God. He came to earth and became the Son of Man, but He never ceased being God.

He was born from the virgin Mary, fully God and fully Man.

Jesus Himself claimed a unique relationship with God as His Father.

He told the Jews that God was His Father. They wanted to kill Jesus because he healed on the Sabbath, but when He responded by saying, "My Father has been working until now, and I have been working" they became even more furious and tried to kill Him, "because he was even calling God his own Father, making himself equal with God." *(John 5:17).*

Jesus told the Jews, "It is the Father who honours Me, of whom you say that He is your God." Then He astounded and infuriated them by saying,

"Most assuredly I say to you, before Abraham was, I AM." (*John 8:58*). He said this in the temple and the Jews took up stones to throw at Him.

Another time, He was again in the temple, walking in Solomon's porch among the Jewish religious leaders, the priests and the scribes and the Pharisees, when He said to them, "I and My Father are one." *(John 10:30).* Again, the Jews took up stones to kill Him.

In His last conversations with His disciples before He was crucified, He said to them, ""I came from the Father and entered the world; now I am leaving the world and going back to the Father." (*John 16:28)*

Jesus is the Son of God. He is equal with the Father. He is God. The Father sent Him to the earth to die, to be crucified, to be buried and to rise again after three days. He did this for the salvation of the world. This is the heart of the Gospel. This is what Muhammad, the Qur'an and Islam deny.

A Hymn of Worship in the Qur'an

Surah Ash -Shuara 26:77-82

78. He who created me, and guides me.
79. He who feeds me, and waters me.
80. And when I get sick, He heals me.
81. He who makes me die, and then revives me.
82. He who, I hope, will forgive my sins on the Day of the Reckoning."

This is a revelation of God as the only one who creates, guides, feeds, heals, resurrects and forgives sin. This is a beautiful description of Jesus Christ. May all Muslims who read this hymn come to realize He is One who can do all these things. He is the one who will forgive our sins on the Day of Reckoning.

God is coming in the clouds with angels

There is an interesting verse in the Qur'an that speaks of God coming in the shadows of the clouds and angels.

Surah Al-Baqarah 2:210-211

"Do they then wait for anything other than that Allah should come to them in the shadows of the clouds and the angels? The case would already be judged. And to Allah return all matters. Ask the Children of Israel how many clear Ayat (proofs, evidences, verses, lessons, signs, revelations, etc) We gave them."

The Qur'an claims that it is confirming the Law and the Gospels. In the Law and the Gospels, it is Jesus who comes with the clouds and the angels. We are waiting for Him to come in the clouds with the angels.

Daniel 7:13–14,

Daniel prophesied, "Behold, with the clouds of heaven there came one like a son of man...."

Matthew 24:30,

Jesus states, ."..they will see the Son of Man coming on the clouds of heaven with power and great glory."

Revelation 1:7,

John said, "Behold, he is coming with the clouds, and every eye will see him..."

What a challenge we see in the Qur'an for Muslims to believe their books that confirm the Law and the Gospel. What a challenge for them to seek to know God, to come to Jesus Christ and find Him as their Saviour and their Lord, their God who alone can save them.

1 Timothy 1:15–17

"The saying is trustworthy and deserving of full acceptance, that Christ Jesus came into the world to save sinners, of whom I am the foremost. But I received mercy for this reason, that in me, as the foremost, Jesus Christ might display his perfect patience as an example to those who were to believe in him for eternal life. To the King of the ages, immortal, invisible, the only God, be honour and glory forever and ever. Amen."

Despite the opposition and rejection of Jesus as God, may many Muslims have their eyes opened to see the truth.

Questions for Discussion

1. What did Muhammad misunderstand about the Trinity?
2. How can God be a Trinity?
3. How can we know there is a Trinity?
4. What is the difference between Jesus being called Son of God and Son of Man? *Read Daniel 7:13-14*
5. How we prove from the Bible that Jesus is the Son of God?

DILEMMA 13

THE ISLAMIC EXPANSION DILEMMA

Jihad, Crusades and Migration

Islam is expanding across the world. When I was at school, during the 1950's and 1960's there were very few mosques or Muslims in Australia. There were no Muslims in my school. I never even met a Muslim when I went to university. I grew up without ever seeing a mosque or a woman wearing the Islamic veil. The only thing I ever remember learning about Islam was in a hymn called, "Let the song go round the earth, Jesus Christ is Lord." There was one verse, that I still recall:

> "Let the song go round the earth!
> Lands where Islam's sway
> Darkly broods o'er home and hearth,
> Cast their bonds away!"

Today the face of Australia is rapidly changing. Mosques are being built across the nation. Women wearing the veil are commonly seen in our supermarkets. Muslims politicians are in our councils and in our parliaments.

The rapid rise and spread of Islam, not only in Australia, but across the world today is challenging. Islam is becoming a central and divisive issue, threatening the cohesion of communities across the world and marked by a sharp rise in violence and terrorism. This phenomena calls for us to understand the root causes. It truly is a major dilemma!

One of the keys to understanding Islam today is Islamic history. As the philosopher George Santayana said in 1905, "Those who cannot remember the past are condemned to repeat it." That sounds like a cliché, but it is very true.

I (Annette) majored in history at university, but I learned nothing about the history of Islam. It was as if Islam scarcely existed, or was merely some minor, irrelevant religion that had nothing to do with me. Even though I was preparing to go to the largest Muslim country in the world, I didn't think much about it. My concentration was on studying the Bible and the Indonesian language, so that I would be prepared to share the Word of God with Christians.

In 1974 Jeff and I went to Indonesia. I still knew very little about Islam. For the next eight years we lived in the district of Poso, in Central Sulawesi, most of the time living in a Christian area where there were lots of churches but few mosques. We taught in a Christian Bible College, visited churches across Indonesia and still I knew little about Islam.

It was only in the late 1990s that I really began to become aware of Islam. It began with the financial crisis that struck in 1998. Seemingly out of nowhere, there were riots in the streets of Jakarta, where we were living at the time. Then churches began to be burned down. Our church was almost attacked. Then the church we had attended in Poso, Central Sulawesi, was burned down. 20,000 Christians were evicted from the city of Poso. Our old house that we had lived in, was burned to the ground, as were all Christian homes in that city. Whole villages nearby were also completely destroyed. Some of our students and friends were attacked and killed and at times we too were under fire in the middle of battles. The jihad attacks and communal conflict spread across the islands of Maluku, in Java and Sumatra and thousands of refugees fled to the Christian city of Manado in North Sulawesi.

It was a sudden crisis, and for us, unprecedented. As we began to become involved in helping refugees from the conflict, it began to dawn on us that we needed some understanding. After Jeff was invited to participate in dialogues with Muslim leaders and become involved in the peace process to reconcile Christian and Muslim communities, we became aware of our need to better understand Islam, the Qur'an, the prophet Muhammad and the history of Islam. We spent several years taking young evangelists from Indonesia to Egypt, Lebanon, Israel, the West Bank, Jordan and Yemen to study the Arabic language, Islam in its homeland and a culture that was foreign to us.

To understand what is happening in Australia and across the world today, it is essential to learn about Islam and the basic teachings of the Qur'an. It is essential to understand the history of the prophet Muhammad, the advance of Islam, its impact and the way it has spread from the Arabian cities of Medina and Mecca to the ends of the earth. How and why did it happen?

Just take a glance at the first century of Islamic expansion. Between the years 600AD and 700AD, Islam swept the entire Middle East. Muslim armies spread out from the Saudi Arabian peninsula through Palestine into Babylonia and Syria and all the way north into Turkey. They swept east into what is today Iraq, Iran, Afghanistan. Then they swept west into what is today Egypt, Sudan, Libya and the northern coast of Africa. They even went north-west to the gates of Vienna and almost took over Europe. Islam was spreading across Europe, taking Spain and parts of France and Italy. They took large parts of Hungary and Greece and Central Europe. They spread into Africa and its mission was to take the world for Allah. The entire face of the world was changed by the coming of Islam.

Bruce Thornton, professor of classics and humanities at California State University Fresno said, "Islam for a thousand years is one of the most successful imperialist colonial powers on the planet." We thought. and were taught in school, that colonialism was the work of Britain, France, Portugal, Spain, the Dutch. What we were not taught, was Islamic colonialism. It was too far in the distant past, to impact the modern world we lived in and geographically too remote for us to be concerned with its existence.

Now, all over the world, there is a resurgence of Islam. The goal is to take the world for Allah. Their mission is succeeding rapidly and spectacularly. The successes of the the first century of Islamic expansion are being repeated in our times.

After the First World War, the Islamic Ottoman empire had collapsed and been soundly defeated by the Allies, who were mainly Christian countries. Islam retreated. Its power was diminished. Its honour was gone. It lay in ruins. Yet, out of those ruins, Islam began to rise again. Islamic nations were carved out of the wreck of the Ottoman empire. All the modern Islamic nations had their beginnings in the twentieth century.

- Lebanon was created in 1920.
- Turkey appeared in 1923, a secular nation, led by Attaturk.
- Modern Egypt was declared an independent Kingdom by Great Britain in 1922 and eventually became a republic in 1953.
- Saudi Arabia was established in 1932.
- Iraq became a nation in 1932.
- Modern Syria was formed in 1946.
- Jordan was created in 1946.
- Kuwait was formed in 1961.
- The modern Republic of Yemen was formed on May 22, 1990.
- The United Arab Emirates emerged in 1971.

The only non-Muslim nation in the Middle East that was established during that time, Israel, declared its independence in 1948. It was immediately attacked by the surrounding nations of Egypt, Jordan, Syria, Lebanon, and Iraq.

Since that time, the Islamic nations have grown and become prosperous. Their oil has brought them great economic wealth and political power. They have become the financial source of promoting Islam around the world. Their influence has penetrated deeply into Western nations, into their economic, educational and political institutions.

Until World War Two, Islam largely remained confined to the Middle East, northern Africa and some Asian nations like Pakistan, India, Malaysia, Brunei and Indonesia. After the war, a huge increase in Islamic population began to take place in Western Judeo-Christian countries.

In Australia, the Muslim population rose from about 2000 to 1.2 million today.

In the USA, from 20,000 to over 5 million.

In the UK in 1951 there were 21,000 and that number has now increased to about 4 million. Western Europe had just over 1 million Muslims, mainly focused in the Balkans. Today Europe has in its population, over 50 million Muslims.

Why has this massive population increase occurred in the Western Christian nations?

Apart from natural increase, it has mainly taken place because of migration and jihad. In fact, migration is one methos Muslims can conduct jihad as the purpose of the migration is the spread of Islam.

All this is consistent with the 1400 year history of Islam that began in the days of Muhammad. Islamic expansion by jihad and emigration is based on the teachings and example of Muhammad expressed in the Qur'an and Hadith. It is important we understand!

Jihad in the Qur'an and Hadith

Is Islam a peaceful religion? Is it spread peacefully? Former US President George Bush said, "Islam is a religion of peace." He stated that the "face of terror is not the true faith of Islam" and that terrorists "don't represent peace. They represent evil and war." Former Australian Prime Minister Malcolm Turnbull said, "So let's start with this fact. For more than 1,000 years, people have been drawn to Islam's message of peace. And the very word itself Islam comes from the Arabic word "*salam*", peace."

How was Islam spread? Does "Islam" come from the Arabic word that means "peace"?

Islam is spread by jihad. Jihad means "struggle." Jihad is more than just fighting. It involves all the methods of struggle that lead to the goal of Islam, the taking of the world for Allah. But… in the Qur'an almost every use of the word jihad implies the use of armed struggle and fighting. There are **164 Jihad Verses in the Qur'an**. Here is a list of those verses:

2:178-179, 190-191, 193-194, 216-218, 244; 3:121-126, 140-143, 146, 152-158, 165-167,169, 172-173, 195; 4: 71-72, 74-77, 84, 89-91, 94-95,100-104; 5: 33, 35, 82; 8:1, 5, 7, 9- 10, 12, 15-17, 39- 48, 57- 60, 65- 75; 9: 5, 12-14, 16, 19-20, 24-26, 29, 36, 38-39, 41, 44, 52, 73, 81, 83, 86, 88, 92, 111, 120, 122-123; 16:110; 22:039, 58, 78; 24:53, 55; 25: 52; 29: 6, 69; 33:15, 18, 20, 23, 25-27, 50; 42: 39; 47:4, 20, 35; 48:15-24; 49:15; 59:2, 5-8, 14; 60:9; 61:4, 11, 13; 63:4; 64:14; 66:9; 73:20; 76:8

"Compiled by Yoel Natan, 2004, www.Yoel.Info."

In the Qur'an, jihad means armed warfare to spread Islam to the whole world. The Sufis interpreted it as a "spiritual-struggle" against one's vices. **The Encyclopaedia of Islam** defines it: "The spread of Islam by arms as a religious duty upon Muslims in general.… Jihad must continue to be done until the whole world is under the rule of Islam.… Islam must completely be made over before the doctrine of jihad can be eliminated."

Today Muslim apologists will claim that Islam is a peaceful religion. They will say the lesser jihad is fighting in the cause of Allah but the greater jihad refers to the internal, spiritual struggle against one's own ego, selfishness, greed, and evil inclinations. They will say that the contexts of all the jihad verses are defensive, and that the spread of Islam across the world has occurred "through ideological conquest" and the gradual replacing of local cultures and religions not through violence and instantaneous destruction, but peaceful means like trade and religious teaching (*dakwah*). They will tell you that it is quite unlike the violent and warlike Western imperialism and colonialism.

However in the Qur'an, the majority of verses about jihad are about physical fighting, killing and warfare. A major problem is that when we read the verses in English we were promptly told, "That's a misinterpretation. You must read it in Arabic to truly understand it!" So we did. We went to the Middle East for several years and studied Islam and Arabic. Then when we were in non-Arabic countries, like Turkey, Malaysia and Indonesia, the vast majority of Moslems didn't know Arabic either and they too could not read the Qur'an in Arabic.

The following verses show that fighting (*al-qital*) and jihad *(al-jihad)* are a vital part of the Qur'an and integral to Islam. Although Muslim apologists claim that these verses are defensive, and some do have that context, nevertheless they indicate clearly that it is the duty of all Muslims to engage in fighting, both in defense of Islam and in its promotion.

Jihad is prescribed

Surah Al-Baqarah 2:216,

"Fighting is ordained for you, even though it be hateful to you; but it may well be that you hate a thing the while it is good for you, and it may well be that you love a thing the while it is bad for you: and God knows, whereas you do not know."

Fighting is a prescribed duty for Muslims. There is no alternative. God says that it is prescribed, ordained, enjoined on you, made obligatory, even if you don't like it. When we were helping refugees in Indonesia, we were told of villages where Christians and Muslims had lived together in peace and harmony for years. It was only when a group of radical jihadists entered the villages and called for jihad that Muslims faced the choice of either joining in the fighting or being attacked together with the Christians and suffering their houses being burned down and themselves and their families being killed. It was a difficult choice. We know of one village where the Muslims refused to submit to the jihad. They joined together with their Christian neighbours in defending their village on the island of Halmahera against the attack. That was an exception to the rule.

Most Muslim villages felt they had no choice. In another village, the local Muslims didn't want to join the jihad. They were threatened that it was obligatory for all Muslims to join in jihad, otherwise they were not true Muslims. If they didn't join with them, then they too would have to be killed and their houses destroyed. Nearly 100 fled the village that night, walked all night through the jungles and in the morning went into the town of Tobelo, North Maluku. We met them there and heard their story. Eventually, many of them became believers in Jesus.

Jihad has a Goal

Fighting is prescribed with a goal. The goal is that all peoples worship the God of Islam, Allah, and submit to the religion of Islam. It is a goal of the world-wide conquest of Islam.

Surah Al-Baqarah 2:193,

"Fight them till all worship Allah!" The context: "Fight against them until there is no more oppression and all worship is devoted to Allah alone; but if they desist, then all hostility shall cease, save against those who do wrong."

Surah Al-Anfal 8:39,

"Fight them until there is no more disbelief!"

The context: "And fight [Arabic word – *qataluu* which means fight, kill, slay, slaughter] them until there is no more Fitnah (disbelief and worshipping of others along with Allah) and (all and every kind of) worship is for Allah (Alone). That means fight them until everyone submits to Allah.

Surah At-Tawbah 9:35,

"And fight them until there is no Fitnah (mischief), and total obedience becomes for Allah. So, if they desist, then, Allah is indeed watchful over what they do."

The Qur'anic command is "Fight them till all worship Allah!" Fight them till there is no more persecution, opposition or unbelief!

Jihad is against Polytheists

Muslims must kill all polytheists, unless they convert to Islam.

Surah At-Tawbah 9:5,

"But once the Sacred Months have passed, kill the polytheists wherever you find them, capture them, besiege them, and lie in wait for them on every way. But if they repent, perform prayers, and pay alms-tax, then set them free. Indeed, Allah is All-Forgiving, Most Merciful."

Jihad is against Jews and Christians

Even the "People of the Book" who believe in God and the Last Day are not exempt from being attacked and killed in the jihad.

Surah At-Tawbah 9.29,

"Fight those who believe not in Allah nor the Last Day, nor hold that forbidden which hath been forbidden by Allah and His Messenger, nor acknowledge the religion of Truth, (even if they are) of the People of the Book, until they pay the Jizya with willing submission, and feel themselves subdued."

Muslims must fight against all the People of the Book, that is, Jews and Christians who reject Islam, until they either pay the *jizya*, the Islamic tax on unbelievers, and submit themselves to Islamic rule or until they are killed. Three choices are given to Jews and Christians:

1. Convert to Islam! Become a Muslim!
2. Submit to Islam! Accept inferior status, become a *dhimmi* (a person who is subjugated) and pay the *jizya (*the protection tax)!
3. Face the sword – be killed!

Surah At-Tawbah 9:111,

"And the Statement of Allah): "Verily, Allah has purchased of the believers their lives and their properties; for the price that theirs shall be the Paradise. They fight in Allah's Cause, so they kill and are killed. It is a promise in truth which is binding on Him in the Taurät (Torah) and the Injil (Gospel) and the Qur'an. And who is truer to his convenant than Allah? Then rejoice in the bargain which you have concluded… And give glad tidings to the believers."

The Hadith also command the followers of God to perform jihad. Muhammad states that he has been commanded to fight against people until they become Muslims.

Sahih al-Bukhari 25,

"Allah's Messenger said: "I have been ordered (by Allah) to fight against the people until they testify that none has the right to be worshipped but Allah and that Muhammad is Allah's Messenger, and offer the prayers perfectly and give the obligatory charity, so if they perform that, then they save their lives and property from me except for Islamic laws and then their reckoning (accounts) will be done by Allah."

Sahih Muslim 22,

"The command to fight the people until they say "La ilaha illallah Muhammad Rasul-Allah", and establish Salat, and pay the Zakat, and believe in everything that the prophet (saws) brought. Whoever does that, his life and his wealth are protected except by its right, and his secrets are entrusted to Allah, the most high. Fighting those who withhold Zakat or other than that is one of the duties of Islam and the Imam should be concerned with the Laws of Islam."

The Meaning of Dhimmitude

Christians who submit to Islam and pay the tribute tax, the jizya, are permitted to live under Islamic protection as "*dhimmis*", that is subjugated peoples. If they insist on remaining Christians and acknowledge their inferior status, they will lose some of their legal rights and status as citizens. They do not have the same legal rights as Muslims. They are prohibited from building new churches or synagogues, and often prohibited from repairing existing ones. They are are forbidden to hold public celebrations. They are forbidden to evangelise Muslims. In the past, they were forced to wear different clothing, use different modes of transport, show public deference to Muslims, such as yielding the street and not building houses higher than those of Muslims. Any criticism of the Qur'an or Islamic law annulled the protection pact.

This is how Christians and Jews have survived in the past in places like Yemen, Jordan, Egypt, Malaysia, Brunei and others. Unfortunately, elements of dhimmitude are already creeping into Western countries, evident in the increasing suppression of free speech, of criticism of Islam, and the pressure against evangelism. Dhimmitude is a spirit of self-acknowledged inferiority and submission to Islamic regulations.

In 2007, a letter entitled "A Common Word between Us and You" was addressed by 138 Muslim scholars to the Christians of the world. In the spirit of dhimmitude, 300 prominent Christian leaders, signed it, including such well-known figures as David Yonggi Cho, Robert Schuller, Bill Hybels, Rick Warren and John Stott signed it. Consistent with the worldview of dhimmitude, they adopted a tone of grateful self-humiliation and self-inculpation, using expressions such as:

- "It is with humility and hope that we receive your generous letter"
- The Muslims' letter was "extraordinary" and written in "generosity"
- "We ask forgiveness of the All-Merciful One and of the Muslim community around the world." *(https://www.meforum.org/the-dhimmitude-of-the-west-a-new-trajectory)*.

One of the symptoms of Dhimmitude can be seen in Britain where the police and other agencies have responded to a pandemic of grooming and sex-trafficking gangs, in which the large majority of traffickers have been Muslims, and the victims, non-Muslim young teenage girls, have been estimated to be in the tens of thousands or more. There has been a reluctance to pursue investigation and prosecution.

Another example of the spirit of dhimmitude was noted in the United Kingdom.

"In Bradford (in the UK), a Christian family converted from Islam have had their lives threatened ... Their car has been arsoned and they have been threatened with violence. The Bishop of Bradford met this family with his interfaith advisor. At this meeting he stated that the Diocese of the Anglican Church would not welcome such converts into it ... He did not want Muslim converts [coming] into the Anglican Church. The convert was extremely disappointed and deeply saddened by the stance of the bishop. He felt that the bishop was more concerned with his relationship with the Muslim leaders in Bradford than with his plight with him as a convert. He felt deeply betrayed." *(The Third Choice: Islam, Dhimmitude and Freedom. Mark Durie. Deror Books, Melbourne, p. 220).*

We ourselves have experienced similar situations where Christian churches are very reluctant to have Muslim converts attend. Churches in Malaysia and churches in Jordan that we have visited have expressed to us these sentiments. There is such fear at the consquence of having a too close relationship with any Muslim convert. This was especially so in Yemen, where it was the death penalty for any Yemeni who converted to Islam.

We need to be aware of what is happening around us. If we do not watch and be sober, as the Bible warns us, we can easily be led into deception and be overcome, and entrapped without us even knowing or understanding what is going on.

Migration in the Qur'an and Hadith

Migration is a way of spreading Islam. It was a strategy used to spread Islam in the days of Muhammad, used during 1500 years of Islamic history and is still being used today. This strategy is based on Qur'anic teaching.

Surah Ali-Imran 3:195,

"So those who left their homes and were driven forth from their homes and persecuted in My way and who fought and were slain, I shall truly remove their evil and make them enter Gardens in which rivers flow — a reward from Allah. And with Allah is the best reward."

Surah An-Nisa 4:97,

"Was not the earth of God spacious enough for you to flee for refuge?"

Surah An-Nisa 4:99-100,

"As for the helpless men, women and children who have neither the strength nor the means to escape, God may pardon them. Surely God pardons and forgives. Those who migrate for the sake of God shall find many places for refuge in the land in great abundance" And whoever flees in Allah's way, he will find in the earth many a place of escape and abundant resources. And whoever goes forth from his home fleeing to Allah and His

Messenger, then death overtakes him, his reward is indeed with Allah. And Allah is ever Forgiving, Merciful."

Surah Al-Anfal 8:74-75,

"And those who believed and fled and struggled hard in Allah's way, and those who gave shelter and helped — these are the believers truly. For them is forgiveness and an honourable provision. And those who believed afterwards and fled and struggled hard along with you, they are of you."

These four verses from the Qur'an will help us to understand the importance of migration. They speak of refugees. They help explain why refugees are willing to board boats and face death in the seas, why they are willing to leave home and families to enter Western nations. It is true many face horrific situations of war and conflict in their own countries

Why are Muslims all over the world migrating to the West? Why don't they migrate to other Islamic nations where they will find a similar culture, traditions and language? The Hadith also encourages migration for the sake of Allah. Migration is a part of jihad. It is a way to either die on the journey and be rewarded by Allah or find a place of escape and abundant resources.

One of the sayings of the Prophet was: "God has made the entire face of the earth as a Mosque for me and its soil as pure." (*Sahih al-Bukhari 335 and Sahih Muslim 521.*) Islam claims the whole world for Muhammad and Allah.

Muhammad gave five commands to the Muslims

Hadith number 2863 Kitab al Amthael reported by Tirmizi, also reported by Imam Ahmed ibn Hanbel as Hadith number 17344,

"I charge you with five of what Allah has charged me with: to assemble, to listen, to obey, to immigrate and to wage Jihad for the sake of Allah."

Of those commands, two of them directly involve the expansion of Islam today, "Immigrate and wage Jihad."

In Islam, migration will continue until the end of the world, when the sun rises from the West. In Arabic the word ***"hijrah"*** means migration. Islam began with migration. All Islamic dates begin with the year 622 A.D. which is called the year of *Hijrah*, the year of migration. All Islamic dates will end with the end of the world. Islam begins and ends with migration.

Sunan Abu Dawud 2479,

"Migration will continue until the sun rises from the West. Hijrah would not be stopped until repentance is cut off, and repentance will not be cut off until the sun rises from the West."

The Islamic doctrine of emigration (in Arabic – *Hijrah*) encourages Muslims to migrate to a new country, separate and set up religious and ethnic enclaves, seek special status and privilege such as halal food, special treatment for religious holidays and customs, begin to supplant the native population, subvert, subdue and subjugate non-Muslims, paving the way for total Islamization and the implementation of Shariah Law.

Spreading Islam by Islamic Evangelism – *da'wah*

Islamic Evangelism is called *da'wah*. It is the Islamic preaching as a way to call people to become Muslims and follow Islam, the Qur'an and Muhammad. Da'wah means invitation or call. It is the duty of Muslims to call people to Islam.

Surah An-Nahl 6:125,

"Call thou to the way of thy Lord with wisdom and good admonition, and dispute with them in the better way. Surely thy Lord knows very well those who have gone astray from His way, and He knows very well those who are guide."

Surah Fussilat 43:33,

"Who is better in speech than one who calls (men) to Allah, works righteousness, and says, "I am of those who bow in Islam."

"*Da'wah*" is the effort to show how good and true the message of Islam is. It is part of the jihad. Together with the other methods of spreading Islam through natural increase, immigration and terrorism through jihad, it is being effectively employed to change the face of the Judeo-Christian nations and prepare them to submit to Islam.

Conversions through *da'wah* alone, in the West have been few and far between. The massive population increase of Islam in the West is mostly attributed to immigration and higher birth rates. Islam is concentrating on establishing a strong and stable base, increasing its economic and political power, rather than trying to win Christians to convert to Islam.

Let us look at how Islam has expanded throughout its history, beginning with the Prophet Muhammad, then the four Caliphs and then under the Islamic Caliphates which lasted for 1500 years.

Stage 1. The Expansion under Muhammad by Emigration

In 610 Muhammad received his first revelations in a cave and began his ministry in Mecca. After twelve years of receiving his revelations and preaching his message, he had only gathered about 100 followers, mostly poor and persecuted. He had suffered mocking and rejection. His followers were economically and politically weak, rejected and scorned and persecuted. Some Muslims of Mecca had to flee as refugees. He had failed in those 12 years to advance or progress. The revelation he had in Mecca was peaceful. The verses in the Qur'an from the Meccan period honour the Jews and Christians, but he gained very little support from them. Mohammad needed a new start. He established the principle of migration that precedes jihad.

The beginning of Islam: The Emigration – 622 AD

Although Muhammad had been largely rejected in Mecca, there were a group of wealthy converts who welcomed him to Medina. They made a pledges to him. The Second Pledge of Aqabah (622 AD) was a pivotal oath of allegiance taken by about 70 Muslims from Yathrib (Medina) to Muhammad. They promised to protect him from any threats, treat him as their own family, and support Islam, even at the cost of their wealth and lives. This pledge, often called the "Pledge of War," paved the way for the Prophet's migration *(Hijrah)* to Medina

Muhammad and his followers from Mecca sought refuge in Medina. This move is called in Arabic the *Hijra, the Migration,* and is counted as the first year in the history of Islam. The Islamic calendar and all Islamic dates begin with the migration of Muhammad and his men from Mecca to Medina in 622 AD. The Islamic year is based on the lunar cycles.

The year 2026 AD (Anno Domini, the year of the Lord) is the year that is counted as the year 1447 AH (After Hijrah) for Muslims.

Migration is part of the doctrine of jihad, the struggle for Islam. Migration is so important that the Islamic calendar and all Islamic dates are based upon the Hijrah, Mohammed's migration from Mecca to Medina. Every date is counted to be before or after Hijrah. Why? Because it was migration that lead to the creation of the Islamic State in Medina and it was jihad that made the Islamic State triumphant. It was Allah who commanded the migration. Muhammad received the following verse:

Surah An-Nisa 4:100,

"And whoso goes forth from his house as an emigrant to God and His Messenger and then death overtakes him, his wage shall have fallen on God."

Muslims are still migrating today for the cause of Allah. There may be those who do not understand the doctrine, but they are part of the growth and expansion of Islam.

The Expansion of Islam in Medina 622-632

After the migration, Muhammad gradually acquired wealth and converts, and within six years he had gained control of the city, established the Islamic state and evicted Medina's three Jewish tribes who had been living there. Migration became an effective strategy to spread his religion, his influence and his power. For the last 1400 years, migration has remained one of the key strategies for spreading Islam across the world.

Before the *hijrah,* Muhammad had been forbidden to fight. After the hijra, Muhammad was commanded by Allah to spread Islam with the sword. In Medina he had a basis for power.

In the history of Ibn Ishaq it is stated: "The apostle had not been given permission to fight or allowed to shed blood before the second pledge of Aqaba. He had simply been ordered to call men to God and to endure insult and forgive the ignorant…He gave permission to His apostle to fight and to protect himself against those who wronged them and treated them badly. Then the following verse was revealed: "Permission to fight is given to those (i.e. believers against disbelievers), who are fighting them." *Surah Al-Hajj 22:39.* ***("The Second Pledge of 'Aqaba" on Unraveling Islam.)***

Muhammad was weak in Mecca and forbidden by Allah to fight. He did not have the numbers, the weapons, the power to defend or attack. Therefore Allah told him to be peaceful and to put up with the insults and the oppression. When he had gained power and military might, he was then commanded by Allah to take up arms and fight.

The Hadith records:

Sahih Bukhari 25

"the Messenger of Allah said: I have been commanded to fight against people till they testify that there is no god but Allah, that Muhammad is the messenger of Allah, and they establish prayer, and pay Zakat and if they do it, their blood and property are guaranteed protection on my behalf except when justified by law, and their affairs rest with Allah."

During his ten years in Medina, the breath, width, and depth of violence increased. Below is a general progression of Muhammad's efforts to obey Allah and spread Islamic domination through the use or threat of force:

- Raiding parties were sent out against non-Muslim villages and caravans. Over the space of ten years, between 622AD and 632AD, many Islamic sources claim that there were 100 such raids, although some say there were only 80. The raids which he did not personally participate were called *sariyyah*, often translated as "expeditions" or "patrols." He sent out 73 such raiding parties. The raids that he himself led were called *ghazawat,* of which there were 27.
- Murders and assassinations were carried out throughout the Arabian Peninsula
- Targeted religious persecutions took place of several Jewish tribes within and without Medina until they were killed, evicted or converted
- Military wars and conquests, subjection, rapes, massacres, and the total destruction of non-Muslim Arab tribes
- Military campaigns were engage in to spread Islam's domination far and wide

Jihad Battles Fought by Muhammad

During this time among these battles weres some major wars led by Muhammad that were highlights of the spread of Islam:

> **Battle of Badr.** In 624 a decisive early battle in Islamic history took place. A small Muslim force of about 313 men from Medina defeated a much larger army of about 1,000 men of the Quraysh from Mecca. It established the Muslims as a formidable force and marked a turning point in the rise of Islam.

Battle of Uhud. In 625, 3,000 Meccan soldiers faced 700 Muslim troops. The Muslims suffered heavy losses. It is considered a major setback for the Muslims.

Battle of the Ditch. In 627 a battle took place which was also known as the Battle of the Trench or Al-Khandaq. It was a 27-day siege of Medina, where a 3,000-strong Muslim force successfully defended against an allied army of nearly 10,000 by digging a defensive trench on their exposed northern flank.

Battle of Khaybar. In 628 there was a military conflict between early Muslims led by Prophet Muhammad and the Jewish tribes inhabiting the oasis of Khaybar, 150km from Medina. Muslims besieged the heavily fortified settlements, securing victory and ensuring northern security, resulting in Khaybar's submission, often seen as a strategic triumph.

Battle of Mutah. In 629 a critical, early conflict took place between Prophet Muhammad's Muslim army and the Byzantine Empire with its Ghassanid allies in the area of Jordan.. The Ghassanids were a South Arabian Christian tribal confederation. Over 3,000 Muslims, led by Zayd ibn Harithah, fought a vastly larger force in retaliation for the killing of a Muslim envoy by a Ghassanid official, signaling a bold expansion of the Islamic state's authority.

Battle of Hunayn. In 630 the Muslims under Prophet Muhammad and the allied Hawazin and Thaqif tribes, a conflict took place shortly after the Conquest of Mecca. Despite an initial ambush that caused a chaotic retreat among the Muslim army, Muhammad lead his armies to a major victory, significant spoils, and the expansion of Islam.

Siege of Taif. In 630 the Siege of Ta'if was a military engagement between Muhammad's forces and the fortified Thaqif tribe in Ta'if, following the Muslim victory at Hunayn. The Muslims besieged the city for 20-30 days, employing catapults, but ultimately lifted the siege without capturing the city because it was well-fortified and provisioned.

Tabuk Expedition. In 630 Muhammad led 30,000 soldiers north to invade the Byzantine Empire. To challenge reported threats from the Byzantine Empire and its Christian Arab allies aimed at stopping the spread of Islam. The Expedition of Tabuk was the final military campaign led by the Prophet Muhammad, aimed at countering a potential Byzantine invasion from the north. A massive force of roughly 30,000 Muslims marched to Tabuk in northern Saudi Arabia, but no battle took place, as the Byzantine army did not arrive.

The conquest of Mecca in 629 was achieved in a swift, near bloodless victory without warfare. The Meccans were so terrified of Muhammad and his troops that they surrendered without a fight. As Muhammad himself said, "I have been made victorious with terror." *(Sahih al-Bukhari (2977) and Sahih Muslim (523a).* 10,000 Muslim troops took control of the city from the Quraysh, ending years of conflict.

Muhammad died in 632. On his death bed, he gave the command that there was to be no two religions left on the Arabian Peninsula.

Sahih Muslim 1767,

"I heard the Messenger of Allah say: 'I will expel the Jews and Christians from the Arabian Peninsula and will not leave any but Muslims'."

Sahih al-Bukhari 3053,

"Narrated by Ibn 'Abbas regarding the last three instructions of the Prophet: "Turn the pagans out of the Arabian Peninsula; respect and give gifts to the foreign delegations as you have seen me dealing with them." (The third order was forgotten by the narrator)."

Jews have lived in Yemen for about 3000 years. We visited a Sheik in Sanaa who showed us, hanging on his living room wall, a genealogy showing his descent from Solomon and the Queen of Sheba. Whether it was genuine or not, it showed the long history of the Jewish influence in Yemen. Jews numbered over 50,000 in the early 20th century. In 1949 many emigrated to Israel. When we first went to Yemen in 2007, there were about 400 Jews living there. By 2016 only about 50 to a few hundred Jews were believed to still be there. As of 2024–2026, it is estimated that only one Yemenite Jew, Levi Marhabi, who has been detained by Houthi authorities, remains in Yemen.

The expulsion of Jews, based on the decree of Muhammad about 1400 years ago, has finally been achieved in Yemen.

Stage 2. Expansion under the first 4 Caliphs 632-661

After Muhammad's death, his example was followed by the first four caliphs. These four men had been close to Muhammad, were trained by him and were experts in Islamic warfare. They followed his teachings and as they spread their authority into new areas, they offered the inhabitants three choices:

1. Convert: become Muslims by saying the confession of faith, "There is no God but God and Muhammad is the Prophet of Allah. In Arabic this confession is called the "shahadah."
2. Pay the Jizya tax: live as "dhimmis," or second class citizens, pay special taxes and accept a lower status in society and submit to Muslim rule and laws.
3. Jihad: fight to the death.

The Qur'an contains a very clear and unequivocal message.

Surah At-Tawbah 9:29 *states,*

"Fight those who believe not in Allah nor the Last Day, nor hold that forbidden which hath been forbidden by Allah and His Messenger, nor acknowledge the religion of Truth, (even if they are) of the People of the Book, until they pay the Jizya with willing submission, and feel themselves subdued."

Caliph 1: Abu Bakr 632-634

The era of Apostasy Wars and the Conquering of the Arabian Peninsula

After the death of Muhammad, Abu Bakr was appointed the Caliph, the ruler of the Muslims. Abu Bakr was father of Aisha and thus father in law of Muhammad.

Abu Bakr's Caliphate lasted for 27 months, during which he proclaimed a jihad against apostate tribes of the Arab Peninsula who revolted after the death of Muhammad. These wars are known in Arabic as the "Ridda Wars" (or Apostasy Wars). Tens of thousands of Arabs were slaughtered until their tribes re-submitted to Islam. The Ridda Wars ended around 634. In the last months of his rule, Abu Bakr sent general Khalid ibn al-Walid on conquests against the Sassanid Empire in Mesopotamia and against the Byzantine Empire in Syria.

When Muhammad died in 632, the western half of Arabia was Muslim. Two years later after the death of Abu Bakr, the entire peninsula had been converted to Islam, and Muslim armies had moved up into the desert between Syria and Mesopotamia.

Caliph 2. Umar 634-644

Expansion into Persia, Egypt, Syria, North Africa

Under Umar, the caliphate expanded at an unprecedented rate, ruling the Sasanian Empire in Persia and more than two-thirds of the Byzantine Empire. Umar launched the wars to stop Muslims from fighting each other. By the end of his reign, Arab armies, which included defeated rebels and former imperial auxiliary troops, conquered the Byzantine provinces of Syria around 636 and Egypt in 641. They took all of north Africa. Mesopotamia was conquered in 650 and the attacks against the Sasanian Empire resulted in the conquest of Persia in fewer than two years (642–644).

Egypt

The military campaign to conquer Egypt began in 639 AD. Led by Amr ibn al-As, a small Arab force of approximately 4,000 soldiers crossed from Palestine into Egypt, marking the start of a swift transition from Byzantine to Muslim rule. The conquest was largely completed by 641–642 AD with the surrender of the main Roman stronghold of Alexandria. Within ten years of Muhammad's death Egypt had been conquered by the Muslims.

Persia

The Muslim conquest of Persia, which began the process of bringing Islam to the region, started in 633 AD. It took a longer than the conquest of Egypt. It took almost 20 years. This led up to the fall of the Sasanian Empire, which was eventually fully conquered by 651 AD.

The Levant, Egypt, Cyrenaica, Tripolitania, Fezzan, Eastern Anatolia, almost the whole of the Sassanid Persian Empire, including Bactria, Persia,

Azerbaijan, Armenia, Caucasus and Makran, were incorporated into the Islamic State.

Islamic forces conquered Christian North Africa through a combination of rapid military expansion led by the Rashidun and Umayyad Caliphates, starting with the conquest of Egypt in 639–642 AD. Arab armies, driven by religious zeal and motivated by political expansion, defeated Byzantine forces in Cyrenaica and Tripoli before advancing through the Maghreb to Carthage by 698 AD.

Local populations of Jews and indigenous Christians, lived as religious minorities and were taxed with the jizya to finance the Byzantine–Sassanid Wars. They often aided Muslims to take over their lands from the Byzantines and Persians, resulting in exceptionally speedy conquests. As new areas were conquered, they also benefited from free trade with other areas of the growing Islamic state, where, to encourage commerce, taxes were applied to wealth rather than trade.

Caliph 3. Uthman 644-656

Expansion into Armenia, Asia and Cyprus

After Umar was assassinated in 644, Uthman ibn Affan became the next caliph. Uthman was the Caliph who burned all the Qur'ans in existence except the one that today is claimed to be the original Qur'an.

Uthman's armies conquered much of Armenia, pushed further north west into Asia, and conquered and ruled Cyprus in 654AD. The Islamic Caliphate expanded significantly, reaching its greatest extent at the time, stretching from North Africa in the west to Persia, Khorasan, and Transoxiana in the east. Major conquests included full control of Persia in 651AD, Cyprus in 649AD, parts of North Africa, and coastal Mediterranean areas. During his reign the Muslims became very powerful and wealthy.

The Arab-Byzantine Wars

The Byzantine Empire was hindering the Muslims. Because of their harassment from the sea, a navy was set up in 649 by the Muslims. They manned the navy with Monophysitise Christians, Egyptian Christian Copts and Jacobite Syrian Christians sailors plus the Muslim troops, and were able to defeat the Byzantine navy in 655 and open up the Mediterranean to Muslim ships.

Islam's blockade of and conquest of the Mediterranean contributed to the sudden and catastrophic decline in Western European civilization which has come to be known as the Dark Ages.

The Byzantines were devastated by the Arab assaults. They were deprived of some of its most prosperous provinces, namely, Syria, Palestine, Egypt and North Africa. The Byzantine Empire was reduced it to less than half its former size both in area and in population. Cities were abandoned, bronze coins were no longer used and barter replaced coinage, the papyrus supply from Egypt dried up and the intellectual class after the seventh century were reduced to a "small clique." Libraries, academies and a great quantity of Classical literature were destroyed by the Muslims. The mid-seventh century was a great catastrophe for Europe.

Caliph 4: Ali 656-661

Consolidation of Power

Ali ibn Abi Talib, a cousin and son-in-law of Muhammad, replaced Uthman who was assassinated. He moved the capital to Kufa in Iraq. Muawiyah I, the governor of Syria, and Marwan I demanded the arrest of those who killed Uthman. Marwan I created a conflict, which resulted in the first civil war called the "First Fitna." Ali was assassinated in 661.

Ali's reign was characterized by civil strife (the First Fitna), during which he was focused on maintaining the unity of the existing Islamic state, restoring justice, and battling domestic rebellions.

This was the end of the era of "the Four Rightly Guided Caliphs", known also as the Rashidun Caliphate. This era spanned approximately 30 years from the death of Muhammad in 632 AD to the death of Ali in 661 AD. This period marked the initial expansion of the Islamic state, with the four leaders Abu Bakr, Umar, Uthman, and Ali ruling from Medina.

Stage 3: Expansion under the Ummayad Caliphate 661-750

Islamic Centre moves to Damascus and Islam spreads around the Mediterranean

After the Caliph Ali's death, Muawiyah I, Governor of Syria established the Umayyad caliphate, with its capital in Damascus. The Ummayads rapidly expanded the rule of Islam into North Africa, Spain and Central Asia through military conquest. The political centre of Islam shifted from Medina to Damascus. Power was consolidated by making Arabic the official language, replacing Byzantine officials with Arabs, and introducing Islamic coinage.

Muslim migration under the Umayyad Caliphate was a central component of its expansionist policies. Migration transformed the demographic and cultural landscape of the Middle East, North Africa, and the Iberian Peninsula. Arab military elites, tribal groups, and their families moved from the Arabian Peninsula into newly conquered territories.

Islam spread out across the neighbouring lands through jihad wars and then immigration, transplanting Muslims into new areas to control and rule the new territories that had come under Islamic rule.

The Muslims conquered the city of Kabul and occupied **Afghanistan** in 664. They pushed into the Maghreb, the region of **North Africa** on the coast of the Mediterranean Sea in 665. In **Jerusalem** they built the Dome of the Rock on the temple Mount in 691.

The fight against the Byzantines escalated. In 674-78 the first Siege of Constantinople took place but the Muslims were repelled with the invention and deployment of "Greek Fire." In 692 at the Battle of Sebastopolis in Asia Minor, the Byzantine Empire under Justinian II was soundly defeated.

From 711-718 the Muslim Conquest of **Spain** took place. Muslim armies under Tariq ibn Ziyad crossed the Strait of Gibraltar and began to conquer Spain using North African Berber armies. he led a large army from the north coast of Morocco, consolidating his troops at a large hill now known as Gibraltar. The name "Gibraltar" is the Spanish derivation of the Arabic name Jabal Ṭāriq meaning "mountain of Tariq", which is named after him. The Visigoths of Spain were defeated when the Umayyads conquered Lisbon. Spain was the farthest extent of Islamic control of Europe (they were stopped at the Battle of Tours). Spain would not be reconquered completely by the Christians until 1492. In 783 the Umayyad conquerors set up their centre in Cordoba. They built a huge mosque on the site of the Catholic Basilica of Saint Vincent of Lérins. Muslims still long for a return to Andalus (Islamic Spain), particularly Córdoba, which they consider a "lost paradise" symbolizing a golden age of intellectual, cultural, and spiritual achievement.

The Muslims pushed up into Europe again. In 717-18 the second Siege of Constantinople took place. The Muslims again failed to take Constantinople but the attack weakened the Byzantine Empire.

The Muslims began to invade **France** in 719. On October 10th 732, Charles Martel halted their northward march into central France with a decisive victory at **the Battle of Tours.** The battle was fought on October 10, 732 between forces led by Charles Martel and a massive invading Islamic army near the city of Tours, France. This battle marked a turning point in history. If it had not been for the French victory over the Arabs, Islam would have continued its march into Europe. The Battle of Tours is highly significant. It was a major setback to the advance of Islam and halted its spread into Europe. It was a symbolic clash between Christianity and Islam that helped to determine the religious future of the continent.

The Extent of the Ummayad Caliphate

By 750, under the Umayyad caliphate, the Muslim world had spread through North Africa up to southern France, north to the Caucasus and east into modern-day Afghanistan and Pakistan. In the east, Islamic armies under Muhammad bin Qasim made it as far as the Indus Valley. Muslim expansion in Central Asia reached to Bukhara and Samarkand. At its largest extent, the Umayyad dynasty covered more than 5,000,000 square miles (13,000,000 km2) making it one of the largest empires the world had yet seen, and the fifth largest empire ever, spanning the continents of Europe, Africa and Asia.

By the year 750, a hundred years after the conquest of Jerusalem, at least 50 percent of the world's Christians found themselves under Muslim rule. Eventually no indigenous Christianity in the region of Northwest Africa remained. Christian communities had vanished from the region.

Muslim invaders had destroyed over 3200 Christian churches in the first 100 years of Islam. It is estimated that over 700 bishropics in Western North Africa were eliminated. In the third century Tertullian had indicated a high density of churches there, suggesting over 20,000 bishops. Muslims had conquered the whole of the previously Christian North Africa.

By the early 8th century, all of north Africa and Spain to the west, and the lands of central Asia and India to the east, were also brought under Islamic rule. Some people doubt that the Muslims used compulsion and forced people to submit to Islam.

The use of force is documented clearly by the major historian of that era, Al-Tabari:

Al-Tabari, "The History of al-Tabari", State University of New York Press" vol. 10, page 2,

"You [Muslims] were the most severe people against his enemies who were among you, and the most troublesome to his enemies who were not from among you, so that the Arabs became upright in God's cause, willingly or unwillingly, and the distant one submitted in abject humiliation until through you God made great slaughter in the earth for His Apostle, and by your swords the Arabs were abased for him."

Stage 4. Expansion under the Abbasid Caliphate 750-1258

The Islamic "Golden Age"

In 750 the Abbasids, descendants of Muhammad's uncle, Abbas, overthrew the Ummayad caliph and set up their own Caliphate. The Ummayads were massacred by the Abbasids. Almost the entire Umayyad dynasty was killed, except for prince Abd al-Rahman who escaped to Spain and founded a dynasty there. The Abbasids created a new capital city in Baghdad.

Baghdad became the centre of the Islamic Golden Age. The Abbasids set up the "House of Wisdom", a library with 400.000 books at its peak, a translation institute, and research centre. It became an intellectual hub for advancements in science, medicine, mathematics. It preserved, and expanded upon Greek, Persian, and Indian knowledge in mathematics, astronomy, medicine, and philosophy.

The Abbasid dynasty consolidated the gains of the earlier Caliphates. They spread their rule through Mediterranean islands and in 827 AD conquered Sicily.

Expansion continued

India

The first stage in the conquest of India began just before the year 1000 AD. with the conquest of Afghanistan. It was followed by the annihilation of the Hindu population and the region is still called the Hindu Kush, that is, "Hindu slaughter." Islamic armies conquered and ruled Northern India for some 500 years from 1200AD to 1700AD. Islam's conquest of India was a protracted and a bloody affair. Looting, burning of cities, and destruction of local economies, led to high mortality. Entire cities were burnt down and the populations were massacred, with hundreds of thousands killed in every campaign, and similar numbers deported as slaves. According to some claims, the Indian subcontinent population decreased by 80 million between the year 1000AD, when the conquest of Afghanistan took place, and 1525AD, the end of Delhi Sultanate.

Sub Saharan West Africa

Islamization in Sub-Saharan West Africa began gradually around the 8th–9th centuries, primarily driven by Muslim Berber traders crossing the Sahara. It initially spread along trade routes, taking root in urban centers and among ruling elites. In the following centuries Muslim trading networks consolidated their power and African kingdoms converted to Islam.

East Africa

Islamic imperialism in East Africa was primarily driven by Omani Arabs and Persians from the 7th century onwards. They established bases on the coast, transformed trade routes, introduced the slave trade and spread Islam. Muslims immigrated into the area and built trading posts along the coast, transforming towns like Kilwa, Mombasa, and Mogadishu into bustling, Islamized trading hubs. Islamic power was briefly contested by the Portuguese in the 16th-17th centuries. Later, this Islamic influence was replaced by European colonial powers, British and German in the late 19th century.

Italy

In 827 the conquest of Syracuse in Sicily took place. Gradually Sicily was conquered by the Muslims and their presence in Sicily lasted until the

Norman conquest in the 11th century. In **831** Palermo fell and became a garison city of the Muslim army. They began to attack the Italian peninsular In **846** Rome was attacked by troops landing at the port of Ostia. St. Peter's Basilica was raided and plundered while Pope Sergius II and the helpless Roman garrison retreated behind the city walls. In **847** the Muslim Conquest of Bari took place in southern Italy. The Muslim presence on the Italian peninsula proper lasted 25 years. **863** In a rare break from the pattern of this era, the Byzantines went back on the offensive, with mixed results over the next 200-300 years of warfare. In **915**, at the Battle of Garigliano, Pope John X personally led an army against Islamic forces in southern Italy.

Under the Abbasids and the North African Aghlabid dynasty (800-909), Muslim rule was extended to Rhodes, Crete, Kabul, Bukhara and Samarkand and expanded in North Africa.

Southeast Asia

Southeast Asia was conquered initially through trade and emigration. Beginning around the 13th century, Arab, Persian, Indian and Chinese merchants traded and migrated to Southeast Asia bearing spices, cotton fabrics, precious stones and minerals. They settled as immigrants, intermarried and gradually introduced Islam along the areas on the coast. Local people converted to Islam for economic advantages.

The Muslims also fought jihad wars to gain control. Jakarta was conquered by Muslim forces on June 22, 1527, when Fatahillah, a commander from the Sultanate of Demak, defeated the Portuguese and the Sunda Kingdom. Following the victory, Fatahillah renamed the city Sunda Kelapa to Jayakarta, meaning "precious victory" or "complete victory" and which today is Jakarta, the capital city of Indonesia. Gradually over several centuries the islands of Indonesia became the world's largest Muslim-majority nation.

Stage 5. The Age of the Crusades - 1095

The Crusades were first declared on the 27th November 1095AD. Why did the Crusades take place? They began after five centuries of jihad attacks where over two thirds of the previously Christian world had been conquered, annihilated or forcibly converted to Islam. Throughout the centuries Christian pilgrims to the Holy Land had been harassed and massacred. The Christians were subject to paying the jizya tax. In the 8th century all displays of the Cross in Jerusalem had been banned. In the following years there were many attacks on the Christians and Jews who lived in Jerusalem and the pilgrims who travelled to the Holy Land.

Attacks against Christians

There were many attacks on Christians that led to the declaration of the Crusades.

- **722** All the hands of Christians and Jews in Jerusalem were branded.
- **789** Muslims beheaded a monk in Bethlehem, plundered the monastery and slaughtered many more Christians
- **923** A new wave of destruction of churches was launched by Muslim rulers
- **937** Muslims rampaged in Jerusalem on Palm Sunday, plundering and destroying the Church of Calvary and the Church of the Resurrection
- **1004** A violent wave of church burning and destruction, confiscation of Christian property and ferocious slaughter of Christians and Jews took place.
- **1004-1014** 30,000 churches were destroyed and vast numbers were forcibly converted or killed

- **1009** The Church of the Holy Sepulchre and the Church of the Resurrection were ordered to be destroyed. Humiliating and burdensome decrees were heaped upon Christians and they were finally ordered to accept Islam or flee.
- **1077** The Seljuk Turks swept into Jeruslem and murdered over 3000 people. The Emperor of Byzantium appealed to help to the Western Churches.

These constant attacks on the Christians and the pilgrims in the Holy Land, eventually led to the call for a defensive response.

The Call to Start the Crusades

1095 At the Council of Clermont, the speech by Pope Urban II started the Crusades. He said,

"As the most of you have heard, the Turks and Arabs have attacked our brethren in the east and have conquered the territory of Romania [the Greek empire] as far west as the shore of the Mediterranean and the Hellespont, which is called the Arm of St. George. They have occupied more and more of the lands of those Christians, and have overcome them in seven battles. They have killed and captured many, and have destroyed the churches and devastated the empire. If you permit them to continue thus for awhile [sic] with impunity, the faithful of God will be much more widely attacked by them. On this account I, or rather the Lord, beseech you as Christ's heralds to publish this everywhere and to persuade all people of whatever rank, foot-soldiers and knights, poor and rich, to carry aid promptly to those Christians and to destroy that vile race from the lands of our friends."

Prior to the First Crusade, roughly two-thirds of the land that had historically been Christian in the Levant, was conquered by Muslim forces. The main Crusades to the Holy Land lasted for nearly 200 years, spanning from 1095 to 1291. During that time there were eight or nine crusades by the Europeans in an effort to oust the Muslims and secure Jerusalem and the areas around about so that it would be safe for the Christian pilgrims.

The Crusaders were eventually defeated but the Abbasids had been weakened and began to lose power. The Mongols sacked Baghdad in 1258 and the Abbasid Caliphate collapsed. Meanwhile, the Seljuk Turks and the Ottomans in Turkey asserted their dominance.

Stage 6. Expansion under the Ottomans 1299-1924

In 1299 the earliest Ottoman state was formed in Anatolia, Turkey. From there they expanded westward into the European continent. The Ottoman Caliphate replaced the Abbasid Caliphate and was to last for over 600 years. Like those preceding, it was expansionist. Jihad attacks were made against the nations.

The Balkans

1352 The Turks crossed the Bosphorus. The Ottoman force met and defeated 4,000 Serbs.This was the Ottomans' first victory in Europe and an ominous portent. Two years later they captured Gallipoli which marked the beginning of the Ottoman conquest of the Balkans, culminating a century later in the Fall of Constantinople. In **1371** again the Ottomans attacked the Serbs and this time won the Battle of Maritsa. In 1389, the Ottomans crushed the Serbs in the Battle of Kosovo in the south of modern-day Yugoslavia. In **1385** at the Battle of Savra, Albania fell under Ottoman rule. Albanian Jihad (1332 - 1853). By the early 20th century, Islam was most deeply rooted in Bosnia and Herzegovina, Albania, Kosovo, and parts of North Macedonia, where indigenous populations had adopted the faith. The Balkan Wars (1912–1913) saw the end of Ottoman rule in most of the region, causing many Muslims to become minorities overnight or migrate.

This migration impacted Australia. Several hundred Albanian Muslims migrated to Australia in the mid-1920s, with some coming in the 1930s and post-World War II. Seeking economic opportunities, these migrants settled mostly in rural Queensland to work on tobacco farms in Mareeba, and to fruit farms in Victoria, especially around Shepparton.

They established some of Australia's first mosques. The first purpose-built mosque in Victoria is the Albanian Mosque in Shepparton, which was officially opened in 1960. The first mosque established in Queensland outside of Brisbane, was built in Mareeba in 1970.

Bulgaria 1396-1878

In 1396 At the Battle of Nicopolis (Bulgaria) on the Danube River, the gates of Eastern Europe were opened to the Muslims. This battle is looked upon as the last crusade where Europe put on a combined resistance to throw the Ottoman Turks out of Bulgaria and stem further Muslim incursions into Europe. Bulgaria after 70 years of fighting had fallen to the Ottomans. In 1444 The Ottomans routed European forces in Eastern Bulgaria at the Battle of Varna and ended the "Crusade of Varna," the last major Christian initiative to expel the Ottomans from Europe for centuries. Bulgaria was liberated as a result of the Russian-Turkish War in 1877-1888. Bulgaria had been ruled by the Muslims from 1396 until 1878. These five centuries have remained in the national mentality as "the Turkish slavery."

Turkey 1453-1924

On Wednesday, 29th May 1453 Constantinople, the capital city of the Byzantine Empire fell to an invading army of the Ottoman Empire. The Hagia Sophia, originally built as a cathedral in 537 AD, was violently seized and converted into a mosque. This marked the end of the Byzantine Empire and the triumph of Islam. It had profound consequences for both Christian Europe and Islam. The Ottoman Empire ruled as the Islamic Caliphate, from 1517 until its dissolution in 1924 after the end of World War I. During that time it ruled over many countries, including Egypt, Greece, Turkey, Bulgaria, Romania, Macedonia, Hungary, Israel, Lebanon, Syria, sections of the Arabian Peninsula, and even parts of North Africa.

Greece 1458-1832

The Muslims advanced southwards into Greece and captured Athens. The Ottomans took over Greece. All non-Muslims were forbidden to ride a horse which made traveling very difficult. Many Greeks fled Greece or fled up into the mountainous regions which were difficult of access for the Turks.

The Greeks were heavily taxed and this tax included a "tribute of children." One male child in five within every Christian family was taken away from the family as a "blood tax" and enrolled in the corps of *Janissaries* for military training in the Sultan's army. The Janissaries were Christian boys aged 8 to 14 who were taken, converted to Islam, and trained rigorously, sometimes to return to their own countries and fight against their countrymen.

Girls were also taken in order to serve as *odalisques* (girl slaves who became concubines) in harems.

Repressive sharia laws were introduced and occasionally the Ottoman government committed massacres against the civilian population.

No Greek's testimony could stand against a Turk's in a law court. Life became ruralized and militarized. Many Greeks were reduced to subsistence farming.

Turkish settled extensively in Thrace and Greek Macedonia. Athens became on its most part a run-down village, its peasant Greek population extremely poor and isolated, not allowed near the Acropolis where the more wealthy Muslim Turks were settled.

The Greeks were under Ottoman rule, often referred to as *Tourkokratia*, or the "four hundred years of slavery." It began in the mid-15th century with the fall of Constantinople in 1453 and lasted until the Greek War of Independence broke out in 1821. On March 25 (now Greek Independence Day) in 1821, a national uprising was proclaimed and a war for independence ensued. In October 1827, the British, French and Russian fleets, destroyed the Ottoman fleet at the Battle of Navarino. By the Convention of May 11, 1832, Greece was finally recognized as a sovereign state.

Hungary 1541-1699

Suleiman defeated Louis II of Hungary at the Battle of Mohács, and began to set up Ottoman rule in Hungary. In 1541 he took the towns of Buda and Pest (which today together form the Hungarian capital Budapest) with a largely bloodless trick: after concluding peace talks with an agreement, troops stormed the open gates of Buda in the night. It was a decisive event for the history of Central Europe. Ottoman rule (roughly 1541–1699) devastated Hungary, splitting it into three parts, decimating the population through constant warfare, and causing a massive economic downturn.

The Siege of Vienna in 1529

This was the first attempt by the Ottoman Empire, led by Suleiman the Magnificent, to capture the city of Vienna, Austria. The siege signalled the pinnacle of the Ottoman Empire's power and the maximum extent of Ottoman expansion in central Europe. It was here that Europe again halted the expasion of Islam. It was another turning point in history.

In 1571 Cyprus fell to the Ottomans. Crete fell in 1669 after a twenty year siege.

Russia 1444-1918

The Russian crusade against Islam lasted from 1444 up to 1918. The Russians waged a four-century long crusade against Islam. Had it not been for the Russian resistance from 1444 up to 1918, the whole of Russia would have been Muslim today. The Russo-Turkish Wars were a series of ten wars fought between the Russian Empire and the Turkish-ruled Ottoman Empire during the 17th to 19th centuries. Their conflict during World War I should also be counted as an eleventh and, so far, the last Russo-Islamic war in the series. They destroyed the Jihadi threat to not only to Russia but also to Europe.

Now the jihadi threat has returned and is increasing again. Russia faces a persistent jihadist threat, primarily from groups like ISIS-K, fueled by resentment over Russian military interventions in Chechnya, Syria, and Africa.

The Ottoman Jihad Massacres

There many massacres that took place during the time of the Ottomans. Many of them were carried out by the Jannisaries, the army made up of Christian boys who had been kidnapped from Christian families, forced to convert, drafted for life, and then forced to return to their villages and attack and kill their families.

Austria, 1683

Muslim armies burnt villages in Austria, enslaved women, children, working men, decapitated the old and sick, sacked churches and trampled crucifixes. In the Perchtoldsdorf Massacre, villagers who had barricaded themselves in a church fortress accepted a deal for safe passage from the Ottoman army, led by Grand Vizier Kara Mustafa Pasha. Upon surrender, the Ottoman forces broke their word, taking the men into the market square to be massacred, while women and children were taken into slavery.

During the two-month siege of Vienna (July 14 – September 12), widespread pillaging and slavery occurred. Ottoman troops raided the surrounding countryside.During that time, an estimated 57,220 people were kidnapped and taken away as slaves from the Austrian and Hungarian border zone.

Greek island of Chios, 1822

In 1822, a brutal massacre took place on the island of Chios during the Greek War of Independence, Ottoman forces killed an estimated 20,000 to 52,000 Greek inhabitants. Out of a population of roughly 100,000–120,000, an additional 45,000 to 52,000 were sold into slavery, which left only a few thousand remaining on the island.

Assyria, 1842-1847

The Ottomans killed 10,000 Assyrian Christian men, and enslaved 10,000 women and children. The attacks involved widespread burning of villages, mass slaughter of men, and the taking of women and children as slaves.

Bulgaria 1876

In April 1876, Bulgarians launched a major, premature uprising against Ottoman rule, known as the April Uprising, which was brutally suppressed by Ottoman irregular troops, killing 15,000–30,000 people and causing a massive international outcry. Though the revolt failed to achieve independence immediately, the "Bulgarian Horrors" triggered global condemnation, directly leading to the 1877–78 Russo-Turkish War and eventual Bulgarian independence.

Armenia and Assyria 1894-1896

Between 1894 and 1896, the Ottoman Empire, under Sultan Abdul Hamid II, carried out widespread massacres targeting Armenian and Assyrian Christians, killing an estimated 80,000 to 300,000 people. Known as the Hamidian massacres, these state-sponsored atrocities involved systematic murders, forced conversions, rape, and destruction of villages, largely carried out by Ottoman soldiers and Kurdish regiments in the eastern province

Armenian Genocide 1915

While being deported and sent on death marches, 1,500,000 Armenian and 250,000 Assyrian Christians died: Women were raped and crucified, children were enslaved, 200,000 who converted were spared. Churches were made into barns. Estimates suggest between 250,000 and 750,000

Assyrians were massacred by the Ottoman Empire and its allies between 1915 and 1923, commonly known as the Sayfo (Assyrian Genocide). In 1918, 15,000 Armenian Christians were killed in Baku, many being used for bayonet practice.

In 1918, Baku was a focal point of extreme violence and conflict, marked by the "March Days" (massacre of Azerbaijanis by Bolsheviks and Dashnaks) and the "September Days" (slaughter of Armenians by the Ottoman-Azerbaijani forces).

The Caliphate killed its own Christian subjects. There were about up to 2.5 million Christians who were killed, starved, or died from atrocities during the Ottoman Christian persecution (1894–1924) that was designed to wipe out the Christian minorities. This is still a sensitive issue in Turkey where they continue to deny that this genicide ever happened.

Stage 7. The Defeat of the Caliphate

World War I ended in 1918. With the defeat followed the dissolution of the Ottoman Empire on March 3, 1924, The abolition of the Islamic caliphate, and the creation of the secular Republic of Turkey was a major turning point and cataclysmic disaster for Islam.

Islamic areas that had been ruled for centuries by the Caliphate now came under the rule of the *kafir*, the heathen, unbelieving nations of Britain and France. Muslim political unity was broken, causing a profound crisis in the Islamic vision of unity, authority, and identity. The Caliphate, an institution that had existed for 1,300 years, had been dissolved. The ultimate symbol of the Muslim *Ummah* (community) had vanished. Islam was left fractured and leaderless.

Stage 8. The Modern Expansion

The Rise of Islam in the Twentieth Century

From 1924 until today there has been no Caliphate. However, the Caliphate dream has not been extinguished or abandoned, nor has the continuing jihad.

The Muslim Brotherhood was founded in Egypt by Hassan al-Banna in March 1928 as an Islamist religious, political, and social movement that became a foundation for all the radical movements today. It has also spread its influence and inspiration for jihad throughout the Islamic world.

Israel was formed as a nation in 1948 and became the focal point of Islamic hatred and grievances. Israel has remained the thorn in the side of Islam. The day after the proclamation of Israel it was immediately attacked by Islamic states. The attacks and wars against this tiny nation continue until today. The ultimate vision of Islam is the elimination of the Jews.

The Ayatollah Khomeini founded the Islamic Republic of Iran in 1979. It was the first attempt at an Islamic state in the modern era and inspired the rise of Islamic power. Iran changed from a modern democratic nation to become an autocratic Islamic republic that is threatening to destroy the surrounding nations as well as the United States and the Western world.

Oil money funded the rise to riches of Saudi Arabia and the Gulf States and allowed the rise and rapid spread of Islamic political power and influence.

The first wave of Muslim immigration into Western nations opened up. Muslims came as refugees, then as entrepreneurs, businessmen, doctors and lawyers. For the first time Islam appeared in the Western Judeo-Christian nations. Muslims moved into Europe, the United Kingdom, the United States, Canada, Australia and New Zealand. Mosques sprang up in cities and towns all over the world that never before had a Muslim presence.

Stage 9. Facing Islam in the 21st Century

Immigration and the Islamic Invasion

On 11th September 2001, the Twin Towers in New York City and the Pentagon in Washington were attacked. Since that day, Islam and Islamic terror have continued their relentless expansion.

On 30th June 2014, the first Caliphate since the demise of the Ottomans was declared. The Islamic State, known as ISIS appeared on the world stage, briefly cause havoc and then was decisively defeated. However, it remains underground, quietly fomenting unrest and waiting for the moment to rise again.

Meanwhile, modern radical Islamist Jihad movements are still spreading across the globe into every nation.

- Jemaah Islamiyya based in Indonesia, with networks across Southeast Asia, including Malaysia, the Philippines, Thailand, and Singapore.
- Boko Haram in Nigeria
- Al Shabaab in Somalia
- Al-Qaeda in the Arabian Peninsula
- Muslim Brotherhood throughout the Middle East
- Hizbullah in Lebanon
- Hamas in Palestine
- CAIR in the USA
- Hizbut-Tahrir in the UK
- ISIS global expansion
- And many others – do a Google search.

At the same time, Islamic immigration is transforming the face of all of the Western democracies.

The website ***www.thereligionofpeace.com*** keeps track of the number of violent jihad attacks as best it can. As of April 2026, the site lists in detail more than 49,200 fatal jihad attacks since September 2001. It is worth a visit.

Understanding the Four Steps of Islamic Conquest

Dr Peter Hammond outlines four steps of Islamic Conquest in his book, ***"Slavery, Terrorism and Islam."*** He documents the way Muslims slowly develop a presence in various countries, build up their population, become more aggressive and assertive about exercising Sharia law.

Step one: Infiltration

It begins with immigration. Muslims begin moving to non-Muslim countries. They are welcomed as peace-loving and desiring harmony. They may have little impact on the host culture. The Muslims have high birth rates and their presence increases. They tend to congregate in areas and gradually establish their homes and businesses in the same area.

As their numbers grow, cultural differences begin to appear. Appeals for humanitarian tolerance begin to be issued. Mosques begin to be built. Halal food begins to appear in the supermarkets. Offers of "interfaith dialogue" to indoctrinate non-Muslims emerge.

The Muslim population increases to over 2 percent. Most Western nations have now passed that threshold.

Most Western nations have now passed that threshold.

Step 2: Consolidation of Power

The Muslim population is no longer a silent, unobtrusive, peaceful minority but they have found their voice. This is when calls to criminalize

"Islamophobia" as a hate crime and threats of legal action for perceived discrimination begin.

As the Muslim population increases, they seek minority rights, demand halal food, and demand the accommodation of their beliefs within school and workplaces. Muslim immigrants and host country converts continue demands for accommodation in employment, education, social services, financing and courts.

Proselytizing increases. Jihadi cells centred in radical mosques begin to recruit young Muslims. Alienated segments of the population are targeted to be attracted to Islam. Efforts are made to revise and Islamize history. Attempts are made to indoctrinate children to the Islamist viewpoint. Increased efforts are taken to intimidate, silence and eliminate all criticism of Islam by to introducing blasphemy and hate laws in order to silence critics.

There is a continued focus on enlarging the Muslim population by increasing Muslim births and immigration. Charities are used to recruit supporters and fund jihad. A political base begins to develop and Muslims begin to be elected to local councils and to the national parliaments. Islamic financial networks fund political growth, acquisition of land, building of mosques and schools. Tolerance of non-Muslims diminishes. Efforts are made to undermine and destroy the power base of non-Muslim religions including and especially Jews and Christians.

Is there a pattern here? Theo van Gogh was murdered in the Netherlands for 'insulting' Islam. The Organization of the Islamic Conference demanded 'anti-blasphemy' laws through the United Nations. France is set afire regularly by Muslim youths. Honour killings are rising. Anti-Semitism is increasing. Islamic intolerance and the covert, cultural jihad to remake host societies into sharia-compliant worlds is taking place. Individual freedoms are being curtailed. The freedom of speech to criticize Islam is being criminalized.

Step 3: Open conflict with the government leadership and culture

Threats are made against those who oppose Islam. Acts of terror and violence erupt in order to force the society to conform to Islamic demands. Attempts to impose Sharia law and associated cultural restrictions begin. Recognition of women wearing the hijab, of Islamic holidays, of the fasting month of Ramadhan begin to be demanded. Conflicts over gender equality and secularism break out. Acts of barbarity to intimidate citizens and foster fear and submission occur intermittently.

As conflict increases there are open and covert efforts to cause economic collapse of the society. All opposition is challenged and either eradicated or silenced. Muslims increase their political power and are able to covertly bring in sharia laws. They become mayors of cities. The host society's secular laws and culture are rejected and defied. Churches, synagogues and other non-Muslim institutions may be burned down. Women are restricted further in accordance with Sharia law. Assassinations and bombings may take place.

Step 4: Totalitarian Islamic Theocracy

The end goal is the setting up of an Islamic Republic and the imposition of Sharia law. Upon reaching a certain, higher percentage of the population, the state is taken over, and Sharia law is implemented, leading to the removal of other religious practices, the toppling of democratic government, the usurpation of political power and the loss of all democratic freedoms.

The most obvious example is what happened in Iran under the Ayatollahs and in Afghanistan under the Taliban.

This framework argues that the aim of Islam is not just religious, but its purpose is to establish a political and legal system over non-Muslim nations. Islam becomes the only religious-political-judicial-cultural ideology. Sharia becomes the "law of the land. All non-Islamic human rights are cancelled. Enslavement and genocide of non-Muslim population takes place. Freedom of speech and the press is eradicated. All religions other than Islam are forbidden and their buildings and symbols are destroyed.

"Muhammad's original migration model," Aynaz Anni Cyrus points out, "is still being followed: enter as a guest, grow into a bloc, demand accommodation, then rule by numbers." *(https://pjmedia.com/bruce-bawer-2/2026/04/06/a-taxonomy-of-jihad-how-does-islam-conquer-n4951500#google_vignette)*

Islam theology recognizes two houses, *Dar al-Islam*, the House of Peace, referring to lands under Muslim rule, and *Dar al-Harb*, the House of War, referring to lands outside of Muslim rule. The goal of Islam is that all nations will become *Dar Al-Islam.* Yes, according to Islamic theology and scriptural interpretation, a central goal of Islam is for all humanity to submit to Allah, which is believed to lead to peace, justice, and the fulfillment of the purpose of human creation.

The 2023-2026 Middle East Conflict – October 7, 2023, to the present

Much will be discussed in the future of this war involving Iran and its proxies – Hamas, Hezbollah, Houthi, Islamic Jihad and other smaller groups through Gaza, Lebanon, Syria, Iraq and Iran. It is a war against the little Satan – Israel and the big Satan – the USA.

It is a war of survival for Israel and even Western civilization. Many protests in the Western World crying "From the River to the Sea" have caused havoc in many cities and countries. Currently Israel and the USA are in a major War with Iran and seek to destroy its nuclear and missile capacities. Attempts at peace treaties or temporary truces may seem to succeed, but Bible prophecy says that this will not be the end. There is a coming great revival in the Middle East and more wars before we reach the climax of the ages, but it can't be too far away.

Islamic expansion for the present will cease in the Middle East but may very well accelerate in Western countries. We need to watch and pray because the Lord will have His way.

Psalm 2:1-12,

"Why do the nations rage, And the people plot a vain thing? The kings of the earth set themselves, And the rulers take counsel together, against the LORD and against His Anointed, saying, "Let us break Their bonds in pieces and cast away their cords from us." He who sits in the heavens shall laugh; the LORD shall hold them in derision. Then He shall speak to them in His wrath, and distress them in His deep displeasure: "Yet I have set My King On My holy hill of Zion." I will declare the decree: The LORD has said to Me, 'You are My Son, Today I have begotten You. Ask of Me, and I will give You The nations for Your inheritance, And the ends of the earth for Your possession. You shall break them with a rod of iron; You shall dash them to pieces like a potter's vessel.'" Now therefore, be wise, O kings; Be instructed, you judges of the earth. Serve the LORD with fear, And rejoice with trembling. Kiss the Son, lest He be angry, And you perish in the way, When His wrath is kindled but a little. Blessed are all those who put their trust in Him."

Questions for Discussion

1. After studying Islamic history, what is our response?
2. What is the reality of Islamic expansion today?
3. What can we do to take the Gospel to all peoples and nations and those in our country now?
4. How can we impact our friends and neighbours with the Gospel?
5. What is God saying to us about our calling, our gifting, our role and relationships in fulfilling the Great Commission?
6. How important do you think it is that we experience *Acts 1:8* so that we can fulfill *Matthew 28:19-20?*

DILEMMA 14

ERRORS AND CONTRADICTIONS DILEMMA

Both Christians and Muslims claim respectively, that their sacred writings, the Bible and the Qur'an, were inspired by God. So it can be quite a dilemma for both Christians and Muslims if errors and contradictions are pointed out. It can be considered an insult against God and destructive to the relevant religious belief system. This makes it a sensitive issue. Nevertheless, it is important for us to know if the holy books that we are reading and trusting are truly of divine origin or just the invention of man, or even worse, inspired by Satan. As you can see, this is an extremely sensitive, yet very important dilemma that we are confronted with.

Generally speaking, Christians view the Qur'an as not from God but rather inspired by Satan. On the other hand, Muslims generally believe that the Bible, originally, was inspired by God, but later on was corrupted by the Jews and Christians, and therfore today, the Bible is false and not to be trusted. In many Muslim countries the Bible has been banned as it is believed to be a destructive book to the Islamic faith. Likewise, in many strict Muslim countries, Christians are fearful of possessing or reading the Qur'an believing that it will corrupt their own faith, or even endanger their lives, if it is believed they are mishandling it, and therefore dishonouring the Qur'an.

This is a serious dilemma indeed and is therefore very important to be understood.

We would advise all Christians to never disrespect Muslims in your community by telling them that their prophet is from Satan and that the Qur'an is inspired by Satan. We believe that God wants to bring the power of salvation and the love of Jesus to all mankind, Jews, Muslims, Buddhists, Hindus, Communists, Animists and even Christians. Give people the dignity of making their own decisions regarding the origins of their faith and their holy books because their eternal future – heaven or hell – is based on their decisions and not what may be forced on them by someone else. Everyone has the right to choose their own eternal destiny.

The Concept of Revelation in the Bible and the Qur'an is Different

Before we examine some contradictions or claimed errors in the Bible and the Qur'an, we need to understand that these two books have totally different concepts of their origin and revelation.

1. ***The Qur'an is believed to be an eternal, preserved and unchangeable book in the heavens containing all the revelations of God***

Surah Al-Burooj (85):21-22;

"This is a Glorious Qur'an (Inscribed) in a Tablet Preserved!"

The original Qur'an is in heaven but it was sent down directly to Muhammad through the agency of the angel Gabriel. The Qur'an has no human input and is perfectly preserved by God. No mistakes can be found in it. It is believed to have been revealed word for word, in the Arabic language, exactly as it is in the heavens. That's why no word can be changed. The Qur'an also includes a specific challenge for readers to examine its contents for errors or contradictions. They are guaranteed that they will find no errors because it is a perfect and glorious revelation.

Surah An-Nisa 4:8,

"Then do they not reflect upon the Qur'an? If it had been from [any] other than Allah, they would have found within it much contradiction."

We will respond to that challenge and examine whether or not there are any errors or contradictions.

2. The Bible does not claim its revelation came in the same way as the Qur'an, but came as the Holy Spirit moved on different people to write God's message

The Bible came piecemeal over a 1600 year period of time. It came book by book, through some 40 different people from a variety of walks of life. Some were kings, others were prophets, fishermen, shepherds, poets, historians and disciples of Christ.

Biblical revelation is not a Book that comes down from Heaven but the record of Divine interaction and fellowship with man in whom the Eternal Purpose of God is being processed. It's revelation is its MESSAGE!

The Old Testament was written between the 17th and the 5th century BC on the only parchments available at that time, pieces of Papyrus, which decayed rather quickly, and so needed continual copying for over 4000 years. There is a huge amount of ancient manuscripts that prove the accuracy of the transmissions.

There are 5,300 Greek New Testament manuscripts or fragments; 10,000 Latin Vulgate manuscripts and at least 9,300 other early translations. In all we now have more than 24,000 ancient manuscript copies of the Bible. Then in 1947, Muslim Bedouin shepherds found hidden manuscripts at a place called Qumran near the Dead Sea. Every Book of the Hebrew Old Testament was found except for the Book of Esther. What was found was identical to over 99% of the Bible of today. It has not been changed. We still have almost perfect copies of the originals.

Three of the oldest manuscripts of the Bible are:

- **The Codex Vaticanus,** one of the oldest manuscripts of the Greek Bible (Old and New Testament), written in about 350 AD.
- **The Codex Sinaiticus,** a handwritten copy of the Greek Bible written about 330-360 AD.
- **The Codex Alexandrinus,** a fifth-century manuscript of the Greek Bible, containing the majority of the Septuagint and the New Testament.

There is a problem with the Qur'an as there is an absence of any ancient manuscripts in the first two centuries of Islam.

The Dilemma becomes Apparent

Several hundred years after the time of Muhammad, Muslims began to read the Bible and discovered that the Qur'an contradicted the Bible, but the Qur'an said that it confirmed the Bible as the true revelation of God. If the Qur'an confirmed the truth of the Bible but the Bible contradicted the Qur'an, then there is a problem.

To solve this dilemma, Muslims claimed that the book of the Jews, (the Law or the *Torah* (the Old Testament) and the book of the Christians (the Gospel or the *Injil* (the New Testament) have been changed, but this only added to the dilemma.

If the Qur'an confirmed the Bible as the true revelation from God and the Bible rejected large portions of the Qur'an then the Qur'an must be false.

If indeed the Bible has been changed and corrupted as Muslims claim, while the Qur'an affirms the inspiration, authority and preservation of the Bible, and Allah demands that we submit to the Law (Old Testament) and the Gospel (New Testament) then the Qur'an must be false as it requires us to submit to a false revelation.

This remains a major dilemma for Muslims today!

If the Qur'an confirms the Bible and the Bible is true, then the Qur'an must be false because the Qur'an says the Bible is true. They can't both be true.

If the Qur'an confirms the Bible and the Bible has been altered and corrupted, then the Qur'an must be false for confirming a false book.

Are there Errors or Contradictions in the Bible?

Yes, there are errors and contradictions in the Bible. Christians readily admit that there have been 'scribal errors' in the copies of the Old and New Testaments. From the time of Moses until the time of Martin Luther and the invention of the printing press by Johannes Gutenberg around 1440–1450 the printing of books was done by hand, one word at a time. With the Reformation came the acceleration of printing Bibles.

Mistakes were made in translations and in copying ancient texts. Not too many and nothing that changed the doctrines of the Bible. As scholars began reading the Bible and comparing with ancient manuscripts, several hundred errors were found. Most of them were very minor, and none of them changed the message of the Bible. To Christians, the main emphasis on Biblical revelation was the message not the literal words. Idioms in one language did not have the same meaning in another language. Christian leaders established an area of science called "Biblical Criticism". This was not to criticize the Bible, but to critically investigate the accuracy of transmission and translation of the Bible. Christians demanded that we have an as accurate as possible translation of the original texts. Some errors still exist today but they are all minor and have no effect on the message of the Bible. Scholars continue to search to correct even the most minor translation problems that still exist.

A well know Muslim scholar Shabbir Ally wrote that there are *101 Contradictions* that he found in the Bible. All these 101 contradictions were examined, one by one, by a number of Christian scholars including

Jay Smith, Alex Chowdhry, Toby Jepson and James Schaeffer. Most of these contradictions were easily solved due to the ongoing discovery of ancient manuscripts. Some of the contradictions were due to copyist errors. Some were not contradictions but just misunderstandings of the historical context. Some were simple misunderstandings of the Hebrew or Greek usage. Some were due to just a simple misreading of the text or misunderstanding the doctrine that was being taught.

Answers to each of those **101 Contradictions in the Bible** can be viewed at:

www.bible.ca/islam/islam-bible-contradictions-refuted.htm

Not all of the contradictions have answers as there are still some problem texts. The unresolved texts have no impact on the message of the Bible, however scholars continue to research these issues as new and older manuscripts are discovered. None of the unresolved issues have any impact on the message of the Bible.

Let's examine a couple of the translation or interpretational problems found in the Bible.

1. When did the disciples receive the Holy Spirit? Was it on the Day of the Resurrection as in *John 20:22* or on the Day of Pentecost as in *Acts 2:4?*

The two accounts recorded here are not a contradiction. In *John 20:22*, Jesus is bringing the disciples into the new birth, born of the Spirit, like what happened in the Garden of Eden with the creation of Adam. See *Genesis 2:7*. This was the new birth. In the Greek it was an *aorist imperative* which means a one off, instant event. It was not repeatable. People only get born-again once. In *Acts 2:4,* it is talking about the baptism in the Holy Spirit which is to equip people for service.

Passover *(John 20:22)* speaks of the new birth while Pentecost *(Acts 2:4)* speaks of being equipped with God's power for service. The baptism of the

Holy Spirit is a *present imperative* which means it is an ongoing, continual filling with the Holy Spirit, just as the Candlestick had to be filled with oil every morning and evening. *Exodus 27:20-21; Leviticus 24:1-4.*

2. Was Jesus on the cross as in *Mark 15:33,* or in Pilate's court as in *John 19:14,* at the sixth hour on the day of the crucifixion?

This is not a contradiction for in the Jewish calendar days (Sunset to Sunset) were split into two parts – Night – 6.00pm to 6.00am and the Daytime from 6.00am to 6.00pm. On the Jewish Calendar, the 3rd hour is 9.00am and the 6th hour is midday.

On the Roman Calendar, a day went from Midnight to Midnight. The 6th Hour would be 6.00am. From 6.00am it allows time for Pilate to conduct his trial, send Jesus to Agrippa, have Jesus return to Pilate, and then by 9.00am Jesus is on the Cross.

Mark 15:25 – at the 3rd hour on the Jewish Calendar, i.e. 9.00am Jesus was put on the Cross.

Mark 15:33 – from the 6th hour (12.00 noon) till the 9th hour (3.00pm) there was the darkness.

In total Jesus was 6 hours on the Cross and He died at 3.00pm as the Lamb of God, the same time of the evening sacrifice in the Temple when on this Passover Day, the priests were slaying the lamb. No contradiction. Just a glorious truth.

Errors or Contradictions in the Qur'an

In the Qur'an errors or contradictions can be a much more serious issue. Yes, there are contradictions in the Bible and above we have referred to the 101 situations identified by Shabbir Ally, and we have provided access to the answers of those situations. We hope that you will examine those contradictions and the answers to them.

There are three reasons for this:

1. Because it is claimed that every word was sent down exactly according to what God (Allah) has recorded in His Eternal Qur'an in Heaven and it seems as though there are unexplained situations that seem to be errors.
2. Because it is also claimed that there can be no errors because none of His words can ever be changed:
   Al Anaam 6:34, "There is none that can alter the words of Allah."
   Al Anaam 6:115, "None can change His words."
   Yunus 10:64, "No change can there be in the words of Allah."
   Al Khaf 18:2, "None can change His words."
3. Because God (Allah) has challenged us to find any errors or contradictions and that we will not find any:

Surah An-Nisa 4:82,

"Then do they not reflect upon the Qur'an? If it had been from [any] other than Allah, they would have found within it much contradiction."

Therefore, if any of these three areas are proved to be wrong then it challenges the authenticity of the Qur'an and provides strong reasons to reject Islam and the message it is bringing. This becomes a major dilemma for Muslims. We will therefore look at multiple examples where there are serious problems that demand answers. There are many more than what we will discuss, but we have chosen some that you may find interesting to discuss with your Muslim friends.

1. The problems with inheritance

Surah An-Nisa (4):11-12,

"Allah (thus) directs you as regards your Children's (Inheritance): to the male, a portion equal to that of two females: if only daughters, two or more, their share is two-thirds of the inheritance; if only one, her share is a half. For parents, a sixth share of the inheritance to each, if the deceased left children; if no children, and the parents are the (only) heirs, the mother has a third; if the deceased Left brothers (or sisters) the mother has a sixth. (The distribution in all cases ('s) after the payment of legacies and debts. Ye know not whether your parents or your children are nearest to you in benefit. These are settled portions ordained by Allah; and Allah is All-knowing, Al-wise.

In what your wives leave, your share is a half, if they leave no child; but if they leave a child, ye get a fourth; after payment of legacies and debts. In what ye leave, their share is a fourth, if ye leave no child; but if ye leave a child, they get an eighth; after payment of legacies and debts. If the man or woman whose inheritance is in question, has left neither ascendants nor descendants, but has left a brother or a sister, each one of the two gets a sixth; but if more than two, they share in a third; after payment of legacies and debts; so that no loss is caused (to any one). Thus is it ordained by Allah; and Allah is All-knowing, Most Forbearing."

Let's summarize what this passage says:

A man dies leaving behind his two living parents, a wife and two or more daughters. How is the inheritance divided?

- His father gets $1/6^{th}$;
- His mother gets $1/6^{th}$;
- His wife gets $1/8^{th}$;
- The daughters get $2/3^{rds}$ between them

When you add the distribution of the inheritance the total is more than 100%. In fact it adds up to 112.5%. When I questioned Sheik Abdul Hafith, our Islamic teacher at the Sana'a Institute for Arabic Studies about this dilemma, he replied: "You need a degree from the Islamic University to understand this. It is divine mathematics!"

2. How can Mary (Maryam) be the sister of Moses and Aaron and the daughter of Imran since they lived 1500 years apart?

Mary, the mother of Jesus, called Maryam in the Qur'an is confused with Miriam, the sister of Moses and Aaron. It is obvious that the writer of the Qur'an was ignorant of the history of the Israelites in Egypt and had no knowledge of the timeline. Consequently, the writer of the Qur'an thinks that Maryam the sister of Moses and Aaron is the mother of Jesus. Since Mary was a virgin giving birth to Jesus, an event happening nearly 1500 years after the time of Aaron, Moses and Miriam, then this would have been the oldest person ever to live.

In Surah Maryam which describes the events relating to the birth of Jesus, Mary is clearly called the sister of Aaron.

Maryam (19):28,

"O sister of Aaron! Thy father was not a man of evil, nor thy mother a woman unchaste!"

The father of Maryam, Aaron and Moses in the Qur'an was Imran. So the two Marys in the Bible and the Qur'an, although 1500 years apart, are merged to become the same person.

Surah Ali 'Imran 3:35-36,

"Remember when Imran's wife prayed to her Lord saying, "I have made a vow to dedicate to Your service whatever is in my womb. Lord, accept it from me. You are All-hearing and All-knowing". When the baby was born she said, "Lord, it is a female." God knew this. Male and female are not alike. "I have named her Mary. I pray that You will keep her and her offspring safe from Satan, the condemned one."

Surah Al Tahriin 66:12,

"And Mary the daughter of 'Imran, who guarded her chastity; and We breathed into (her body) of Our spirit; and she testified to the truth of the words of her Lord and of His revelations, and was one of the devout (servants)."

3. How can Pharoah and Haman be friends in their plans to destroy the Jews since Haman was a Persian who lived 1000 years later on a different continent?

In the Qur'an, Haman worked for Pharoah.

Surah Al-Qasas 2):38,

"And Pharaoh said: O chiefs! I know not that ye have a god other than me, so kindle for me (a fire), O Haman, to bake the mud; and set up for me a lofty tower in order that I may survey the god of Moses; and lo! I deem him of the liars."

The tower built up to God was built in Babel about 750 years before Moses and was never associated with Pharoah. The Qur'an, several times, has confused historical records and it would seem that history was not a very strong point in the Arabian desert.

Surah Al-Qasas 28:4-6,

"Truly Pharaoh elated himself in the land and broke up its people into sections, depressing a small group among them: their sons he slew, but he kept alive their females: for he was indeed a maker of mischief. And We wished to be Gracious to those who were being depressed in the land, to make them leaders (in Faith) and make them heirs, To establish a firm place for them in the land, and to show Pharaoh, Haman, and their hosts, at their hands, the very things against which they were taking precautions."

Historically, Pharoah was the Ruler of Egypt while Haman was an Advisor under King Ahasueros in Persia about 2500 kilometres to the east of Egypt. Furthermore, this Pharoah and Haman lived over 1000 years apart. It seems clear that the author of the Qur'an did not know the history, geography or timelines of these events.

4. Were there 6 days or 8 days for creation?

In several Surahs of the Qur'an **(Surah Al-Araf 7:54; Yunus 10:3; Hud 11:7 and Al-Furqan 25:59)** it states clearly that God created the heavens and the earth in six days. Compare the following verses.

Surah Fussilat 41:9-12 it says it was 8 days.

"Say: Is it that ye deny Him Who created the earth in **two Days**? And do ye join equals with Him? He is the Lord of (all) the Worlds. He set on the (earth), mountains standing firm, high above it, and bestowed blessings on the earth, and measure therein all things to give them nourishment in due proportion, in **four Days**, in accordance with (the needs of) those who seek (Sustenance). Moreover He comprehended in His design the sky, and it had been (as) smoke: He said to it and to the earth: "Come ye together, willingly or unwillingly." They said: "We do come (together), in willing obedience."So He completed them as seven firmaments in **two Days**, and He assigned to each heaven its duty and command. And We adorned the lower heaven with lights, and (provided it) with guard. Such is the Decree of (Him) the Exalted in Might, Full of Knowledge."

So – 2 Days plus 4 Days plus 2 Days equals 8 Days! But in the other passages it states it took only 6 Days.

Surah Al-Araf (7):54 *(Yusuf Ali Translation),*

"Your Guardian-Lord is Allah, Who created the heavens and the earth in six days, and is firmly established on the throne (of authority)

5. Another problem with the creation of the Heavens and the Earth is which one was created first? It depends on which Surah we read.

In one Surah, the Earth was created first and then the Heavens were created.

Surah Al-Baqarah 2:29,

"He it is Who created for you all that is in the earth. **Then turned He to the heaven, and fashioned it** as seven heavens."

Another Surah reverses the order. God created the Heavens first and then the Earth:

Surah An-Naziat 79:27-30,

"Are ye the harder to create, or is the heaven that He built? He raised the height thereof and ordered it; And He made dark the night thereof, and He brought forth the morn thereof. And **after that He spread the earth."**

6. Does the sun set in a spring of murky water?

The Qur'an informs us of the discoveries of science. One of the most amazing discoveries is where the sun sets each night. According to the Qur'an it sets in a spring of black muddy water.

Surah Al-Kahf 18:86,

"Until, when he reached the setting of the sun, he found it set in a spring of murky water."

If you can't find the end of the rainbow, maybe we should try finding the spring of murky water where the sun sets!

7. A major Medical Problem – Disease and Healing in the wings of flies.

Sahih Al-Bukari reported the following authenticated hadith of the prophet Muhammad. It was narrated by Abu Huraira in ***Volume 4, Book 54, Number 537*** where he records that the Prophet Muhammad said:

"If a house fly falls in the drink of anyone of you, he should dip it in the drink, for one of its wings has a disease and the other has the cure for the disease."

If true, this would be a major breakthrough in controlling many diseases.

8. The Qur'an informs us how far away is God's Throne?

The answer to this question is not simple as there are a variety of answers. It seems that even the Qur'an is unsure as to which answer is true.

In one Surah, it takes 1,000 years to reach His Throne. In another Surah it takes 50,000 years.

Surah As-Sajdah 32:5,

"He rules (all) affairs from the heavens to the earth: in the end will (all affairs) go up to Him, on a Day, the space whereof will be (as) **a thousand years of your reckoning**."

Surah Al-Ma'arij (70):4 *(Yusuf Ali Translation),*

"The angels and the spirit ascend unto him in a Day the measure whereof is **fifty thousand years.**"

9. Did Noah and his family escape the Flood?

In the Biblical record, Noah escaped with his wife, his three sons and their wives.

Genesis 6:17-18,

"I Myself am bringing floodwaters on the earth, to destroy from under heaven all flesh in which is the breath of life; everything that is on the earth shall die. But I will establish My covenant with you; and you shall go into the ark—you, your sons, your wife, and your sons' wives with you."

Genesis 7:7,

"Noah, with his sons, his wife, and his sons' wives, went into the ark because of the waters of the flood."

According to the Qur'an Noah escaped the flood, but one of his sons drowned for refusing to join them on the ark.

Surah Hud 11:42-43,

"So the Ark floated with them on the waves (towering) like mountains, and Noah called out to his son, who had separated himself (from the rest): "O my son! embark with us, and be not with the unbelievers!" The son replied: "I will betake myself to some mountain: it will save me from the water." Noah said: "This day nothing can save, from the command of Allah, any but those on whom He hath mercy! "And the waves came between them, and the son was among those overwhelmed in the Flood."

10. John the Baptist

In the Qur'an, the angel, announcing the birth of John the Baptist (Yahya) to his father, saying that we are giving him a name never given to anyone else before him.

Surah Maryam 19:7,

Allah said, "O Zakariya (Zachariah)! Verily, We give you the glad tidings of a son, His name will be Yahya (John). We have given that name to none before (him)."

However, the Qur'an is mistaken as the name "Yahya" in the Arabic or "Johanan" in the Hebrew form of John was **quite a common name** and was mentioned in the Old Testament. See *2Kings 25:23*.

There are many more examples, but the above accounts demonstrate that there is a severe dilemma in assessing the accuracy of the Qur'an in its historical records, scientific assertions and evaluations of ascertaining the accuracy of divine revelation. There is an excellent article by an ex-Muslim, who shares the dilemma he faced in finding so many discrepancies in the Qur'an. You can read Farooq Ibrahim's powerful testimony online:

answering-islam.org/Authors/Farooq_Ibrahim/discrepancies.htm

There is also an excellent Youtube video on Blunders in the Qur'an by *@testifyapologetics* that you should take time to watch - *www.youtube.com/shorts/0TiFvBDLdrI*

A Major Problem with the Hadith

An excellent resource is *@Relentless Reasoning*. Their research is very challenging and concise. They expose a major problem that dismantles not only the Qur'an, but also the Hadith, without which the Qur'an cannot stand. This is an extremely important dilemma that is vital for Christians to understand. See their information in full on the internet: *medium.com/@relentlessreasoning18/part-12-islams-canon-crisis-5e7bd08fb568*

Quoting from the above source we have an excellent summary:

"But historically, legally, doctrinally, practically —

Islam lives or dies by the Hadith.

"Without hadith:

- There is **no** shahada formula
- **No** five daily prayers
- **No** prayer times
- **No** Rak'ahs
- **No** wudu rules (ritual washings)
- **No** pilgrimage rituals
- **No** zakat percentages
- **No** hijab rules
- **No** hudud punishments
- **No** marriage rules
- **No** divorce laws
- **No** inheritance laws
- **No** Islamic state structure
- **No** explanation of the Qur'ān

- **No** biography of Muhammad
- **No** Sunnah at all
- **No** Islam that can function"

In ***Sahih Muslim 3004***, Muhammad commanded the Muslims: "Do not write anything from me except the Qur'ān." He specifically forbad them from writing the Hadith, but they wrote them anyway."

The conclusion in the research is that the historical errors in the Qur'an and even more so in the Hadith totally destroys the foundations of Islam. The article has a very clear conclusion stating that "Islam has no reliable text. Islam has no recoverable canon. Islam has no verifiable history."

This indeed suggests that this is an insurmountable dilemma!

Be aware of two Islamic Doctrines that can confuse us

1. The Doctrine of Taqiyya

In Islam, truth is not absolute. Lying, deceiving and distorting the truth is the essence of *taqiyya* as long as it is lying for the cause of Allah. Muslims do not consider this to be a lie before Allah. They see it as a strategy.

Sahih Bukhari (49:857),

"He who makes peace between the people by inventing good information or saying good things, is not a liar."

Lying is permitted when the end justifies the means. In fact Allah declares that He is the greatest of deceivers.

Suran Al Imran 3:54 *(Direct English translation and Rashad Translation),*

"They plotted and schemed, but so did Allah and Allah is the best schemer."

"And they deceived and Allah deceived and Allah is the best of deceivers."

wa makaru wa makara allah wa allah khairu ulmakareen

The Arabic word **makar** means **deceive**.

The Bible says that "God is not a man that He should lie", *Numbers 23:13.* God is truth, and Jesus is declared to be "the truth", *John 14:6.* Jesus challenged the Pharisees for their hypocrisy saying to them:

John 8:44,

"You are of your father the devil, and the desires of your father you want to do. He was a murderer from the beginning, and does not stand in the truth, because there is no truth in him. When he speaks a lie, he speaks from his own resources, for he is a liar and the father of it."

Yasser Arafat and Taqiyya

Arafat, the founder of the PLO, referred repeatedly to the use of *taqiyya* by Muhammad when explaining his agreement with the Oslo accords and his negotiations at Camp David with Israeli Prime Minister Ehud Barak. To Islamic audiences Arafat would say that he used *taqiyya* as a negotiation tactic. When the Israelis heard a recording of his statements at an Islamic leaders summit, they broke off all negotiations with Arafat. It should be noted that in 2026, the Iranians have used the same tactic.

2. The Doctrine of Abrogation

Some errors in the Qur'an can be explained with this doctrine. Allah says that Allah sometimes gives a lesser revelation as the people are not yet able to receive the full truth. At a later time when the people are able to receive it, Allah gives a replacement text. With this principle, the old, or less than truthful revelation is replaced with the more truthful or complete revelation.

Surah Al-Baqarah 2:106,

"Whatever a Verse (revelation) does We abrogate or cause to be forgotten, We bring a better one or similar to it. Know you not that Allah is able to do all things?"

(Rashad Translation),

"When we abrogate any miracle, or cause it to be forgotten, we produce a better miracle, or at least an equal one. Do you not recognize the fact that GOD is Omnipotent?"

(Pickthall Translation),

"Nothing of our revelation (even a single verse) do we abrogate or cause be forgotten, but we bring (in place) one better or the like thereof. Knowest thou not that Allah is Able to do all things?"

(Yusuf Ali Translation),

"None of Our revelations do We abrogate or cause to be forgotten, but We substitute something better or similar: Knowest thou not that Allah Hath power over all things?

If you understand this principle which is practiced in many discussions and negotiations with Muslims, especially when making peace treaties, it will help you to understand many contradictions that have occurred in history.

Muhammad and Abrogation

An ancient example of abrogation was when the Prophet Muhammad made a peace treaty, the Treaty of Hudaybiyyah (628 AD) with the Meccans not to attack Mecca for 10 years, but two years later Muhammad returned with his army and took Mecca. He then destroyed all the Meccan idols and Mecca became an Islamic city.

When we understand these principles of *taqiyya* and *abrogation* then it gives another perspective for us to consider when analyzing errors and contradictions in the Qur'an.

Discussion Questions:

1. Discuss three errors in the Qur'an.

2. Discuss three errors in the Bible?
3. Which contradiction in each of the Bible and the Qur'an most affected you?
4. What are the differences between for we receive the Qur'an revelation? Is it any different than how the Bible receives its revelations?

DILEMMA 15

THE LAMB OF GOD DILEMMA

We come across an intriguing dilemma with the appearance of John the Baptist in both the Bible and the Qur'an. In the Qur'an, John the Baptist is called ***Yahya***, a greatly respected prophet.

This is confirmed by the Qur'an. The Prophet Yahya was given special wisdom from his youth:

Surah Maryam 19:12,

> "Ya Yahya, kuthil kitab" wa ataynahul hukma sabiyyan"
> "O John! Hold fast the Scripture." And We
> gave him wisdom while yet a child."

In the Bible, Jesus called John the Baptist the greatest of the prophets.

Luke 7:28,

Jesus said: "I say to you, among those born of women there is not a greater prophet than John the Baptist."

What was this special wisdom that was given to Yahya (John the Baptist)? It is here we will see this dilemma come out into the open. It will reveal what truly is original religion and this is where we will begin.

What is Original Religion?

If we were to engage in a dialogue on questions directly relating to Jesus, Muhammad, the Qur'an, the Bible, the Crucifixion etc., we might end up in a sharp and unhelpful debate. We want to be open and engage our friends and create an interest, and a "I want to know more" atmosphere, and that's what this question is designed to do. So, we go right back to the beginning where there is some agreement between the Bible and the Qur'an. Both books record accounts of the Creation, Adam and Eve, Cain and Abel and Abraham and his sons. So, this is where we will begin.

The Fall: Adam & Eve

The root cause of sin in the world is the satanic self-centeredness planted in the hearts and minds of Adam and Eve and was revealed in the temptation and subsequent fall.

1John 2:16,

"For everything in the world, the lust of the flesh, the lust of the eyes, and the pride of life, comes not from the Father but from the world."

However, in Islam, the three elements that the Bible sees as the root cause of evil, i.e. the lust of the flesh, the lust of the eyes, and the pride of life, are actually seen as desirable attributes for eternal life in the Muslim heaven.

Surah Az-Zukhruf 43:71

"All that the souls may desire and that may delight their eyes will be available therein (in heaven). You will live therein forever."

This reveals the difference in moral standards between the Bible and the Qur'an.

From the beginning, God warned Adam of the consequences of disobedience to the Divine command.

Genesis 2:16-17,

"The LORD God commanded the man, saying, "Of every tree of the garden you may freely eat; but of the tree of the knowledge of good and evil you shall not eat, for in the day that you eat of it you shall surely die."

After Adam and Eve sinned, they tried to cover-up their sin and nakedness by making a covering made from fig leaves. They thought that their efforts would hide their sin, but our best efforts can never save us.

Genesis 3:7,

"Then the eyes of both of them were opened, and they realized they were naked; so they sewed fig leaves together and made coverings for themselves."

We also read a similar account in the Qur'an, where Adam and Eve tried to cover their nakedness by sewing leaves together. Even in the Qur'an, there had to be Divine intervention if they were to be saved. The efforts of Adam and Eve were insufficient to save themselves.

Surah Ta-Ha 20:121,

"They both ate of the tree, and so their nakedness appeared to them: they began to sew together, for their covering, leaves from the Garden: thus did Adam disobey his Lord, and allow himself to be seduced."

Man's best efforts could never save themselves. It would take Divine intervention to save mankind.

When did Adam die?

Genesis 5:5,

"All the days that Adam lived were nine hundred and thirty years; and he died."

So, Adam and Eve did not die in the 24-hour day that they sinned for there was an act of Divine intervention. First God came seeking man and secondly, God made a sacrifice to provide redemptive clothing for them.

God's Response to the Fall of Man

Genesis 3:9-10,

"Then the LORD God called to Adam and said to him, "Where are you?" So he said, "I heard Your voice in the garden, and I was afraid because I was naked; and I hid myself."

Adam's effort to hide their sin and nakedness was insufficient to deal with sin. It took divine intervention. God sacrificed an animal, probably a lamb, to provide a blood-soaked redemptive clothing that saved Adam and Eve from death. This amazing intervention of God demonstrates God's love, planning and eternal purpose for the salvation of mankind who will believe in and accept His act of grace.

This becomes a redemptive example that we can use in witnessing to our Muslim friends, because in both the Bible and the Qur'an, man could not save himself. It took Divine intervention and a blood sacrifice, a substitutionary sacrifice. Sin demands death, so the lamb died to provide Adam and Eve a blood-stained covering to hide their sin and shame and bring them salvation from immediate judgement and death.

Genesis 3:21,

"The LORD God made garments of skin for Adam and his wife and clothed them."

The Qur'an also reveals that it was God who provided the clothing for Adam and Eve. Notice these remarks from *http://al-injil.net/blog/2012/04/24/taurat-Qur'an-to-injil-lesson-1-the-sign-of-adam/*

This article states the Islamic position:

"In both accounts [The Taurat and The Qur'an], the characters are identical (Adam, Eve, Shaytan (Devil), Allah); the place is the same in both accounts (the Garden); in both accounts Shaytan (Devil) lies and tricks

Adam and Eve; in both accounts Adam and Eve put on leaves to hide the shame of their nakedness; in both accounts Allah then comes and speaks to the others and pronounces judgment; in both of the accounts Allah then shows them mercy by providing raiments (i.e. clothing) to cover 'the shame' of their nakedness. The Qur'an prefaces this by saying to the 'Children of Adam' (which would be us!) that this is 'among the signs of Allah'."

"If we study carefully what Allah does (again in both accounts) we see that He does three things:

1. Allah makes them mortal – they will now die.
2. Allah expels them from the Garden. They must now live in a much more difficult place on Earth.
3. Allah gives them clothes of skins.

What is fascinating about these three things is that all of us even to this day still share in them. (1) Everyone dies. (2) No one – prophet or otherwise – has ever returned to the Garden; and (3) everyone continues to wear clothes. These three things are so 'normal' for everyone that we almost miss noticing this fact that what Allah did to Adam and Eve is still being felt by us to this very day, thousands of years later. It is as if the consequences of what happened that day are still affecting us today in these ways at least.

Another thing to note here is that the raiment (clothes) from Allah was a Mercy from Him. Yes, He judged them, but he also provided mercy. Allah did not have to give this to them. And Adam and Eve did not earn the raiments through righteous behaviour that earned 'merit' against their disobedient act (in fact their behaviour throughout in both Taurat and Qur'an is far from righteous).

Adam and Eve could only receive Allah's provision without meriting or deserving it. But someone did pay for it. The Taurat more specifically tells us that the raiment from Allah were 'skins'. Thus, they came from an animal. Up until this point there was no death, but now some animal (perhaps a sheep or goat, in any case an animal whose skin was suitable for making a covering of clothes) did pay – with its life. An animal died so that Adam and Eve could receive Mercy from Allah.

The Qur'an then tells us further that this raiment did cover their shame, but the raiment that they really needed was 'righteousness', and that in some way the raiment that they did have (the skins) is a sign of this righteousness, and this is a sign for us. I quote this in detail so you can follow what I am observing from the passage.

Surah Al-Araaf 7:26,

"O you Children of Adam! We have bestowed raiment upon you to cover your shame, as well as to be an adornment to you. But the raiment of righteousness – that is the best. Such are among the signs of Allah, that they may receive admonition,"

Perhaps a good question for us to keep in mind from this is: how do we get this 'raiment of righteousness'?"

Surah Al-Araaf 7:26,

"We have sent down to you garments to conceal your shame, and for adornment, but the garment of righteousness is best. This is of the Signs of Allah, that they may take heed."

Therefore, in the Jewish, Christian and Islamic world, there is this view that the "clothing" God gave, was an animal. It was a sacrifice and it was the Mercy of God. In the Qur'an, Allah says that Jesus was given to be the Mercy of God. Therefore, the act of God providing clothing for Adam and Eve, in place of the clothing they made for themselves, as a redemptive act of God giving His Mercy. It was therefore prophetic of the coming Messiah (Almasih) who indeed is the Mercy of God, the only sinless prophet and the only one able to save mankind from their sin.

According to the Qur'an, when the Archangel Gabriel came to Mary and informed her that she would give birth to the Messiah, Mary was shocked and replied:

Maryam 19:20-21,

"How shall I have a son, seeing that no man has touched me, and I am not unchaste?" He said: "So (it will be): Thy Lord saith, 'that is easy for Me: and (We wish) to appoint him (Jesus) as a Sign unto men and a Mercy from Us': It is a matter (so) decreed."

This internet discussion shows that even in Islamic circles there is a recognition by some, that a redemptive sacrifice was necessary. The example of Adam and Eve clearly shows us this.

Because of the sacrifice of the Lamb, Adam and Eve did not die yet were still put out of the Garden of Eden. Even when sin is forgiven, there are sometimes physical consequences. The experience of Adam and Eve also reveals a theme that runs through the whole of the Bible, that there are two alternate ways to try and get saved, become acceptable to God and to gain access to heaven.

What are the Two Ways we can try to reach God?

1. **The first way is by our own good works** - Adam and Eve made their own clothing from fig leaves and tried to be acceptable to God, but this was rejected by God. Throughout the Bible, even our very best efforts are unacceptable to God. We can never save ourselves.

Isaiah 64:6,

"All of us have become like one who is unclean, and all our righteous acts are like filthy rags."

2. **The second way is by accepting God's redemptive sacrifice.** God slew an animal to clothe Adam and Eve with the animal skins to cover their shame. This was indeed the Mercy of God, and prophetic of the Messiah who was given to mankind as the mercy of God. He alone would be the "animal" sacrifice that would save

believing mankind from sin as prophesied by the prophet Yahya (John the Baptist).

John 1:29,

"John saw Jesus coming toward him and said, "Look, the Lamb of God, who takes away the sin of the world!"

A. The Sacrifices of Cain and Abel – Genesis 4 and Surah Al-Ma'idah 5:27-31) – One Lamb for God

Adam and Eve initially had two sons, Cain and Abel called *Qabil* and *Habil* in the Qur'an. Later Adam and Eve had many sons and daughters *(Genesis 5:5).* Intermarriage was permitted at that time as it was necessary for the continuation of the human race. At this stage they did not have damaged DNA and their offspring were healthy. This answers the question of where Cain got his wife, He married his sister. Sibling marriage was later forbidden in the Law of Moses, *(Leviticus 18:9).*

As Cain and Abel matured they were required to bring a sacrifice to the Lord. In their upbringing they heard, probably many times, the account on how Adam and Eve had failed to save themselves, yet were saved from death and the judgement of God through the act of Divine Mercy when God slew animals, probably lambs, to provide blood-soaked skins to cover their nakedness.

The response to this testimony from Adam and Eve was very different in the two boys. It is possibly reflected in the two different professions that the boys chose as they grew up.

Genesis 4:2-3,

"Abel was a keeper of sheep, but Cain was a tiller of the ground."

What's the distinction between these two choices and what are the clues?

(i) Abel's Sacrifice

Firstly, Abel's response to his parents' testimony was to acknowledge that he too was a sinner and needed the mercy of God just like his parents. He remembered that their best efforts were not good enough to save them. They needed the intervention of God. The clue we have is found in ***Hebrews 11:4,***

"**By faith Abel** brought God a better offering than Cain did. **By faith he** was commended as righteous, when God spoke well of his offerings. And **by faith Abel** still speaks, even though he is dead."

The clue is that Abel responded by faith and faith is not an accident. Faith comes from listening and acting according to God's Word. Abel chose to be a keeper of the sheep. It would seem to be a strange choice given that mankind were still forbidden from eating meat. They were vegetarians until the time of Noah's flood, *(Genesis 9:3-4).* Also, there would be no clothing industry for just four people! Was he looking after the sheep with the eye of faith that one day, he too, would have to offer a lamb to God on behalf of his own sin?

Romans 10:17,

"Faith comes by hearing, and hearing by the word of God."

Abel heard the word of God in the testimony of his parents and responded by faith, offering a blood-soaked lamb as the sacrifice for his sin and his offering was pleasing to God. To us Abel's offering looked cruel and ugly. Why kill an innocent lamb? Was this a prophetic act by Abel. From the testimony of his parents and his faith response, perhaps there was also prophetic illumination.

Genesis 4:4-5,

"Abel also brought of the firstling of his flock and of their fat. And the LORD respected Abel and his offering, but He did not respect Cain and his offering. And Cain was very angry."

(ii) Cain's Sacrifice

Cain's attitude and response to the call to bring a sacrifice was very different to that presented by Abel. Cain had heard the same testimony from his parents that had so impacted Abel, but what impacted Cain, it seems, was very different. Possibly he thought that his parents hadn't tried hard enough. Fancy just using fig leaves! Cain was going to prove that we could be acceptable to God by our own good works. He was going to prepare the best fruit of the ground. It would consist of herbs, spices, vegetables, flowers, and fruit. It would be the most beautiful, colourful and wonderfully aromatic sacrifice ever produced. God would surely be pleased by his great efforts.

However, Cain overlooked one important point about the testimony of his parents. The ground had been cursed, as it says in ***Genesis 3:17,***

"Cursed is the ground for your sake."

Cain's offering was rejected by God. His best efforts, like his parents, had fallen short, and the sin in his nature manifested itself.

Genesis 4:8-12,

"Cain rose up against Abel his brother and killed him. Then the LORD said to Cain, "Where is Abel your brother?" He said, "I do not know. Am I my brother's keeper?" And He said, "What have you done? The voice of your brother's blood cries out to Me from the ground. So now you are cursed from the earth, which has opened its mouth to receive your brother's blood from your hand. When you till the ground, it shall no longer yield its strength to you."

Not only did Cain kill his brother, he also became a liar. The curse also came on him. Note the characteristics identified with the nature of Satan.

John 8:44,

"You are of your father the devil, and the desires of your father you want to do. He was **a murderer** from the beginning, and does not stand in the truth, because there is no truth in him. When he speaks a lie, he speaks from his own resources, for he is **a liar** and the father of it."

The two characteristics in Cain as a murderer and a liar reflected the one controlling his nature. This is the fruit of rejecting faith and God's mercy in the slain lamb and trying to rely on one's own good works. This is the way of Cain. Who today seems to be walking in the way of Cain?

Jude 1:10-13,

"But these speak evil of whatever they do not know; and whatever they know naturally, like brute beasts, in these things they corrupt themselves. Woe to them! For they have gone in **the way of Cain,** have run greedily in the error of Balaam for profit, and perished in the rebellion of Korah. These are spots in your love feasts, while they feast with you without fear, serving only themselves. They are clouds without water, carried about by the winds; late autumn trees without fruit, twice dead, pulled up by the roots; raging waves of the sea, foaming up their own shame; wandering stars for whom is reserved the blackness of darkness forever."

The consequences of walking in the fleshly lusts of this world bring eternal damnation. Trying to please God with our own good works seems honourable but the heart of man is desperately wicked and will eventually rise up and destroy us. The Bible is very clear about the fruit of the flesh.

Galatians 5:19-21,

"Now the works of the flesh are evident, which are: adultery, fornication, uncleanness, lewdness, idolatry, sorcery, hatred, contentions, jealousies, outbursts of wrath, selfish ambitions, dissensions, heresies, envy, murders, drunkenness, revelries, and the like; of which I tell you beforehand, just as I also told you in time past, that **those who practice such things will not inherit the kingdom of God**."

The only path to salvation is through repentance from sin and faith in Jesus Christ. This will transform your life and bring you the fruit of the

Holy Spirit: love, joy, peace, longsuffering, kindness, goodness, faithfulness, gentleness, and self-control, *(Galatians 5:22-23).*

It should be noted that the account of Cain and Abel in the Qur'an is very different from the Bible. In the Qur'an, Cain and Abel both had twin sisters. Cain's sister was said to be beautiful and Abel's sister was ugly. Allah and Adam made an agreement that there would be a competition to determine which son would marry which daughter. When Cain lost the competition he was given the ugly twin of Abel and Abel was given the beautiful twin of Cain. This is why Cain killed Abel and exploded in anger because he wouldn't get the pretty girl, *Surah Al-Maidah (5):27-32.*

An Islamic commentary on this event, recorded in *Qur'an.com/5:27/tafsirs/en-tafsir-maarif-ul-Qur'an*:

"What happened was that the girl born with the first boy, Qabil, was beautiful while the girl born with the second boy, Habil, was ugly. When came the time of marriage, the ugly girl born with Habil fell to the lot of Qabil according to rules. This enraged Qabil. He turned hostile to Habil and started resisting that the girl born with him should be the one given in marriage to him. Sayyidna Adam, in view of the legal rule of procedure, did not accept the demand. However, to remove the division between Habil and Qabil, he proposed that they should both offer their respective sacrifice for Allah. Whoever. has his sacrifice accepted will be the one to have that girl. The reason is that Sayyidna Adam was certain that the sacrifice to be accepted will be the sacrifice of the one who has the right to marry her, that is, the sacrifice of Habil. ...

Now, the situation was that Habil was the owner of a flock of sheep and goats. He offered the sacrifice of a good spring lamb. Qabil was a farmer. He offered some grains as his sacrifice. As customary with them, a fire did come from the sky and ate up the sacrifice offered by Habil - and the sacrifice offered by Qabil remained lying where it was, untouched.

Thereupon, hit by failure and disgrace, Qabil was further enraged. Unable to restrain it, he told his brother openly: "I will kill you".

B. Abraham's sacrifice *(Islamic Feast of Eidl Adha)* – Genesis 22 and Surah Asy-Syafaat (37) – One Lamb for one person

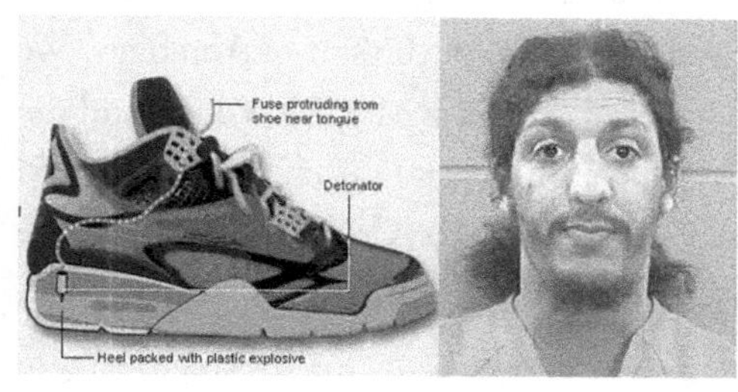

In Sana'a, the capital of Yemen, where we studied Arabic and Islam in an Institute run by Al-Qaeda. The goal of this Institute, *Sanaa Institute for Arabic Language (SIAL)*, was to win foreigners to Islam and where possible, train them to become martyrs for Islam. One graduate was Richard Colvin Reid known as "Richard the shoe bomber". He tried to blow up American Airlines Flight 63 in 2001.

Another was Farouk Abdul Muttalab, the underwear bomber. He tried to blow up a plane over Chicago in 2012. He had explosives built into his underpants in Sana'a, Yemen then flew to Amsterdam. There he changed planes on to Northwest Airlines Flight 253 to Detroit, Michigan. When he went to explode the bomb, the explosives had become so damp that it failed to fully explode and just ignited a fire in his underpants.

We were in the Institute at the same time as Abdul Muttalab. Both of those terrorists failed and both are in prison in the USA.

One day in class, a few days before *Eid Al Adha* (The Feast of the Sacrifice), our teacher said to us: "We Muslims believe that Abraham was offering his son, Ishmael. You Christians say it was Isaac. We do not believe that. What do you say?"

We were familiar with the tricks played by our teachers who almost daily would ask us to acknowledge that Muhammad was the final prophet. We answered and said, "You are right. It was not Isaac that was sacrificed, but it is also true that it was not Ishmael that was sacrificed." He interrupted asking, "Why do you say that?" We continued. "It was neither Ishmael nor Isaac that was sacrificed. It was the lamb caught by its horns in the thicket. The lamb was the substitute, who died instead of the son of Abraham. We see that this is an amazing prophecy of the coming Messiah who would die for each of us as the Saviour of the world! This exactly what was prophesied by the great prophet Yahya in the Gospel, *John 1:29.*"

This answer shocked him and he didn't pursue the subject any further. He had never heard this before.

Let's return to the Biblical account which identifies Isaac as the son who was going to be offered on Mount Moriah. Incidentally, the chapter in the Qur'an that talks about this event does not mention Ishmael at all. It is all about Isaac. When it says that Abraham offered his son, without mentioning his name, Muslims say, "O, that is Ishmael".

Surah As-Saaffat 37:100-107,

"O my Lord! Grant me a righteous (son)!" So We gave him the good news of a boy ready to suffer and forbear. Then, when (the son) reached (the age of) (serious) work with him, he said: "O my son! I see in vision that I offer thee in sacrifice: Now see what is thy view!" (The son) said: "O my father! Do as thou art commanded: thou will find me, if Allah so wills, one practising patience and constancy!" So when they had both submitted their wills (to Allah), and he had laid him prostrate on his forehead (for sacrifice), We (Allah) called out to him "O Abraham! "Thou hast already fulfilled the vision!" - thus indeed do We reward those who do right. "Thou hast already fulfilled the vision!" - thus indeed do We reward those who do right. For this was obviously a trial - **And We ransomed him with a momentous sacrifice.**"

We will discuss this last phrase in more detail shortly. The rest of this Surah talks about Isaac and not Ishmael. The Bible account also clearly said that the son being offered is Isaac.

Genesis 22:2,

"Take your son, your only son, Isaac, whom you love, and go to the region of Moriah. Sacrifice him there."

On the way up the mountain, Isaac recognized that something was missing. They had everything needed for the sacrifice except for the lamb to be sacrificed. They had the wood and the knives so Isaac asked his father:

Genesis 22:7-8,

"Isaac spoke to Abraham, his father and said, "Where is the lamb for a burnt offering?" And Abraham said, "My son, God will provide for Himself the lamb."

What an interesting answer. We could play with these words.

"My son God" – Jesus is the prophesied Son of God.

"will provide himself a lamb" (KJV) – is it prophesying that God Himself would become the lamb and offer Himself?

That's playing with words, but there is still a message there that the lamb to be slain would be provided by God Himself.

This is Jehovah Jireh, the LORD providing the substitute lamb. Yes, for God the Father so loved the world that He gave His only begotten Son to be the sacrificial Lamb of God that would be our Redeemer, our Substitute.

As Abraham was about to slay his only begotten son, God intervened. There are only two "only-begotten" sons in the Bible – Isaac and Jesus.

God said to Abraham:

Genesis 22:12-13,

"Do not lay your hand on the lad, … Abraham lifted his eyes … and there … was a ram caught in a thicket by its horns. So Abraham … offered it up for a burnt offering instead of his son."

Eidl Adha: The Feast of the Sacrifice

This event of the offering of Abraham's son became the most important Feast in Islam. It's more important than Ramadan, the month of fasting, although Ramadan is way more well known. **Eidl Adha** is the occasion when Abraham would offer his son to God by slaying him on Mount Moriah. This is the mountain today known as the **Temple Mount** in Jerusalem where today we find the Islamic shrine called, the **Dome of the Rock**.

Abraham and his son – Was it Isaac or Ishmael?

Even though most Muslims believe it was Ishmael that was offered by Abraham, a well known Indonesian liberal Muslim scholar, **Ulil Abshar Abdalla** *(http://www.kabarbangsa.com/2015/10/ulil-abshar-abdalla-yang-dikurbankan.html),* categorically states that it was Isaac. He gives three reasons:

1. The Qur'an does not name Ishmael as the son that was offered so it is more logical to accept that the "official" son of Abraham's "official" wife would be the object of Abraham's test than the son of a slave woman.
2. The original account is taken from the Torah (Old Testament), *Genesis 22,* and names the son to be sacrificed as being Isaac and not Ishmael.
3. Many famous early Islamic scholars including two of the rightly guided Caliph's stated that it was Isaac that was offered i.e. Umar and Ali. He also mentions Al-Abbas (Muhammad's uncle), Ibn Masud, Ka'b al-Ahbar. And from the disciples of Muhammad's companions called the *tabiin*: Qatadah, Said ibn Jubair, Masruq, Ikrimah, al-Zuhri, Al-Suddi, and Muqatil.

In the Qur'an – Isaac is the chosen son not Ishmael *(Surah Hud (11):69-73; Surah As-Syafaat (37):99-113; Surah Ath-Thariyat 51:24-30)* nevertheless, most Islamic scholars state that the son offered was Ishmael. The most important part of the story is not the name of the son being offered, but the test to Abraham's faith, and that Abraham's son was redeemed by the blood of the sacrificial lamb/ram.

Surah Hud 11:69-73,

"Our messengers came unto Abraham with good news. ... And his wife, standing by laughed when We gave her good tidings [of the birth] of Isaac, and, after Isaac, of Jacob. She said: Oh woe is me! Shall I bear a child when I am an old woman, and this my husband is an old man? Lo! this is a strange thing!"

The most amazing aspect of the Islamic Feast of Eidl Adha is the remembrance of the substitionary sacrifice that saved the life of Abraham's son. This is what was prophesied by God's intervention in saving Adam and Eve through the sacrifice that provided their covering. Now the son of Abraham is saved by a substitutionary sacrifice, and this continues the prophetic message that the Messiah will be that Lamb that saves us. We cannot save ourselves. It takes the gift of the Mercy of God i.e. Jesus, the Lamb of God.

Isaiah 53:7,

"He (the Messiah) was led as a lamb to the slaughter."

John 1:29,

"Behold (the Messiah)! The Lamb of God who takes away the sin of the world!"

The Qur'an declares that this sacrifice offered by Abraham, provided by God, was a substitutionary sacrifice for his son. Earlier we referred to the substitutionary redemption that occurred on Mount Moriah. Let's examine further what it declares.

Surah Asy-Syafaat 37:107,

"We ransomed him with a tremendous victim."

Surah As-Safaat 37:107,

"wa-fa-dayna-hu bi-thib-hin ʿa-thiim"

In Arabic, the word *ʿathiim* = "great, Supreme, exalted" and is one of the 99 names of God. Look at how this word is translated by three other Islamic scholars and interpreters:

Khan: And We ransomed him with ***a great sacrifice***
Pickthal: Then We ransomed him with ***a tremendous victim.***
Sherali: And WE ransomed him with ***a mighty sacrifice***

What is the Meaning of the Name *Al-Atheem:*

The adjective used to describe this sacrifice is "ʿal-atheem". Islamic scholars speak of this term in such a way that it can only be God Himself. It is in fact one of the 99 Names of God that are revealed in Islam. In Google Search you will find that this word is: "In English: The Great One, The Supreme. This name of Allah represents that Allah is The Magnificent. There can be none who is Greater than Allah. None can ever be more or as Powerful as Allah."

An internet article from an Islamic site explains how exalted this name is. It can only apply to God. This Lamb that was sacrificed is none other than ALMIGHTY GOD.

http://understandQur'an.com/and-the-answer-is-%E2%80%AAal-atheem%E2%80%AC.html "The One Who is greatest, mightiest, grandest and above all. He has absolute greatness in both His attributes and self, all His actions are Perfect. He is the one deserving the attributes of exaltment, glory and purity from all imperfection. His Might and Grandeur is surely beyond our grasp!"

How to live by this Name?

"Realize that Al-Atheem is greater than any problem you have, so turn to Him only for a solution at all times! Contemplate His Greatness when you feel you are about to sin. Make it a habit to think about the meaning when you … realize His magnificence each time you pronounced it, in and outside *salah* [the 5 compulsory prayers]!"

Who is Al-Atheem?

Surah Asy-Syura 42:4,

"To Him belongs whatever is in the heavens and whatever is in the earth, and He is the Most-High, the Magnificent (Al-Atheem)."

How can they not accept that Jesus, the Messiah, is the true Al-Atheem, the Almighty God and Saviour of the World?

C. The Passover Lamb – One Lamb for a Family

The Passover account and the deliverance of Israel from Egypt is the most significant event in Moses' confrontation with Pharoah. However, the Qur'an fails to mention the Passover account at all. Why does the Qur'an avoid the Passover message? It acknowledges Moses and the deliverance from Egypt but not how it occurred. We need to understand the Passover is a central component and invaluable link in the story of the Lamb bringing deliverance and salvation. We have seen this with Adam and Eve, Cain and Abel as well as the story of Abraham and his son.

NEW BEGINNING – NEW BIRTH

This event is so important that God changed the calendar. The month called Abib or Nisan, was the 7th month in Israel's ***agricultural calendar***, but God changed it to become the 1st month of their spiritual calendar. It was a new beginning, prophesying a new birth!

Exodus 12:2,

"This month shall be your **beginning** of months; it shall be **the first month** of the year to you."

Passover was a new beginning for Israel just as it is for every individual who comes to know Jesus as their Lord and Saviour. That's why we need to be born again. Our physical birth gives us a natural family on Earth but when we are born again we are born into God's eternal family and He becomes our Heavenly Father.

NEW BIRTH

2Corinthians 5:17,

"Therefore, if anyone is in Christ, he is **a new creation**; the old has gone, the new has come!"

Why was the Lamb kept for 4 DAYS before being sacrificed?

The Passover Lamb had to be kept for 4 days. These 4 days were prophetic of the 4 days, or 4000 years, from the Fall of Adam and Eve until Jesus was crucified on the Cross. Jesus is *the* Passover Lamb as the Apostle Paul declared.

1Corinthians 5:7-8,

"For even Christ our passover is sacrificed for us: Therefore, let us keep the feast."

The four prophetic days are 4000 years in God's calendar.

2Peter 3:8,

"Beloved, do not forget this one thing, that with the Lord one day is as a thousand years, and a thousand years as one day."

The Lamb had to be kept for FOUR DAYS before being slain, as declared by the Lord to Moses.

Exodus 12:3-6,

"Tell the whole community of Israel that on tenth of this month each man is to take a lamb for his family, one for each household ... Take care of them until the fourteenth day of the month, when all the people of the community of Israel must slaughter them at twilight."

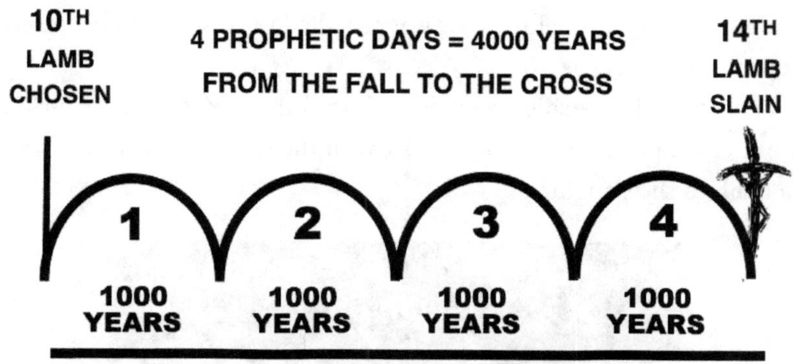

D. One Lamb for the Nation

Leviticus 16:15,

"He shall then slaughter the goat (or sheep) for the sin offering for the people."

Isaiah 52:13-14,

"Behold, My Servant (Messiah) shall deal prudently; He shall be exalted and extolled and be very high. Just as many were astonished at you, So His visage was marred more than any man, And His form more than the sons of men."

The Lamb is a MAN = The Messiah

Isaiah 53:7-8,

"He was led as a lamb to the slaughter. ... For the transgressions of My people He was stricken."

In the incredible prophecy of the Messiah from *Isaiah 52:13-15* through *Isaiah 53*, it is clear that the Messiah is a human being, a man who will suffer for the sins of Israel, God's chosen nation. He will face a brutal punishment. He will be killed, yet He will rise again from the dead. This was prophesied 800 years before Jesus was crucified yet it was fulfilled perfectly in every detail.

There were 14 specific statements: 7 from the view of man (v.1-6); and 7 from God's perspective (v.8-12). Between the two 7's it says: "He was led as a lamb to the slaughter."

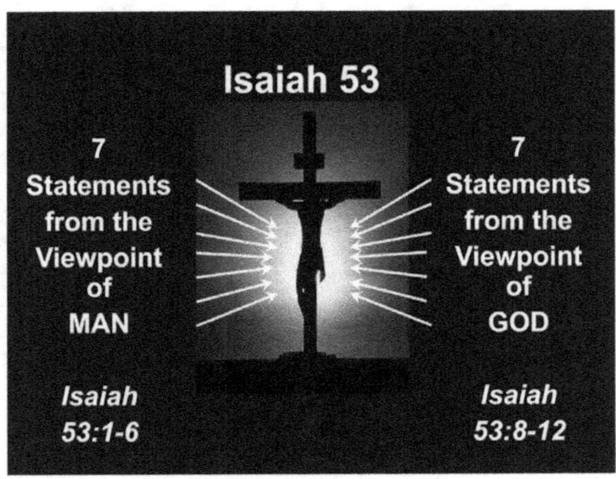

The testimony of the Prophet Yahya (John the Baptist)

Jesus the Messiaah (Isa Almasih in the Qur'an) declared that John the Baptist, the Prophet Yahya, to be the greatest prophet.

Luke 7:28,

Jesus said: "I say to you, among those born of women there is not a greater prophet than John the Baptist."

This is confirmed by the Qur'an. The Prophet Yahya was given special wisdom from his youth:

Surah Maryam (19):12

يَا يَحْيَى خُذِ الْكِتَابَ بِقُوَّةٍ وَآتَيْنَاهُ الْحُكْمَ صَبِيًّا

"O John! Hold fast the Scripture." And We gave him wisdom while yet a child."

What is the wisdom of the Prophet Yahya (John the Baptist)?

5 Amazing Revelations:

1. Yahya had the wisdom to continue to read, believe and understand the Old Testament Scriptures, the Law, the Psalms and the Prophets, *Surah Maryam (19):12.*
2. Yahya had the wisdom to identify the coming of Jesus the Messiah as the coming of the Straight Path and in doing so confirmed the Prophet Isaiah as one of the prophets whose message we must believe,

John 1:23,

"John (Yahya) replied in the words of Isaiah the prophet, "I am the voice of one calling in the wilderness, 'Make straight the way for the LORD.'"

3. Yahya had the wisdom to know that the Messiah was more than a man for the Messiah is eternal and only God is Eternal. So Yahya had the wisdom to know that the Messiah is God who would become a man and be known as the Son of God.

   John 1:15,

   "John (Yahya) testified concerning him. He cried out, saying, "This is the one I spoke about when I said, 'He who comes after me has surpassed me because he was before me.'"

   John 1:32-34,

   "John (Yahya) bore witness, saying, "I saw the Spirit descending from heaven like a dove, and He remained upon Him. I did not know Him, but He who sent me to baptize with water said to me, 'Upon whom you see the Spirit descending, and remaining on Him, this is He who baptizes with the Holy Spirit.' And I have seen and testified that this is the Son of God."

4. Yahya had the wisdom to understand the prophetic message of the coming Messiah, i.e. that the Messiah would be a man who would suffer greatly, bearing the sins and diseases of all mankind, and that He would bear the wrath and judgement of God against sin. The Messiah would be God's Lamb bringing salvation to mankind. As a result the Messiah would die and then rise from the dead and prolong His days,

Isaiah 53:6-11,

"The LORD has laid on him (the Messiah) the iniquity of us all. He (the Messiah) was oppressed and afflicted, yet he (the Messiah) did not open his mouth; he (the Messiah) was led like a lamb to the slaughter ... He (the Messiah) was cut off from the land of the living; for the transgression of My people he (the Messiah) was punished. He (the Messiah) was assigned a grave with the wicked, and with the rich in his death, though he (the Messiah) had done no violence, nor was any deceit in his mouth. Yet it was the LORD's will to crush him (the Messiah) and cause him (the Messiah) to suffer, and though the LORD makes his (the Messiah's) life an offering for sin, he (the Messiah) will see his offspring and prolong his days, and the will of the LORD will prosper in his hand. After he (the Messiah) has suffered, he will see the light of life and be satisfied; by his knowledge my righteous servant will justify many, and he (the Messiah) will bear their iniquities."

Isaiah revealed that it was God who would sacrifice Jesus, the Messiah, as the sacrificial Lamb, for the salvation of all mankind who would believe in Him.

5. Yahya had the wisdom to be able to identify who the Messiah was. It was Jesus and that Jesus would be God's Lamb taking away the sin of the world,

John 1:29,

"John (Yahya) saw Jesus coming toward him, and said, "Behold! The Lamb of God who takes away the sin of the world!"

Indeed, the Prophet Yahya (John the Baptist) was a mighty prophet of God with amazing revelation and wisdom. This is why many followed him and were baptized by him. Even though he pointed his disciples towards

Jesus, the Messiah, some continued to follow Yahya. After his death his followers became known by the name ***Sabians***. When Paul came to Ephesus, he met such a group, and had to further establish the foundations of their faith *(Acts 19:1-7)*.

The Sabians, the disciples of John the Baptist (the Prophet Yahya), have continued throughout the history of the Middle East. They are mentioned three times in the Qur'an *(Al Baqarah (2):62; Al-Maidah (5):69; Al-Hajj (22):17)* as belonging to the "people of the Book" along with Jews and Christians. Even today, mainly in Turkey, Syria and Iraq and in some migrant communities in Western countries, there are still remnants of the Sabians, some of whom are now identified as Mandeans.

In the Original Religion, God revealed the original way to salvation

1. **Adam and Eve** – man saved by divine intervention and the provision of the blood-soaked skins of a lamb and not by their own efforts
2. **Cain and Abel** – faith not works pleases God. Cain tried really hard, but was not accepted. Abel offered a substitutionary lamb by faith and was accepted by God.
3. **Abraham and his son** – God intervened to provide a glorious *(atheem)* substitute sacrifice, a lamb/ram caught by its horns in the thicket.
4. **John the Baptist (Yahya)** – given the wisdom to reveal many truths about salvation and the identity of the Messiah, revealed thye Messiah as the Lamb of God who redeems mankind from sin and Satan, bringing forgiveness and salvation from sin.

God revealed that salvation is dependent upon Divine intervention. We saw that with Adam and Eve. We saw it the intervention to spare Isaac. We have seen that man's efforts can never save himself. We can only be saved by a substitute sacrifice, the Lamb of God, the Messiah. The theme from Genesis to Revelation continues to grow and we discover that for all of history there is only one Saviour, the Lamb of God, Jesus.

E. One Lamb for History

The Apostle Peter summarizes all that has gone before and then adds one new exciting truth.

1Peter 1:18-20,

"Knowing that you were not redeemed with corruptible things, like silver or gold, from your aimless conduct received by tradition from your fathers, **but with the precious blood of Christ, as of a lamb** without blemish and without spot. He indeed was foreordained before the foundation of the world, but was manifest in these last times for you."

Redemption does not come from corruptible things like wealth, our conduct or our traditions.

Redemption only comes through a perfect sacrifice, a lamb without spot or blemish.

Redemption was planned, foreordained from eternity because knew we would sin and would need a Saviour.

That's why Jesus came. Before there was sin, God had prepared the medicine, the shed blood of Christ on the Cross.

Redemption was fully manifest after 4000 years of human history. In the whole of history, there is only ONE SAVIOUR. There is only ONE WAY, ONE STRAIGHT PATH, and that is Jesus.

Jesus is the one Lamb for all history! The miraculous prophetic revelation of the Lamb continues to grow.

He is the ONE LAMB provided by God to save Adam and Eve – *Genesis 3*

He is the ONE LAMB offered by Abel to please God – *Genesis 4*

He is the ONE LAMB to die as the substitute for Isaac – *Genesis 22*

He is the ONE LAMB to die for the nation of Israel – *Leviticus 1-6 and Isaiah 53*

He is the ONE LAMB to die for the whole world – *John 1*

He is the ONE LAMB to die for whosoever believes – the Ethiopian – *Acts 8*

He is the ONE LAMB for all history – *1 Peter 1*

And now we find that for the whole Universe there is just ONE LAMB – *Revelation 5*

F. One Lamb for the Universe

Revelation 5:6,

"I saw a Lamb, looking as if it had been slain, standing in the center of the throne, encircled by the four living creatures and the elders. He had seven horns and seven eyes, which are the seven spirits of God sent out into all the earth."

This Lamb is sitting in the throne of the Universe and His description shows that He is none other than the Lord God Almighty who is Omnipotent, Omniscient and Omnipresent.

Look at the awesome characteristics this Jesus possesses. He has:

7 Horns = The Lamb is OMNIPOTENT – All Powerful!
7 Eyes = The Lamb is OMNISCIENT – All Knowing!
7 Spirits = The Lamb is OMNIPRESENT – Ever Present Everywhere!

This Jesus who was born in Bethlehem, fled to Egypt, raised in Nazareth, baptized in the River Jordan, baptized in the Holy Spirit, proclaimed the coming Kingdom of God, offered Himself as the one true sacrifice on the Cross to save us from sin, **is now seated in the Throne of the Universe.** And He invites us saying, "Come unto Me."

Hallelujah! What a Saviour!

Now He wants to take this revelation one step further and bring us into eternity. In Eternity, in the New Jerusalem, we find that the Lamb is mentioned SEVEN TIMES. He is the King of kings and the Lord of lords. If you want to escape hell and live with God in His glorious and joyful eternity, then you had better quickly accept Jesus as your Lord and Saviour since He is the Straight Path. He is the Mercy of God. He is the only way and as the Lamb of God, He sits in the Throne of Eternity. Run to Him now while there is still time and opportunity!

G. One Lamb for Eternity: New Jerusalem - 7x - Revelation 21-22

1. 21:9 – The Lamb is the Eternal Bridegroom
2. 21:14 – The Lamb is the Eternal Foundation with His 12 Apostles
3. 21:22 – The Lamb is the Eternal Temple
4. 21:23 – The Lamb is the Light and Glory of Eternity
5. 21:27 – The Lamb has the Eternal Book of Life
6. 22:2 – The Lamb is the Source of Eternal nourishment
7. 22:3 – The Lamb is the Eternal King

Review God's Lamb from Genesis to Revelation

1. Genesis 3 - Adam and Eve - 1 Lamb provided by God
2. Genesis 4 - Cain and Abel - 1 Lamb for God
3. Genesis 22 - Abraham - 1 Lamb for 1 person
4. Exodus 12 - Passover - 1 Lamb for 1 family
5. Leviticus 1-5;16 - Sacrifices - 1 Lamb for 1 nation

6. Isaiah 53 - Prophetic Lamb - 1 Lamb for all the elect
7. John 1:29 - Lamb Identified - 1 Lamb for the whole world
8. Acts 8 - Lamb for Gentiles - 1 Lamb for whosever will believe
9. 1Peter 1 - Historical Lamb - 1 Lamb for all history
10. Revelation 5 - Lamb's Throne - 1 Lamb for the entire universe
11. Revelation 12:11 - Lamb's Triumph - 1 Lamb for total victory
12. Revelation 21-22 - Eternal Lamb - 1 Lamb for all eternity

Give careful consideration to the origins and central message of what is "Original Religion" and how you can use this to share the Gospel with your friends. This can be a powerful message in sharing with our Muslim friends as to how there is no way we can save ourselves and that original religion shows us, both in the Qur'an and in the Bible, that in original religion, it takes God's intervention and gift of His Mercy to save us from sin, hell and eternal judgement.

Questions to discuss:

1. What do you think motivated Abel to become a shepherd?
2. Why was Cain so angry that he killed his brother?
3. What motivated Cain to lie to God?
4. What do you understand from the theme of the Lamb of God?
5. How does the understanding of the *al-ʿatheem* impact you?

DILEMMA 16

ESCAPING HELL DILEMMA

As a 16-year-old teenager I faced a personal dilemma. I wasn't sure if there was a God, an afterlife or heaven. However, I had an overwhelming fear of spending eternity in the fires of hell. I once lit a match and put my finger above the flame to see how long I could stand it. I don't think I lasted one second. The pain was unbearable. I snatched my hand away. That made me even more convinced that I didn't want to go to hell, if hell existed. I was not religious but there was something inside my mind that tormented me about the torturous agony of hell and never being able to escape. I now believe that it was the Holy Spirit planting in my spirit and mind a consciousness of eternity and that I was standing on the wrong side of eternity. It was the gentle, loving touch of God who had begun to woo me to Himself. If there really was a hell, I certainly didn't want to go there, not even for one second.

I didn't believe in Jesus, but I heard things from the Religious Education teacher at my school at Boronia High School. I saw some Christian comics with stories about Jesus, but I didn't believe they were true. I knew that evil resided in my life. I knew from my thoughts and actions. I was a liar, a thief, ran a gambling ring at school. I tried to derail a train, threw rocks from the top of a quarry down on to what is now called Burwood Highway in Ferntree Gully.

There was a struggle in my life as I didn't like the things I was doing. I made a New Year's Eve resolution to change but even on the first day I couldn't keep my resolution. By January 3 I had forgotten all about the resolution. I couldn't keep it. The good thing about that was that it was laying a foundation of belief that I could never change myself or save myself. It was setting me up for when I would hear the Gospel of Jesus Christ.

My dilemma was that I wanted to escape hell but I had no idea how I could do that.

The Fear of Hell and Judgement

In the Bible and the Qur'an it speaks of a Day of Judgement. Some of what is taught in the Bible can also be found in the Qur'an while the details are quite different. It is clear from any comparison that the Bible is the original source of revelation, and that is acknowledged in the Qur'an. Some of those concepts have been adapted and adopted into the teachings of Islam.

Muslims believe in hell-fire torture!

Ahmadiyya Muslims, who are generally regarded as a false cult by Sunni and Shi'a Muslims, believe that hell is a form of purgatory from which all will escape after suffering the purging fires of purification and will eventually be allowed into paradise. It may take 1000 years or 100,000 years but eventually everyone will make it. This is not accepted in Sunni nor Shi'a Islam who believe that the fires of hell are eternal.

What the Sunni and Shi'a believe is the concept of Muslim believers going through a temporary period of purification in hell-fire, called *Barzakh*, an unseen realm of temporary suffering, like the Catholic purgatory, between this worldly life and the hereafter. It's a barrier that prevents returning to this life. It's an intermediate stage before gaining admittance to eternity, either in heaven or hell.

The Maulana Qur'anic commentary (1951) is a classic example of Ahmadiyya Muslim teaching in their attempt to be accepted by orthodox Islam. However, orthodox Islam believes in the everlasting nature of hell-fire suffering. We mention both of these views as you will come across both concepts in your discussions with Muslims. The Islamic concept of hell can be found in the following references:

Surah An-Nisaa 4:55-56,

"Sufficient for them as punishment is the blazing fire of Hell. Those who reject our Signs, We shall soon cast into the Fire: as often as their skins are roasted through, We shall change them for fresh skins, that they may taste the penalty."

Did you catch that? God will throw us into the fires of hell until our skin is burned off and then God will restore our skin to be fresh again so that we can then go through the fires again and again and have our skin burned off – repeatedly!

Surah Adh-Dhukan 44:45-49,

"Like molten brass; it will boil in their insides. Like the boiling of scalding water. A voice will cry: "Seize him and drag him into the midst of the Blazing Fire! Then pour over his head the Penalty of Boiling Water, "Taste this!"

The torture and agony of hell is continually repeated and the agents of that torture seem to be delighting in causing people to experience this continuous, eternal, agony.

Imam Ghazzali, a famous Islamic scholar in *Ihya Uloom Ed-Din (p.1.64; p.1.124; p.2.59),*

"There will be terrible punishment in hell for a hypocrite learned man. His bowels will gush forth and he will roam with his bowels as a donkey moves around a mill-stone. Muhammad said: If a man explains the Qur'an according to his opinion, let him seek his abode in hell."

Purgatory – Islamic and Catholic

Purgatory according to Catholic Church doctrine, is an intermediate state after physical death in which those destined for heaven "undergo purification, so as to achieve the holiness necessary to enter the joy of heaven." Some Muslims also believe hell is a temporary place of punishment for some, eternal for others.

However, sinning Muslim believers who end up in hell will stay temporarily but eventually will be removed, if Allah permits them to enter Paradise. But there are no guarantees!

Barzakh, the place or state, where one's soul is kept after death and before the Day of Judgement.

Surah Ar-Rahman 55:19-20,

"He has let free the two bodies of flowing water, meeting together: between them is a barrier *(barzakh)* which they do not transgress."

Surah Al-Furqaan 25:53,

"It is He Who has let free the two bodies of flowing water: One palatable and sweet, and the other salt and bitter; yet has He made a barrier between them, a partition that is forbidden to be passed."

In between the islands of Borneo (Kalimantan) and Sulawesi, as well as between Bali and Lombok, there is a natural sea barrier called the Wallace Line. It divides Asia from Melanesia. Most of the marine life do not cross this line including the sea creatures and the vegetation due to the deep currents. In the spiritual realm the *Barzakh* is similar to that. It's a barrier between human life and the eternal destiny in the afterlife.

Surah Al-Mu'minuun 23:99-100,

"Until, when death comes to one of them, he says: "O my Lord! send me back (to life), in order that I may work righteousness in the things (The unrighteous will ask for another chance. But it will be too late then. The time for repentance will then have passed.) "By no means! It is but a word he says." (Their request will mean nothing. It will be treated as an empty word of excuse. They had plenty of chances in this life. Not only did they reject them, but they did not even believe in Allah or ask for His assistance.) Before them is a Partition (*Barzakh:* a partition, a bar or barrier; the place or state in which people will be after death and before judgement. Behind them is the barrier of death, and in front of them is the *barzakh* partition, till the Day they are raised up."

The concept could be similar to the two parts of Hades that was described by Jesus and possibly even the source of the Islamic doctrine of the *Barzakh.*

The Story about Lazarus and the Rich man

In ***Luke 16:22-26,*** Jesus described the deaths of two men and how in Hades (the realm of the dead) there is an uncrossable gulf between the place of believers (bosom of Abraham) and the place of unbelievers (the fires of torment). This was the state of Hades before Christ died and rose from the dead.

"So it was that the beggar died, and was carried by the angels to Abraham's bosom. The rich man also died and was buried. And being in torments in Hades, he lifted up his eyes and saw Abraham afar off, and Lazarus in his bosom. "Then he cried and said, 'Father Abraham, have mercy on me, and send Lazarus that he may dip the tip of his finger in water and cool my tongue; for I am tormented in this flame.' But Abraham said, 'Son, remember that in your lifetime you received your good things, and likewise Lazarus evil things; but now he is comforted and you are tormented. And besides all this, between us and you there is a great gulf fixed, so that those who want to pass from here to you cannot, nor can those from there pass to us."

On one side, it was called *the Bosom of Abraham.* This is where those believing in the teachings of the Bible resided after death waiting the Day of Judgement. On the other side was unbelievable pain and suffering of unbelievers in what we would call the fires of hell. Those there too are waiting the Day of Judgement. This is similar to the Islamic *barzakh*.

Amazing Events at the Death, Resurrection and Ascension of Jesus

When Jesus died on the Cross there was a great earthquake and many graves in Jerusalem were opened.

Matthew 27:50-52,

"Jesus cried out again with a loud voice, and yielded up His spirit. Then, behold, the veil of the temple was torn in two from top to bottom; and the earth quaked, and the rocks were split, and the graves were opened; and many bodies of the saints who had fallen asleep were raised; and coming out of the graves after His resurrection."

When Jesus died, He went into Hades. What happened?

1. *He disarmed Satan and took back from him the Keys of Death and Hell*

   Colossians 2:14-15,

   Jesus "wiped out the handwriting of requirements that was against us, which was contrary to us. And He has taken it out of the way, having nailed it to the cross. Having disarmed principalities and powers, He made a public spectacle of them, triumphing over them in it."

2. *He rose from the dead, raising the dead from those opened graves and appeared for the next 40 days*

Matthew 27:53,

"coming out of the graves after His resurrection, they went into the holy city and appeared to many."

Matthew 28:18,

After His resurrection Jesus said, "All authority has been given to Me in heaven and on earth."

Satan had been disarmed. Jesus now has the Keys of Death and Hell. All power is now in Christ's hands. Jesus spent the next 40 days with His disciples then came the Day of His Ascension to the Father in heaven.

Ephesians 4:8,

(NIV) "When he ascended on high, he took many captives."

(NKJV) "When he ascended on high, He led captivity captive."

When Jesus ascended He emptied the area of Hades called "the Bosom of Abraham" and took them with Him to heaven. No longer do the believing dead wait in Hades.

2Corinthians 5:8,

"We are confident, yes, well pleased rather to be absent from the body and to be present with the Lord."

In Islam is it more difficult for Women to be saved than for Men?

It seems that not many Muslim women will get to heaven. Maybe that's why Allah creates so many *houris*, created beings to be the sex slaves of Muslim men in Paradise. Women, it seems, will only get to Paradise if they are exceptionally devoted to Allah, die as martyrs or fully please their husbands.

"Abdullah Ibn 'Amr narrated: O women! Give alms and ask pardon [from Allah] frequently, as I have seen that the majority of the dwellers of hell were you (i.e. women)." One of them asked, 'Why, Messenger of Allah, are we the majority of the dwellers of hell? He replied, 'You curse frequently and are ungrateful to your husbands. I have not seen anyone more deficient in intelligence and religion than you."

Al-Bukhari, Hadith 6, Zakat 44; Muslim, Iman 132, 'Iydain 4.19; Ibn Maja, Fitan 19; al-Darimi, Wudhu' 104, Salat 224; Ahmad Ibn Hanbal, 1:307, 423, 425, 436; 3:318.

Sahih Bukhari 2:18:161,

"Narrated 'Abdullah bin Abbas: … The Prophet replied, "I saw Paradise and stretched my hands towards a bunch (of its fruits) and had I taken it, you would have eaten from it as long as the world remains. I also saw the Hell-fire and I had never seen such a horrible sight. I saw that most of the inhabitants were women."

Hadith Kanz al-'ummal, 22:10-11,

"Muhammad said: "Out of 99 women, one is in paradise and the rest are in hell. A believing woman is the same among women as a white-footed raven among the ravens. Fire has been created for the senseless and women are the most senseless of all."

How do women get to Paradise?

The Qur'an acknowledges that women can get into heaven though nothing is really said about what they can get.

Surah Ali 'Imran (3):195,

"And their Lord hath accepted of them, and answered them: "Never will I suffer to be lost the work of any of you, be he male or female: Ye are members, one of another: Those who have left their homes, or been driven out therefrom, or suffered harm in My Cause, or fought or been slain, - verily, I will blot out from them their iniquities, and admit them into Gardens with rivers flowing beneath; a reward from the presence of Allah, and from His presence is the best of rewards."

According to many Islamic scholars, women can only get to Paradise if their husbands want them. That men can take their wives is also clear though there doesn't seem to be anything about women being able to enter Paradise without their husbands. These wives then become like the *houris* and get restored to being virgins after every time they have sex with their husbands.

Surah Az-Zukhruf 43:70,

To the men it is said: "Enter the garden, you and your wives; you shall be made happy."

In an essay on ***"The Muslim Woman and her Husband"*** *(http://www.islamicbulletin.org/free_downloads/women/the_muslim_woman_and_her_husband.pdf)* we are told on page 6 that "the Muslim woman does not forget that her obedience to her husband is one of the things that may lead her to Paradise."

This is what Muhammad said in the Hadith reported by Ahmad and al-Tabarani.

Majma' al-Zawa'id, 4/306, Bab haqq al-zawj 'ala'l-mar'ah,

"If a woman prays her five daily prayers, fasts the month (of Ramadan), obeys her husband and guards her chastity, then it will be said to her: 'Enter Paradise by whichever of its gates you wish.'"

In another Hadith Umm Salamah said that wives pleasing their husbands may enter Paradise.

Ibn Majah, 1/595, Kitab al-nikah, bab haqq al-zawj 'ala'l-mar'ah; al-Hakim, 4/173,

"The Messenger of Allah said: 'Any woman who dies, and her husband is pleased with her, will enter Paradise.'"

What is a Woman's Capacity to love a Man or for a Man to love Women?

This relates to the question of polygamy both here on earth and in Paradise. According to Mufti Dr. Abdur-Rahman ibn Yusuf, a British Islamic scholar, God created women with the capacity to only love one man, but men were created with the capacity to love many women. So, in Paradise, Allah's gift to women, is their one husband.

See - *https://www.google.com.au/search?q=Mufti+Abdur-Rahman+ibn+Yusuf+&ie=utf-8&oe=utf-8&gws_rd=cr&ei=vnqhVoToJ4yl0ATEjqLQDQ*

Men are allowed to have up to four wives at the one time, although Muhammad was allowed to have an unlimited number of wives. However, in Paradise, the men will have many *houris*, apart from their wives, to satisfy their sexual needs. The *houris*, and the wives that make it to Paradise, will be renewed as virgins after every time having sex *(Hadith: Silsilat al-Sahihah: 3351)*. However, the wives will not know that their husbands are having sex every day with the *houris* as Allah will hide it from them.

Surah An-Nisa 4:3,

"If ye fear that ye shall not be able to deal justly with the orphans, Marry women of your choice, two or three or four; but if ye fear that ye shall not be able to deal justly (with them), then only one, or (a captive) that your right hands possess (i.e. your slave girls), that will be more suitable, to prevent you from doing injustice."

When the balance of the Qur'an and the Hadith are assessed on the various statements made concerning women. They are at least promised to be happy and accepting of their fate. Maybe not now, but at least after they have reached Paradise.

In Sana'a, Yemen, in our class with Sheik Abdul Hafith, he told me (Jeff) of the benefits of Paradise and all the *houris* I could have. He told me that I could have sex 100 times a day before coming home to my wife. Annette became agitated and said, "I don't like the idea of my husband having sex with 100 houris every-day before coming home to me." Abdul Hafith replied, "That's okey, you won't know. Allah will wipe it from your memory so that you will think you are the only one." Annette was getting angry and I began holding her arm but she still said, "Your God is a deceiver!" I calmed her down, then Adul Hafith gave Annette a pamphlet explaining all this. On the way home Annette was fuming and looking at the pamphlet she said, "This just makes it worse." I wonder how many Muslim women feel the same way and that they are being humiliated and degraded by such a teaching?

For Christian women, talking with Muslim women, this could be an opportunity to explore the possibility of sharing the Gospel?

How can we introduce the Gospel to a Muslim by discussing the concepts of the Day of Judgement, Hell and Eternal Damnation?

One way of approaching our Muslim friends is to ask about the Islamic greeting. Here's a helpful way to begin a conversation. To be able to do this, you would need to have some understanding of a few Arabic sentences and the grammar otherwise it would not be effective.

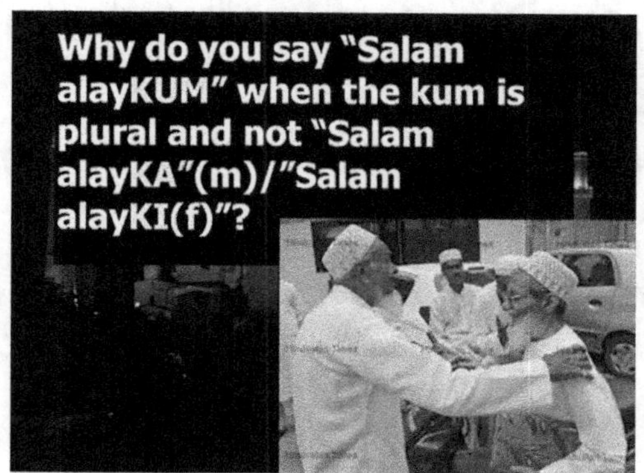

A good way to introduce a discussion could be to use the topic of the angels, the books of our good and evil deeds, and the Day of Judgement with a Muslim friend. You could begin by asking the question,

"Why do you say "Salam alay**KUM**" when the **kum** is plural and not "Salam alay**KA** (masculine) **or** Salam alay**KI** (feminine)"?

The Arabic ending **KA** is singular masculine while **KI** is singular feminine but they always say alay**KUM** because they are also greeting the angels on each of your shoulders.

Don't ask all the questions at once, but use them to develop a conversation. Remember you are an inquirer asking them to help you understand. Don't attack and don't be like an interrogator, but rather as a fellow journeyman seeking the truth.

Your next questions could be about the two angels – Atid and Raqib

What are the angels doing on your shoulders? What will be done with the books of our good and evil deeds? Which book is heaviest in your life? If things don't work out so well, do you have a back-up plan? If we can't do enough good works to save ourselves, is there a way out? How much do you think God cares about this problem and do you think He loves us enough to do something about it? What would you like God to do? Would you like to know how Jesus overcomes that problem? etc.

How do people get judged and how can they escape this terrible damnation?

Learn about the two special angels – Atid and Raqib. They are called the two respected angelic scribes or in Arabic the *Kiraman Katibin.*

Surah Al-Araf 7:8-9,

"And the weighing on that day (Day of Resurrection) will be the true (weighing). So as for those whose scale (of good deeds) will be heavy, they will be the successful (by entering Paradise). And as for those whose scale will be light, they are those who will lose their own selves (by entering Hell) because they denied and rejected Our signs (proofs, evidences, verses, revelations, etc.)."

Surah Al-Anbiya 21:94,

"So whoever does righteous good deeds while he is a believer, his efforts will not be rejected. Verily! We record it in his Book of deeds."

It's a Matter of Personal Responsibility!

Surah Al-Isra 17:13-14,

"Every man's fate We have fastened on his own neck: On the Day of Judgment We shall bring out for him a scroll, which he will see spread open. (It will be said to him:) "Read thine (own) record: Sufficient is thy soul this day to make out an account against thee."

You have to read out all your own sins – how embarrassing!

Surah Al-Haaqa 69:25,

"And he that will be given his Record in his left hand, will say: "Ah! Would that my Record had not been given to me!"

How Many of our Deeds are Recorded? Absolutely every detail!!!!

Surah Qaf 50:17-18,

"Behold, two (guardian angels) appointed to learn (his doings) learn (and noted them), one sitting on the right (ATID) and one on the left (RAQIB). He utters not a word but there is by him a guardian angel ready to record it."

Surah Yunus 10:21,

"When we bestow mercy upon the people, after adversity had afflicted them, they immediately scheme against our revelations! Say, "GOD's scheming is far more effective. For our messengers are recording everything you scheme."

Surah Az-Zukhruf 43:80,

"Do they think that We hear not their secrets and their private counsels? Indeed (We do), and Our messengers (recording angels) are by them, to record."

Surah Al-Infitar 82:10-12,

"But verily over you (are appointed angels) to protect you, kind and honourable, writing down (your deeds). They know all that you do."

Surah Al-Jathiya 45:28-29,

"You will see all the people kneeling down. Everyone will be summoned to the Book (containing the record of their deeds). They will be told, "On this day you will be recompensed for what you have done. This is Our Book. It will tell you the truth. We have made a copy of all that you have done."

Scales of Justice

The two recording angels, Atid and Raqib, will bring their books to place on the Scales of Justice.

Surah Al-Anbiya 21:47,

"We shall set up scales of justice for the Day of Judgment, so that not a soul will be dealt with unjustly in the least, and if there be (no more than) the weight of a mustard seed, We will bring it (to account): and *enough are We to take account.*"

Surah Al-A'raaf 7:8-9,

"And the judging on that day will be just; so as for those whose good deeds are heavy, they are the successful. And as for those whose good deeds are light, those are they who ruined their souls because they disbelieved in Our messages."

Surah Al-Kahf 18:49,

"And the Book is placed, and thou seest the guilty fearful of that which is therein, and they say: What kind of a Book is this that leaveth not a small thing nor a great thing but hath counted it! And they find all that they did confronting them, and thy Lord wrongeth no-one."

JANAH (Paradise) or JAHANAM (Hell)

One Angel (Atid) sits on your right shoulder and records all your good deeds, good thoughts, and good words, while another Angel (Raqib) sits on your left shoulder and records all your bad deeds, bad thoughts and bad words. On the Day of Judgment, the results are read out before God who then decides if you are going to JANAH (Paradise) or JAHANAM (Hell).

Surah Al-Mu'minuun 23:103-104,

"And those whose scales are light (of good deeds), they are those who lose their own selves. In Hell will they abide. The Fire will burn their faces, and therein they will grin in agony, with displaced (disfigured) lips."

Will you be light in the scales?

The Recording Angels are commanded to cast the disbelievers into hell fire.

Surah Qaaf 50:23-27,

"His companion (Qarin – twin genie) will say: "Here is (the Record) ready with me!" [Allah said:] "Both of you (recording angels) throw into

Hell, every stubborn disbeliever. [Allah said to the Qarin:] "Hinderer of good, transgressor, doubter, who set up another god with Allah? [Allah says to the recording angels:] "Now (both of you) cast him in the severe torment."

This is a fearful scenario!

What's the answer to being light in the scales?

After all the sin we have committed, is there any way that we can gain salvation? Yes there is! The writings that are against us in the book of evil deeds needs to be wiped clean! How?

The Concept of the "Books" comes from the Bible! Revelation 20:11-12.

The Book of Life mentioned in *Revelation 20:11-12* is not mentioned in the Qur'an. That's where our name needs to be written. We can agree that the book recording our evil deeds is far heavier than the book recording our righteous deeds for even our most righteous deeds are as "filthy rags" before God, *Isaiah 64:6; Romans 3:10-23.* No-one can save themselves, but God in His great love, took away our sins in the Divine Exchange on the Cross!

The Cross sets us free: *Colossians 2:13-14,*

"And you, being dead in your trespasses and the uncircumcision of your flesh, He has made alive together with Him, having forgiven you all trespasses, having wiped out the handwriting of requirements that was against us, which was contrary to us. And He has taken it out of the way, having nailed it to the cross."

Compare *John 3:16-18; 3:36; 5:24.* Salvation is by faith and God's grace and mercy. It is not by works. Accepting Jesus as our Lord and Saviour is the ONLY WAY to overcome the problem of sin and the scales of justice coming down to condemn us.

The concept of the measuring scales originates in the Bible!

Proverbs 16:11,

"Honest weights and scales are the LORD's; All the weights in the bag are His work."

Read the story of Belshazzar in *Daniel 5:1-30,* "TEKEL: You have been weighed in the balances, and found wanting ... That very night Belshazzar ... was slain."

The concept of God recording in the Books also comes from the Bible!

Read these verses: *Luke 10:20; Philippians 4:3; Revelation 3:5; 13:8; 20:11-15.*

The Cross of Christ liberates us by eliminating the writing that was against us! Confessing our sin and receiving Christ as our Saviour cleanses us from ALL sin and judgement. *Romans 10:9-10; Matthew 10:32-33; Luke 12:8-9; 1John 1:7-9.*

I was talking with a young man named Muhammad in Yemen who told me that the Book with all his bad deeds was heavier than the Book with his good deeds, so I asked him what was he going to do about it?

Muhammad said, "When I am old I will go to Mecca on the hajj (the pilgrimage) and that will wipe away many of my sins. Then I will be a faithful Muslim, pray the five times a day, pay the zakat and be a good Muslim."

But what if you die before going to Mecca?

Muhammad replied, "Then I'll be in trouble."

So I asked, "Do you have a Plan B?

What do you mean Plan B? Muhammad asked.

I then mentioned that in the Qur'an all Muslims are commanded to believe in the Bible, the Law, the Prophets, and the Gospel as in ***Surah Al Baqarah 2:136.*** It also tells us in ***Colossians 2:13-14,*** that Jesus "has made alive together with Him, having forgiven you all trespasses, **having wiped out the handwriting of requirements that was against us,** which was contrary to us. And He has taken it out of the way, having nailed it to the cross."

I told him that by believing in Jesus, all the writings in the Book of our bad deeds are 100% wiped out. If all the bad things in the Book that is against us are heavier than the Book of our good deeds, when we accept and believe in Jesus, He wipes all those bad deeds away, because He has "wiped out the handwriting of requirements that was against us."

Anyway, I said, think about it and if one day you're really worried that you might end up in the fires of hell, think about Plan B. Anyway, let's get together again tomorrow for coffee and we'll talk about it some more.

Muhammad replied, "No, not tomorrow, right now. Pray for me, I want to accept Jesus."

This was a real WOW! Moment. The Holy Spirit had opened his heart and he saw it. He wanted forgiveness. He wanted the mercy of God. He wanted Jesus.

It doesn't always happen like this. We need to allow the Holy Spirit to do His work. Don't push it. Don't rush. Let the Holy Spirit go to work in his heart and in his mind while you continue to pray for him. This is very effective.

Ask them to think about which Book is the heaviest one in their life and what steps they are taking that will guarantee their salvation? Then pray for them!

The Book with all the evil thoughts and deeds is truly the heaviest in everyone's life. No-one is able to save themselves. *Isaiah 59:2; 64:6; Romans 3:20-23; 6:23.*

God's Amazing Grace! God, in His love, has seen our total inability to earn our salvation so He sent us a Saviour! *John 1:29.* That's why we need Jesus. He wipes away all the evil deeds of sin and writes our name in the Book of Life. All others go into eternal damnation.

Will going on the Hajj Pilgrimage save me?

There is a common misconception among many Muslims that going to Mecca on the Hajj is a cure all guarantee of salvation and forgiveness for all their sins. It is not. Note the following comments, quoted below, from an Islamic commentary on gaining forgiveness through the Hajj on *www.utrujj.org/does-hajj-or-umrah-clear-all-your-sins/*

"Major Sins vs. Minor Sins"

"Scholars have clarified that these hadiths generally refer to minor sins. Major sins (known as kabāʾir) are not automatically forgiven by Hajj or ʿUmrah unless true repentance (tawbah) is made.

Imam Nawawi (may Allah be pleased with him) explains:

"The scholars said that what is meant is that minor sins are expiated by acts such as Hajj, Umrah, prayer, and fasting. As for major sins, they require specific repentance."

Conditions of true repentance

For a major sin to be forgiven, sincere repentance must meet three conditions:

1. Stop committing the sin immediately.
2. Feel regret for having committed it.
3. Firmly resolve never to return to it.

And if the sin involved violating the rights of another person, a fourth condition is added:

4. Rectify the harm, either by returning what was taken, seeking forgiveness, or compensating them.

Allah says:

"And turn to Allah in repentance, all of you, O believers, that you might succeed." (Surat An-Nur 24:31)

Sins between you and Allah vs. Sins between you and people

It's also critical to distinguish between:

- Sins between you and Allah – e.g. missed prayers (ṣalāh), not fasting, etc.
- Sins between you and others – e.g. backbiting, theft, injustice in business.

Hajj or ʿUmrah does not automatically forgive:

- *Missed prayers*: These are debts to Allah, and should be made up as qaḍāʾ (missed prayers).

The Prophet said:

"The first thing a person will be asked about on the Day of Judgement is his prayer." (Nasai'i)

Rights of others

Allah will not forgive sins involving another human until that person forgives or the wrong is corrected.

The Prophet said:

"Whoever has wronged his brother with regard to his honour or anything else, let him seek his pardon before the Day comes when there will be no dinar or dirham." (Bukhari)"

In other words, going on the Hajj pilgrimage does not automatically wipe away sins.

The Day of Judgement

The Bible describes vividly the Day of Judgement in the Book of Revelation.

Revelation 20:11-15,

"Then I saw a great white throne and Him who sat on it, from whose face the earth and the heaven fled away. And there was found no place for them. And I saw the dead, small and great, standing before God, and books were opened. And another book was opened, which is the Book of Life. And the dead were judged according to their works, by the things which were written in the books. The sea gave up the dead who were in it, and Death and Hades delivered up the dead who were in them. And they were judged, each one according to his works. Then Death and Hades were cast into the lake of fire. This is the second death. And anyone not found written in the Book of Life was cast into the lake of fire."

The Bible tells us there two days and two types of Resurrection. They are 1000 years apart:

The first resurrection is for all who believe in and follow Jesus.

The second resurrection is for everyone else. It is for all who have rejected Jesus Christ as the Son of God and only Saviour of the world.

Two Resurrections – 1000 years apart!

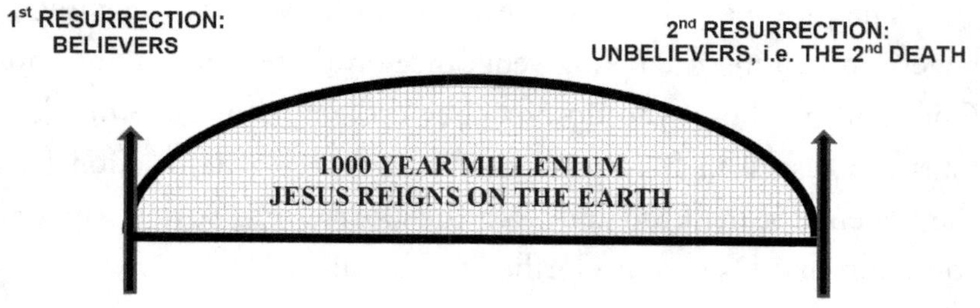

Do not reject God's offer of Salvation!

All who reject God's offer of salvation are cast into the Lake of Fire but those who accept Him will live in His glory: ***Matthew 13:40-43; Jude 1:14-15.***

Know & Understand! All the ungodly will be destroyed at the 2nd Coming of Jesus. Only believers will be spared in the end-time final judgement. ***Matthew 24:37.***

In the days of Noah, in the whole world, only 8 believed and all those were saved in the Ark of Salvation. Likewise, when Jesus returns, only the believers who have been changed ***(1Corinthians 15:50-53)*** will be able to survive the fire of the glory of God, "for our God is a consuming fire," ***Hebrews 12:29.***

Jesus will return in flaming fire.

It will be impossible for non-believers to survive:

2Thessalonians 1:7-10,

"When the Lord Jesus is revealed from heaven with His mighty angels, in flaming fire taking vengeance on those who do not know God, and on those who do not obey the gospel of our Lord Jesus Christ. These shall be punished with everlasting destruction from the presence of the Lord and from the glory of His power, when He comes, in that Day, to be glorified in His saints."

When Jesus returns at the end of the Great Tribulation:

1. The Antichrist and the False Prophet will be immediately cast into the eternal Lake of Fire. *Revelation 19:20.*
2. Satan will be bound in the bottomless pit for 1000 years. After the 1000 Year Millennial reign of Christ, Satan will face his final

judgement and he too will be cast into the Lake of Fire, *Revelation 20:2-3.*

Only by believing and accepting Christ's sacrifice now can we escape on the Day of Judgement. He invites us all to come to Him while there is still opportunity, *Matthew 11:28-30.*

The Last Two Islamic Tests of Making it to Heaven – Crossing the Bridges!

In Islam, when the final moment of judgement arrives, it is said that we still have two tests we have to pass if we are to enter Islam's eternal Paradise.

First is crossing the thread to Paradise called the Sirat Bridge

The **Sirat Bridge** is a fine thread over Hell (*Jahannam*) that all souls must cross on the Day of Judgment to reach Paradise (*Jannah*). It is described in the Hadith as being:

- Finer than a hair and sharper than a sword.
- A slippery path with clamps and hooks that will catch people based on their deeds.
- Suspended over the fire of Hell.

In Wikipedia you will find it provides the following description:

"On Judgement Day, after the dead have been resurrected, assembled, and judged by God, the saved and the damned now being clearly distinguished, the souls will traverse over hellfire via the bridge of *As-Sirāt*. The faithful will "move easily and swiftly **across a broad path**", led first of all by Muhammad and other leading lights of the community on their way to *Jannah*; those judged guilty of sin but still considered to be *mu'minun* (lit. 'believers') will fall from the bridge into *jahannam* (lit. 'hellfire') but remain there only for a limited period of purgation; unbelievers, however, will find the bridge has become "sharper than a sword and thinner than a hair" and darkness blinds their way. Their inevitable fall from the bridge will be an "inescapable descent" into their fiery destination of everlasting punishment."

The Second Stage to reaching Heaven *(Jannah)* is the Qantarah Bridge

The Qantarah Bridge is described as "a special bridge in Islamic eschatology where believers who have successfully crossed the Sirat Bridge will stop to settle mutual disputes, injustices, and grudges from their earthly lives. It acts as a final purification process to ensure believers enter Paradise *(Jannah)* with purified hearts. It is situated after the *Sirat Bridge* over Hell and before the entrance to Paradise.

Only those destined for *Jannah* reach this stage. Once purified on the Qantarah Bridge, they are admitted into Paradise. While all people (including hypocrites and sinners) attempt the Sirat Bridge, only the righteous pass it to reach the Qantarah Bridge."

The Bible gives us Two Choices – the Narrow Way or the Broad Way?

Matthew 7:13-14,

"Enter by the narrow gate; for wide is the gate and broad is the way that leads to destruction, and there are many who go in by it. Because narrow is the gate and difficult is the way which leads to life, and there are few who find it."

Jesus taught us that to accept Him and to walk in the narrow way is difficult. It means taking up the cross and walking in the footsteps of Jesus. Many will oppose us, but the end of the journey is everlasting life.

The broad way is the easy choice. It may seem popular, but the end of that path is eternal destruction.

Be wise in the choice you make.

Some Questions for Discussion:

1. Which path are you on in your journey to eternity?
2. When you die, do you know for sure where you are going?
3. How can you be sure that God will accept you?
4. Is there anything you need to do now to make sure you are ready for the Day of Judgement?
5. What questions would you like to ask your Muslim and Christian friends?

DILEMMA 17

CONQUERING SPIRITUAL POWERS DILEMMA

Ever since we went to Indonesia in 1974 and later to other Islamic countries around the world we have met many different varieties of Muslims. We discovered that we cannot lump them all into one block. There are huge differences in their beliefs and practices. Some are theological. Many are cultural. When we moved to a different country or city or community, the dilemma we faced was to discover what kind of Muslims are we interacting with?

Different groups of people responded in different ways. No one method of approach seemed suitable for the variety of people we met. The passion of Christ's love motivated us to discover how best to share the saving power of the Gospel with people that God loved so much. This was a dilemma we had to work through. We had to get to know the people and to love them unconditionally and understand them compassionately and to live with them sacrificially.

The Bible tells us that we are to die to self. That can mean many things. It can mean our culture, our social behaviour, our attitudes or our lifestyle. Jesus, the Creator of Heaven and Earth, the Lord God and Saviour of mankind gave us the perfect example. He was willing to humble Himself, leave the power and rights of His divinity to become a human being and suffer the rejection, humiliation and agony of the Cross because He loved us and wanted to save us. Our dilemma was the challenge that could we too take up His Cross and walk in His footsteps to bring Christ to the people we lived amongst.

It's a War between Christ and Satan

There is an ongoing battle between Christ and Satan for the possession of the human soul. It began in eternity past, before the creation of the heaven and earth, when the Triune God of the Father, the Son and the Holy Spirit declared the intention to have a community in His own image and likeness.

Genesis 1:26-28,

"God said, "Let Us make man in Our image, according to Our likeness; let them have dominion over the fish of the sea, over the birds of the air, and over the cattle, over all the earth and over every creeping thing that creeps on the earth." So God created man in His own **image; in the image of God He created him; male and female He created them. Then God** blessed them, and God said to them, "Be fruitful and multiply; fill the earth and subdue it; have dominion over the fish of the sea, over the birds of the air, and over every living thing that moves on the earth."

This was an eternal commitment from the Eternal Triune God – "Let **US**" make man in "**OUR** IMAGE" according to "**OUR** LIKENESS".

Satan's rebellious reaction and declaration of war against the Divine plan has echoed across history in his 5 "I WILLS",

Isaiah 14:13-14:

"**I WILL** ascend into heaven,

I WILL exalt my throne above the stars of God;

I WILL also sit on the mount of the congregation on the farthest sides of the north (Mt. Zion cf. *Psalm 48:1-2);*

I WILL ascend above the heights of the clouds,
I WILL be like the Most High."

Satan set his will against the Will of God, and became the enemy both of God and Man.

Satan doesn't care for the creation, but he hates God and he hates mankind. He is no gentleman. He is cruel and vicious, and as Jesus said that Satan has been a ***liar*** and a ***murderer*** from the beginning, *John 8:44.*

In his rebellion, Satan brought chaos, destruction, darkness and death, *Genesis 1:2; Jeremiah 4:23-28; Isaiah 14:9-16; Ezekiel 28:11-19,* and for this he was cast down to the Earth. The War of Eternity had begun!

Jesus warned us that Satan is on the hunt and he's out to destroy us. He wants us all damned in hell, but Jesus wants us to be saved. That's why Jesus came to die on the Cross. He created us. He loves us. He suffered the agony of the crucifixion for us. God, the Father, the Son and the Holy Spirit, have invested all of heaven's resources in this war to save us and transform us into the glorious image of Christ. Satan is doing everything he can to stop this. He fights dirty. He slanders. He brings division. He plays with the flesh, ego, pride and ambition – especially amongst Christian leaders who wrestle and strive for position, wealth and personal glory. That's why so many "successful" leaders fall. Satan plays dirty. He will do anything to see that we are confused, frustrated, divided, splintered, accusing one another, damned and destroyed.

The Apostle Peter warned the early church of the attacks we would face and we should take it seriously. It's real!

1Peter 5:6-9,

"Yes, all of you be submissive to one another, and be clothed with humility, for "God resists the proud, but gives grace to the humble." Therefore humble yourselves under the mighty hand of God, that He may exalt you in due time, casting all your care upon Him, for He cares for you. Be sober, be vigilant; because **your adversary the devil walks about like a roaring**

lion, seeking whom he may devour. Resist him, steadfast in the faith, knowing that the same sufferings are experienced by your brotherhood in the world."

Paul also warned us to be prepared and equipped,

Ephesians 6:10-13,

"Finally, my brethren, be strong in the Lord and in the power of His might. Put on the whole armour of God, that you may be able to stand against the wiles of the devil. For we do not wrestle against flesh and blood, but against principalities, against powers, against the rulers of the darkness of this age, against spiritual hosts of wickedness in the heavenly places. Therefore take up the whole armour of God, that you may be able to withstand in the evil day, and having done all, to stand."

The Apostle John was given the revelation of the coming, intensified war that would find its culmination in the Last Days.

Revelation 12:7-11,

"And war broke out in heaven: Michael and his angels fought with the dragon; and the dragon and his angels fought, but they did not prevail, nor was a place found for them in heaven any longer. So the great dragon was cast out, that serpent of old, called the Devil and Satan, who deceives the whole world; he was cast to the earth, and his angels were cast out with him. Then I heard a loud voice saying in heaven, "Now salvation, and strength, and the kingdom of our God, and the power of His Christ have come, for the accuser of our brethren, who accused them before our God day and night, has been cast down. And they overcame him by the blood of the Lamb and by the word of their testimony, and they did not love their lives to the death."

For the last time the devil was cast down to the earth. The battle is expanding. We see it everywhere today. The devastation is increasing. His anger against the glorious, overcoming Church is exploding. He knows there is **only a little time left**, so first he attacks the glorious woman but she is transported out to her place of divine protection. He can't touch her, so he goes after the lukewarm, unanointed Christians to bring them into submission or to behead them.

Revelation 12:12-17,

"Therefore rejoice, O heavens, and you who dwell in them! Woe to the inhabitants of the earth and the sea! For the devil has come down to you, having great wrath, because **he knows that he has a short time**." Now when the dragon saw that he had been cast to the earth, he persecuted the woman who gave birth to the male Child. But the woman was given two wings of a great eagle, that she might fly into the wilderness to her place, where she is nourished for a time and times and half a time, from the presence of the serpent. So the serpent spewed water out of his mouth like a flood after the woman, that he might cause her to be carried away by the flood. But the earth helped the woman, and the earth opened its mouth and swallowed up the flood which the dragon had spewed out of his mouth. And the dragon was enraged with the woman, and he went to make war with the rest of her offspring, who keep the commandments of God and have the testimony of Jesus Christ."

Note what happens. It's an End Times scenario. It's not 2000 years ago. It's our generation. The devil knows that he only has a short time. What happens to the unanointed Christians? Perhaps they are like the five foolish virgins of *Matthew 25:1-13*, a parable which is also an End Times scenario. Are these the Christians who failed to measure up to the measure of Christ referred to in *Revelation 11:1-2?* Wasn't this the mission of the Five-fold Ministries of *Ephesians 4:11-13* to bring us "to the measure of the stature of the fullness of Christ."

The battle is on. These are dangerous times and we need to be bold in our declaration of the Gospel. The Church has been "seeker friendly" for too long and has been trampled under foot. We need to rise up in faith, be renewed in boldness in the dynamic baptism of the Holy Spirit, filled with the love and compassion of Jesus for the lost and walk in the wisdom of God the Father that we might understand His strategies for our generation. We must preach the Cross and the Resurrection! Boldly!

The Testimony of Dr David Wood and Dr Nabeel Qureshi

David Wood was a wild young man for which he was imprisoned for several years. In prison he heard the Gospel and became a believer in Christ. Later, in his university studies, he became friends with a devout Muslim, Nabeel Qureshi, who tried to convert him to Islam. Similarly, David Wood was trying to convert Nabeel to Christ. After several years Nabeel came to faith in Jesus and became a dynamic public speaker and first-class apologist in debates with international Islamic scholars. His videos on Youtube are well worth watching.

David Wood had also become an internationally known public speaker and Christian apologist thriving in debates with top Islamic apologists from around the world. During his time with Nabeel at university, David had earlier wondered why Nabeel hadn't yet become a Christian. Eventually Nabeel became a believer in Jesus and his radical transformation was noted by many Christian leaders.

Two years after becoming a Christian, Nabeel told David why it took so long for him to accept Christ as his Lord and Saviour. David was shocked to hear his testimony. Nabeel told David, "I heard your preaching and arguments for the Christian faith. It convinced me 98% that you were telling the truth, so why didn't I convert. Well, I still believed 100% in Islam. I believed in the truth of the Qur'an. I believed in the scientific miracles recorded in the Qur'an. I believed the Qur'an was the eternal Book of God sent down from heaven. I believed in the moral superiority of the Prophet Muhammad as the final Prophet. So why should I abandon Islam and become a Christian?"

Nabeel went on to give David a rebuke about his preaching and debating style. "David, you have to stop just saying how true and great the Christian faith is. You have to start destroying the Islamic belief system. You say this and this in Islam is not true. Then prove it. Show people where it's wrong. I didn't leave Islam because I thought it was all true. It was only after I knew of all the errors in Islam."

Around the same time a lady approached David at one of his events and had a similar message. "David, what does it say in *1Corinthians 10:3-5?* "For though we walk in the flesh, we do not war according to the flesh. For the weapons of our warfare are not carnal but mighty in God for pulling down strongholds, casting down arguments and every high thing that exalts itself against the knowledge of God, bringing every thought into captivity to the obedience of Christ."

These incidents caused David to change his style. He knew he had to pull down strongholds, and cast down erroneous arguments. David began to go on the attack and he saw that there were many more Muslims coming to faith in Christ. Yes, David was still preaching the Gospel, but now he was also defending the truths of the Gospel and destroying the arguments used against it. His Youtube videos have attracted millions of viewers around the world and in many strong Islamic countries, the chains are loosening and many captives are being set free. We need that same anointed boldness to explode throughout the Body of Christ.

Many Different Aspects of Islam

As we investigate different aspects of Islam we pray that this testimony and challenge will motivate us to be bold. It takes courage to investigate and to discuss especially when there are serious threats against us. At the time of writing, one of my students is in severe danger. He posted a factual report on the Prophet Muhammad, but Muslims decide to get offended. This student was arrested and imprisoned. He is currently being tortured to recant and return to Islam. He is being beaten and prodded with sharp instruments. He is being physically forced to kneel and say Islamic prayers and to say the Islamic confession of faith, the Shahada.

Over the years several of our students who have become believers in Jesus have been arrested and suffered severe brutality and torture. Through their testimony in the prisons many hundreds have come to faith in Jesus. They are so bold. They are following Jesus.

Jesus told us that there would be persecution and it would become more and more severe. Restrictions will be put on our faith. We will be accused of hate speech, being fanatics, divisive and undesirable elements in the community. We too will be arrested and imprisoned but fear not, Jesus told us this would happen. Are we willing to take up the Cross and follow Christ.

Revelation 2:10,

"Do not fear any of those things which you are about to suffer. Indeed, the devil is about to throw some of you into prison, that you may be tested, and you will have tribulation ten days. Be faithful until death, and I will give you the crown of life."

The martyrs in the Book of Revelation spoke with the Lord about the End-Times,

Revelation 6:9-11,

"When He opened the fifth seal, I saw under the altar the souls of those who had been slain for the word of God and for the testimony which they held. And they cried with a loud voice, saying, "How long, O Lord, holy and true, until You judge and avenge our blood on those who dwell on the earth?" Then a white robe was given to each of them; and it was said to them that they should rest a little while longer, until both the number of their fellow servants and their brethren, who would be killed as they were, was completed."

Yes, we must walk with wisdom, but wisdom does not mean silence. We must stand for the truth with all love, compassion and boldness. We must not force or intimidate people who think differently from us. They must be free to make their own decisions and we must be free to share the alternative choices that each of us must confront.

We reject Islam as a belief system coming from God, but we love Muslims. They are humans created by God, just like us. We need to give them the dignity to be free to make their own decisions. However, if we are not free to share with them our faith, and they have no other alternative choices, then in fact they are prisoners and are in bondage to a system that keeps them bound without the true benefits of freedom. This is a real danger that is spreading around the world.

Let us seek to understand the wide variety of Muslims that are around us in our various communities.

Folk Islam

In most of this book we have been investigating more formal Islam, or Qur'anic Islam. In this section we want to look more into the mystical elements in Islam usually known as Folk Islam. It can be a serious dilemma that we face in knowing what sort of Islam we are dealing with. Each group considers that they are true Muslims and their beliefs are based on the Qur'an, yet many never read the Qur'an. They have memorized the compulsory prayers, and the basic pillars of the faith, but know little beyond that.

There are fundamentalist, liberal, mystical and secularist Muslims. Understanding the difference is important in knowing the best approach for a particular individual in introducing the Gospel to them. One mystical element in Islam is often referred to as Folk Islam.

Folk Islam is basically a non-Qur'anic form of Islam giving rise to sets of beliefs followed by the majority of ordinary Muslims around the world. In countries like Indonesia, Muslims following folk Islam are called *abangan* or *Kejawen* which can be quite mystical and syncretistic. They maintain the 5 basic pillars of Islam (Prayer, the Fast, Hajj, Alms, the Shahada Testimony) but beyond that they have their spiritual beliefs that affect everyday life which may or may not be endorsed by the Qur'an.

In many respects, the majority of Muslims are very animistic, even occultish, and this aspect of Islam is often not discussed in "Islamology" as most teachers of Islam concentrate on the Qur'anic Islam rather than the non-Qur'anic version of Islam. Qur'anic Islam is much more rigid in its beliefs adhering more diligently to the writings of the **Qur'an** and the **Sunnah** (Orthodox consensus), the verbally transmitted record of the teachings, deeds and saying. of the Islamic prophet Muhammad. Added to this are various reports about Muhammad's companions and these are confirmed in the **Hadith** (the traditions) and the **Sira** (the biography of Muhammad).

Many Muslims conceive the world as alive with spirits and make offerings to these spirits, the same way as pagans do. **Johan Tangelder**, a Reformed missiologist states that many Muslims "believe that these spirits relate not only to the physical and mental well-being of a person, but also to the success and failure in agriculture and business. For these Muslims their religious practices are nothing less than Islam. They believe that they are faithful and true to the basic teachings of the Qur'an. There have been instances when foreign - fundamentalist Islamic teachers have tried to point out that many of their local religious practices were un-Islamic, but in each case the local religious leaders repudiated these charges by saying that they (the foreigners) didn't have a correct understanding of Islam."

Why does Folk Islam exist?

Folk Islam is practiced because formal Islam does not answer the questions of everyday life, but only deals with ultimate issues of life, i.e., origins, heaven, hell, purpose. It is cognitive, legalistic, and institutional. On the other hand, Folk Islam gives an answer to everyday concerns of health, guidance, and success.

In the West we often dismiss stories of "spirits" or "ghosts" or "demons" as figments of imagination or of superstition. In the Islamic world these entities are very real spirits, more commonly referred to as jinn, from which we get the term *genie.* The Bible declares the reality of the spirit world and rebellious angels under the leadership of Satan. *Matthew 8:29; 25:41; Revelation 12:9; 2Peter 2:4; Jude 1:6.*

Folk Islam will make use of whatever works, even if it is Christian. Folk Islam follows the original belief systems of scattered tribal people around the world, to which Islam has become attached. Its root is animism with a religious cover. It's a complex system of causes and remedies, with differing expressions in different countries and cultures.

Animistic Practices Hiding in Islam

A key element in the Islamic public proclamation is that "there is no compulsion in religion".

Al-Baqara 2:256,

"There is no compulsion in religion." "la ikraha fi addeen"

Folk Islam nests inside official orthodox Islam and the Qur'anic shell provides sufficient justification for the existence of the varieties of animistic Islam. In Western countries, we often dismiss stories of "spirits" or "ghosts" or "demons" as figments of imagination or of superstition. In the Islamic world these entities are very real.

For an excellent overview of Folk Islam, we recommend you obtain and read **Bill Musk's book, *The Unseen Face of Islam.*** It is essential reading in understanding this subject. We have freely taken full advantage of his research and experience in the material we use in this book, and so should you.

As you study Islam, both formal and mystical, as missiologists like Bill Musk and Johan Tangelder point out in their books, you will discover that the practice of animism extends to the use of the Qur'an. Various Surahs and verses are reputed to be powerful for such problems as headaches, fevers, blindness, and toothaches. For example, ***Surah 113*** is believed to be a deterrent to all sorts of disease. ***Surah 114*** has the power to counter psychic afflictions, and ***Surah 13:28*** is a sure cure for headaches. And throughout the Islamic world, the Qur'an is used as a charm in itself. Miniature copies of the Qur'an are pinned on to children's clothing as talismans to protect them.

Common elements of Folk Islam:

1. The "Evil Eye"
2. The Jinn
3. The Veneration of the Saints
4. Divination, Sorcery and Magic
5. Festival Devotions
6. Exorcisms
7. Domains of Power
8. The *Baraka* – the Blessing

1. The "Evil Eye"

The force of the "Evil Eye can devastate lives. It is that certain look that a person uses with evil intent towards another person. In Australian indigenous culture it could be similar to "pointing the bone". Envy/jealousy is a key part and brings harm and comes from a mere envious look. It's the opposite of *baraka* (blessing). *Baraka* is imparted by touch. The "Evil Eye" is regularly associated with various calamities, personal failures, sicknesses, unhappiness and even death.

Worldwide, Muslims have developed counter measures:

- Magic charms,
- Glazed ceramic beads of bright turquoise
- Hand of Fatima
- Cards containing Qur'anic verses, etc.

Diagnosing the Evil Eye

For Muslims, diagnosis is important for determining the required healing medicine:

1. Investigate any special history
2. Use a seer, fortune teller to unlock its mysteries
3. Hold a breaking of an egg ceremony to help identify the cause

Healing from the effects of the Evil Eye:

1. Burning of incense
2. Reading verses from the Qur'an – e.g. ***Surah 113*** and ***Surah 114.***
3. Visiting the graves of the saints to obtain *baraka* (blessing)
4. Drinking bottles of water with verses of Qur'an written on them is a powerful magic charm, etc.

The "Evil Eye" is not in the Qur'an but is detailed in the *Hadith* (the traditions), as a powerful element globally in Islam. Muslims regularly wear amulets with Arabic inscriptions like: *"al-hasud la yasud"* i.e. "the envier will not overcome." For the average Muslim, protection is more important than cure.

The remedy for the "Evil Eye" is the usage of the term *ma sha'allah* which means "what God has willed." By saying this, the praise is directed away from the person to God, thus protecting the person from the perils of the evil eye.

2. The Jinn

Jinn are everywhere and involved in everything. Satan is called one of the jinn.

Al-Kahf (18):50, "We said to the angels, "Bow down to Adam": They bowed down except Satan. He was one of the Jinn, and he broke the Command of his Lord."

Jinn are beings somewhere between humans and angels. They may be believers or non-believers. They are intensely jealous of humans and seek constantly to injure them.

The term **Qarin** is very interesting. It represents a human's child with an identical jinn's child – so be on guard! Jinn like to do an exchange of babies.

Many Muslims will protect a mother and her newly born child for 40 days after the birth to protect the child from being taken by the jinn and being replaced with a naughty child. Some families will accuse their naughty children as being naughty jinn and will fear that their real baby is in the hands of the jinn.

A common jinn is called *marid (ill, disease)* – this jinn is considered the most powerful jinn who always strives to kill its victims. Strong magical power is needed to combat the destructive power of the *marid* jinn.

Jinn occupy geographical and time locations

- rubbish pits, certain trees, marshes, wells, caves, graveyards, toilets, dark rooms, the night, also certain dangerous animals like sharks, snakes and crocodiles.
- Muslims, where possible, avoid these places, or if they must pass these areas, will go well protected by magic charms and incantations.

Jinn feature prominently in the Qur'an. ***Surah Al-Jinn (72)*** is dedicated to Jinn.

Jinn are:

- Created by God (6:100)
- Made from fire (15:27)
- Can be good or evil (72:11)
- Steal God's worship (34:41)
- Judged on the Last Day (72:14-15)
- Hell is full of humans and jinn (11:119)
- Jinn have babies matching humans as their twins, *qarin*, (50:23-27).

Demons (jinn) are not to be played around with. They are deadly, destructive agents of Satan and their purpose is to destroy faith and life.

See what happened to the sons of Sceva: *Acts 19:11-20.*

3. Veneration of Saints

Even though the Qur'an does not support the veneration of saints, most ordinary Muslims believe in the power of saints as intermediaries or agents of blessing, whether they are dead or alive. Intermediary saints were validated in early Islam by intercession to Muhammad and Fatima. Among most ordinary Muslims, the evident power of the *baraka* (blessing) of saints is its own validation, i.e. the end justifies the means! It is validated by needy Muslims in terms of its known effectiveness.

Johan Tangelder, a reformed theologian, confirms that in Folk Islam saints fulfill an important role: "A major distinction is between the dead and the living saints. Whitewashed, domed shrines dot the landscape of much or rural Africa and the Middle East. Both the corpses of saints and their shrines - even the ground, water, or foliage surrounding their graves - are endowed with large deposits of *baraka*. Folk Muslims believe it is a magical power that can be created by ritual and manipulated for human benefit."

Anwarul Karim says, "It is the saint who can avert calamity, cure disease, procure children for the childless, bless the efforts of the hunter and even improve the circumstances of the dead." In return, devotees express their gratitude and dependence in the form of vows, visits to shrines, and celebration of saints' days.

Can these practices be found in the Bible or among Christian communities?

Perhaps the origin of the veneration of "saints" in some circles of Christendom are the amazing and miraculous events surrounding some events in the Bible:

- Elijah's bones touched the corpse and the man was raised from the dead – *2Kings 13:21*
- Peter's shadow healed the sick – *Acts 5:15*
- Paul's clothing used to cast out demons and heal the sick – *Acts 19:12.*

In contending with false systems of veneration we perhaps need to understand the power of God that resides in the true fellowship of the saints i.e. the Body of Christ - **the power of a "one another" lifestyle,** *1Corinthians 12:7-27; 14:26.* There is an amazing power of God's blessing in the fellowship of the saints, i.e. the living believers in Jesus. Where two or three are gathered together, Jesus is there and prayer will be answered! *Matthew 18:19-20; James 5:13-16.*

We do not need to venerate the dead and call them saints, for all true believers are the saints of God and are now privileged to be able to live in fellowship with God and with each other.

The Fellowship of the Saints is a Biblical Lifestyle:

- Romans 13:8, "love one another"
- Romans 14:19, "edify one another"
- Romans 15:1, "admonish one another"

- ➢ Ephesians 4:2, "bearing with one another"
- ➢ Ephesians 4:32, "forgiving one another"
- ➢ Hebrews 10:24, "consider one another"
- ➢ James 5:16, "confess to one another"
- ➢ James 5:16, "pray for one another"
- ➢ John 13:14, "wash one another's feet"

4. Divination, Sorcery and Magic

For many Muslims, divination, sorcery and magic are dynamic and powerful methods, providing real answers to the crises of daily life. Divination is used to find the cause of sicknesses and often involves trances. A waning moon could mean the sickness will get worse while a waxing moon will indicate improvement. Magic, incantations and potions, for hate or love, for protection or aggression, for pregnancy or healing are valid parts of daily living.

As **Johan Tangelder** correctly observes, "The folk-Islamic view of the world presents a great challenge for Christian mission outreach ministries. The world of popular Islam demonstrates the reality of the kingdom of darkness. Its demonic nature must be exposed and dealt with."

Muslims are looking for real answers as everything is subjected to the evil eye, to jinn, to sorcery etc. They are desperate to find remedies. If it works, some will even attend churches to pray to saints, or attend large evangelistic healing campaigns.

How should we respond?

Do we have answers to meet these needs? This is a key area to be productive in witnessing to Muslims. They want to know if your Jesus is more powerful than the spirits, than the jinn, than the witch-doctor.

I was a speaker at the FGBMFI Convention in the city of Surabaya, the Capital of East Java. About 7000 were in attendance. During the service, while we were praying for the sick, the police came in and physically stopped us from praying for the sick. They did this moments after we prayed for a leper with leprosy visible all over his body, face and arms. He was miraculously and instantly healed. The audience erupted in cheers and praise to the Lord.

The police moved in and said, "You have to stop. You have no licence to practice medicine!"

At least they acknowledged that it worked. This is why many Muslims are coming to faith in Christ. Not just in Surabaya but in many parts of Indonesia, and other Muslim countries around the world. Muslims everywhere and especially in Iran, are seeing the awesome power God has, and see it being manifested in visions, dreams and appearances of Jesus. Iranian migrants, in many countries, are also seeing it in His church. **This is why the church must wake up.**

If we are to have healthy evangelism then we must have healthy churches. We need to return to biblical foundations of love, unity and live in the power of the Holy Spirit. **Nothing less will penetrate the wall of darkness.**

5. Festival Devotions

Muslims celebrate festivals as public affirmations of their commitment to Islam. But they see Christians have moved their festival celebrations to focus on Santa Claus, flying reindeers, elves, Christmas Trees, rabbits and Easter eggs! What message are we sending them? Why are we abandoning the true message and miracles and prophetic appearances occurring in connection to the birth of Christ, and the powerful events surrounding the Passover – His death, burial and resurrection? What spirit causes us to abandon the most powerful messages in the Gospel story and turn them into cartoon events? **Isn't it time that we put Christ back into Christmas and truly celebrated the events of Passover** rather than using them as an opportunity just to have an extended holiday?

6. Exorcisms

The belief system in controlling spirits and jinn goes hand in hand with being possessed. This sometimes happens in mass. We have seen this happen in Indonesian Islamic schools or other public gatherings. It is reported in the daily newspapers. These "possessions" are called *keserupan.*

This then calls for exorcisms or the cancelling of a contractual partnership with jinn and spirits and can be a very difficult, dangerous and expensive process. Powerful charms and amulets are needed by Muslims for protection. Failed exorcisms have sometimes driven people in desperation to come to the church for help. Christ gave us His power to defeat these evil spiritual forces, but today, many Christians, abandon clear biblical revelation, and ignore the power of the spirit-world, and even more-so, they ignore the awesome power of the Holy Spirit that has been given to us.

Victorious power encounters are an amazingly effective spiritual tool to bring Muslims to faith in Christ. God has given this power to you. Don't ignore it! Don't intellectualize it but believe the revelation of God's Word, and prove that Jesus is real, alive and able to meet their needs.

Mark 16:17-18,

"These signs will follow those who believe: In My name they will cast out demons; they will speak with new tongues; they will take up serpents; and if they drink anything deadly, it will by no means hurt them; they will lay hands on the sick, and they will recover."

Luke 10:19,

"Behold, I give you the authority to trample on serpents and scorpions, and over all the power of the enemy, and nothing shall by any means hurt you."

In many parts of Indonesia we have seen amazing demonstrations of the power of God setting people free. We have witnessed amazing deliverances among cannibals from among the Dayaks of Kalimantan (Borneo) and the

Bataks of Brastagi, North Sumatra. In other parts of Indonesia we have seen a variety of manifestations but always Christ has revealed His power to deliver, save and heal.

7. Domains of Power

Times and Seasons

Muslims have strong beliefs in the controlling forces in certain times, seasons, places and directions. The 2nd month in the Islamic calendar is considered the most dangerous. One reason for that is Muhammed's sickness that killed him occurred in this month.

The king of the jinn specializes in attacking people born in the month of Safar (2nd month). Special sacrifices and protective measure need to be taken. The 9th month, Ramadan is the best month and the 27th, the Night of Destiny, is especially blessed. Thursdays and Fridays are the best days because angelic activities are higher, while Wednesdays and Saturdays are the most dangerous because demons are more active.

These concepts influence ordinary Muslims. They will travel or not travel depending on these influences. It will determine decisions on when to marry, circumcise their sons, open a new business etc. Divinations are used to determine the appropriate time, season, date for every major event.

Places and Directions

Places and even directions – left or right – are important factors in determining events in their lives. The left indicates negative influences while the right indicates positive influences. They believe that going to the wrong place or in the wrong direction can considerably impact their lives, wealth, health or sexual ability. So, it is best to sleep on one's right side and face Mecca.

What is our response as Christians? We need to take control over homes, cities, nations as the Bible declares in the promise given to Abraham and possess the gates of the nations.

Genesis 22:16-18,

"By Myself I have sworn, says the LORD, because you have done this thing, and have not withheld your son, your only son — blessing I will bless you, and multiplying I will multiply your descendants as the stars of the heaven and as the sand which is on the seashore; **and your descendants shall possess the gate of their enemies. In your seed all the nations of the earth shall be blessed, because you have obeyed My voice."**

2Chronicles 7:14,

"If My people who are called by My name will humble themselves, and pray and seek My face, and turn from their wicked ways, then I will hear from heaven, and will forgive their sin and heal their land."

Take dominion through prayer - throughout a home, a city or a nation. Take control, exercise your authority in Christ and change the course of history. It happened with the Berlin Wall. It happened with a powerful and wealthy Indonesian businessman, Ir. Ciputra. It happened with Graeme and Ruth Smart in a staggering spiritual warfare in their family and their home.

Take control by marking the boundaries of homes, cities, nations and learning to possess the gates, as promised by God. Look at Mordecai, Jacob, Boaz, Samson, and the Abrahamic covenant. Take hold of the keys – ***Matthew 16:19***, and learn to be the true *ekklesia* of God!

Don't let spiritual forces control you, for in Christ we have ALL power and authority, *Matthew 28:18,* and in Christ we can do "all things", *Philippians 4:13.*

8. The *Baraka* (blessing) – *A Hebrew and Arabic word*

The concept of *baraka* (blessing) is fundamental to the worldview of most Muslims. In Islam, the *baraka* (blessing), is a much sought after commodity. *Baraka* maybe gained or lost. It is most intense in Mecca above the Ka'aba at the gateway to heaven. That's the point of the hajj – to gain more of the *baraka.*

The Battle for Human Souls

As discussed above, there is a war between Christ and Satan for human souls. Many different expressions in different countries, religions, cultures and languages, *John 10:10.* We need Power Encounters! *Mark 1:26-28.* But Power Encounters are insufficient. Casting out an evil spirit is not enough. A cleansed house must be filled with light. A man cleansed of an evil spirit but not filled with light, leaves a door of access for the evil spirit to return with 7 others and reoccupy the house. The person is worse off. We witnessed this happening in Dixons Creek, Melbourne. It was frightening and dangerous.

Power encounters begin the process but must be followed with steps to fill the house with the light of Christ. Power Encounters must include immediate after-care service, *Luke 11:24-26.* Don't wait for new believers to settle down! They need immediate "after-care" service just like any newborn baby!

1. Fill the new believer with Jesus for He is the Light of the World: *John 8:12; 12:35-36.*
2. Fill the new believer with God's Word for it is the Light of the soul: *Psalm 119:105; 2Peter 1:19.*
3. Fill the new believer with the fellowship of the saints for they too are the light that God has placed among us. The new believer needs

to be part of the community of believers: *Matthew 5:14-16; 1John 1:7.*

The Muslim has daily needs. They need answers. They are desperate. But what are we offering as the church?

- A religion that lost its power at the end of the 1st Century?
- A religion that no longer believes in spiritual forces?
- A religion that only wants intellectual answers?
- A religion where Jesus has been locked outside the door?

Are we irrelevant today?

Many Muslims have greater faith in the supernatural than educated, sophisticated modern Christians. Have we adopted a logical and humanistic worldview that sees these Muslims as uneducated since we see sickness as simply a matter of germs and bacteria and not because of the evil eye, the jinn or spirit phenomena?

When we take such an unbiblical stance, we become irrelevant to a needy world where only the power of Jesus can satisfy the hungry soul. How do we reach a thirsty soul? Do we recognize that Muslims function in an experience-oriented worldview that many "sophisticated" Christians reject as superstition?

Can we enter their world, like Jesus entered ours, in order to bring them salvation?

- Was Moses stronger than the gods of Egypt in his battle to set Israel free?
- Was Elijah stronger than the gods of Baal binding the nation in idolatry?
- Was Paul stronger than the 7 sons of Sceva?

- Is Jesus more powerful than Satan, the jinn and the evil spirits? Prove it!

What do we have to offer?

- People are sick and in need of healing. Where will they find their answer – in magic cures or in Jesus?
- They are under pressure and are being attacked by spiritual forces messing up their lives and their families. Where will they find their answer – in alliances with evil spirits and jinn or the Holy Spirit?
- The future is uncertain and troubling and decisions need to be made. Where will they get their guidance – from Fortune Tellers or from divine revelation through the Bible, the Holy Spirit and His people?

The victory of Ephesus – Acts 19

Ephesus was the capital of an idol-worshipping cult worshipping the goddess Artemis. It took power encounters to deliver that city.

- Extraordinary miracles – *Acts 19:11*
- Healings – *Acts 19:12*
- Deliverances from evil spirits – *Acts 19:12*
- 7 sons of Sceva defeated – *Acts 19:13-17*
- Repentance and confession – *Acts 19:18*
- Public burning of magic books – *Acts 19:19*
- Gospel spread - grew in power – *Acts 19:20*
- 30 years later, Artemis was totally defeated under the powerful ministry of the apostle John! (See *The Christianizing of the Roman Empire* by Ramsay MacMullen).

Discipling of New Believers

1. Many new Muslim Background Believers need ongoing one on one reinforcement of their new-found faith like Champion Gatherings; I'm a Follower of Christ (IFC); Leadership Boot Camps (LBC); 4 Growth morning devotion Steps: Accept, Contemplate, Take action, Share (A.C.T.S)., etc.
2. New believers, like at Ephesus, need to renounce their magic books and occult activities of the past – *Acts 19:18-19.* Look at the results! Do you want to see that happen today? How will it happen?
3. Like the Gadarenes, new believers need to be encouraged to witness for Christ – *Mark 5:19; Romans 10:9-10*
4. Ongoing power encounters – water baptism, growing in the fruit of the Holy Spirit, filled with the Holy Spirit, operating in the gifts of the Holy Spirit, fellowship with other believers and telling others how the Lord has taken them out of darkness and into His light – *Galatians 5:25; Hebrews 10:25; 1Peter 2:9*
5. They need to continue to study of the Word of God – *John 8:32; Psalm 119:11,105.* Teach them to be teachable. Teach them to study. Teach them to share with other believers. Teach them to teach others.

Discussion Topics

In a group, read the story of the Gadarenes – *Mark 5:1-19.*

Why was this man left in this terrible condition?

1. Was it because there had never been any power-encounters? Maybe they didn't believe in them! Maybe it was best just to put him in an asylum! Here's a novel idea, why not just deliver him?

2. Maybe there were no possessors of faith, power and authority to bind the man and set him free? Is that true in our church today? *Matthew 28:18.*
3. Jesus has the power and the authority and He has given it to us. Matthew - *Acts 1:8.* Will we act upon that power and authority or will we fear what man might think? *Luke 10:19-20; Mark 16:17*
4. Jesus tells the delivered man to go and be a witness of what the Lord has done. What would we say if it was a Muslim accepting Jesus? *Mark 5:19.* Would we tell him to go and be a witness or to keep it hush, hush? Discuss.

DILEMMA 18

ISLAMIC ESCHATOLOGY DILEMMA

End Time Prophecies in the Qur'an and the Hadith

Both Christians and Muslims believe in the end times. Both the Bible and the Qur'an prophesy of the end times. There are some similarities. Both are looking to the coming of Jesus, the Day of Resurrection and the Day of Judgment.

For Muslims, belief in the Last Day is one of the six basic beliefs, the six fundamental pillars of Islam. The Qur'an demands such belief. What does the Qur'an say about the Last Day, the Day of Judgment and the Day of Resurrection? How much does it influence the lives and actions of Muslims?

It is estimated that one-tenth of the Qur'an speaks about the last days and the afterlife, the matters of eschatology. End time teaching is a core component of the Qur'anic message. The last days and the signs of the end, the resurrection of the dead, the final judgment, the punishment of hell fire and the reward of Paradise, are prominent messages throughout the Qur'an.

The Qur'an provides the core theological doctrine about the afterlife and judgment. However, many of the specific, detailed signs or narratives surrounding the Islamic teaching of the "end times", including the coming of the Mahdi, the return of Jesus and detailed accounts of the Antichrist (Arabic - the *Dajjal)*, are discussed in the Hadith, the stories of what Muhammad said and did, rather than in the Qur'an itself.

Christians need to understand the worldview of the Muslims. It will help to understand and communicate with our Muslim friends and neighbours. It will help us understand what is happening around the world with the rise of radical and fundamental terrorist groups. It will help us understand their motivations and final goals. It will help us engage in conversations and share the Gospel with them.

The Importance of the End Times

The vision of the end times figures prominently in the Qur'an and the Hadith. Muslims are constantly reminded of the coming day of judgment, when they must face the terrible day of reckoning. Every prayer, every day, centres around the King of the Day of Judgment *(Malik Yawm ad-Deen).*

Prayer is central to the life of all devout Muslims. They must perform five obligatory prayers every day. They pray:

1. Before dawn – the *Fajr* prayers (2 *rakah).*
2. At noon – the *Dhuhr* (4 *rakah*).
3. Mid-afternoon – the *Asr* prayers (4 *rakah*).
4. Before sunset – the *Maghrib* prayers (3 *rakah).*
5. An hour after sunset – the *Isha* prayers (4 *rakah).*

Those prayers include mentioning belief in the day of judgement, 17 times a day.

Each of these prayer times involves saying a set of prayers (*rakah*). The set of prayers is a single, complete unit of prayer in Arabic that consists of a sequence of actions and recitations. It includes standing, bowing, and two prostrations.

A full prayer consists of two to four *rakah*. Each *rakah* is the same. They add up to 17 prayers which are all the same and are prayed every day, every week, every month, every year for all their lives.

During every *rakah* they recite the whole of the first surah in the Qur'an. This is based on what Muhammad said in the Hadith.

Sahih Al-Bukhari 723,

"Allah's Messenger said, "Whoever does not recite Al-Fatiha in his prayer, his prayer is invalid.""

The central verse of this surah, verse 4, mentions the King of the Day of Judgment *(MalikYawm ad-Deen).*

This is the prayer:

Surah Al Fatihah 1-7,

1. In the name of Allah, the Gracious, the Merciful.
2. Praise be to Allah, Lord of the Worlds.
3. The Most Gracious, the Most Merciful.
4. King, (Ruler or Owner) of the Day of Judgment. (*Malik Yawm Ad-Deen*)
5. It is You we worship, and upon You we call for help.
6. Guide us to the straight path.
7. The path of those You have blessed, not of those against whom there is anger, nor of those who are misguided.

Every devout Muslim knows this Surah by heart and can recite it in the Arabic language. Christians pray the Lord's Prayer at different times, in different circumstances, maybe once a week, maybe rarely. It is not a religious requirement. Muslims recite *Surah Al-Fatihah* seventeen times a day.

To believe in Allah and the Last Day is a priority in Islam. If Muslims are to be saved on the Day of Judgment, they must find the "straight path." Seventeen times a day they pray for guidance to the "straight path."

According to the Bible there is only one "straight path." That straight path is the "narrow way" that leads to life. That "way" which is the truth and the life, is Jesus Christ. Muslims are genuinely seeking that way. Maybe this is why so many Muslims are having visions of Jesus. He is answering their prayers. He is guiding them to the path of those who are blessed. He is showing them who is the "King of the Day of Judgment".

The phrase "God and the Last Day" is central to Islamic belief. Believing in God and the Last Day has many benefits. It is of supreme importance to the Muslims. There are many promises to those who believe in God and the Last Day. Muslims must believe in "God and the Last Day" to be accounted righteous.

The Qur'an says that Muslims and even Christians, Jews and Sabeans who believe in "God and the Last Day" and act righteously, will have nothing to fear of grieve.

Surah Al-Baqarah 2:62,

"Those who believe, and those who are Jewish, and the Christians, and the Sabeans—any who believes in Allah and the Last Day and acts righteously—will have their reward with their Lord; they have nothing to fear, nor will they grieve."

Surah Al-Maidah 5:69,

"Those who believe, and the Jews, and the Sabians, and the Christians—whoever believes in Allah and the Last Day, and does what is right—they have nothing to fear, nor shall they grieve."

The importance of believing in "Allah and the Last Day" is highlighted in verses that say that such people are righteous, that they make the best decision and have the most excellent determination, that they will not stray into error but receive a great reward and that they are the people who attend the mosques. If people do not believe in "Allah and the Last Day" they need to be fought against.

Who are those who believe in "Allah and the Last Day"?

- **They are the righteous.**

  Surah Al-Baqarah 2:177,

  "But righteous is he who believes in Allah, and the Last Day, and the angels, and the Scripture, and the prophets."

- **They are those who make the best decision.**

  Surah An-Nisa 4:59,

  "O you who believe! Obey Allah and obey the Messenger … if you believe in Allah and the Last Day. That is best, and a most excellent determination."

- **They will not stray into error.**

  Surah An-Nisa 4:136,

  "Whoever rejects Allah, His angels, His Books, His messengers, and the Last Day, has strayed far in error."

- **They will receive an immense reward.**

  Surah An-Nisa 4:162,

  "… the believers in Allah and the Last Day—upon these We will bestow an immense reward."

- **They will be able to attend mosque.**

  Surah At-Tawbah 9:18,

  "The only people to attend Allah's places of worship are those who believe in Allah and the Last Day, …"

- **They will not be fought against.**

  Surah At-Tawbah 9:29,

  "Fight those who do not believe in Allah, nor in the Last Day."

How important is this doctrine of the Last Day, taught in both the Qur'an and the Hadith! Islam teaches that the Last Day is an inevitable, impending reality known only to Allah. Its coming will be preceded by minor signs like moral decay and natural disasters. Then, the emergence of the Islamic Messiah (the *Mahdi)* will take place and be followed by major signs like the coming of the Antichrist (the *Dajjal*), the return of Jesus to turn the world to Islam and the rise of the Beast (*ad-Dabbat*). The Last Day will be a cataclysmic day of judgment, also described as "the Hour" (*As-Sa'ah*).

There are many prophecies about this coming time of judgment in the Qur'an. The day of Resurrection (*Yawm al-Qiyama*) and the Last Day (*Yawm al-Akhir*) are mentioned over seventy times in the Qur'an. That day also has many other titles.

The Day of Judgment (*Yawm Ad-Deen*). (*Surah Al-Fatihah 1:4*)

The Day of Recompense. (*Yawm Ad-Deen*). (*Surah Al-Ma'arij 70:26) Sd-Deein)*

The Day Reckoning (*Yawm Al-Hisab*).

The Day of Gathering *(Yawm Al-Jam*).

The Day of Regret: *Yawm Al-Hasrah.* (*Surah Maryam 19:39).*

The Day of Judgment or Division: (*Yawm Al-Fasl).* (*Surah Ad-Dukhan 44:40*).

The Day of Meeting: (*Yawm At-Talaaqi*). *(Surah Ghafir 40:15).*

A Known day: (*Yawm Ma'luum).* (*Al-Waqiah 56:50).*

The titles of the following surah all have to do with the last day, and all hold descriptions of that day. Most of them are short and many of them are Meccan surahs.

Surah Ad-Dukhan 44 – **The Smoke.**

Speaks of the day that will bring forth a visible smoke and a painful torment.

Surah Al-Waqiah 56 - **The Inevitable Event.**

Details the inescapable nature of the Day of Resurrection, the separation of people into three groups, and the recompense.

Surah Al-Haqqah 69 - **The Inevitable Reality.**

Depicts the finality of the Day and the destruction of nations that denied it.

Surah Al-Ma'arij 70 - **The Ascending Stairways.**

Discusses the day when the sky will be like molten metal and no friend will ask about another.

Surah Al-Qiyamah 75 - **The Resurrection.**

This Surah is entirely focused on the Resurrection, swearing by the Day and describing the scenes of the soul's departure and the gathering of humanity.

Surah Al-Mursalat 77 - **Those Sent Forth**.

Mentions "The Day of Decision" several times to warn those who deny the truth.

Surah An-Naba' 78 - **The Tidings**.

Opens with a mention of the "momentous news" (Judgment Day) and describes it as a decided appointment.

Surah An-Naziat 79 **- Those Who Drag Forth.**

Describes the sudden terror of the Trumpet blast.

Surah At-Takwir 81 **- The Overthrowing.**

Describes the sun, stars, and mountains being brought to an end, and the resurrection of souls.

Surah Al-Infitar 82 **- The Cleaving Asunder.**

Describes the heavens breaking apart, the stars falling, the seas overflowing and the graves breaking open. It is the day of reckoning when the angels who have written down their deeds will produce the records and people will enter paradise or hell.

Surah Al-Mutaffifin 83 **- The Defrauders.**

Specifically mentions the "tremendous Day" (*Yawn 'Azeem*) on which mankind will stand before the Lord.

Surah Al-Inshiqaq 84 **- The Splitting Open.**

Describes the sky cracking and the earth leveling, where every soul will meet its record.

Surah Al-Ghashiyah 88 **- The Overwhelming.**

Discusses the overwhelming Day when the humiliated enter the hot blazing fire and the joyful who will rejoice in lofty Paradise in luxury

Surah Az-Zalzalah 99 **- The Earthquake.**

Describes the earth being shaken and mankind being shown their good and evil deeds.

Surah Al-Qari'ah 101 **- The Calamity/Striking Hour.**

Describes the immense terror of the Day of Judgment when people will be scattered like moths and weighed in the balances.

Christians also believe in the coming day of judgment. The prophets all prophesied of that day. Jesus taught of the day when He is coming again in the clouds. The apostles wrote of that day of resurrection in their epistles.

The Book of Revelation tells of the coming of the Day of the Lord when there will be signs of His coming, a time of great tribulation and then the glorious appearance of Jesus Christ in the clouds with the saints when He will destroy the wicked, conduct the last judgment and reign forever with His people in eternity.

The Motivation of the End Times

The vision of the end times is an important motivation for Muslims. just as it is for Christians.

Belief in the end times, can motivate kindness, charity and good behaviour. It can inspire Muslims to become more religious and to fulfill all their obligations according to the Qur'an.

For many devout Muslims, it is a motivation that shapes their daily behaviour. They desire to increase their good deeds so that on the day of judgement their good deeds will outweigh their bad deeds. They want to do good. They are fearful of the threat of Hell. Such Muslims will pray five times a day, give alms, keep the Ramadhan fasting month and if possible, go on a pilgrimage to Mecca, (the *hajj*). They will try to be kind and charitable and they may also recite the Qur'an and Islamic sayings, such as "*Bismillah*" (in the name of Allah), "*Alhamdulillah*" (praise be to Allah), "*Astaghfirullah*" (forgive me Allah) and "*Subhanallah*" (glory be to Allah). They believe that saying these phrases, (*dhikr*) are acts of worship for which they will be rewarded. They will try to follow up bad deeds with good ones, in order to wipe out the bad.

Although according to Islam, faith is considered essential, Muslims believe that it is their deeds that will make them acceptable to God and enable them to enter heaven. They long to be pleasing to God. They hunger and thirst for righteousness. This hunger and thirst in the hearts of Muslims is opening the door for God Himself to speak to them through dreams and visions. There are many reports of Muslims praying to God and seeing a vision of a figure in white robes appear. That figure is Jesus. Their vision of the end times opens their heart to find the Lord.

Belief in the end times can also motivate violence and terrorism.

For devout radical movements like Hamas, Islamic Jihad, Hezbollah, Islamic State, the Taliban and the Muslim Brotherhood, belief in the end times is a motivation to jihad. They use eschatological narratives, such as the coming of the Mahdi and the triumph of Islam to stir up political action, to legitimize violent actions or go to war in a jihad. Their vision of the end times especially incites them to eradicate the Jews. It inspires the Palestinians to Intifada. It encourages ISIS to attempt to establish a Caliphate, an Islamic Kingdom. The details differ between the Sunni and the Shia but overall, their end time vision is basically similar. They believe that because their good deeds will never be enough, that jihad, especially dying as a martyr in a jihad, will guarantee their entrance into heaven. Their vision can impel them to suicide bombing, arson, rape and murder in the name of Allah for the goal of the triumph of Islam.

It can give rise to a balancing act between fear and hope.

Because of the very vivid depictions of both hell and heaven in the Qur'an, Muslims can be torn between the fear and terror of terrible torture and punishment on one hand and the hope of luxurious pleasures and delights in Paradise on the other.

It can also produce an attitude or resignation and apathy.

Because their future destiny is already foretold and everything is up to God, they may just lose interest in anything but the immediate situation and give up easily. They may shrug their shoulders and say, "*Inshallah*!" ("If God wills"). We encountered this attitude among the victims of the Aceh tsunami in 2005 where people who had lost their homes and families passively accepted it as "God's will." It reduced their capacity and energy to rebuild their lives or to help those who had suffered from the calamity.

Impending signs of the end can also result in greater religious observance. This has been notable around the world.

We observed how, after the attack on the World Trade Centre in New York in 2001, there was a noticeable increase in Indonesia of the wearing of the veil by Muslim women and the observing of the fast of Ramadhan by Muslims. It was as if the events of 911 signalled an eschatological sign that turned the thoughts of Muslims to the end of days and the triumph of Islam and inspired a deeper return to religious faith and observance.

The Minor Signs

The Hadiths indicate that there will be specific signs that the end is near. These are signs foretold by Muhammad and reported by his companions. They were written down about 200 years after he lived.

Key hadiths about the signs of the end

Sahih Al Bukhari 80,

"From among the portents of the Hour are (the following): 1. Religious knowledge will be taken away (by the death of Religious learned men). 2. (Religious) ignorance will prevail. 3. Drinking of Alcoholic drinks (will be very common). 4. There will be prevalence of open illegal sexual intercourse."

Sahih al Bukhari 81,

"...Women will increase in number and men will decrease in number so much so that fifty women will be looked after by one man."

Sahih Al Bukhari 5590,

"The prophet said "From among my followers there will be some people who will consider illegal sexual intercourse, the wearing of silk, the drinking of alcoholic drinks and the use of musical instruments, as lawful."

Sahih al Muslim vol 4 1503-1504,

"Religious knowledge will be taken away, religious ignorance will prevail, drinking of alcoholic drinks will be common and there will be a prevalence of open illegal sexual relationships."

Sahih Muslim 8,

"He (the Holy Prophet) said: That the slave-girl will give birth to her mistress and master, that you will find barefooted, destitute goat-herds vying with one another in the construction of magnificent buildings."

Sahih al-Bukhari 1036,

"The Prophet said, "The Hour (Last Day) will not be established until (religious) knowledge will be taken away, earthquakes will be very frequent, time will pass quickly, afflictions will appear, murders will increase and money will overflow amongst you."

These hadith describe widespread moral, religious, social, ethical, and environmental decay. Key signs include religious knowledge being lost through the death of scholars and increasing immorality, adultery (*zinah*) and sexual promiscuity. Society will degenerate marked by alcoholic orgies, the spread of musical instruments and men wearing gold and silk. There will be moral decay with increased dishonesty, murders and killing. There will be economic chaos with barefoot Bedouins competing in building tall buildings. There will be earthquakes and afflictions.

These events act as warnings that the Last Hour is approaching and the major signs are at hand. Many Muslims believe they are seeing all these minor signs already in the earth. While minor signs have already occurred, the major signs are seen as the final warning.

Christians too believe they are seeing the signs of the last days. Jesus taught His disciples about the end times. He spoke of the period of initial signs of His coming as the "beginning of sorrows." (*Matthew 24:3-14.)*

The Coming of the Mahdi

Muslims are waiting for the coming of the Mahdi. They see that as the next event to take place on the prophetic calendar. A 2012 poll found that over 50% of respondents in several Muslim-majority countries expected the Mahdi to return during their lifetime. He is said to be a righteous leader, a descendant of Muhammad who will come to rid the world of evil, of injustice and oppression, to restore justice, to unify Muslims and establish a worldwide Islamic kingdom, the caliphate. He will appear shortly before Jesus returns.

According to the hadith, Muhammad prophesied of the coming of the Mahdi, "...the Prophet said: "The world will not pass away until the Arabs are ruled by a man from my family whose name matches my name". (*Sunan Abi Dawud Hadith 4282*).

Another hadith describes the appearance and rule of the Mahdi. "... "The Mahdi will be of my stock and will have a broad forehead and a prominent nose. He will fill the earth with equity and justice as it was filled with oppression and tyranny, and he will rule for seven years". *(Sunan Abi Dawud 4285).*

The Mahdi is a leader, a descendant of Muhammad who will appear when the world is filled with injustice, to restore peace and justice. He is a messianic figure, expected to appear in the last days to establish a global kingdom of justice, peace, and righteousness. He is believed to be a descendant of the Prophet Muhammad, who will eradicate evil and oppression after the world has been filled with anarchy, turmoil, and moral degradation.

Sunnis believe in him although he is not mentioned in the Qur'an or in the most authentic Hadith collections of Al-Bukhari and Sahih Muslim. Shias believe the Mahdi is the twelfth Imam who has been in hiding since the 9th century and will return to lead the Islamic kingdom. This belief has inspired many of the radical Sunni and Shia movements.

The terrorist movements around the world have been inspired to engage in jihad to prepare the way for the Mahdi and to transform their societies and their nations into Islamic states that will be willing to submit to the coming Caliphate. They firmly believe they are following the message of Allah and fulfilling His will in taking part in the preparations for the coming of the Mahdi.

The Prophecy about Jews in the Last days

An essential part of the prophecies of the end times is the role of the Jews. They must be fought against and defeated. This has been a highly motivating vision for the radical terrorist movements, especially Hamas. They believe that the killing of the Jews is a sign of the last days and signals the destruction of Israel and the victory of the Muslims. The future is a prophesied war against a perpetual enemy, the Jews, in which Islam being aided by Allah will win.

One of the most famous Sunni Muslim Hadith (tradition) speaking of the End Times and the conflict with the Jews says it this way:

Sahih Muslim 2922,

"Allah's Messenger said: "'The Hour (of Resurrection) will not be established until Muslims fight the Jews, and Muslims will kill them. The Jews will hide behind stones and trees, and the stone or tree will say: 'O Muslim, O servant of Allah, there is a Jew hiding behind me; come and kill him,' except for the Gharqad tree, for it is the tree of the Jews.'

Sahih Al-Bukhari 2926,

Allah's Messenger said, "The Hour will not be established until you fight with the Jews, and the stone behind which a Jew will be hiding will say. "O Muslim! There is a Jew hiding behind me, so kill him."

Hamas quoted this hadith in their 1988 Charter. This highly motivates them. For them, it is the command of Allah. Hamas named their latest offensive, "Operation Al Aqsa Flood". That is the name of the mosque, Al Aqsa Mosque on the Temple Mount in Jerusalem. They believe that it, and all Jerusalem for that matter, belong to Islam and will ultimately be reconquered by an Islamic army and put once again under Islamic control.

Hamas is motivated by a radical Islamist ideology that views victory over Israel and its destruction as an apocalyptic fulfillment of their vision. It aims to end the state of Israel and replace it by an Islamic state. It is rooted in the Islamic prophetic ideology where the struggle of jihad is required for an ultimate, divine victory. Hamas sees the "liberation of Palestine, from the River to the Sea, as a religious obligation, not just a political goal. Their ultimate purpose is to establish an Islamic state to replace Israel. There is no way they can accept peace with Israel or "normalize" relations with the Jews.

Hamas branded their current fight as "Operation Al-Aqsa Flood". They aim to extend the battle to the West Bank, Jerusalem, and beyond. It is their vision and mission to conduct a violent campaign to take Jerusalem (*Al-Quds*) which they claim as Islam's third most holy site.

Their core belief is that Islam will eventually triumph, making way for the rule of the Mahdi, restoring a "perfect Islamic society" and establishing a global caliphate, often viewed as the final outcome of a struggle against both external enemies and "apostate" governments within the Muslim world.

Likewise, all the other Islamic radical groups around the world see themselves vanguards in the jihad to overthrow all secular non-Islamic regimes in order to prepare the world for the coming of the Mahdi and the return of Jesus. The struggle for Palestine and Jerusalem is seen as the central battleground in this cosmic conflict.

The Prophecy about Muslims in the Last Days

Another sign which is much less talked about is the prophecy about Muslims in the last days. This one does not make a lot of sense but it is included in the most authentic hadith.

Sunan Abu Dawud 4297,

"The Prophet said, "A day will come when the nations of the world will gather against the Muslims like hungry people rushing to a dish of food." His companions asked: "Will we be few in number, O Messenger of Allah?" He replied: "No, you will be many... but like foam on floodwater - weightless, divided, weak.""

Other Hadiths state that Islam will crawl back into its hole between the two mosques (Mecca and Medina). It indicates that faith will retreat to Medina in times of danger, just as a snake crawls back into its hole.

Sahih Muslim 146,

"It is narrated on the authority of Ibn 'Umar ('Abdullah b. 'Umar) that the Messenger of Allah observed: Verily Islam started as something strange and it would again revert (to its old position) of being strange just as it started, and it would recede between the two mosques just as the serpent crawls back into its hole."

Sahih al-Bukhari 1876,

"Allah's Messenger said, "Verily, Belief returns and goes back to Medina as a snake returns and goes back to its hole (when in danger)."

Some Muslims scholars say that means that Islam, which once spread throughout the world from a small beginning, will eventually shrink, retreat, and concentrate itself back in its original birthplace—the Hijaz (specifically Medina and Mecca)—at the end of time.

This is one of the more enigmatic prophecies of the end times and creates quite a dilemma for Muslims.

The Major Signs

Several hadiths say there will be ten major signs.

Sahih Muslim. 2901,

"Allah's Apostle was in an apartment and we were beneath that, that he peeped in and said to us: What are you discussing about? We said: (We are discussing about the Last) Hour. Thereupon he said: The Last Hour would not come until the ten signs appear: land-sliding in the east, and land-sliding in the west, and land-sliding in the peninsula of Arabia, the smoke, the Dajjal, the beast of the earth, Gog and Magog, the rising of the sun from the west and the fire which would emit from the lower part of 'Adan. Shu'ba said that 'Abd al-'Aziz b. Rufai' reported on the authority of Abu Tufail who reported on the authority of Abu Sariha a hadith like this that Allah's Apostle did not make a mention of (the tenth sign) but he said that out of the ten one was the descent of Jesus, son of Mary (peace be upon him), and in another version it is the blowing of the violent gale which would drive the people to the ocean.."

There seems to be general agreement among Muslims after the Mahdi comes. that the major signs will include:

1. The coming of the Anti-Christ, the Dajjal.
2. The descent of Jesus.
3. The rise of Gog and Magog (*Yajuj and Majuj*
4. Landslides taking place in the east.
5. Landslides in the west.
6. Landslides in the Arabian Peninsula.
7. The smoke.
8. The rising of the sun in the west.

9. The beast.
10. The fire.

The Rise of the Islamic Antichrist, the Dajjal

After the appearance of the Mahdi, Muslims are also expecting the coming of the false Messiah, the Dajjal (*Ad-Dajjal),* the False Messiah). He is an antagonistic figure who will corrupt the faith of many, claim divinity, and cause widespread havoc and testing on earth. He will come to deceive humanity. He will claim to be a prophet and then later, claim to be God Himself. The Dajjal is among the first of the ten major signs of the Hour, bringing unparalleled temptation (*fitnah*) and corruption to the world.

The Dajjal is mentioned frequently in the Hadith. He will show signs and wonders, and many people will follow him. In the end he will be killed by Jesus. There are physical descriptions of him. He is described as a young, stout man with a reddish complexion, thick curly hair, and blind in one eye. He is seen as an enemy of Jesus, a false Messiah.

Muhammad had a vision of the Dajjal, the Antichrist.

Sahih Muslim 169C

"Muhammad said, "I saw near the Ka'bah a man of fair complexion with straight hair, placing his hands on two persons. Water was flowing from his head or it was trickling from his head. I asked: Who is he? They said: He is Jesus, son of Mary or al-Masih son of Mary. The narrator) says: I do not remember which word it was. He (the Holy Prophet) said: And I saw behind him a man with red complexion and thick curly hair, blind in the right eye. I saw in him the greatest resemblance with Ibn Qitan I asked: Who is he? They replied: It is al-Masih al-Dajjal."

The Coming of Jesus

According to many hadiths, the Mahdi will arrive first, followed by the Dajjal. Only after then, Jesus will descend from heaven where He now is, and will join the Mahdi to fight against and defeat the Dajjal.

Muslims believe Jesus will come back as a Muslim and descend to the Umayyad mosque in Damascus, the fourth holiest site in Islam. He will be dressed in yellow robes. Together with Jesus, the Mahdi will defeat the Antichrist. The Descent of Jesus (*Isa*) will take place in Damascus. He will defeat the *Dajjal* at the gate of Ludd (Lod), which is about 15km south of Tel Aviv, establish Islam as the prevailing religion, and break the cross, kill all the pigs and abolish the jizya tax. He will abolish the jizya because there will be no more Christians or Jews left as all people will accept Islam and there will no longer be any need for taxation in exchange for state protection.

He will kill the pigs and break the cross and every one of the People of the Book, all the Jews and Christians, will believe in Him. Thus, there will be one community on earth, the people of Islam. The Mahdi then will on live and rule for six or seven years. After his death, he will be replaced as leader of the Muslims by Jesus who will be a just ruler.

This is based on the hadith.

Bukhari Hadith 2476,

"Allah's Apostle said, "The Hour will not be established until the son of Mary (Jesus) descends amongst you as a just ruler, he will break the cross, kill the pigs, and abolish the Jizya tax. Money will be in abundance so that nobody will accept it".

Muslims believe Jesus will come before the Day of Resurrection and Judgment. His return will be one of the signs of that coming Day. Much of this teaching is based on the hadith. After the death of the Mahdi, Jesus will rule the world and establish peace and justice. He will join the Mahdi in the fight and kill the false Messiah, al Masih al Dajjal. after which Gog and

Magog will disperse and cause trouble in the earth. Gog and Magog will finally be defeated by the forces of Jesus. God, in response to Jesus' prayers, will send a worm in the napes of their necks and kill them all.

Jesus will rule for forty years, get married, establish peace and justice and die a natural death and be buried alongside Muhammad, Abu Bakr and Umar in Mecca in the fourth reserved tomb of the Green Dome of Mecca.

The Qur'an does not explicitly state in a single, direct verse that Jesus will return to Earth. However, many Islamic scholars interpret specific verses as indications of his second coming.

Jesus is described as a "sign of the Hour".

Surah Az-Zukhruf 43:6,

"And (Jesus) shall be a Sign (for the coming of) the Hour (of Judgment): therefore have no doubt about the (Hour), but follow ye Me: this is a Straight Way."

The Qur'an states that all the People of the Book will believe in him before his death.

Surah An-Nisa 4:159,

"And here is none of the People of the Book but must believe in him (Jesus) before his death. And on the day of resurrection, he will be a witness against them."

Thus, all Christians will believe in and accept the Islamic Jesus.

The Prophecy about Gog and Magog in the Last Days

The prophecy about Gog and Magog seems to be based on the Biblical text. In the Old Testament, Gog and Magog are described as an army invading Israel from the north. (*Ezekiel 38–39*). In the New Testament Gog and Magog emerge in huge numbers and attack the camp of the saints in Jerusalem after the Millennium. (*Revelation 20:7–8*).

According to the Islamic sources, Gog and Magog will spread mischief on earth and no one will be able to resist them. They are irrepressible tribes that will wreak havoc and cause widespread havoc and destruction. Gog (*Yajuj)* and Magog (*Majuj)* are two disbelieving tribes from among the sons of Adam. They have wide faces and small eyes. They used to spread mischief on earth, so Allah gave Dhu'l-Qarnayn (a righteous ruler sometimes identified as Alexander the Great) the power to build a barrier to detain them. They will keep on digging at it until Allah gives them permission to come out at the end of time, after 'Isa has killed the Dajjal.

It appears Gog and Magog come after Jesus.

Gog and Magog will emerge in huge numbers and will drink up the lake of Tiberias (in Palestine). They will spread mischief on earth and no one will be able to resist them. Jesus and the believers with him will take refuge in Mount Tur. They will pray and then Allah will destroy Gog (*Yajuj)* and Magog (*Majuj)* by sending worms that will eat their necks. Then Allah will send rain to wash away their bodies into the sea and cleanse the earth of their stench. *(Sunan Ibn Majah (Hadith 4079 and 4080) and Sahih Muslim (part of Hadith 2937).*

Three Land-slidings: Occurring in the East, West, and Arabia.

These events are often described as severe "sinkings" or "collapse of the earth," indicating mass casualties in these locations.

They are expected to occur toward the end of time, alongside other major signs like the appearance of the Dajjal, the return of Jesus, and the rising of the sun from the West.

The Smoke

The smoke (Arabic: *Ad-Dukhan*), is also usually listed as one of the last major events in Islamic eschatology. The Smoke is one of the ten major signs preceding the Day of Judgment. It is described as a thick, visible smoke or mist that will envelope the entire earth for 40 days and nights, causing severe illness for disbelievers while affecting believers only with light cold-like symptoms.

Surah Ad-Dukhan 44:10-11,

"So be on the watch for a day when heaven shall bring a manifest smoke covering the people; this is a painful chastisement".

According to the Hadith, Muhammad explained that this smoke will fill the area between the east and west. It is considered a severe punishment from God, that will cause great distress and fear.

The Sun Rising from the West: The closing of the gate of repentance.

This event represents the closing of the "door of repentance." Good deeds or embracing faith after this event will not be accepted. It is one of the final major signs, occurring after other events such as the appearance of the Dajjal (Antichrist) and the descent of Jesus.

It is believed that this incident will show Allah's power to alter the laws of nature. Some modern interpretations suggest this could coincide with a geomagnetic reversal (poles flipping), while others focus solely on the metaphysical, miraculous nature of the event.

As stated in the *Al-Anam 6:158*, on that day, "no good will it do to a soul to believe in them then, if it believed not before".

The Coming of the Beast

The Antichrist is not mentioned in the Qur'an, although there is a prophecy of the rise of a Beast. In Islamic eschatology, the Antichrist, the Dajjal, appears first, followed by the appearance of the Beast (*Dabbat al-Ard).*

The Beast is mentioned in the Qur'an. He is considered to be one of the final signs, emerging from the earth, when the world is already heavily corrupted. When the Beast arises, the doors of repentance are closed. He will speak to humanity, marking believers and disbelievers, signifying the end of the time for repentance. He seems to be modelled to some degree on the Beast of Revelation chapter 13.

An Naml 27:82,

"And when the Word has fallen on them, We will bring out for them from the earth a beast which will say to them that the people are uncertain of Our revelations."

The Beast, *"Al-Dabbah"*, is a great creature which Allah will cause to emerge when the people become corrupt. He will speak to mankind and exhort them, having the ability to reason and speak. He will make marks on the people's noses which will distinguish the believers from the disbelievers.

The Fire: A fire from Yemen driving people to their final gathering

The fire from Yemen is a final major sign of the end times in Islamic eschatology, described in the Hadith as emerging from the bottom of Aden. This massive blaze will emerge late in the sequence of signs, forcing humanity to move toward a final gathering place. It is a massive, intense blaze that acts as a supernatural or "gathering" fire, moving even while people sleep, forcing everyone ahead of it.

In a long narration about the signs of the Hour, the Prophet Muhammad said: "...and the last of that will be a fire which will emerge from Yemen and drive the people to their place of gathering." *Sahih Muslim (2901a).*

The Order of Events

There is little indication of the order of events in the Qur'an or in the Hadiths. Basically, there will be the minor signs, then the major signs and then the Hour will arrive. Between the minor signs and major signs, the Mahdi will arrive on the scene and set up the Islamic Kingdom. This has been the inspirational doctrine that has given such impetus to the current radical Islamic movements around the world. They are preparing the ground for the arrival of the Mahdi who will set up the next and final Caliphate when the kingdom of Islam will conquer and rule the world.

The Dajjal is among the first of the ten major signs of the Hour. He will bring in unparalleled temptation (*fitnah*) and corruption to the world. He will oppose the Mahdi. Then Jesus will come and help the Mahdi fight and kill the Dajjal. The Beast appears after the Dajjal's reign and is considered to be one of the final signs. He appears when the world is already heavily corrupted and the doors of repentance are closed.

A Hadith in Sahih Muslim mentions the signs together, but scholars note that among the ten, the rising of the sun from the west and the emergence of the Beast are often considered the last to appear.

The Description of the Hour

In Islamic belief, "the Hour" refers to the moment that is to come when every human being must face God for the final reckoning before receiving rewards or punishment. "The Hour" is mentioned 39 times in the Qur'an. This is the final Hour that follows all the minor and major signs. It is the event that the whole of history is heading towards.

It will come suddenly

Surah Al-Araf 7.187,

"They ask you ˹O Prophet˺ regarding the Hour, "When will it be?" Say, "That knowledge is only with my Lord. He alone will reveal it when the time comes. It is too tremendous for the heavens and the earth and will only take you by surprise." They ask you as if you had full knowledge of it. Say, "That knowledge is only with Allah, but most people do not know."

Its coming is only known by God

Surah Al-Azhab 33:63,

"The people ask you regarding the Hour. Say "Its knowledge is with God."

Muhammad did not know when it would come and had no knowledge to say anything about it.

Surah An-Naziat 79:42,

"They ask you (O Muhammad) about the Hour – when will be its appointed time? You have no knowledge to say anything about it. To your Lord belongs (the knowledge of) the term thereof. You are only a warner for those who fear it."

It will be marked by cataclysmic signs in the heavens and on earth

Surah At-Takwir 81:1-14,

1. When the sun is rolled up. 2. When the stars are dimmed. 3. When the mountains are set in motion. 4. When the relationships are suspended. 5. When the beasts are gathered. 6. When the oceans are set aflame. 7. When the souls are paired. 8. When the girl, buried alive, is asked: 9. For what crime was she killed? 10. When the records are made public. 11. When the sky is peeled away. 12. When the Fire is set ablaze. 13. When Paradise is brought near. 14. Each soul will know what it has readied.

Heaven and earth will shatter

Surah Al-Intifar 82:1-4,

"1. When the sky breaks apart. 2. When the planets are scattered. 3. When the oceans are exploded. 4. When the tombs are strewn around. 5. Each soul will know what it has advanced, and what it has deferred."

Earthquakes will take place, followed by judgment

Surah Al-Zalzalah 99:1-8

"When the earth is shaken with its quake. 2. And the earth brings out its loads. 3. And man says, "What is the matter with it?" 4. On that Day, it will tell its tales. 5. For your Lord will have inspired it. 6. On that Day, the people will emerge in droves, to be shown their works. 7. Whoever has done an atom's weight of good will see it. 8. And whoever has done an atom's weight of evil will see it."

The inevitable earthquake and judgement will take place

Waqiah means "the Event". This surah describes what will happen on the day of judgment and then goes on to describe in detail heaven and hell.

Surah Al-Waqiah 56:1-10,

1. When the inevitable occurs. 2. Of its occurrence, there is no denial. 3. Bringing low, raising high. 4. When the earth is shaken with a shock. 5. And the mountains are crushed and crumbled. 6. And they become scattered dust. 7. And you become three classes. 8. Those on the Right—what of those on the Right? 9. And those on the Left—what of those on the Left? 10. And the forerunners, the forerunners.

It is an hour of great shaking

Surah Al-Hajj 22.1-2,

"O humanity! Fear your Lord, for the violent quaking at the Hour is surely a dreadful thing. The Day you see it, every nursing mother will abandon what she is nursing, and every pregnant woman will deliver her burden ˹prematurely˺. And you will see people ˹as if they were˺ drunk, though they will not be drunk; but the torment of Allah is ˹terribly˺ severe."

It is a day of destruction

Surah Al-Isra 17.58,

"There is no city but We will destroy before the Day of Resurrection, or punish it with a severe punishment. This is inscribed in the Book."

It is a terrifying day for everyone

Al Anfal 8.25,

"And fear a trial which shall surely not smite in particular the evildoers among you; and know that God is terrible in retribution."

A Hadith describes the depths of the fear and terror that will effect people on that day.

"The people will sweat so profusely on the Day of Resurrection that their sweat will sink seventy cubits deep into the earth, and it will rise up till it reaches the people mouths and ears." *(Al Bukhari vol 8, 354).*

The Events of the Day

The Day of Resurrection and Judgement

The Day of Judgment (*Yawm-al-Qiyamah)* is the same day as the Day of Resurrection (*Yawm-ad-Diin*). That is the day when all human beings will be raised from their graves to face God's judgment. They will be judged according to their works. All their deeds will be put on a scale (*Al-Mizan*) and the good and the bad will be weighed against each other. They will receive their records of deeds and stand for judgment. They will be divided into two main groups: those whose good deeds outweigh the evil will enter Paradise (*Jannah*) and those whose bad deeds outweigh the good will enter Hell (*Jahannam*).

The Trumpets will blow

Surah Az-Zumar 39:68,

"And the Trumpet will be sounded, whereupon everyone in the heavens and the earth will be stunned, except whomever Allah wills. Then it will be sounded another time, whereupon they will rise up, looking on."

Surah An-Naziat 79:6-7,

"Consider the Day when the quaking Blast will come to pass, followed by a second Blast."

The Qur'an mentions the blowing of the trumpet multiple times (around 10 times), generally interpreted as two distinct events—one for death and one for resurrection. The angel, Israfil will then blow the trumpet again, and all souls will rise from their graves, marking the start of the resurrection.

The Resurrection and Gathering will occur

All humans, from the beginning of time, will be raised from their graves and assembled. It will be a time of intense fear and accountability, where people will wait, unshaded, under a sun brought close.

Surah Al-Haqqah 69:18

"That Day shall you be brought to Judgement, not a secret of yours will be hidden."

The Judgment will take place

Judgement *(Ad-Din)* means the judging and the dispensing of the reward or punishment. Allah said, (On that Day Allah will pay them the recompense (of their deeds) in full). *(An-Nur 24:25)*.

According to the Hadith, The Day of Judgement will occur on a Friday. The Prophet Muhammad mentioned:

Sahih Muslim 854,

"The best day on which the sun has risen is Friday; on it Adam was created, on it he was made to enter Paradise, on it he was expelled from it. And the last hour will take place on no day other than Friday."

The Reckoning will take place

Each individual will be held accountable for their life, specifically regarding their wealth, youth, and knowledge. They will be asked about their deeds. The Qur'an refers to the Day of Reckoning (*Yawm al-Hisab*) when Allah holds all humans accountable for their earthly deeds. Every person will receive a record of their life, with righteous souls receiving an "easy reckoning," while the unjust face a rigorous interrogation.

The Records of Deeds

Individuals will receive a book, recorded by angels, containing every action they performed. Those who receive it in their right hand will experience an easy, joyful reckoning, while those receiving it in their left hand or behind their back will face despair.

The Weighing of the Scale

Good and evil deeds will be weighed in a scale *(Al-Mizan)*. If good deeds outweigh evil, they will be rewarded; if not, they face punishment unless forgiven by God. They are scales of justice. They are set up by God.

Surah Ar-Rahman 5:7-8,

"And the sky, He raised; and He set up the balance… So do not transgress in the balance."

Surah Al-Anbiya 21:47,

"We shall set up the scales of justice for the Day of Resurrection, so no soul will be wronged in the least..."

The weighing will take place.

Surah Al-A'rāf 7:8-9,

"And the weighing [of deeds] that Day will be the truth. So those whose scales are heavy – it is they who will be the successful. And those whose scales are light – they are the ones who have lost their souls..."

There will only be two outcomes.

Surah Al-Mu'minūn 23:102-103,

"Then those whose scales are heavy [with good deeds] – it is they who are the successful. But those whose scales are light – those are they who have lost their souls..."

This is the day that all Muslims fear. It is the day when all their good deeds and their bad deeds are put in the scale to be measured, one against the other. The result, for those with scales heavy with good deeds, is a life of sensuous, blissful luxury in Heaven (*Jannah*). The result, for those whose scales are light with good deeds, is the awful terror and horror of the flames of a fiery Hell (*Jahanam*).

Surah Al Qariah means the Shocker, or the Striking Hour and describes what the day will be like.

Surah Al-Qāriah 101:6-9,

1. The Shocker.
2. What is the Shocker?
3. What will explain to you what the Shocker is?
4. The Day when the people will be like scattered moths.
5. And the mountains will be like tufted wool.
6. As for he whose scales are heavy.
7. He will be in a pleasant life.
8. But as for he whose scales are light.
9. His home is the Abyss.
10. Do you know what it is?
11. A Raging Fire.

The Crossing of the Bridge

There is a bridge over Hellfire that all must cross. It is called the *Sirat.* In the hadith it is said to be razor sharp and thinner than a hair. Every man must cross it. The righteous will cross it quickly, while those with any sin will fall or be dragged into the fire.

Final Destiny

Chapter Ten discussed the details of what the final destination, either heaven or hell, will be like. *Jannah* is heaven, the eternal abode of pleasure for the believers and the righteous. *Jahannam* is hell, the place of torment for disbelievers and those whose sins outweighed their good deeds.

Intercession

The Qur'an claims that there will be the opportunity for intercession (*Shafa'ah*), on that day. Prophet Muhammad will be allowed to intercede for believers.

Surah Ta-Ha (20:109),

"No intercession will be of any benefit with Him, except by those granted permission by Him".

Surah Al-Anbiya 21:28,

"They do not intercede except for whom He approves, and they tremble in awe of Him".

Surah Maryam 19:87,

"[on that Day] none will have [the benefit of] intercession unless he has [in his lifetime] entered into a bond with the Most Gracious."

The day is described as inevitable, just, the moment when all human actions are finalized, with God (Allah) acting as the ultimate Judge.

The Qur'an claims that it is confirming and recording what is written in the Law, the Gospels and the Psalms.

Surah Al-Anbiya 21:104,

"And (remember) the Day when We shall roll up the heaven like a scroll rolled up for books. As We began the first creation, We shall repeat it. (It is) a promise binding upon Us. Truly, We shall do it. And indeed We have written in the Psalms ([that is all the revealed Holy Books – the Taurat (Torah) the Injil (Gospel), the Psalms, the Qur'an] and after written in the Adh Dhikr [Al Lauh Al Maufuz] (the Book that is in heaven with Allah)], that My righteous slaves shall inherit the land (i.e. the land of Paradise)."

The King of the Day of Judgment

Who is the King of the Day of Judgment? Allah is Al-Malik (King or Owner). Allah is the True Owner (Malik) (of everything and everyone).

Surah Al Mumthanah 59:23,

"Allah said, "He is Allah, beside Whom *La ilaha illa Huwa,* the King, the Holy, the One free from all defects."

Both Sahih Al Bukhari and Sahih Muslim recorded Abu Hurayrah saying that the Prophet said for Allah, the most awful man, the worst person and the target of His wrath on the Day of Resurrection is the man who is called, "the King of kings".

Sahih al-Bukhari 6205,

"Allah's Messenger said, "The most awful name in Allah's sight on the Day of Resurrection, will be (that of) a man calling himself *Malik Al-Amlak* (the King of kings)".

Sahih Muslim 2143b,

"The most wretched person in the sight of Allah on the Day of Resurrection and the worst person and target of His wrath would of the person who is called *Malik al-Amlak* (the King of kings) for there is no king but Allah."

However, the Bible tells us that the most glorious One who is coming on the Day of Resurrection is the King of kings.

The book of Revelation tells us however, that it is Jesus is coming in power and glory in the clouds of heaven and He has a name written on His robe and on His thigh which is KING OF KINGS AND LORD OF LORDS. *(Revelation 19:16).* He is identified as the one coming to judge and maeke war, clothed with a robe dipped in blood and His name is called The Word of God. *(Revelation 19:11-13).*

They also recorded that the Messenger of Allah said, "On the Day of Judgement Allah will grasp the earth and fold up the heavens with His Right Hand and proclaim, 'I Am the King!"

Sahih al-Bukhari 7382, Book 97, Hadith 12,

"Narrated Abu Hurairah (Radi Allahu Anhu): The Prophet said, "On the Day of Resurrection Allah will hold the whole earth and fold the heaven with His right hand and say, 'I am the King: where are the kings of the earth?"

According to the Qur'an, there is only who is identified with the name, "The Word of God", and that is Jesus, son of Mary. He is the Word of God. King of kings.

According to the Bible, there are two armies that clash on that day. One is led by Satan, the Beast and the False Prophet. The other army is led by the King of kings. (Revelation chapters13 and 19).

Who will be King on that day?

Will it be Allah proclaiming, "I am King!" Or will it be the target of His wrath who is called, "The King of kings"?

The Warning

Surah Al-Anbiya 21:1,

"Allah said: "Closer and closer to mankind comes their Reckoning: yet they heed not and they turn away."

"The Prophet Muhammad said, "Give good tidings to those who walk to the mosques in darkness for having a perfect light on the Day of Judgment." (*Sunan Abi Dawud 561.)*

Today there are many Muslims who are walking to the mosques in darkness who need a perfect light on the day of judgment. Let us give them the good tidings of the Lord Jesus Christ. He is the King of kings. He is the Judge of all mankind.

Muslims are pointed constantly to the King of the Day of Judgment. They think of Him as being the God of Islam, far away, distant, uninvolved in their personal lives. Muslims believe the two angels are sitting on their shoulders, writing down all their good and bad deeds. Muslims believe that they will have to face the judgement, the scales, the sirat bridge across the flames of hell. They must face the day of judgment.

Muslims practice *dhikr* (remembrance of Allah) by repetitively uttering sacred phrases, names of God, or supplications, either silently or aloud to maintain conscious awareness of the Divine. Commonly practiced after daily prayers (salah), in the morning/evening, or during daily tasks, it often involves counting 33 or 99 repetitions using fingers or prayer beads (*tasbih*). This is the way that Muslims can approach God. Many do so with searching hearts. Muslims believe they can know God (Allah) through His attributes, the Qur'an, and creation. They are servants or slaves seeking to do good and serve Him and attain full submission.

They constantly seek the mercy and compassion of God. They are constantly reminded that He is the Merciful, the Compassionate. There are 114 surahs in the Qur'an. 113 of those surahs begin with the words, "In the name of God, the Merciful and Compassionate" (*Bismillah Ar-Rahman, Ar-Rahiim).*

The Gospel shows us that we can know His mercy and compassion by coming to know God personally and intimately, rather than just knowing about Him. This knowledge is made possible through Jesus Christ, who came to reveal God as Father. Jesus gives us His Holy Spirit who comes to live inside us. Through searching the scriptures, the Book, the Old and New Testaments and questioning, searching, comparing verse with verse, together with prayer, and obedience, our lives can be transformed from mere intellectual belief into an experiential relationship of knowing God. We can be born into God's family as His sons and daughters. We can be filled with His Holy Spirit who lives within us and will work within us to change us and makes us like Jesus. We can become children of God who walk with Him, and live in His presence, each day. We can be made ready for His coming, ready for His appearance as the King of kings and Lord of lords on the Day of judgment.

Both Muslims and Christians all over the world are contemplating the Last Days and the coming of Jesus to this earth.

Questions for Discussion:

1. Are we ready for the end times and the day of resurrection and judgment?
2. Are we sharing our faith with our friends and neighbours?
3. Do we want the return of Jesus in our generation?
4. Do we know what our destiny will be when we face the Day of Judgment?

DILEMMA 19

BIBLE PROPHECY DILEMMA

The Message of the Bible

God's message to mankind is love. He loved the world and gave His only Son that none should perish. *John 3:16.* That includes all the nations of the world. That includes all the people of every religion. He loves Muslims.

We attended an Easter celebration where Jeff was preaching in the city of Palu, Central Sulawesi in 2024. It was held in an outdoor stadium and about 50,000 people were present. A Muslim leader had been invited to speak and give greetings. During his message he stated, "Jesus didn't just come to save Christians. He came for Buddhists and Hindus and Muslims as well." It was a startling message! It was an amazing confession! It is the truth! Jesus came for all the peoples of the earth, of all ethnic backgrounds, of all religious heritage. Jesus came to call all people to Himself. God has a purpose for everyone on earth. He loves everyone. He loves every nation. He has an eternal plan that includes all nations. By the next day he was facing death threats being accused of blasphemy. There are many people being challenged by the age in which we live and many are seeking the certainty of salvation.

The Origin of all Prophecy is the Eternal Purpose

God's eternal purpose is to produce a people in His image and likeness, a family consisting of sons and daughters of God from every family, tribe, nation and race. God expressed that purpose when He created man.

Genesis 1:26-27.

Then God said, "Let Us make man in Our image, according to Our likeness. God blessed them and said to them, "Be fruitful and increase in number; fill the earth and subdue it. So God created man in his *own* image, in the image of God created he him; male and female created he them."

It is God's desire for the Earth to be filled with people in His image and likeness. To that end He has been working from the beginning. He has declared this to be His will. He has sent messengers to proclaim His purpose. He has raised up prophets to foretell what the future will bring. He has sent His Son to enable that purpose to be fulfilled. He has poured out His Spirit to equip men and women to work with Him towards that goal.

The First Man on the Earth

In the very beginning God created two individuals, a man and a woman, Adam and Eve. They were created in His image and likeness and placed in the Garden of Eden, *Genesis 1:26-28.*

However, the serpent entered the Garden, deceived the woman and enticed the man and the woman into rebelling against God and committing sin. When they had sinned, God came searching for them. God did not destroy them, but He provided coverings of the skin of an animal for them. He covered their sin by His own grace. He promised them that the Serpent would be trodden underfoot by the seed of the woman. This is the grand theme of the Bible! Mankind will be saved and restored back into relationship with God, and the enemy will be defeated and destroyed, *Genesis 3:1-15.*

The First Nations on the Earth

Ten generations from Adam, the earth was filled with wickedness and violence, so that God sent the flood in the days of Noah. The wicked were destroyed and the righteous who had faith, were saved. After the flood, when only eight people were saved, men began to increase in number again. Noah's three sons, Shem, Ham and Japheth became the founders of the races, *Genesis 10.* Several generations later at Babel, the different races were scattered throughout the earth and nations began to be formed, *Genesis 11.*

The Firstborn Holy Nation

Twenty generations after Adam, God chose a man to be the father of the firstborn nation Israel, *Genesis 12:3.* God promised Abraham that in him all the families of the earth would be blessed, *Genesis 22:17-18.*

Paul explains to the Galatian church how that promise was fulfilled.

Galatians 3:8,

"And the Scripture, forseeing that God would justify the Gentiles by faith, preached the Gospel to Abraham beforehand, saying, "In you all the nations shall be blessed."

Israel, the literal nation made up of the genetic descendants of Abraham, Isaac, Jacob and the twelve tribes became what God called, His "firstborn." Israel is the firstborn among the nations.

Exodus 4:22,

"And you shall say to Pharaoh, Thus. says the LORD, Israel is my son, even my firstborn."

Israel was called to be a special treasure above all people, a kingdom of priests, and an holy nation.

Exodus 19:5-6,

"Now therefore, if you will indeed obey My voice and keep My covenant, then you shall be a special treasure to Me above all people; for all the earth is Mine. And you shall be to Me a kingdom of priests and a holy nation."

Israel was chosen to be a nation where God would show His faithfulness to His covenant, as a demonstration to all the other nations of the earth of His redemptive power and to show that He keeps His word and that what He says will surely come to pass.

Deuteronomy 7:6-10,

"For you are a holy people to the Lord your God; the Lord your God has chosen you to be a people for Himself, a special treasure above all the peoples on the face of the earth. 7 The Lord did not set His love on you nor choose you because you were more in number than any other people, for you were the least of all peoples; 8 but because the Lord loves you, and because He would keep the oath which He swore to your fathers, the Lord has brought you out with a mighty hand, and redeemed you from the house of bondage, from the hand of Pharaoh king of Egypt."

Isaiah declares that Israel was formed to be a light to all the nations.

Isaiah 49:6,

"Indeed He says, It is too small a thing that You should be My Servant to raise up the tribes of Jacob, and to restore the preserved ones of Israel; I will also give You as a light to the Gentiles, that you should be My salvation to the ends of the earth.'"

The New Man

Forty-two generations after Abraham, Jesus was born. He was the seed of the woman, promised to Adam and Eve. He was the seed of Abraham, promised to bring blessing to all the nations of the world. He was the second Adam, the new man. He was the seed of David, the son of David, born to be the king of the Kingdom of God. He was born into the nation of Israel to be the light that would bless all the nations of the world. When He was eight days old, Jesus was taken to the temple and Simeon prophesied that he would be a light to lighten the Gentiles, and to be the glory of God's people Israel.

Luke 2:32,

"For my eyes have seen Your salvation, which You have prepared before the face of all peoples, a light to bring revelation to the Gentiles, and the glory of Your people Israel."

At the end of His ministry Jesus commissioned His disciples to take the Gospel to all nations, *Matthew 28:19-20; Acts1:8.* He prophesied that this Gospel of the Kingdom will be preached in all the world for a witness unto all nations; and then the end will come, *Matthew 24:14.*

The New Nation

God began to form a new nation on the day of Pentecost when the Holy Spirit was poured out on the 120 in the upper room, *Acts 2:1-4.* On that day the effects of Babel that scattered the nations began to be reversed as the Holy Spirit was poured out and the disciples began to speak in other languages. The Spirit of God began to be poured out on all peoples. A new nation was beginning to be formed.

Jesus had already announced to the scribes and Pharisees, the religious leaders of the Jews, that the kingdom of God would be taken from them and be given to a new nation.

Matthew 24:33,

"Therefore I say to you, the kingdom of God will be taken from you and given to a nation bearing the fruits of it."

Several years later at the first international church conference in Jerusalem, the disciples had begun to understand and comprehend what was happening.

Peter declared how God had used him to open the door to the Gentile nations, *Acts 15:6-11.* Paul and Barnabas testified of the signs and wonders God had performed among the Gentiles, *Acts 15:12.*

Then James explained what was happening. He declared that God was visiting the nations to take out a people for His name, the new nation of God. He declared that this was consistent with the teachings of the prophets, especially the prophet Amos, *Acts 15:13.*

Acts 15:14-17,

"After this I will return, and will build again the tabernacle of David, which is fallen down; and I will build again the ruins thereof, and I will set it up: That the residue of men might seek after the Lord, and all the Gentiles, upon whom my name is called, saith the Lord, who doeth all these things."

This was the prophecy of Amos that James declared was fulfilled in their day.

Amos 9:11-12,

"On that day I will raise up the tabernacle of David which has fallen down, and repair its damages; I will raise up his ruins, and rebuild it as in the days of old: That they may possess the remnant of Edom, and all the Gentiles, who are called by my name, says the LORD who does this thing."

The Tabernacle of David was the tent that David erected to house the ark of the Covenant, the place of the glory and presence of God, *2Samuel 6:17; 1Chronicles 15:1, and 1Chronicles 16:1.* The priests of Israel ministered in praise and worship around that tent twenty-four hours a day. The restoration of the tabernacle of David is a prophecy of the Church, the place where two or three gather in the name of the Lord Jesus Christ and He is there in the midst, *Matthew 18:15-20.* It is the place of His presence, His glory and exuberant worship in Spirit and in truth.

The Church, consisting of Jews and Gentiles, thus became the new people of God, the chosen generation, the royal priesthood, the holy nation and peculiar people, *1Peter 2:9.* Through the Church the blessing of Abraham comes on the Gentiles through Jesus Christ, *Galatians 3:14.* Jew and Gentile through faith in Christ become the one new man, the one new temple of God, *Ephesians 2:11-22.* Jew and Gentile become the one new olive tree with the same root and origins, *Romans 11.*

Thus, the prophecy of Amos is fulfilled. The Tabernacle of David is built again as a center for worship to the Lord. David had built the Tabernacle in Zion, the city of God, the city of the great King.

Jesus is the stone that the builders rejected, that has been laid in Zion, *Psalm 118:22; Matthew 21:42; Mark 12:10-11; Acts 4:11;1 Peter 2:7.*

It is there in Zion, that the Temple is built, not one made of hands, because God does not dwell in such temples, *Acts 7:48; Acts 17:24.* This Temple was far greater than the first Temple built by David and Solomon, far greater than the restored Temple built by Ezra, Nehemiah, Zerubbabel and finished by Herod. This new Temple was far greater because it is global and covering all nations!

It is the Temple of His Body, *John 2:21; 1 Corinthians 3:16–17; 1 Corinthians 6:19–20, Ephesians 2:20-22.*

The cornerstone has already been laid in Zion, *Isaiah 28:16, Romans 9:3; 1Peter 2:6.*

Jesus has already come riding into Zion heralded as King, *Matthew 21:1–11,* fulfilling the prophecy of Zechariah, *Zechariah 9:9.*

The Old Testament prophets prophesied that people of every nation and tongue will gather in Zion, the place of the ultimate Temple, built on the stone that the builders rejected, the Temple whose cornerstone has already been laid in Zion, *Isaiah 2:2-3; Micah 4:1-2; Zechariah 8:22; Isaiah 60:3,* and not made with the hands of man, *Acts 17:23-24; 2Corinthians 5:1; Hebrews 9:11; Hebrews 9:24.*

The intention of the Old Testament prophecies was not limited to physical, natural fulfillments. They have to do with the eternal purpose of God, of the gathering and building together of a company of people from all nations, who will be His dwelling place forever. Is this the true Third Temple?

All the Nations

Amos prophesied that the "Gentiles" and "all the nations" will be a people for His name. Who are the "Gentiles"? While in a broad sense "Gentiles" (Hebrew – *goyim*) means all the nations of the earth that are not Israel, in the Bible we see that very specific nations are mentioned. Let us look at these nations and their origins. Although these nations do not exist in the same way as they did in Biblical times, in the territories that they occupied we now see new nations and kingdoms that show the same spiritual DNA of those former nations.

How interesting it is that all these nations today are Islamic nations! Israel is geographically a dot surrounded by nations that are all Islamic. Some of these nations have a special place in the prophecies in the Old Testament, just as Israel has.

Many of the nations mentioned in the Bible originate from the "table of nations" which is recorded in *Genesis 10.* It is here that the nations begin to exist.

Genesis 10:5,

Of Japheth it is said, "By these were the isles of the Gentiles divided in their lands; everyone after his tongue, after their families, in their nations."

Genesis 10:20,

Of Ham it is said, "These are the sons of Ham, after their families, after their tongues, in their countries, and in their nations."

Genesis 10:31,

Of Shem it is said, "These are the sons of Shem, after their families, after their tongues, in their lands, after their nations."

Genesis 10:32.

Then we see the emphasis again: "These are the families of the sons of Noah, after their generations, in their nations: and by these were the nations divided in the earth after the flood."

Here in *Genesis 10* from this "table of nations" beginning with Noah and his three sons. There are about 70 names listed, from whom all the nations can count their ancestry as mankind spread out across the world, after the Flood.

Here is a list of some of them with their modern equivalents that exist today:

Egypt

The sons of Ham were Cush, Mizraim, Put, and Canaan, *Genesis 10:6.* Mizraim is the ancient name for Egypt. Egypt is mentioned many times in the Bible. Today the nation and people of Egypt still exist in the same territory as they did in Bible days.

Cush

Whenever Cush is mentioned it refers to the ancient area that is today occupied by Ethiopia, Eritrea, Yemen and Sudan.

Put

Put was located in the area today that is Libya in northern Africa.

Canaan

Genesis 10:15-18,

"And Canaan begat Sidon his firstborn, and Heth, And the Jebusite, and the Amorite, and the Girgasite, And the Hivite, and the Arkite, and the Sinite, And the Arvadite, and the Zemarite, and the Hamathite."

Today the people who occupy the land that was originally Canaan and claim the right to occupy it today, are called *"Palestinians"*. Although they may not be racially the same, they are certainly spiritually, the descendants of Canaan.

Babel

Genesis 10:8-10,

"And Cush begat Nimrod: … And the beginning of his kingdom… was Babel, and Erech, and Accad, and Calneh, in the land of Shinar."

Today the nations of Iraq and Syria occupy these lands.

Nineveh

Genesis 10:11.

"Out of that land went forth Asshur, and builded Nineveh."

Nineveh is situated in Iraq, near the city of Mosul, birthplace of Saddam Hussein. The kingdom of Assyria was ruled from its capital, Nineveh. Two prophets were sent with prophecies to this nation, Jonah and Nahum. After Jonah's message, Nineveh repented and was saved. Over one hundred years later, they had returned to their wickedness and God sent another prophet Nahum, who prophesied their destruction. God is looking for a people who will repent and seek Him. Opportunities are given for repentance, but if rejected, judgment and destruction will follow, as we see, happened in Nineveh.

Elam/Persia

The children of Shem, Elam, *Genesis 10:22.* The Medes are mentioned in the book of Daniel. They captured and replaced the kingdom of Babylon. It was in Persia that we read of the story of Esther. Today, the area of Elam and Persia are part of the modern nation of Iran. Many of the Iranians see themselves as Persians, direct descendants of the people in that area.

Moab and Ammon

Lot's daughters bore Moab and Ammon, the fathers of the nations of Moab and Ammon, *Genesis 19:37-38.* These two nations were often mentioned as enemies of Israel. Today, the territory, which used to be occupied by them, is ruled by the kingdom of Jordan.

Nebaioth and Kedar

Genesis 25:13,

"These are the names of the sons of Ishmael … Nebaioth; and Kedar, and Adbeel, and Mibsam." Arabs claim to be the literal descendants of Ishmael. Most Arabs today are Muslim. The Muslims also claim to be the spiritual descendants of Ishmael. In prophecy therefore, we can see Kedar and Nebaioth as representing the Muslim people who occupy the area of the Middle East.

Edom

Esau was given the name Edom. "And Esau said to Jacob, Feed me, I pray thee, with that same red pottage; for I am faint: therefore was his name called Edom," *Genesis 25:30.* The Edomites therefore are descendants of Edom. Their land is also called the land of Seir, *Genesis 32:3.* Edom are the inveterate enemies of Israel. Today this spirit of hatred for Israel and God's people can be seen in the radical Islamic terrorists that are scattered around the nations. They have the same determination to kill the people of God.

Esau/Ishmael

Genesis 28:9,

"Then went Esau unto Ishmael and took unto the wives which he had, Mahalath the daughter of Ishmael, Abraham's son, the sister of Nebaioth, to be his wife."

The joining together of the families of Ishmael and Esau produced an alliance of the physical descendants of Abraham that were left out of the Covenant promise and became bitter enemies of Israel. This combination of peoples can be seen to represent Islam in its mixture of peaceful and radical elements.

Tyre and Sidon

The cities of Tyre and Sidon were located in the area of what today is called the nation of Lebanon. These cities are also frequently referred to in the Bible and are scenes of the judgment of God.

Prophecy to the Nations

The nations mentioned above are the ones that are most frequently mentioned in the prophecies in the Bible. They are prophesied about in Isaiah, Jeremiah, Ezekiel, Amos and in the Psalms. Many of these prophecies have been literally fulfilled in history and yet still await an ultimate fulfillment at the end of this age.

As Peter said,

Acts 3:20-21,

"And he shall send Jesus Christ, which before was preached unto you: whom the heaven must receive until the times of restitution of all things, which God hath spoken by the mouth of all his holy prophets since the world began."

Because we live in these times of restitution, we need to understand not only what God is doing in the Church or in the natural nation of Israel, but also what God is doing among the nations of the earth, as prophesied by the Old Testament prophets.

The Nations will be Judged

There are many prophecies about judgment on the nations, just as there are prophecies about judgment on Israel and the Church as the people of God. David prophesied that the nations would be broken with a rod of iron.

Psalm 2:1-9,

"The kings of the earth set themselves and the rulers take counsel together against the Lord and against His anointed… Ask of Me and I will give you the nations for your inheritance… You shall break them with a rod of iron."

This prophecy was partially fulfilled in the first coming of Jesus. Peter proclaimed that it is fulfilled in the coming of Jesus as the Messiah.

Acts 4:26,

"The kings of the earth took their stand, and the rulers were gathered together against the Lord and against His Christ."

David prophesied that the rulers would stand against Him and try to destroy Him. Nevertheless, the ultimate fulfillment still awaits the end times when all nations will take their stand against Him. He has not yet broken them with a rod of iron. Meanwhile we can join Him in prayer and intercession to take the nations as our inheritance.

Psalm 83 – The Ten Nations

In *Psalm 83* there is a prophecy of ten nations coming together and uniting to attack Israel. According to Bill Salus, author of the books *"Isralestine"* and *"Revelation Road"*, the specific nations can be identified as follows:

NAME IN PSALM 83	MODERN EQUIVALENT
Tents of Edom	Palestinians & South Jordan
Ishmaelites	Saudi Arabia
Moab	Palestinians & Central Jordan
Hagarenes	Egyptians
Gebal	Hezbollah & North Lebanon
Ammon	Palestinians & North Jordan
Amalek	Sinai
Philistia	Hamas of Gaza
Tyre	Hezbollah & South Lebanon
Assyria	Syria & Northern Iraq

Some see this prophecy as a prophetic scenario showing a coalition of nations, including Jordan, Egypt, Lebanon, Syria, Iraq, Saudi Arabia and the Palestinian peoples that will join forces to attack Israel. We have already witnessed attacks from these nations on Israel.

Joel Richardson claims there are some problems with this analysis. The Hagarenes were not descendants of Hagar but a people who lived in the region of northern Jordan, east of Gilead, *1Chronicles 5:10.* Also Amalek is an area south of Hebron which is located in Israel today. Joel Richardson says that the only modern nations solidly included in *Psalm 83* are Jordan, Lebanon, Saudi Arabia and the Palestinian territories.

However we may interpret these prophecies, it is obvious today that all the areas around Israel have been conspiring to destroy her, thus fulfilling this prophecy. We saw this literally fulfilled in 1948, when after declaring independence as a state, Israel was immediately attacked the following day, 15th May 1948, by the armies of Jordan, Lebanon, Egypt, Syria and Iraq.

The Prophecies of Isaiah

There are 12 specific prophecies about the nations that are recorded by Isaiah, *Isaiah 13-23.* These prophecies are significant, as they were written down, not for the people who lived in the times they were recorded, but for those of us who live in the last days. These prophecies about the following nations included messages of judgement for sin, calls to repentance and promises for those who respond and become the people of God.

- Babylon – IRAQ *Isaiah 13–14:23*
- Assyria – ISIS *Isaiah 14:24-27*
- Filistia – PALESTINIANS *Isaiah 14:28-32*
- Moab – JORDAN *Isaiah 15–16*
- Damascus – SYRIA *Isaiah 17:1-11*
- Cush – ETHIOPIA *Isaiah 17:12 – 18:7*
- Egypt – EGYPT *Isaiah 19–20*
- Babylon – (2nd prophecy) IRAQ *Isaiah 21:1-10*
- Duma/Edom – ARABS *Isaiah 21:11-13*
- Arabia – SAUDI ARABIA *Isaiah 21:13-17*
- Jerusalem – ISRAEL *Isaiah 22*
- Tyre – LEBANON *Isaiah 23*

The Prophecies of Jeremiah

Jeremiah is specifically called "the prophet against the nations", *Jeremiah 46:1.* He prophesies against the same nations as Isaiah, *Jeremiah 46-51.*

- Egypt – EGYPT *Jeremiah 46*
- Philistia – PALESTINIANS *Jeremiah 47*
- Moab – JORDAN *Jeremiah 48*
- Ammon – JORDAN *Jeremiah 49:1-22*
- Damascus – SYRIA *Jeremiah 49:23-33*
- Elam – IRAN *Jeremiah 49:34-39*

• Babylon	– IRAQ	*Jeremiah 50–51*

The Prophecies of Ezekiel

Ezekiel also prophesies against the nations., *Ezekiel 25-31.* He gives very clear reasons for the declaration of judgment against them.

• Ammon	– JORDAN	Ezekiel 25:1-7
• Moab	– JORDAN	Ezekiel 25:8-11
• Edom	– ARABS	Ezekiel 25:12-14
• Philistia	– PALESTINIANS	Ezekiel 25:13-17
• Tyre	– LEBANON	Ezekiel 26-28
• Egypt	– EGYPT	Ezekiel 29-31

Terrorist Nations

In *Ezekiel 32:18-30,* there is a specific identification of "the Nations that cause terror in the land of the living." All of these nations today are the source and key origin of the Islamic terrorism that is threatening all the nations of the earth.

• Egypt	– EGYPT.
• Assyria	– SYRIA, IRAQ.
• Elam	– IRAN.
• Meshech & Tubal	– TURKEY.
• Edom	– ARABS.
• Sidonians	– LEBANON.

The Prophecy of Habakkuk

Habakkuk specifically sees the rise of Babylon.

Habakkuk 1:5-6.

"Look among the nations and watch – Be utterly astounded! For I will work a work in your days, which you would not believe, though it were told you. For indeed I am raising up the Chaldeans…"

Perhaps the most astounding event we have been witnessing in the last 50 years is the rapid rise of Islamic terrorism.

The Prophecy of Obadiah

The short one-chapter prophecy of Obadiah is a prophecy against the people of Edom.

Obadiah 1:1,

"We have heard a report from the Lord and a messenger has been sent among the nations saying, "Arise and let us rise up against her for battle."

Perhaps we can hear the calling of God today to rise up against the "Edomites" who have attacked the people of God. Perhaps we can hear the call for saviours to come up on Mount Zion, to preach the Gospel to Edom so that "the kingdom will be the Lord's", *Obadiah 1:21.* This is a prophecy to be fulfilled in the Day of the Lord.

The Prophecy of Nahum

The prophecy against Nineveh is mainly one of judgment. Nineveh had repented at the preaching of Jonah but about a hundred years later they had returned to their sins and Nahum was called to prophecy Nineveh's sudden and tragic destruction.

This was literally fulfilled in 612 BC, and until the 19th century Nineveh lay in ruins, hidden from sight, so that some believed the city was merely mythical. Yet could this prophecy not have a further fulfilment?

Nahum 1-2,

"A wicked counsellor rises", 1:11; "his images fall", 1:14; "the chariots rage", 2:4; "run like lightning" 2:4; "the gates of the rivers are opened", 2:6; "the palace is dissolved", 2:6; "spoil is taken, 2:9; "the old lion hides in his dens", 2:11-12."

Indeed, the short three chapters pf Nahum have amazing parallels with the 2003 war against Iraq. Maybe they also hold prophetic words against the modern Assyria, with ISIS? In April 2016 it was reported that the Mashqi Gate, one of a number of grand gates, which guarded the ancient Assyrian city of Nineveh, was destroyed by ISIS. ISIS was taking the territory of the old kingdom of Assyria. Today, ISIS has been all but wiped out but its spirit still survives.

The Nations will be Delivered

Not only are there prophecies of judgment against the nations, there are also promises of salvation and redemption. The basis of all these promises lies in the Abrahamic Covenant. God promised to Abraham, "In you shall all families of the earth be blessed", *Genesis 12:3.* This promise was also confirmed to Jacob, *Genesis 28:14.* Today, we are seeing this promise fulfilled as the Gospel of Jesus Christ is being preached to all nations, all tribes, all families.

In fact, there are special promises made to the descendants of Hagar and Ishmael, even though they are not included in the Abrahamic Covenant.

Twice God gives promises directly to Hagar, ***Genesis 16:9-15,***

"I will multiply your descendants."

Of Ishmael when he is cast out, God says to her, "I will make him a great nation," *Genesis 21:18.*

God also promises to Abraham, Behold, I have blessed him, and will make him fruitful, and will multiply him exceedingly. He shall beget twelve princes, and I will make him a great nation," *Genesis 17:20; 21:13,*

The literal fulfillment of this promise we can see in the Arab peoples. Though today they may form a number of different political states, nevertheless Arabs today see themselves as one nation, the Arab nation. The Spirit of God is beginning to work in the Arab nations causing a great turning to the Lord.

Nations will be Born Again

God does not only have plans and prophecies for the nation of Israel. He has planned for all the nations of the earth. In heaven gathered around the throne are people from every tribe and people, every language and nation. The plan and purpose began with the firstborn nation, Israel, but continues to gather in people from all the other nations who will listen to God's voice and turn to Him in repentance and faith. The Psalmist refers to those from other nations who will become part of the people of God.

Psalm 87:1-7,

"I will make mention of Rahab and Babylon to them that know me: behold Philistia, and Tyre, with Ethiopia; this man was born there. And of Zion it shall be said, This and that man was born in her: and the highest himself shall establish her."

The peoples mentioned here are Rahab (Egypt), Babylon (Iraq), Philistia (Palestinians), Tyre (Lebanon), Ethiopia (Sudan/Ethiopia/Yemen). This Psalm shows that members of these people will also be born in Zion, the city of God. They will be born again and become no longer strangers, Gentiles, but members of God's holy nation. They will become citizens of the heavenly Zion.

Hebrews 12:22,

"But you have come to Mount Zion and to the city of the living God, the heavenly Jerusalem, to an innumerable company of angels."

The New Testament Church was composed of Jews first, then Greeks and then people from many different nations who were joined together in our Lord Jesus Christ to become one people, called out of darkness into His marvelous light, called out of the kingdom of Satan into the Kingdom of His dear Son.

Nations will be saved

God specifically prophesies of Assyria, Egypt and Israel.

Isaiah 19:18-25,

"In that day ... He will send them a Savior and a Mighty one and he will deliver them... The LORD of hosts shall bless, saying, Blessed be Egypt my people, and Assyria the work of my hands, and Israel mine inheritance."

Middle-East Nations will be United

The prophets also declare that there shall be a highway from Assyria to Israel. The nations which travel on that highway will become one people.

Isaiah 11:16,

"And there shall be a highway for the remnant of his people, which shall be left, from Assyria; like as it was to Israel in the day that he came up out of the land of Egypt."

Nations will Worship the LORD (YHWH) together

There will be a gathering of all nations to worship the LORD. People will come from Assyria and from Egypt.

Isaiah 27:13,

"And it shall come to pass in that day, that the great trumpet shall be blown, and they shall come which were ready to perish in the land of

Assyria, and the outcasts in the land of Egypt, and shall worship the LORD (YHWH) in the holy mount at Jerusalem,"

Nations will Sing and Praise the LORD together

Not only those of Israel will praise the LORD (YHWH). Arabs, the people of Kedar (Saudi Arabia), will also join in praise and worship.

Isaiah 42:11,

"Let the wilderness and the cities thereof lift up their voice, the villages that Kedar doth inhabit: let the inhabitants of the rock sing, let them shout from the top of the mountains."

Nations will Minister unto the LORD together

When darkness covers the earth and God's people rise and shine with His glory, the nations will come to that light. Multitudes from all over the Arab world will come and proclaim the praises of the LORD. It is specifically when this prophecy is fulfilled that the house of God, the Church of our Lord Jesus Christ will become the "house of My Glory".

Isaiah 60:7,

"All the flocks of Kedar shall be gathered together unto thee, the rams of Nebaioth shall minister unto thee: they shall come up with acceptance on mine altar, and I will glorify the house of My glory."

Nations will Bow Down to the LORD together

The word of the Lord declares that the peoples of all nations will bow down before Him and confess that Jesus Christ is the Lord. They will confess that He is the Son of God. This is prophesied in the Old Testament:

Isaiah 45:23,

"I have sworn to Myself, The Word has gone out of My mouth in righteousness, and shall not return, that to Me every knee shall bow, every tongue shall take an oath."

It is proclaimed in the New Testament:

Philippians 2:10-11,

"That at the name of Jesus every knee should bow, of those in heaven, and of those on earth, and of those under the earth, and that every tongue should confess that Jesus Christ is Lord, to the glory of God the Father."

Romans 14:11,

"For it is written: As I live, says the Lord, every tongue shall confess to God."

Thus, the day will surely come when every knee will bow and every tongue will proclaim that Jesus Christ is Lord!

Therefore, we see that in the last days, in the midst of horrific judgments being poured out amongst the nations, both from among the representative nations of the Middle East which are specifically mentioned in the prophecies of the Bible, plus from all the nations throughout the whole world, God is going to bring out a people for Himself.

From among these nations, both in the Middle East and all throughout the earth, there will be multitudes of people who are:

* Born Again!
* United!
* Saved!
* Worshipping!
* Singing and Praising!
* Serving!
* Bowing down!
* IN CHRIST!!

Read the awesome prophesy of ***Revelation 5:9,***

"And they (the redeemed of all time) sang a new song, saying: "You are worthy to take the scroll, and to open its seals; For You were slain, and have redeemed us to God by Your blood out of **every tribe** and **tongue** and **people** and **nation**."

Revelation 7:9-10,

"After these things I looked, and behold, **a great multitude which no one could number, of all nations, tribes, peoples, and tongues,** standing before the throne and before the Lamb, clothed with white robes, with palm branches in their hands, and crying out with a loud voice, saying, "Salvation belongs to our God who sits on the throne, and to the Lamb!"

Joel 3:13-14,

"Put in the sickle, for the harvest is ripe. Come, go down; for the winepress is full, The vats overflow—For their wickedness is great.: Multitudes, multitudes in the valley of decision! For the day of the LORD is near in the valley of decision."

Multitudes are going to be in the great End Time ingathering from all the nations of the world. Are we ready for it? Are we preparing for it? Do we have a heart and a vision for it? There is great judgement coming and people must decide. Who is on the Lord's side? Who will serve the King? Eternal destinations are at stake; and you and I are God's chosen vessels to be alive at this time. The harvest separates the good and the evil. And the wheat from the chaff.

There will truly be a great multitude of fish.

John 21:6,

"He (Jesus) said to them, "Cast the net on the right side of the boat, and you will find some." So they cast, and now they were not able to draw it in because of ***the multitude of fish***." Multitudes in the Valley of Decision!

Matthew 13:47-50,

"The kingdom of heaven is like a dragnet that was cast into the sea and gathered ***some of every kind,*** which, when it was full, they drew to shore; and they sat down and **gathered the good into vessels**, but **threw the bad away**. **So it will be at the end of the age.** The angels will come forth, separate the wicked from among the just, and cast them into the furnace of fire. There will be wailing and gnashing of teeth."

The harvest has a two-edged sword! The Valley of Decision is all around us. Help your neighbour, your family, friends, community to make the right decision. These are the days of Noah and we need to urge people to come into the Ark. Time is short. Eternity is at stake!

The Words of Jesus will be fulfilled

When we see this happening, we will know that the end is near.

Matthew 24:14,

"And this Gospel of the kingdom shall be preached in all the world, for a witness unto all nations; and then the end shall come."

The words of the Prophets will be fulfilled

When we see these things happening, we will know that the words of the prophets are being fulfilled and Jesus Christ will soon be returning.

Acts 3:20-21,

"And he shall send Jesus Christ … Whom the heaven must receive (retain) until the times of restitution of all things, which God has spoken by the mouth of all his holy prophets since the world began."

The Eternal Purpose will be Fulfilled

When we see these things happening on earth, we will know that the will of the Father, the eternal purpose of God is being fulfilled. For His will surely will be done on earth as in heaven, His kingdom will be coming on earth and there will be a people formed for Himself out of every tribe and tongue and people and nation. They will sing with triumph.

This will be the song of people from all over the earth, including the Arabs and the Israelis, including those from Muslim backgrounds who have received Christ, from every nation. God has an eternal purpose, and His purpose will come to pass on the earth!

What is our vision?

What is our hope?

Are we willing to go and preach the Gospel to the nations?

Great and mighty things are about to break out on the earth, and the people of God must be ready. We must believe the prophetic word of Scripture. We need to be equipped. We need the full anointing of the Holy Spirit, *Acts 1:8*. We need the courage to take up the Cross and follow Christ, *Matthew 16:24*. The end is near, but our work is not finished!

QUESTIONS FOR DISCUSSION

1. In the past, how accurate has the Bible been in prophesying the future? Has anything changed?
2. Which prophecies in the Bible do you see as the most important and relevant for Christians today?
3. What do you believe the Bible reveals should be our main priorities in these Last Days and why do you believe that? Be specific.
4. Discuss which should come first and why? The Rapture? The finishing of the Great Commission? Global revival? Escaping the Antichrist and the Great Tribulation?

DILEMMA 20

EFFECTIVE WITNESSING DILEMMA

Introducing Ishmael to God the Father

Today, there are over 2 billion Muslims who are lost, fatherless, cast out, humiliated, rejected, hurting, and lashing out. Our dilemma is to know how we can hear and respond to their cry. Ishmael seeks to please God and earn respect before God as a servant-slave by giving absolute submission to God and earning acceptance through good works. Their cry is never satisfied. They don't understand that good works can never be good enough. They are thirsty, but they cannot see the well of water. They have no father to give them bread. They are wandering, restless, searching. Will you show them the way to the water? Will you help them find the bread? Our dilemma is to learn how we can do this.

Basic steps you can take to reach Ishmael

1. Believe God's Word about Ishmael

Do not reject or abandon Ishmael! God didn't and He has a specific purpose for the descendants of Ishmael.

Habakkuk 2:3,

"For the vision is yet for an appointed time; But at the end it will speak, and it will not lie. Though it tarries, wait for it; Because it will surely come, It will not tarry."

Ezekiel 12:22-23,

"Son of man, what is this proverb you have in the land of Israel: 'The days go by and every vision comes to nothing'? Say to them, "This is what the Sovereign LORD says: I am going to put an end to this proverb, and they will no longer quote it in Israel." Say to them, "The days are near when every vision will be fulfilled."

This applies to Israel and also to the nations of the world. God has a plan. He has a vision. And He wants us to be His instruments to fulfil it. That was made clear in the Great Commission verses – *Matthew 28:18-20; Mark 16:15-20; Luke 24:47; John 20:21; Acts 1:8; Acts 26:17-18.*

Acts 3:19-21,

"Repent, then, and turn to God, so that your sins may be wiped out, that times of refreshing may come from the Lord, and that he may send the Christ, who has been appointed for you - even Jesus. He must remain in heaven until the time comes for God to restore everything, as he promised long ago through his holy prophets."

Do not abandon Ishmael! God has a specific purpose for the descendants of Ishmael. Believe God's Word to fulfill His promises about Ishmael and his descendants!

Ishmael was promised great blessing. Why?

Genesis 17:20,

"And as for Ishmael, I have heard you. Behold, I have blessed him, and will make him fruitful, and will multiply him exceedingly. He shall beget twelve princes, and I will make him a great nation."

Notice again some points in Isaiah 60:5-6,

(5) "… the abundance of the sea shall be turned to you, the wealth of the Gentiles shall come to you."

(6) "… They shall bring gold and incense, And they shall proclaim the praises of the LORD."

All this from Ishmael! It seems they may help fund global evangelism!

End-Time Middle-East Revival – 3 nations – Assyria – Israel – Egypt

Isaiah 19:22-25,

"And the LORD will strike Egypt, He will strike and heal it; they will return to the LORD, and He will be entreated by them and heal them. In that day there will be a highway from Egypt to Assyria, and the Assyrian will come into Egypt and the Egyptian into Assyria, and the Egyptians will serve with the Assyrians. In that day Israel will be one of three with Egypt and Assyria—a blessing in the midst of the land, whom the LORD of hosts shall bless, saying, "Blessed is Egypt My people, and Assyria the work of My hands, and Israel My inheritance."

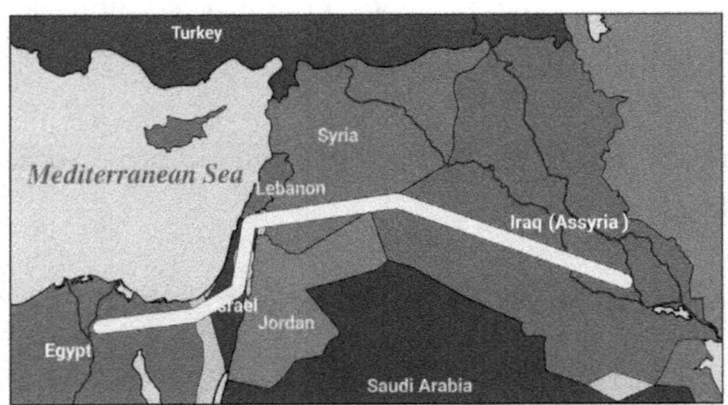

A highway from Egypt through Israel to Assyria (Iraq) - Isa 19:23

Revival is coming to the Middle East

There will be a great and absolutely amazing revival in all the world. It will be in every nation, including in the Middle East – Arabs and Israelis. Some key scriptures: *Isaiah 2:1-3; 19:19-25; 60:1-22; Amos 9:8-15; Matthew 13:36-43; 23:39; Revelation 5:9-10; 7:1-17.* Even Saudi Arabia and Yemen will turn to the Lord, *Isaiah 60:6-7.*

2. We need to love Ishmael like Jesus loves them – unconditionally

John 3:16,

"For God so loved **the world** that He gave His only begotten Son, that whoever believes in Him should not perish but have everlasting life."

That includes Arabs! They were there on the Day of Pentecost too!

Acts 2:9-11,

"How is it that we hear, each in our own language in which we were born? Parthians and Medes and Elamites, those dwelling in Mesopotamia, Judea and Cappadocia, Pontus and Asia, Phrygia and Pamphylia, Egypt and the parts of Libya adjoining Cyrene, visitors from Rome, both Jews and proselytes, Cretans **and Arabs** - we hear them speaking in our own tongues the wonderful works of God."

What is our heart for the lost of Ishmael?

1Corinthians 9:19-21,

"Though I am free and belong to no man, I make myself a slave to everyone, to win as many as possible. To the Jews I became like a Jew, to win the Jews... To those not having the law I became like one not having the law … so as to win those not having the law. To the weak I became weak, to win the weak. **I have become all things to all men so that by all possible means I might save some."**

Remember the story of Jonah and the cry of Nineveh! Jonah didn't believe they were worthy to be saved. He wanted them wiped out. Are we any different in our heart attitude towards Ishmael?

Jonah 4:10-11,

"But the LORD said, "You have been concerned about this vine, though you did not tend it or make it grow. It sprang up overnight and died overnight. But Nineveh has more than a hundred and twenty thousand people who cannot tell their right hand from their left, and many cattle as well. Should I not be concerned about that great city?"

3. Be an open book – a living letter

This is the living expression of our faith, hope and love outworked in our daily lives. This is OUR PERSONAL TESTIMONY. Don't bring them the message in 'the' Book unless first they can read the message in the Book of your life! Tell your personal story! Tell them how you have experienced the transforming power of Christ's love.

Psalm 107:2 (NIV),

"Let the redeemed of the LORD tell their story, those he redeemed from the hand of the foe."

1Peter 2:9,

"that you may declare the praises of him who called you out of darkness into his wonderful light."

2Corinthians 3:2-3,

"You yourselves are our letter, written on our hearts, known and read by everyone.

You show that you are a letter from Christ, the result of our ministry, written not with ink but with the Spirit of the living God, not on tablets of stone but on tablets of human hearts."

4. A Vital Key in Breaking through the barriers is Intercession

Every year in Indonesia churches and ministries have 40 day fasts around Ramadan! And there are awesome results! As priests we need to bring people to Christ in prayer before we bring Christ to them! On one occasion during the fast, Jesus appeared to a group of Muslims in a mosque in Gorontalo, North Sulawesi. Jesus urged them to accept the Gospel, to believe in Him and be baptized. These shocked men walked down the street to the nearest Church. They went in, told the pastor what Jesus had said. The frightened, and very suspicious pastor said that Jesus must have meant the next church down the road. The same thing happened. The churches were afraid that this might be a deception which would result in their church being attacked. Eventually they fell into our hands. For their protection we took them to Rantepau in Toraja, South Sulawesi where they were mentored in Christ.

1Peter 2:9, "You are a chosen people, a royal priesthood."

2Corinthians 5:18, Jesus has given us, "the ministry of reconciliation."

A woman giving birth must PUSH. Do you want to see Muslims born into the Kingdom of God? Do you P.U.S.H? **P**ray-**U**ntil-**S**omething-**H**appens. Our God is a God of miracles and we need to believe Him, and we need to be willing to pay the price.

Look at the amazing prophecy in Isaiah. There is going to be a great revival in the nations!

Isaiah 66:6-8,

"Hear that uproar from the city, hear that noise from the temple! It is the sound of the LORD repaying his enemies all they deserve. "Before she goes into labor, she gives birth; before the pains come upon her, she delivers a son. Who has ever heard of such a thing? Who has ever seen such things? Can a country be born in a day or a nation be brought forth in a moment? Yet no sooner is Zion in labor than she gives birth to her children."

James 5:16, "The prayer of a righteous man is powerful and effective."

Prayer is not a religious ritual, it is a power encounter with the living God. When people pray, things happen! Prayer can change the destiny of people and nations! Walter Wink said, "History belongs to the intercessors", *Walter Wink (2010). "The Powers That Be: Theology for a New Millennium", p.187, Harmony.* Wink emphasized that through believing prayer and intercession we bring the future into being. We need to believe like this for Ishmael.

Through prayer, identify the most effective breakthrough gates!

Keys are for Doors and Gates. Identify the Gates to the person or community you are wanting to reach. Take the authority of the Keys and open the Door!

Matthew 16:19,

"I will give you the keys of the kingdom of heaven; whatever you bind on earth will be bound in heaven, and whatever you loose on earth will be loosed in heaven."

Genesis 22:17; and 24:60,

The promise to Abraham's seed – "You shall possess the gates of your enemies."

See the examples of *Jacob – Genesis 28:11-19; Mordechai – Esther 5-6; Boaz – Ruth 4:1-11; Daniel – Dan.2:49.* Jesus has the keys and He is giving them to us! Use them!

There are many gates!

The economic gate, religious gate, political gate, education gate, military gate, entertainment gate, mercy gate, healing gate, sports gate, religious gate etc. Possess the gates and possess the land! Open the gates – we have the keys!

God's heart cry in Ezekiel highlights the spiritually crippled nature of many churches and church leaders. The city is under attack from the powers of darkness. Satan and his hordes can freely enter and exit through wide open gates. God places an advertisement in the Bible – for "someone" who loves their city and nation enough to stand in the gap. Who applied for the position? No one! How tragic!

Ezekiel 22:30,

"I looked for someone among them who would build up the wall and stand before me in the gap on behalf of the land so I would not have to destroy it, but I found no one."

So sad – Christians not willing to respond. What about you? Are you willing to rerspond?

Will you be the one to respond to God's call, God's advertisement? It's like the call to Isaiah in ***Isaiah 6:8,***

"Whom shall I send? And who will go for us?"

Who has a heart for Ishmael. They are crying, hungry and thirsty. Will you respond to the Lord and say, "Here am I. Send me!"

Identify the gates of Ishmael and Esau – two different spirits!

Ishmael has the cry for a father's acceptance – it's a seeking spirit. Esau has the cry of hatred – it's a spirit of revenge. These 2 spirits exist within Islam today – that's why we need intercession with discernment. *Ephesians 6:12; 2Corinthians 10:4-5*

5. Dependency on the Holy Spirit is a vital Breakthrough Key

John 16:13-14,

"But when he, the Spirit of truth, comes, he will guide you into all truth. He will not speak on his own; he will speak only what he hears, and he will tell you what is yet to come. He will bring glory to me by taking from what is mine and making it known to you."

Matthew 10:19-20,

"When they arrest you, do not worry about what to say or how to say it. At that time you will be given what to say, for it will not be you speaking, but the Spirit of your Father speaking through you."

Luke 12:11-12,

"When you are brought before synagogues, rulers and authorities, do not worry about how you will defend yourselves or what you will say, for the Holy Spirit will teach you at that time what you should say."

It's a *kairos* time!

A moment in time where heaven's grace touches human events giving a special opportunity to change destiny and seize the day!

Ephesians 5:16, "making the most of every *kairos* (opportunity)."

Colossians 4:5, "Be wise in the way you act toward outsiders; making the most of every *kairos* (opportunity)."

Some Kairos moments in History:

- Kublai Khan and Marco Polo and his brothers – C12th
- Korea – 1900 – 1980. From 1% to 35%
- Japan and General MacArthur – 1945
- Growth of believers in Indonesia – 1965-2026

  1945 – 3.9%

  1965 – 4.8%

  1974 – 8.7%

2026 – 18%

Use God's kairos moments!

- *Kairos* moments can be created by God's Sovereignty
- *Kairos* moments can be created by our faith responses to God's Covenant promises
- *Kairos* moments can be created by natural phenomena – tsunamis, earthquakes etc

6. Walk with Ishmael as a fellow journeyman

It's not a contest! It's not a debate! It's a journey where we walk with seekers of truth and help them discover the answers for themselves. Get them to ask questions! Help them find the way. And give them the dignity to make their own choices.

1Peter 3:15-16,

"in your hearts revere Christ as Lord. Always be prepared to give an answer to everyone who asks you to give the reason for the hope that you have. But do this with gentleness and respect, keeping a clear conscience, so that those who speak maliciously against your good behaviour in Christ may be ashamed of their slander."

We want revelation to touch their hearts not just to win an argument. Sow seeds by faith, love and the anointing of the Holy Spirit.

1Corinthians 2:4-5,

"My message and my preaching were not with wise and persuasive words, but with a demonstration of the Spirit's power, so that your faith might not rest on human wisdom, but on God's power."

2Corinthians 3:5-6,

"Not that we are competent in ourselves to claim anything for ourselves, but our competence comes from God. He has made us competent as ministers of a new covenant—not of the letter but of the Spirit; for the letter kills, but the Spirit gives life."

Proverbs 15:1-2(NIV),

"A soft answer turns away wrath, But a harsh word stirs up anger. The tongue of the wise uses knowledge rightly."

1Kings 12:7,

"If today you will be a servant to these people and serve them and give them a favorable answer, they will always be your servants."

Jeremiah 33:3,

"Call to me and I will answer you and tell you great and unsearchable things you do not know."

His wisdom is always available to you when you share Christ with others with a loving heart. Do not be afraid. Do not let the "Esau spirit" keep you from the joy of bringing a precious person into the fellowship of the Kingdom of God.

Proverbs 11:30,

"The fruit of the righteous is a tree of life, and he who wins souls is wise."

7. Effective Evangelism demands Unity in the Body of Christ

Evangelism is not haphazard. It takes prayer and planning. We could call it "prayerperation"! We also need to understand that it is not just "a me and Jesus thing!" It's a Body of Christ goal. The unity of the Body of Christ is imperative in presenting an effective witness. Disunity and division are the killers of successful evangelism.

We saw this in Indonesia. In the town of Tentena, Central Sulawesi in 1974, a military officer committed suicide. He was a Javanese Muslim. His wife had become a Christian. He knew this would cause problems in his family when they returned to Java. He went to two different churches to ask them what was necessary for him to become a Christian. One pastor told him that he would have to be baptized (by sprinkling), learn certain key beliefs and he would become a Christian. He asked about the other Church at the other end of town and was informed, "Don't go there they are a false Church." He went anyway.

At the second Church he asked the same questions about becoming a Christian. The pastor told him that he would have to repent of his sins, accept Jesus as His Lord and Saviour and be baptized (by immersion). When he asked about the other Church at the other end of town, the pastor said, "Don't go there, they are a dead Church."

In his agitated and confused state, he went home and wrote a note to his wife and then committed suicide.

What a tragedy, but I learned quickly that division in the Body of Christ is a great hindrance to evangelism. Instead of sowing seeds of love and faith, we sow seeds of division and confusion. As believers in the Body of Christ we need to repent and come in full surrender to Christ. Too many Muslims are confused by our divisions.

What did Jesus teach us that will convince unbelievers of the truth of Christ's transformative love? We need a love that lives! Jesus taught us to love.

John 13:34-35,

"A new commandment I give to you, that you love one another; as I have loved you, that you also love one another. By this **all will know** that you are My disciples, if you have love for one another."

Jesus amplified this message in His powerful statement in His prayer to the Father.

John 17:20-23,

"I do not pray for these alone, but also for those who will believe in Me through their word; that they all may be one, as You, Father, are in Me, and I in You; that they also may be one in Us, **that the world may believe** that You sent Me. And the glory which You gave Me I have given them, **that they may be one just as We are one**: I in them, and You in Me; that they may be made perfect in one, and **that the world may know** that You have sent Me, and have loved them as You have loved Me."

Jesus prayed for a unity of the same quality that exists between the Father and the Son. People may say that's impossible. In our ability? Absolutely true, but our God is a specialist in impossibilities. If we are true disciples of Jesus, then this is our faith, Nothing is impossible to Him.

Luke 1:37,

"With God nothing will be impossible."

Matthew 17:20,

"Assuredly, I say to you, if you have faith as a mustard seed, you will say to this mountain, 'Move from here to there,' and it will move; and nothing will be impossible for you."

The Father is not on a pension. Jesus has not retired. The Holy Spirit is not in a wheel chair! God has not changed. His power has not changed. His vision and message has not changed. So, what has changed? Could it be us?

Have we become crippled by fear? Are we afraid of being called "bad names"? Have we lost our faith and just want to protect our reputations?

Brothers and sisters, these are the End Times and we are the instruments that God has placed in the world for such a time as this. If we don't step up, who will?

Luke 18:8,

"When the Son of Man comes, will He really find faith on the earth?"

We cannot rely on the United Nations or global Government policies and programs. No! It is the Church, the Body of Christ that is being called to mobilize in the power of the Father's wisdom, the love of our Lord Jesus Christ and in the *dunamis* anointing power of the Holy Spirit!

If the Gospel is true – Prove it! Preach it! Demonstrate it! Eternity is waiting! The heroes of the faith in *Hebrews 11* are waiting for it! They are cheering us on in the grandstands of history in *Hebrews 12.* What will be your response? What will be our response?

8. Be the Salt of the Earth!

Understand the nature of salt and learn to be an effective witness for Christ.

Salt has many characteristics which are discussed in the Bible. Salt reveals the character of God's love.

Leviticus 2:13 – worship is unacceptable without salt. Compare *1John 4:20-21.*

Job 6:6 – Salt makes food taste good. Asian pineapples can be very acidic and sour, but when washed in salt become sweet and delicious. Is our testimony the non-salted version or the sweet salty version? Compare *Psalm 34:8.*

2Kings 2:18-22 – Salt heals – physically. The salt of His love heals spiritually. There are many wounded who need healing. Compare *Mark 9:50;*

Colossians 4:5-6 – Salt helps create *kairos* opportunities and gives us wisdom to answer the questions of those who are seeking. Compare a few verses where the Greek word *kairos* is used to indicate a special opportunity, an opportune moment - *Mark 1:15; Luke 19:44; Galatians 6:10; Ephesians 5:16 etc*

There are many other characteristics of salt and they point to how we can be an effective witness for Christ. Jesus said that if we lose our saltiness then we are no longer useful for the Master's service – *Matthew 5:13.*

Salt breaks through metallic objects, it creates thirst, it is used to channel life-giving electricity through defibrillators and is a powerful preservative. We can all do with a bit more of His salt.

9. Demonstrate God's power with signs and wonders.

Elijah was never going to win Israel back to God by powerful arguments. It took a demonstration of God's miraculous power. *1Kings 18:17-39.*

We need to exercise spiritual gifts *(1Cor.12:7-11; 14:1)*. This is what the Gifts are for! It was the demonstration of His Almighty power.

- That's how Paul won Corinth – *1Corinthians 2:1-5*
- That's how Ephesus was won – *Acts 19:11-20*. Read John's amazing victory recorded in history! Ramsay MacMullen, "*The Christianizing of the Roman Empire*"
- Many MBBs share how Christ came to them or they had a vision or there was a healing etc. Demonstrate His power by interpreting dreams and visions and praying for them when they are sick. Many Muslims have dreams and visions because Jesus is trying to reach their hearts. God will give you His wisdom to interpret the dreams and this will reach right into their spirits.
- See the example of Joseph: The cupbearer and the baker. *Genesis 40:7-23*

Genesis 40:7-8, "Why are your faces so sad today?" "We both had dreams," they answered, "but there is no one to interpret them." Then Joseph said to them, "Do not interpretations belong to God? Tell me your dreams."

Why not ask your Muslim friend what dreams he or she has had lately. Ask if they are causing any concern? Would they like to know what they mean? Offer to pray about the dream and to bring them the interpretation. What? Why not? Let's step out in faith, like Joseph, like Daniel, and see this powerful gift impact the lives of our Muslim friends.

- Another example is Daniel, a man filled with the Holy Spirit.

Daniel 2:22-24,

"He reveals deep and hidden things; he knows what lies in darkness, and light dwells with him. I thank and praise you, O God … You have given me wisdom and power, you have made known to me what we asked of you, you have made known to us the dream of the king." … "Take me to the king, and I will interpret his dream for him."

Daniel 4:8-9,

"But at last Daniel came before me – Nebuchadnezzar - (his name is Belteshazzar, according to the name of my god; in him is the Spirit of the Holy God), and I told the dream before him, saying: "Belteshazzar, chief of the magicians, because I know that the Spirit of the Holy God is in you, and no secret troubles you, explain to me the visions of my dream that I have seen, and its interpretation."

- What about our generation?

Acts 2:17,

"In the last days, God says, I will pour out my Spirit on all people. Your sons and daughters will prophesy, your young men will see visions, your old men will dream dreams."

Now, it's time for us, His Church, to exercise His dynamic power. That's why you were filled with the Spirit – to be His dynamic witnesses, *Acts 1:8.*

We had groups of Iranian and Afghani refugees, who in the past had been under the dominion of the strong man, but we knew the power of the stronger man, Jesus, and He wanted to set them free.

Luke 11:21-22,

"When a strong man (Satan and his servants), fully armed, guards his own palace, his goods are in peace. But when a stronger (Jesus and his people) than he comes upon him and overcomes him, he takes from him all his armour in which he trusted, and divides his spoils."

Today we are facing the globalized strong man's house and he is holding many captives. They are imprisoned in darkness and we are being called to set them free and bring them into the light of God's salvation.

Matthew 12:29,

"How can one enter a strong man's house and plunder his goods, unless he first binds the strong man? And then he will plunder his house."

Reinhard Bonke preached a passionate message focused on saving souls from eternal damnation and bringing them to salvation through Jesus. He declared: "We must plunder hell and populate heaven!"

Our Iranian and Afghani refugees were crowding into our apartment in Kelapa Gading, North Jakarta, to have discussions. These were all Muslims who had never been exposed to the Gospel. They were hungry. Some wanted to know more. Some wanted to trap us and prove that Christianity was false. After many of them came to believe that Jesus truly was the Straight Path and only Way to salvation, on the first occasion of a baptism service for them, more that 50 were baptized. In the years that followed many more were set free to find faith in Christ and many have become evangelists in Australia, Canada, the USA, back in Iran and in several parts of Indonesia.

There is a global war to win the hearts of mankind

We are witnessing a spiritual war and many who are finding Christ are being transformed into radical, loving, passionate disciples for Christ.

Islam divides the world into two Houses:

(a) **The House of Peace – Dar al-Salaam –** lands under total Islamic control with Sharia law. Some countries like Brunei or Provinces like Aceh in Indonesia have this title as part of their identity.

(b) **The House of War – Dar al-Harb** – lands not under Islamic control, like Australia. Their vision is to turn the whole world into Dar al-Salaam. This is why they say, "We love Peace!" What do they mean? They mean global Islamization and this comes under the control of the "Strong Man". Only then, in their definition, will there be "peace". This is NOT the peace that Jesus offers.

We believe in Jesus. He is the "Stronger Man" and He wants to bring true love, true freedom and true peace. Jesus gives a peace that this world cannot give and cannot take away.

John 14:26-27,

"But the Helper, the Holy Spirit, whom the Father will send in My name, He will teach you all things, and bring to your remembrance all things that I said to you. Peace I leave with you, My peace I give to you; not as the world gives do I give to you. Let not your heart be troubled, neither let it be afraid."

Yes, Jesus is the Stronger Man and the question in *Isaiah* is still being asked today, "Who is on the Lord's side?" Silence, fear, and a refusal to be Christ's witnesses says that we are under the control of the "strong man", Satan. We need to break the chains of bondage and be true disciples of the "stronger man", Jesus, for He is the Creator, the only Lord and Saviour and He wants to walk with us and be in us.

Matthew 10:32-33,

"Whoever confesses Me before men, him I will also confess before My Father who is in heaven. But whoever denies Me before men, him I will also deny before My Father who is in heaven."

We have ALL AUTHORITY. Believe it! Use it!

We do not need to be afraid of using our God-given freedoms to find the most effective ways to share the Gospel. Don't be afraid to share the saving love of Christ. As Christians we have been commanded by Jesus to take the Gospel to all nations. They need His love. They need to know Him, and God has chosen us to be His instruments, and He's given us His authority to share it.

Matthew 28:18-19,

"ALL AUTHORITY has been given to Me in heaven and on earth. GO THEREFORE and make disciples of all the nations."

1John 4:4,

"He who is in you is greater than he who is in the world."

God loves all people of every nation, race and belief system but He has provided only one way for people to be saved. He sent His Son, Jesus, and He wants all people to believe in Him so that they might be saved.

Acts 4:12,

"Nor is there salvation in any other, for there is no other name under heaven given among men by which we must be saved."

That name is Jesus!

The focus of this book is our Muslim friends. We want them to know the joy, freedom and love that can be found in Jesus and that they may receive the fulness of God's blessing.

10. The Power of Prevailing Prayer

James 5:15-16,

"The prayer of faith will save the sick, and the Lord will raise him up. And if he has committed sins, he will be forgiven. Confess your trespasses to one another, and pray for one another, that you may be healed. The effective, fervent prayer of a righteous man avails much."

We need this mighty key to break down the wall and to open the gates.

- Prayer for 7 years at the Berlin Wall brought down the Berlin wall.
- Prayer for 15 years brought revival to Wales and the Hebrides.
- Blind Henos prayed for over 20 years filled the cup of mercy with mercy drops of faith and brought a miracle healing to blind Henos Babao, one of our students in Central Sulawesi, Indonesia.

I met Henos in the city of Palu, Central Sulawesi, a few months after he was healed but I was warned not to speak as he would recognise my voice. In Bible School I had prayed for him over 15 times to be healed. Back in his hometown of Bugis, the miracle happened and now I was meeting him again. No longer blind, Henos was told to welcome me, as though I was a stranger. He approached me and shook my hand. I could no longer contain myself, and I spoke just one word – "Henos!"

Immediately Henos collapsed to the ground kissing and hugging my feet and crying out, "My teacher! My father!" I too wept for joy. Blind Henos was in Bible School for two years, now he could see! Prayer power works every hour.

What does Prayer accomplish?

1. *Prayer builds our relationship with God - Ephesians 3:14-19*

Prayer is not a speech to God, it is a conversation with our Creator and Redeemer. See how that relationship that Paul had with the Lord brought them great deliverance on the boat that shipwrecked on Malta – *Acts 27-28.*

2. *Prayer helps us to understand God's Will – 2Timothy 1:7*

As we pray and converse with God, He gives us a sound mind to make good decisions. When we pray, "Your will be done on earth as it is in heaven" we are aligning our will with His will – *Matthew 6:9-15.* Through prayer, God's people learn the strategies and tactics we are to use so that we can win the battle. See what happened when Jehoshaphat prayed in *2Chronocles 20.* They learned the enemy's strategy, and then the Lord revealed His strategy and that day they saw a mighty victory.

3. *Prayer is a weapon in the spiritual war we engage in – Ephesians 6:10-20*

We need to put on the whole armor but the capstone of it all is prayer. It helps us to overcome the enemy, gives us the strength to persevere, the power to speak boldly, and the ability to unveil divine mysteries. Through prayer the Holy Spirit spoke and sent Paul and Barnabas on their apostolic missionary journeys – *Acts 13-14.*

4. *Prayer opens revelation so that we can see what God is going to do – Daniel 2:28*

Look at the lives of Daniel and Joseph. Their relationships with the Lord grew through prayer. Their personal conversations with Him, in prayer, brought awesome personal deliverances as well as national victories. Then the Lord opened their eyes to see into the future and gave them revelations for their generation and for the Last Days.

Do not underestimate the power of prayer in your sharing the love of Christ. God hears our prayers. He stands with us. He imparts wisdom, knowledge, miraculous power, and strategies that will see many come to faith in Christ. ***J. Edwin Orr*** once said that "every revival in history could be traced to find at its source a group of people gathered for prayer." ***Walter Wink*** said, "History belongs to the intercessors."

11. Give a Challenge to your Muslim Friends

There are three basic challenges that you could share with them based on what the Qur'an says can make a person a better Muslim

i. *Ask a Christian to explain the Gospel to you*

Christians and Jews are called "the People of the Book" referring to the Old Testament (Law, Psalms, Prophets) and the New Testament (the Gospel).

Surah 10:94,

"So if you are in doubt about that which we've revealed to you, then ask those who have been reading the scripture before you. The truth has certainly come to you from your Lord. So never be among the doubters."

Surah Al Baqarah 2:136,

"Say ye: "We believe in Allah, and the revelation given to us, and to Abraham, Isma'il, Isaac, Jacob, and the Tribes, and that given to Moses and Jesus, and that given to (all) prophets from their Lord: We make no difference between one and another of them: And we bow to Allah."

When you ask the Christians, as Allah has told you to do, you'll learn that Jesus is the Son of God, that He died for your sins and rose from the dead. You'll learn that Jesus is the Straight Path and the Mercy of God needed for salvation. God's final messenger to humanity because Jesus is God.

Some think the Qur'an contradicts the Gospel, but the Qur'an never says that. The Qur'an in fact confirms the Gospel and you are commanded to submit to the Qur'an, not question it. If you have doubts, Allah commands you to ask those who have been reading the scripture before you. That means you should ask the Christians.

ii. Encourage Christians to judge by the Gospel

Surah 5:47 *says,*

"So that the people of the Gospel judge by what Allah has revealed in it, and those who do not judge by what Allah has revealed are the rebellious."

Christians have been commanded by Allah, in the Qur'an, to obey and judge by the Gospel. If they do not, they are "the rebellious".

The Christians have had the Gospel for hundreds of years before Muhammad, during the life of Muhammad, and even until today, Christians have the same Gospel.

So don't be among the doubters. Be a good Muslim, tell the Christians to judge by the Gospel.

iii. Talk to the Christians and find out if Muhammad is mentioned in the Bible

Muslims believe that Muhammad is mentioned in the Bible.

Surah al-A`raf 7:157,

"Those who follow the messenger, the illiterate prophet, **whom they find mentioned written in their own Torah and Gospel**, he guides them towards righteousness, forbids them from evil, permits for them all good things, prohibits for them all impure things, and relieves them of their burdens and the shackles that have bound them."

To be a better Muslim, go and ask a Christian where they find Muhammad mentioned in their Gospel.

When we were in Sana'a Yemen we had Muslims who wanted to read the Gospel. They wanted to find Muhammad in the Bible. They spent hours in a room, privately inspecting the Bible, in Arabic, and they found that Muhammad's name is not in the Bible. Not in the Old Testament and not in the New Testament.

The above three questions can be useful for mature Christians to discuss with Muslim friends. It is a dilemma they need to solve, because in each of these three questions, Muslims are commanded by the Qur'an to ask the Christians. The Qur'an also confirms that the Bible is true, authoritative, and to be obeyed by both Christians and Muslims as we read in *Surah Al Baqarah 2:136.*

If you want to see more information on this issue of the three challenges for a Muslim to be a better Muslim and to believe in historical accuracy, watch the following videos on Youtube: *www.youtube.com/watch?v=WG0Ta2K-WI8*

www.youtube.com/watch?v=_CAZfY8R45o

We have seen that Ishmael is a key element of the End-Time Revival

Many Muslims with the spirit of Ishmael are looking for answers and we believe in these last days, in the midst of global crises, wars, economic collapse, persecution, natural disasters and pandemics that *kairos* opportunities are on the way and we need to be ready to use them.

Isaiah 19 and Isaiah 60 are amazing prophecies for the Middle East, including Israel, Egypt, Syria, Lebanon, Saudi Arabia and Yemen, as well as other far off nations, of a great and mighty harvest to come! But we need to see what must happen in the church to enable this to come to pass. The church must be transformed until Christ-likeness is VISIBLE in the church! *John 13:34-35; 17:23.* It will happen when it seems that hopelessness and despair are everywhere, but look up. Believe His Word! It's coming!

Isaiah 60:1-7,

"Arise, shine, for your light has come, and the glory of the LORD rises upon you. See, darkness covers the earth and thick darkness is over the peoples, but the LORD rises upon you and his glory APPEARS over you. **Nations will come to your light**, and kings to the brightness of your dawn. "Lift up your eyes and look about you: All assemble and come to you; your sons come from afar, and your daughters are carried on the arm. Then you will look and be radiant, your heart will throb and swell with joy; the wealth on the seas will be brought to you, to you the riches of the nations will come. Herds of camels will cover your land, young camels of **Midian** and **Ephah**. And all from **Sheba** will come, bearing gold and incense and proclaiming the praise of the LORD. **All Kedar's flocks** will be gathered to you, **the rams of Nebaioth** will serve you; they will be accepted as offerings on my altar, and I will adorn My glorious temple."

John 13:34-35,

"BY THIS ALL WILL KNOW." i.e. visible enough for them to recognize it!

John 17:23,

"THAT THE WORLD MAY KNOW," i.e. visible enough for them to recognize it!

Muslims in mass coming to Christ is a very VISIBLE sign. It's happening in Iran. It's beginning in Saudi Arabia. This will provoke Israel to jealousy and faith! Their turn is coming. They too will have revival.

Israel and Arab Nations will experience an Amazing Revival

Isaiah 19:16-25; Romans 9-11.

Romans 11:11,

"I say then, have they stumbled that they should fall? Certainly not! But through their fall, to provoke them to jealousy, salvation has come to the Gentiles."

Paul wanted to provoke the Jews to jealousy so that some might be saved! But what if there is national repentance?

Romans 11:14-15,

"If by any means I may provoke to jealousy those who are my flesh and save some of them. For if their being cast away is the reconciling of the world, what will their acceptance be but life from the dead?"

Ishmael's conversion will be a blessing to the Body of Christ:

1. To bring many Muslims to faith in Christ.
2. To bring repentance in the church and a renewed zeal for the Great Commission.
3. To bring in more harvesters for the final end-time revival.
4. To release wealth to proclaim the Gospel.

5. To provoke the Jews into jealousy causing many to accept the Messiah.

Jesus loves all nations. He creates *kairos* moments. We have to learn to use them. He has anointed you. Ishmael is waiting – it's his *kairos* time! Have you heard his cry?

What is the greatest Dilemma facing Muslims today?

Muslims believe that Islam was built on three unshakeable foundations:

1. The Prophet Muhammad,
2. The Qur'an as the verbatim word of God, and
3. The city of Mecca as the birthplace of revelation.

But what if the archaeological and historical evidence destroys these foundations? What if the person originally referred to as Muhammad, "the praised one", was actually Jesus and this has lots of evidence right up until the 8th Century? What if it was the Abbasids in the 8th Century, following an heretical Christian sect that denied Jesus deity, crucifixion and the Trinity, and accepted ancient Christian and Arab legends, created a new religion. This new religion needed a founding prophet. The title "Muhammad" meaning the "praised one" was taken away from Jesus, and made to be a man, the prophet of Islam, whom they named "Muhammad". The historical and archeological evidence for this seems overwhelming. See: *The Hidden Origins of Islam, Edited by Karl-Heinz Ohlig and Gerd-R Puin, Prometheus Books, 2010.*

The Qur'an, as we know it, was developed over several centuries, with over 2000 scribal variations, and over 26 different versions of the Qur'an. The history of the city called Mecca, along with the history of the Qur'an and the prophet named Muhammad was revealed step by step over 200 to 300 years until eventually the religion of Islam, with its prophet

Muhammad, and it's centre of worship, Mecca, was unveiled in full. This will prove to be a massive dilemma for Muslims around the world. A very informative video on Youtube can be viewed to learn more on this dilemma.

Youtube: www.youtube.com/watch?v=d_-WWzJs-iQ

What is the greatest Dilemma facing Christians today?

A major problem for Christians is apathy for the Great Commission. Christians, generally, are more interested in enjoying the fruits of salvation than in taking up the cross of Christ and sharing the Gospel with a lost world. Many focus more on a hoped-for rapture than on fulfilling Christ's command to take the Gospel to every person. The rapture will come when the Lord is ready for it to come. It will not come before Christ's mission has been fulfilled.

Matthew 24:12-14,

"And because lawlessness (disobedience to His commands) will abound, the love of many will grow cold (The result of promoting self-interest over the need of others to hear the Gospel). But he who endures to the end shall be saved. And this Gospel of the Kingdom will be preached in all the world as a witness to all the nations, and then the end will come."

Where are we standing? Are we so passionately in love with Christ and the lost of this world, that whatever the cost, we will proclaim the message of salvation in Christ?

Acts 3:18-21,

"But those things which God foretold by the mouth of all His prophets, that the Christ would suffer, He has thus fulfilled. Repent therefore and be converted, that your sins may be blotted out, so that times of refreshing may come from the presence of the Lord, and that He may send Jesus Christ, who was preached to you before, whom heaven must receive until

the times of restoration of all things, which God has spoken by the mouth of all His holy prophets since the world began."

Jesus is not coming back until His mission is complete. Events in the past were prophesied and fulfilled perfectly on time. Unfulfilled events will also be fulfilled perfectly and on time. We must focus more on fulfilling His mission than on trying to speed up the rapture. We must stop being lazy, selfish Christians and turn our focus back to the Great Commission. People need the Lord! They need Jesus. Will you tell them, or will you hide away in self-protection. What did Jesus say? Let this be a warning for all of us as this indeed is a great dilemma for Christians!

Mark 8:34-38,

"When He had called the people to Himself, with His disciples also, He said to them, "Whoever desires to come after Me, let him deny himself, and take up his cross, and follow Me. For whoever desires to save his life will lose it, but whoever loses his life for My sake and the gospel's will save it. For what will it profit a man if he gains the whole world, and loses his own soul? Or what will a man give in exchange for his soul? For whoever is ashamed of Me and My words in this adulterous and sinful generation, of him the Son of Man also will be ashamed when He comes in the glory of His Father with the holy angels."

Our dilemma is to be willing to take up this challenge to be true disciples of Christ, to take up the Cross and to follow Him – all the way!

CONCLUSION

Congratulations on reading through 20 chapters or dilemmas in **Multiple Dilemmas.**

You may feel that you know everything there is to know. Please allow me to disappoint.

When we began writing this book we were focused on a training seminar with 20 sessions. We needed a Manual as a guide for the subjects we would cover in this 10-night series with two sessions per night. We looked at our material and there were over 40 subjects that we would love to teach to equip you for the Great Commission in bringing the Gospel to the tents of Kedar and Nebaioth and the other tribes descending from Ishmael.

We had to limit ourselves to 20 subjects. That leaves many more subjects we have not touched upon. If by God's grace, He gives us the strength, and the time, we will write another book with the rest of the material we have not covered. Some of those subjects include:

1. The Origin of Islam
2. The 5 Pillars of Islam
3. The 6 Fundamental Beliefs of Islam
4. Understanding the denominations in Islam – Sunni, Shia, Sufi, Ahmadiyya
5. Historical original of Muhammad?
6. Official History of Sira Muhammad
7. The Origins, Compilation and Contents of the Hadith
8. Questioning the original Mecca
9. Challenges of History in the Qur'an
10. The Problems of Science in the Qur'an
11. Church Reformers and National Leaders Discuss Islam
12. Miracles, Signs and Wonders
13. Did Paul corrupt the Bible?
14. Christian-Muslim Friendships
15. The Doctrine of Abrogation
16. The existence and role of the Jinn
17. The Practice of Slavery
18. Lying for God's Cause - Taqiyya
19. Growth and Expansion of Jihad
20. Schools of Jurispudence in Islam
21. Standards of sexual morality in Islam

22. Ownership of Palestine in the Qur'an?
23. Mentoring New Believers
24. A Jonah heart or a Jesus heart?

FINAL DISCUSSION POINTS:

1. What approach would you feel comfortable with in introducing and explaining Jesus to your Muslim friends?
2. How do you see revival in Muslim countries impacting the world?
3. Write down, individually, or collectively, what you think could be a short, medium and long-term action plan that you and your friends could begin praying about, or even implementing, today.
4. Do you really want the rapture to happen now before all these exciting things take place?
5. Are you truly willing to be a disciple of Christ and to take up the Cross and to fully follow Him?

With all our love,
Jeff & Annette Hammond
abbahouse2000@outlook.com

SOURCES USED AND RECOMMENDED

Books

www.ingramcontent.com/pod-product-compliance
Lightning Source LLC
LaVergne TN
LVHW010222110826
845148LV00022B/1230

* 9 7 8 1 7 6 4 5 6 2 0 5 8 *